SHAPE-SHIFTING

SHAPE-
SHIFTING

SHIFTING
SHAPE-

Images of Native Americans in Recent Popular Fiction

Andrew Macdonald
Gina Macdonald
MaryAnn Sheridan

Contributions to the Study of Popular Culture, no. 71
Kathleen Gregory Klein, Series Adviser

GREENWOOD PRESS
Westport, Connecticut • London

Library of Congress Cataloging-in-Publication Data

Macdonald, Andrew, 1942–
    Shape-shifting : images of Native Americans in recent popular fiction / by Andrew
Macdonald, Gina Macdonald, and MaryAnn Sheridan.
       p. cm.—(Contributions to the study of popular culture, ISSN 0198–9871 ; no. 71)
    Includes bibliographical references and index.
    ISBN 0–313–30842–X (alk. paper)
    1. American fiction—20th century—History and criticism. 2. Indians in literature. 3.
Popular literature—United States—History and criticism. 4. American fiction—Indian
authors—History and criticism. I. Macdonald, Gina. II. Sheridan, MaryAnn. III. Title.
IV. Series.
PS374.I49M33   2000
813'.54090397073—dc21   00–021048

British Library Cataloguing in Publication Data is available.

Library of Congress Catalog Card Number: 00–021048
ISBN: 0–313–30842–X
ISSN: 0198–9871

First published in 2000

Greenwood Press, 88 Post Road West, Westport, CT 06881
An imprint of Greenwood Publishing Group, Inc.
www.greenwood.com

Printed in the United States of America

The paper used in this book complies with the
Permanent Paper Standard issued by the National
Information Standards Organization (Z39.48–1984).

10 9 8 7 6 5 4 3 2 1

Copyright Acknowledgments

The author and publisher gratefully acknowledge permission for use of the following material:

Excerpt from "Ceremony" from *Ceremony* by Leslie Marmon Silko. Copyright © 1977 by Leslie
Silko. Used by permission of Viking Penguin, a division of Penguin Putnam, Inc.

It was astounding to Joshua how much the times had changed. The Indians now lived in poverty on the poorest of the land, and the only thing fearsome about them was their despair. But the stories of the old days still were told by the white grandfathers, and the stories became enhanced and romantic, and then they became legends. And the Indians today were so far from the stuff of legends that they engendered no respect in comparison, and they were almost totally forgotten. They had become part of the landscape like the creosote bushes and the bear grass and the desert broom, and just as easily ignored and trampled. The distinction between peaceful Indians and savage warriors had long since died, and no white man could tell the difference between a Papago and an Apache. And few people now cared.

—Richard Parrish, *The Dividing Line*, 248

Contents

Acknowledgments

For their inspiration and support, I would like to thank my numerous teachers, especially Tom Berry, students, and family members, without whom my own creation story could not unfold.

—MaryAnn Sheridan

In thanking mentors for whatever virtues this work possesses and in accepting blame for its failures, we must give all credit for the concept of this book to our friend and editor, Kathleen Klein, who, when we were discussing a study of images of Native Americans in detective fiction, said, in effect, Why not write about all the other genres as well? Once over our shock at the daring and ambition of this idea, we came to see its virtue in completing a circle: images of Native Americans run throughout our culture. We remain deeply indebted to Kathy for her confidence in us, her unwavering support, and her fine editorial intelligence. A more intimate and particular debt of gratitude is owed to the late historian and humanist Peter Cangelosi of Loyola University (New Orleans) for influencing our sense of historical "truths" and "facts": Peter shared his wisdom with generosity and old-fashioned graciousness. We are also grateful to the Greenwood editorial staff, particularly Pamela St. Clair, for enthusiastically supporting the development of idea into book and David Palmer for thorough editing. Margaret Coel shared with us her insights into the virtues and pitfalls of detective stories involving Native Americans, and Howard Fast did so about *The Last Frontier* and the problems inherent in writing historical fiction. Our thanks also go to Ellen Kocher Plaisance for valuable feedback on several chapters in draft, to Paulette Richards for providing insights on gender and race issues that helped inform our analysis, to Joseph and Anita Kess for their lively recounting of Canadian popular mythologies, and to Forrest and Ruth Copeland for introducing us to the Native cultures of Vancouver Island.

All artwork is the conceptualization and creation of Jeanie Kay Duvall.

—Andrew and Gina Macdonald

Introduction

Our title might be read to mean that this is a book about real Native Americans, but our true concern is the American Indian, a somewhat different figure. The Native Americans were the indigenous people whom the Europeans colonized and whom immigrants to North America first encountered; the American Indian is the generalized figure the Europeans immediately began to create, sometimes as a merely distorted version of the original Native Americans, sometimes as an almost entirely fictionalized Other Being set up to serve colonial and national agendas.

Since the first encounters of precolonial times, Europeans have shaped, changed, and distorted the indigenous people to serve white people's needs. The very word "Indian" is a conflation of hundreds of tribes, languages, and cultures into one emblematic figure: the Other, the Alien, the generalized Non-European. This figure soon outgrew its very real progenitors to serve the needs of whites: of Puritans seeking certification of their own favored status even as they encountered friendly Natives sometimes regarded as God's unspoiled children; of other Puritans finding in Indian hostility the Antichrist's opposition to their City on a Hill; of French Jesuits seeking support for missions to train childlike innocents; of new Americans of varied ideological stripes who needed wild and free New World symbols or dramatic foils or credible bogeymen to advance their own agendas and projects. The one unchanging historical truth about the impressively varied and complex Native American people is that they were almost always cast by the popular imagination in the singular, as "The Indian," a figure of transcendent simplicity and consistency.

While popular culture is now institutionalized, enjoying a position far more pervasive and developed than in the early years of the republic, its treatment of Native Americans is still much the same. Despite two hundred years of expe-

rience with varied tribes and cultures, despite anthropology, and despite lobbying by rights groups, the figure of the Indian persists—a transformation of
the sociologically and culturally complex into a singular emblem useful for its
various exploiters. Thus, the ecology movement uses the Indian (sometimes with
the cooperation of Native American support groups) as a symbol of living in
harmony with the earth, while romance fiction sees Indian men as unspoiled
paragons of maleness. Westerns depict Indian women as sexually free and ad-
venturesome, and males as either unnaturally cruel or triumphantly noble despite
the harsh demands of an unforgiving environment. The Indian as spy or war
hero is depicted as superhuman, drawing on ancient instincts and the skills of
his forefathers and surviving against all odds, while the Indian detective epito-
mizes the blend of rationality and intuition beloved by Sherlock Holmes. Put
simply, America cannot have its cowboys without Indians. The figure of the
Indian completes any number of popular culture genre formulas in any number
of ways: by providing contrast, by establishing a complementary difference, by
looming large as a model of how to live correctly, by signifying a noble lost
cause, and so on. Therefore, the generalized Indian tells us far more about our
modern selves than about Native Americans, past or present, and deserves attention for this importance. Moreover, the half-breed and the "white" Indian as
conventional figures have come to embody the conflict between East and West,
and to serve as literary devices for making Native American issues and themes
more accessible to whites.

The distinction between Native American and Indian is sharply drawn in
Robert F. Berkhofer's fine work, *The White Man's Indian* (1978), to which we
are deeply indebted, and to some degree we have followed his conceptual model

Thus, the real Native American culture, as opposed to its use and manipulation by mainstream popular fiction, is only a tangential concern of this study;
we will deal with historical and sociological realities only to establish a benchmark against which to measure distortion. We mean no disrespect by this apparent neglect, for none of us is competent to speak for the native community
at large, and in fact, one of our main points is just that: the difficulty of fairly
representing such culturally diverse and far-flung groups of people. A recurring
theme in our critique is the consistent dehumanization of the Other. It takes no
special anthropological expertise to identify this dehumanization, however blind
some consumers of popular culture may be to it. Nor are Indian stereotypes
necessarily intended as malign. The figure of the Indian weeping a single tear
over park land despoiled by litter is clearly intended as a benign icon of caring
for the earth, but conveniently avoids complexity; some native groups were
"litterers," too, and subsuming all into well-meant generalization reduces discourse to meaningless abstraction, ungrounded in known historical practice. Yes,
most Native Americans respected the earth, but to exhort the untidy with such
moral sententiousness turns complex philosophies of nature into bumper-sticker
sloganeering. Particular cultural practices aside, we will stress the need to see
individual native groups and individuals whole, as complete human beings.

The distinction between Native American and Indian is sharply drawn in
Robert F. Berkhofer's fine work, *The White Man's Indian* (1978), to which we
are deeply indebted, and to some degree we have followed his conceptual model

in our thinking about the manipulation of stereotypes. However, since our own purposes in focusing on these two figures are different from Berkhofer's, it is worth pausing to note that like all linguistic distinctions, the division between Native American and Indian is a complex one, with continual tendrils of influence crossing the distinction line and sometimes blurring it entirely. Berkhofer's seminal work was intended to highlight the difference between the facts about the indigenous people and white people's fancy, between reality and symbol in American culture beginning in colonial times. Our own intention is to acknowledge this line of demarcation and then to show how, in our own times, popular fiction has developed genres to exploit the image of the American Indian, sometimes by incorporating true elements of Native American culture, more often by stereotyping or oversimplifying, but always serving the needs of the mainstream culture, the mass readership that marginalizes Native Americans if only because of the overwhelming force of its numbers.

There is a mechanistic fallacy in postulating that a people's history is simply the sum of the facts about them. Sociology, theology, linguistic studies, anthropological or ethnographic descriptions—all provide the matter but not the spirit or mentality of a people. What we are here calling "popular culture" figures or images—the imaginative and fictionalized versions of reality found in mass culture stories—may be severely at odds with material realities while nevertheless retaining a firm grip on the popular imagination. The most notable example from the earliest days of European colonization was the Spanish insistence, in the face of continuing evidence to the contrary, that some Native American cities were paved with gold, a fatal projection of desire.

Most projections of European wishes and values on the Native Americans were far more mundane, and in fact some were subject to change when reality proved intractable. The sex life of the Indian or his strategies of war were subjects of myth, but the stories changed as knowledgeable frontiersmen and -women brought back more experientially based information. The concepts of Native American and Indian were in states of continual adjustment, in other words, and while our interest is in the fictional Indian shaped by white needs and fantasies, it is worth noting that Native American versions of their own identity and culture were also inevitably shaped by white versions of who they were. If only because the white mythologizing apparatus (the press, the coffeehouse, the church, the statehouse) was so efficient, inevitably Native Americans learned about their distant fellows as transmuted through white sources. The process continues in our own time. In addition to Indians grossly distorted by the needs of a genre, we will examine examples of popular fiction that make commendable efforts at accuracy of depiction and interpretation, even at times straining against the requirements of their genre and risking readership rejection as a result.

With these complexities in mind, we turn to our primary subject, the manipulation of the Indian figure in recent popular fiction. As suggested above, this distorted picture of real Native Americans goes back to colonial days, and where relevant we will trace this history, mainly in the abduction/captivity stories and early Westerns. Our primary focus, however, is on more modern genres that are increasingly using Indian characters and settings. There is some irony here, for as the number of full-blooded Native Americans who practice complete versions of their culture has declined, the Indian figure is in yet another of its periods of widespread popularity among the general public. Curiosity about Native Americans and studies programs themselves have swung in and out of favor, but the Indian figure as American icon and totem remains a growth industry.

Recent American popular literature with Native American subjects has experienced a burst of creative energy, with numerous new titles being published that test and reshape genre patterns to address current topics and contemporary agendas. The romance novel, for example, has, more than ever before, produced a set of newly minted "captivity" novels with Native American heroes or heroines, as well as novels focused on rediscovering ancestral roots or discovering feminist principles in the tribal past. Dramatizations of current issues cross genres, incorporating Native American culture, themes, and issues. The horror novel has adopted the power of pre-Christian earth and animal spirits from various Native American religions (for instance, Naomi Stokes's evil shaman in *Tree People* or Muriel Gray's demonic Coyote spirit in *Trickster*). Science fiction has imagined Native American cultures seeded on distant planets by alien cultures yet retaining the ecological wisdom of their Earth counterparts. The detective genre has prospered by changing its focus to accommodate new culturally curious readers, new understandings of crime and aberrancy, and new cultural clashes and competitions. The basic conventions of crime fiction have proven receptive to new Native American investigators who teach readers about cultures and worldviews as they catch criminals, combining traditional native wisdom with the European-inspired detective story and police procedural. Many Westerns and much historical fiction, of course, whether traditional or revisionist, explore modern themes in historical settings and create new fantasies to appeal to modern values.

What unites these disparate genres in their use of Native American characters, cultures, and worldviews is their transformation of the historical figure of the American Indian into popular culture emblems that, although cast in the forms of defined genres, deal with changing issues on the national landscape. Our investigation will show how the Indian figure serves different rhetorical and ideological agendas when set in established genres, how the figure is made to accommodate the purposes of the genre, how the genre itself is changed in turn, and how enduring this window provided by the Indian figure has been, offering a view into American obsessions, fears, hopes, and fantasies. This twinned outlook, of white American linked/played against Indian Other, has changed our view of Native Americans and ourselves throughout our history, and is now providing new and even more compelling visions of American identity.

The title of this book, *Shape-Shifting: Images of Native Americans in Recent Popular Fiction*, puns on the Native American concept of magical transformation. In particular, it refers to a human being changing into another living creature—for example, the shamanistic idea of the Lakota Sioux warriors shape-shifting into buffalo or wolves to enhance hunting skills and to honor the animal hunted. In general, it carries the idea of metamorphosis, of transformation from one form to another, or to some degree, becoming the other, sharing point of view and lifeway.

Thus, our focus will be on key popular fiction genres that make broad use of Native American characters, cultures, and settings, transforming their reality for a variety of purposes, including their genre conventions. Our treatment will be representative rather than comprehensive, providing an overview of the genre conventions and patterns at work in this new fiction and then exploring in more detail the works that expand and transform the genre, such as the novels of Micah Hackler, James Doss and Naomi Stokes, whose detective fiction, to varying degrees, becomes horror/supernatural. The widely varying levels of sociological accuracy, representations of culture, and genre conventions employed in these books with Native American characters offer fascinating analytical opportunities for the critic and reader, raising questions both literary and cultural. How accurate are our current fictional images of North America's native peoples? Are current representations truly improvements over the stereotypes of the past? What are our ways of knowing cultures truly different from the mainstream, and can such ways of life be reconstructed imaginatively in English prose and English literary forms?

We will begin with the American Indian of the imagination. Chapter 1 briefly surveys various influences that caused the imaginative portrait to be formed— the linking from colonial times of the Indian and the European—and the ways these make-believe Indians served the needs of the colonial and later settlers. For the Europeans, Native Americans were never defined simply by the sum of the sociological facts about them but were, rather, potent symbols of what settlers were not or what they wished to be. For some thinkers, they reflected shifting definitions of the nature of humankind in the neutral conditions of the New World, an arena uncorrupted by European history where reason and romanticism, as well as nature and nurture, could be observed at play. For the less philosophically inclined, the natives provided a stern challenge to European models of ways of life, and ultimately to ownership of the new continent. While the military defeat of the indigenous people was accomplished well over a century ago, battles in the imaginative arena continue, with Indian fortunes still shifting as reformed visions of the past are tested out in new genres.

Chapters 2 and 3 provide a cultural foundation for reading Native American literature and explore how representative Native Americans currently view themselves through the prism of their own literature. These self-portraits are not meant to be definitive or comprehensive pictures of Native American life and concerns at the end of the twentieth century, but rather to be touchstones of how people who are so fixedly viewed by others actually see themselves— remembering, of course, that no one in English-speaking society can escape being influenced by "the Indians" of popular culture. They focus in particular on the importance of the Creation story as a mental framework for literary creation. This Native American vision lays the foundation for understanding how much the fictive Indian of our various mainstream genres is indeed a fantasy creation reflecting dominant literary conventions and dominant cultural attitudes and values.

The next chapters examine the various popular literary genres in which the Indian figure is found: the Western, the romance, the crime/detective story, the magic/horror story, and science fiction. Since gender difference is both a universal condition and one expressed variously in different cultures and localities, the startling uniformity among the conventions and rhetoric of the abduction/captivity stories demands attention, first as a European way of dealing with a huge challenge to identity, then as the inspiration for romance fantasies old and new.

Chapter 4, on the Western, examines how the rigid conventions of the classic Western have their origins as much in genre needs as in racial and ethnic stereotyping. Currently, more particularized depictions of Native Americans have created more humanized literary figures, but the genre remains subject to mainstream distortion in its tendency to see through white eyes and to slavishly follow fad and current wisdom. Thus, historically, Westerns have simplified Native American complexity. The utter confusion wrought by dozens of tribes and cultures encountered in the western plains fits poorly with the literary demands of creating a simple, manageable, and therefore dehumanized, villain.

Chapter 5, on the romance, examines the recent growth of cross-cultural romances, particularly captivity romances, with both feminists and defenders of traditional roles seeing in the Indian a launching pad for their ideas about gender relationships. The modern romance genre reflects both a deep human need for fulfillment as an individual within a community and a rejection of the messy realities of true cultural experience in the closest of encounters with alien others. As such, it encapsulates the ambivalence that has always run through white attitudes toward Indians, even in the best and most intimate of relationships.

Chapter 6 moves to a more modern genre, Native American/Indian detective fiction. In the works of Tony Hillerman, the Native American comes through as a truly complex figure, and Hillerman's Navajo and Zuñi investigators exemplify how such characters can become legitimate bridges between cultures, both in the confines of their plots and for their mainly mainstream readers. As guides and cultural signposts, Hillerman's Native American detectives have engendered imitators good and bad, and the recent plethora of alleged Native American sleuths in fact includes many bogus Indian figures, tribal Sam Spades whose cultural depth goes little beyond touristic trappings. The enormous growth of such books in recent years allows an insight into the way new fiction quickly adapts to reset genre requirements or even fossilizes such patterns. Thus, despite some excellent practitioners, the detective genre is in danger of becoming as conventionalized and stereotyped as the Western, with faux ethnic accoutrements substituting for true ethnicity and cultural validity.

In their richest forms, the cultural practices of Native Americans can be used to stretch a genre in new directions. This stretching happens with the detective story when the Native American investigator becomes a shaman or medicine man/woman. European ratiocination (and the quintessential detective genre) is left behind, as the genre shifts shape into a new form. Such works are treated in Chapter 7, on the magic and horror genres. In stories using magic, crimes are solved and problems resolved by the use of Native American medicine or cultural ways; in horror stories, the traditional European horror genre is re-formed to permit Native American demons, devils, or other figures of evil to play major parts. As with the Native American detective story, genre demands may convert fairly legitimate Native American lore into Indian conventionality, as the multiplying figure of the shaman attests.

The last genre chapter, 8, deals with science fiction and fantasy projections, Native American or Indian utopias and dystopias set in the distant past or the far future, all to prove political or social points. As with the other genre distortions, such agendas may have little to do with real Native American concerns. However, they do replay on distant worlds the European encounter with the Other—the Indian as Alien. As mentioned earlier, the Indian-European encounter is far from over, at least in the realm of fiction.

We end with a short chapter on future directions. The Indian figure seems solidly entrenched in some genres, especially the romance and the Western, where readership demands appear to have overruled systematic updating of conventionalized and stereotyped figures. The detective and magic/horror genres have been laboratories for experimentation with more legitimate depictions of Native Americans, but their success has also propagated exploiters of the Indian figure. Fantasy visions of Native Americans tend toward the Indian stereotype when political and social agendas become more important than the characters and situations themselves. Whether 250 years of Indian stereotyping will be overcome by more accurate depictions is still unclear, for even as writers such as Tony Hillerman, Naomi Stokes, Muriel Gray, Margaret Coel, Kathleen Eagle, and others paint scholarly and sensitive portraits of native culture, imitators turn the genres toward the old familiar figure, the Indian.

A glossary of Native American terms used in the text and valuable for the student of Native American culture is included.

1

Writing Indians: Native Americans of the Imagination

The American savages resemble the heroes of Homer and Ossian; their simplicity is equal to their bold freedom and their haughty pride. To understand them one must love them; love fathoms better than intellect.
> —Chahta-Ima (Father Adrien Rouquette), *La Nouvelle Atala*
> (New Orleans, 1897; translation by A. Macdonald).

. . . reality imparts credibility to myth, and myth charges reality with imaginative power.
> —Edward Buscombe, ed., *The BFI Companion to the Western*, 13.

THE APPEAL OF THE "WEST" AND OF THE "INDIAN"

The location of the West has shifted with time from the forested woodlands of the Atlantic Coast, which was a "western" frontier to European colonists, to the Great Plains of the Midwest, down to Texas and up to the Rocky Mountains and to the Pacific Coast communities from Baja California to western Canada and eventually Alaska; the broad present-day meaning of "the West" is simply "beyond the Mississippi." These changing geographical limits suggest that the term "the West" is an idea more than a place, a set of attitudes and expectations more than a geographic reality. However, a constant of this Western image has been the Native American as symbolic of the deep, pervading appeal of Western life first to colonial settlers, then to later Americans, and later to people around the globe who have never set foot in the New World. From Indians came frontier living patterns; the Native people provided models of a proud, free, fiercely independent lifestyle that was appropriated by their nemeses (the mountain men, cowboys, and farmers who supplanted them) and that remains very much a part of the American character. Anarchic freedom unimaginable in Old World orders could be located in living people and functioning societies, not shunted off into Edenic and utopian myths. A part of the American character has always been defined either against or in sympathy with the free Indian life.

In particular, the mounted warrior tribes of the Plains and of the Southwest—the Cheyenne, Sioux, Comanche, and Apache—have become stereotypical symbols of wild freedom. Like the Cossacks and the Golden Horde of Russia or the Mongols of China, the warlike nomads of the Americas struck complex mixtures of admiration and fear in the hearts of observers: awe for their phenomenal horsemanship and military skills, horror and terror when these skills were turned against their admirers. Yet, the idea of the West is more than simply the romantic picture of men and women on horseback traversing a picturesque countryside. The Native American tribes of the East Coast—largely unmounted, and more farmers or fishers than hunters—had their own appeal, one so deep and seductive that many white Europeans incorporated elements of Indian culture into their own lives. Playing Indian, as Philip Deloria calls it in his book of that title (*Playing Indian*, 1998), is a venerable American activity, one highly revealing of the unresolved dialectics that have always defined American culture: the opposed influences of a parent culture and its rebellious progeny, of Enlightenment rationalism and Romanticism's counterpoint, of sentimental visions of society and the brutalities of realpolitik and genocide. In all its contradictions and complexities, the appeal of going native appears in the initial experiences of the Europeans with the indigenous peoples and in the cultures of the later white explorers. Furthermore, it underlies much of the popular literature that features Native American characters, culture, and settings, whether set in colonial times or later.

The Thrill of the Exotic

One part of this appeal was the thrill of the unknown and potentially dangerous possibilities unleashed by exposure to new cultures. Like the illustrations of monstrous beings (dragons, anthropophagi, and other mythological beasts) inhabiting the terra incognita of the first maps, early descriptions of the native peoples of the Americas include portraits of fierce cannibals; pagan witches engaged in devilish practices, their red skins reflecting the red flames of hell; alien beings "more brutish than the beasts they hunt, more wild and unmanly then [*sic*] that unmanned wild countrey, which they range rather then [*sic*] inhabite" (Samuel Purchas, in *Hakluytas Posthumus*, 1625). Gertrude Burlingame witnessed a war dance by the Potawatomi Indians in mid-nineteenth-century Kansas, and even this staged event guarded by U.S. troops and coming so late in the white experience with Native Americans carried great emotional force:

When the time came the tom-toms struck up their weird, hideous music and all at once the Indians came rushing out of their tents [wearing only breechcloths and a coat of red paint and some feathers in their hair]. . . . For an instant my heart stood still at the sight.

. . . The Indians were often called "red devils," and they certainly looked it. They got in the circle, one behind the other, and the dance was a sort of hop with their bodies all bent over and their piercing eyes looking in every direction, like they were looking for the enemy, holding up their tomahawks and every few minutes joining in their war whoops that nearly shook the ground. It was a sight never to be forgotten. (Stratton, 111)

One need not be a Jungian to see in this breathless description a fascination with the id, the submerged part of the self related to the primitive "power-concept" and conveying the ideas of "bodily strength, fertility, magic, influence, power"; after all, many of these elements characterize Native American religions, as settlers were decidedly aware (Jung, 68). Puritan divines' equation of Indian attacks with the symbolic depredations of Satan's armies was simply another manifestation of this ambivalence. While the bloody wars waged by the French and Indians and the massacres of settlers over the years indisputably fed white fears, the fear of attack by a people with an almost supernatural capacity to terrify overcame reasonable cause for anxiety. On her horseback ride from Boston to New York in 1704, the terrorstricken Sarah Kemble Knight saw threats on every side: "The only Glimmering we now had was from the spangled Skies, whose Imperfect Reflections rendered every Object formidable. Each lifeless Trunk, with its shatter'd Limbs, appear'd an Armed Enemy; and every little stump like a Ravenous Devourer" (Perry Miller, 122). The words of a late settler, Mary Gettys Lockard of Kansas, further confirm this psychological response:

In our frontier experience, the thing that continually harrowed the feelings of myself and my mother was the fearful dread of Indians. . . . We had been told that there were no hostile Indians in Kansas, but just the same we could remember the horrible tales of Indian depredations further west that continued to sift in to trouble us. We had a book that gave some of [mountain man] Jim Bridger's philosophy . . . "Wh're you don't see no Injuns, tha're they are the thickest." That gave the fixed idea that Indians rose up from the ground at times and killed everybody in sight. We children talked about Indians so much it got on my mother's nerves not a little, and she had hard work trying to stop our chatter about them. (Stratton, 111–112)

Lockard's remarkable self-understanding of the power of obsession—of this "fixed idea" of Bridger's that what was not seen was in fact most ubiquitous—exemplifies how many white Europeans reacted with dread to a truly different civilization: familiarity bred trepidation, at best. Accounts reveal that questions we now might call matters of etiquette—Native Americans walking into frontier cabins and sod houses with no knock or warning, just as they would into a fellow tribesman's lodge or tepee—were often magnified into hideous psychological threats. The simple inability of many settlers to accommodate to a different set of rules for polite behavior certainly created a good part of the image of the hostile Indian with bad intentions.

Freedom and License as Religious Temptation

The Puritans' conscious use of Indianness in their rhetorical dialectic has been thoroughly explored. The deep, dark virgin forest in which Indians dwelt nearby was a place of pagan freedom, and the Indians were close and living symbols of anti-Christian license and deviltry, equations meant to fortify the shaky Puritan settlements against the internal threats of backsliding, dissent, and decrease of zeal. Indians served as useful Sunday morning touchstones of license for Cotton Mather and his Puritan contemporaries, projections of "whatever is forbidden and horrifying in human nature" (Kovel, 8), a "symbol of instincts run wild" (Kovel, 8) and of man "captivated . . . to Satans tyranny in foolish pieties, mad impieties, wicked idlenesse, busie and bloudy wickednesse" (*Garland*, vol. 19, 231). Mather's sermons and letters warned of "tawny" savages with "Hell fire" in their eyes, leading wives and maidens on "a Long Journey into the Woods" where "those Bruitish men" do "many a Fearful Thing" (*Garland*, vol. 3, 220–221). Clearly, real psychosocial temptations existed in the Indian models of primordial abandon, and could be moralized neatly against Puritan self-images of God-fearing restraint.

Although written closer in time to the Kansas settlements than to the period of its Puritan colonial setting, Nathaniel Hawthorne's "Young Goodman Brown" (1835), a short allegory, nicely captures this psychosexual appeal of a primordial forest inhabited by a mysterious, darkly exotic people, the generic/absent Indians who stimulated the *idée fíxe* of Mary Gettys Lockard's family. The title character leaves his wife, Faith, in town while he spends the night at a "witch-meeting" in the woods, imagining "a devilish Indian behind every tree" (1034) and the devil himself at his elbow. Hawthorne's night forest is a place of infinite evil possibility, one where all the upright burghers and their straitlaced goodwives come to let their hair down. "Fair damsels" and "women of spotted fame" mingle with "hoary-bearded elders of the church [who have] whispered wanton words to the young maids of their households," while "[s]cattered also among their pale-faced enemies were the Indian priests, or powwows, who had often scared their native forest with more hideous incantations than any known to English witchcraft" (1040). In Puritan eyes, the thin strip of civilization along the coast was backed by limitless "heathen" forests where the veneer of Europe was soon stripped away. Hawthorne's restrained and dignified prose evokes the moral license equated with the deep woods, a place where the too-rigid culture of the whites can break loose in every direction. The next morning, all is seemingly back to normal for the weary Goodman—again, the proof of evil threat is the absence of proof.

In Puritan communities such paranoia about impending license was all too painfully reinforced in sons and daughters captured and converted by Indians. However, symbols were more powerful than objective realities; Perry Miller calls the constant fear of massacre in Puritan settlements secondary to the even more frightening possibility of captivity, for captivity meant a loss of cultural identity and acceptance of a pagan worldview: "Captured children were known to go entirely heathen and refuse to come back" (*The American Puritans*, 256). Gary Ebersole, in *Captured by Texts: Puritan to Postmodern Images of Indian Captivity* (1995), correctly identifies change or loss of identity as one of the most deep-seated terrors of colonial Americans: "A vague fear that one might be susceptible to going native, a fear akin to the Protestant religious fear of being tempted into sin, always hovered around the thought of Indian captivity" (182). In an age well acquainted with mortality but innocent of theories of personality, the symbolic death of identity loomed more hideous than physical death.

Typical was the plight of John Williams of Roxbury, Massachusetts, a Harvard graduate "called" to Deerfield in 1686 and abducted with all his children in a massacre by French and Macquas in 1704. Redeemed in 1706, Williams then faced the embarrassment of his daughter Eunice being won over to Indian ways. In a December 1706 lecture, printed as *Reports of Divine Kindness; or Remarkable Mercies Should Be Faithfully Published for the Praise of God the Giver*, Williams reports English children captured some years before having become "very much like Indians and in manner . . . symbolizing with them," a transformation confirmed by Titus King, who was captive from 1755 to 1758: "In Six months time they Forsake Father & mother, Forgit thir own Land, Refuess to Speak there own toungue & Seeminly be Holley Swollowed up with the Indians" (Demos, 69). Those who somehow were eventually returned to their homes were never the same; their perspectives had changed, and the younger they were when captured and the longer they stayed, the more they had assimilated to the way of their captors and the harder it was to return comfortably to their former communities. Unanswered questions of guilt and responsibility, of Indian influences, of sexual encounters, sin, weakened faith, and tainted views made them seem morally dangerous to those around them. Williams's daughter Eunice, adopted by a Mohawk family that treated her well, became so acculturated that she lost her ability to speak English and her desire to return to the Williams family. When she was of age to choose the directions of her life, Eunice, dressed in buckskins, her hair heavily greased in Mohawk fashion, chose marriage to a Mohawk; moreover, she and her lover threatened to live together unblessed by any church if a handy French Catholic priest continued to refuse to marry them.

The Puritan response to this relative of Cotton Mather was first great sympathy and fear for her; then distress at her transformation, which was seen as God's test of their faith; and finally horror that she, a child raised in a Protestant household, had sunk so "low" as to betray her heritage and choose both the "Romish" faith and a "savage" Indian husband (see Demos, *The Unredeemed Captive*, 1994, 69). Negotiators attempting to redeem captives like Eunice Williams reported "the English [captives] are so naturalized to the customs and manners of the French and Indians, and have forgotten the English tongue, and are so many of them married . . . that I think it would be far easier to gain twice the number of French and Indians to go with us than English" (Demos, 117).

The colonialists' initially unshakable faith in who they were was transformed by the wilderness into tests of their sense of uniqueness and of mission. The sudden freedom of unrestrained choice must have been closer to an existential terror than what Ebersole calls a "vague fear," though a constant unease no doubt ran through vulnerable settlements.

The figure of the Indian provided the Puritans with a (dis)loyal opposition—a counterfigure to their own chosen status as God's people—but the temptations of a less repressed, more natural way of life (not simply for abductees) were undeniable. Furthermore, neat dualism could not survive continued immigration and multiplying examples of other cultural choices. As Puritan influence waned, the Indian, always a shifting figure, became a more positive model of how one might live.

Hawthorne's story conceptualized the Puritan attitude toward the wilderness as an active negative force equated with license, especially of a sexual kind. If colonial Boston represented an Apollonian way of life, then the green land to the west was certainly Dionysian. The empty frontier had no prying eyes, no unrelenting peer pressure, no limits or restraints—men and women could drop the social roles of civilized life, expressing their inmost desires and fantasies. Unlike the forests of Europe, the New World frontier was peopled by Indians who, at least in the colonial imagination, lived such lives of freedom and autonomy. For all the creature comforts European civilization offered, the appeal of the wild forest shows something was missing for many, whether the desire to go one's own way apart from others, the challenge of hacking a living out of virgin forest, or the atavistic allure of a simple hunter-gatherer lifestyle.

In fact, contemporary accounts of life with Native Americans frequently contrast the relative latitude of Indian life against white frontier settlements, creating images of idyllic splendor in contrast to the hardscrabble work of colonists. While the lot of tribes dependent on hunting and subsistence farming might be chancier than that of colonial yeomen tending animals and filling barns for the winter, the stress levels among the Indians were possibly much lower, if the evaluations of white captives are to be believed. As a result, the image of the frontier and of Indian life was sometimes depicted very positively. Captive Mary Jemison, for example, remarks on the harmonious communal labor of Seneca women, which obviously relieved individuals of personal responsibility for crop failures; on frequent sexual segregation when men left on hunting and war parties, which must have lessened the strain of gender interactions in everyday communal life; on a general openness and clarity of identity among the tribe, whose members knew precisely who they were collectively and what was expected of them as individuals. Jemison mentions it only in passing, but the relative lack of material property among the Indians relieved them of the endless agrarian burdens of repair and maintenance. Jemison says, charmingly, that washing up was no great task, for there was little to wash; compared with the clutter of manufactured goods even on far-frontier farms, the contents of lodge or tepee could be packed up and moved fairly quickly and easily.

If the frontier along the East Coast offered social freedom and liberation from the tasks of ownership, the land to the west offered even more. In the 1750s James Fenimore Cooper's Natty Bumppo of the *Leatherstocking Tales* (1823–1841) mixed easily with his Indian companions, a new American who could roam the forest as comfortably as his progenitors moved about the harmless lanes of England. This "marriage" of Old World and New suggested the limitless possibilities of having it both ways, "civilized" and "savage." The romantic philosophies of Rousseau, Chateaubriand, Crèvecoeur, and Delacroix no doubt affected the popular understanding enough to make Americans ready to believe in the essential goodness and nobility to be found in unspoiled nature. When the Indian was not a devil, he might be thought a noble savage, even by someone intimately familiar with native life:

No people can live more happy than the Indians did in times of peace, before the introduction of spirituous liquors amongst them. Their lives were a continual round of pleasures. Their wants were few, and easily satisfied; and their cares were only for to-day; the bounds of their calculations for future comfort not extending to the incalculable uncertainties of to-morrow. If peace ever dwelt with men, it was in former times, in the recesses from war, amongst what are now termed barbarians. The moral character of the Indians was (if I may be allowed the expression) uncontaminated. Their fidelity was perfect, and became proverbial; they were strictly honest; they despised deception and falsehood; and chastity was held in high veneration, and a violation of it was considered sacrilege. They were temperate in their desires, moderate in their passions, and candid and honorable in the expression of their sentiments on every subject of importance. (Seaver, *A Narrative*, 72–73)

Mary Jemison's effusive praise of native life may be somewhat suspect, if only in its artfully managed balance of sentence structure, but enough corroborating accounts exist to convince even the most skeptical that free pleasures truly were to be found out west, among the native peoples. Just as the nineteenth-century adventurers Richard Burton, John Speke, Samuel Baker, and many other Englishmen "went native" in India, Africa, and the Middle East, so generations of English Americans became would-be Indians, a phenomenon that continues to the present day. The "white Indian" became a virtual stock character, as he remains in the Western, the romance, and even detective fiction. Moreover, as we shall show in later chapters, playing Indian through the medium of popular fiction remains a quintessentially American pleasure.

The Aesthetic Appeal

Another great appeal was aesthetic. Unspoiled and beautiful America as the new Eden nicely complemented economic motives for moving west. Civilization was continually encroaching on the pristine wilderness, and both practical needs for economic advancement and psychic hungers for a new start drove settlement into Indian territory. Many settlers of the early nineteenth century seemed genuinely astonished at the dramatic beauty of their new surroundings. Even the practical Mary Jemison talks about the physical beauty of the Genesee valley, still sometimes called "the Grand Canyon of the East," a place of solitude and majestic vistas that evidently nourished the spirit of its early settlers as well as provided for their physical sustenance.

Interspersed among the practical, factual records of the Lewis and Clark expedition are moments of sheer wonder. Patrick Gass calls scene after scene "the most beautiful . . . I ever beheld." Meriwether Lewis, on May 31, 1805, marveling at the black stone walls that frame a river, calls them "scenes of visionary enchantment" which look as if they will "never have an end," and muses imaginatively on the grandeur of the shapes and forms rivaling the most wondrous human structures: "vast ranges of walls . . . so perfect indeed . . . that I should have thought that nature had attempted . . . to rival the human art of masonry had I not recollected that she had first began her work." To these observations, Patrick Gass adds, "They seem as if built by the hand of man, and are so numerous that they appear like the ruins of an ancient city." On June 8, 1805, Lewis describes a river's passage through a "rich fertile" valley:

. . . one of the most beautifully picturesque countries that I ever beheld, through the wide expanse of which, innumerable herds of living animals are seen, its borders garnished with one continued garden of roses, while its lofty and open forests are the habitation of myriads of the feathered tribes who salute the ear of the passing traveler with their wild and simple, yet sweet and cheerful melody. (www.pbs.org/lewisandclark/archive/index.htm)

On June 13, 1805 his ears are saluted "with the agreeable sound of a fall of water," and later he reports spray from "the great falls" of the Missouri rising above the plain "like a column of smoke":

To gaze on this sublimely grand specticle . . . forms the grandest sight I ever beheld, . . . irregular and somewhat projecting rocks below receive the water in its passage down and break it into a perfect white foam which assumes a thousand forms in a moment, sometimes flying up in jets of sparkling foam to the height of fifteen or twenty feet and are scarcely formed before large rolling bodies of the same beaten and foaming water is thrown over and conceals them. . . . from the reflection of the sun on the sprey or mist which arises from these falls there is a beautiful rainbow produced which adds not a little to the beauty of this majestically grand scenery. (www.pbs.org/lewisandclark/archive/index.htm)

The visual record of western beauty was well recorded by the itinerant artist and writer George Catlin—the "Leatherstocking of American art"—as he roamed North and South America painting and writing about the indigenous people he encountered (Goetzmann and Goetzmann, 16). Catlin's wonderful paintings and sketches of what he called "Nature's proudest, noblest men" in their innocence before "the grand and irresistible march of civilization . . . this splendid juggernaut rolling on . . . [with its] sweeping desolation" (Goetzmann and Goetzmann, 16–17, 35) may have failed to prevent the natives' inevitable destruction, but they certainly cast a romantic glow on their life that remains to this day. The status of the Indian had moved from fierce opponent of "civilization" to doomed romantic figure, a shift that says far more about those who pictured him than about Native American realities.

THE DIVIDED SELF: PLAYING INDIAN ON THE FRONTIER

It goes without saying that most colonists and early Americans were far more like Goodman Brown than Mary Jemison or the many others who lived at least part of their lives among the Indians. Although abductions numbered in the thousands in the colonial period and the early years of the nineteenth century, they constituted only a statistical blip on the graph of direct (as opposed to symbolic) cultural influence: comparatively few of the millions of Americans inhabiting the continent (about three million at the time of the Revolution) actually gave up white culture and joined Indian groups or lived exactly like them. Even traditional Native American culture itself changed rapidly and irreversibly from the earliest trade contacts with Champlain and the French, as the metal tomahawk head, the iron knife, gunpowder, and the inexhaustible European market for animal skins converted hunter-gatherer or simple agrarian economies into trade organizations that amassed capital and sought to expand dominance of markets.

The psychological influence of Native American culture, however, was another matter. Although most Americans in the eighteenth and nineteenth centuries lived daily lives in some ways not much different from those of their European ancestors, native culture had very large effects on American food, clothing, language, and ways of life. The extent of the influence is most evident in language, where hundreds of words of native origin entered English permanently, especially words for food, flora, fauna, indigenous clothing and dwellings, and geographical features. The depth of this influence has, in general, been unacknowledged, even by linguistic studies, which have tended to focus on the obvious, such as place-names, rather than on the frequent daily uses of words related to American domestic life. (Jack Weatherford's *Native Roots: How the Indians Enriched America* [1991] explores this influence in nineteen chapters covering all aspects of North American culture.) The large number of native words in American English suggests how tightly intertwined native and European cultures were, even as the official texts and documents suggested otherwise. In fact, such texts constituted a solid line of resistance against forces that would have merged the European with the indigenous, creating a new figure on the American landscape.

Deloria argues that the Indian role has been a significant part of the American repertoire since before the Boston Tea Party. Contemporary graphic representations of Native figures make their shifting uses very clear:

At an intersection between noble and savage, tawny white and colored, the figure of the Indian had enormous iconographic flexibility. By arming it, clothing it, shifting its gender, or coloring its face, British cartoonists could depict the colonies as violent, civilized, savage, genteel, aggressive, subservient, rebellious, or justified. Visualizing the figure as an Indian princess . . . allowed one to evoke female sexuality in picturing the fertile landscapes or to show the colonies as available and vulnerable to the desires of English men. (29)

The Tea Party is a seminal event for Deloria, for the colonists' appropriation of the Indian figure to confront British authority signified both their acceptance of their emerging American identity and their denial of their British heritage. The Tea Party is simply the best known of many similar appropriations. From fraternal groups to patriotic ones, from literary conceits to commercial pitches, from conservative bankers to the Boy Scouts, Indian play has been part of the way Americans have at least temporarily quelled the dissonances of American life, reconciling order with freedom and constraint with license. Even quintessential white Texan Sam Houston kept running away from his hardworking family to enjoy a leisurely life of hunting, fishing, and game playing among his Cherokee friends, much to his family's consternation, and as a young adult he took pleasure in dressing in Cherokee buckskins and feathered turban (even on visits to Washington, D.C., to see his friend Andrew Jackson, a nemesis of the Cherokees). His long-standing love affair with a respected Cherokee woman ended only with the Trail of Tears and his immersion in Texas politics. (A fine fictional treatment is Lucia St. Clair Robson's *Walk in My Soul* [1985].)

The scope of appropriation of native figures is so broad and the levels of appropriation so varied that no survey of the practice is possible here. We will, rather, focus on two case studies in which the native story is lost in white constructions, the first a narrative that begins before the Republic was founded, the second a history lived at the beginning of our own modern period. One case involved a white captive and the other, the son of a captive; this white influence provided no bridge to understanding native culture, as we might hope and expect, but justified further appropriation.

Mary Jemison: A Native Life Appropriated

Mary Jemison's story is a straightforward narrative of her experiences, completely free of the Christian devotional frameworks established by Puritan captivity accounts and, at least on the surface, of rhetorical manipulation. Jemison, abducted as a child, completely forgot how to read and had no memory of her previous religious instruction. Given the total absence of native-authored accounts of daily life among the Indians, her narrative would seem to be invaluable, the inside story of a white Indian of very long standing, the tale of a person honored by both cultures, an account free of social and cultural agendas. However, what seems to be a candid, honest report is in fact an appropriated text greatly corrupted in its creation and further distorted in its marketing, a story subject to skepticism on a number of important points. The significance of this fact lies not just in fairly treating the historical Mary Jemison, but also in understanding that the forces which make her story less than reliable also distort and deform the vast majority of stories told about, and even sometimes by, Native Americans. Seeing the Indian figure in American culture is simple; understanding the complex Native Americans who lie behind the figure has been nearly impossible. Current popular fiction simply continues this phenomenon.

Mary Jemison was between twelve and fifteen years old when she was abducted from her parents' farm near Gettysburg in western Pennsylvania in 1755, an area that during the French and Indian War was contested by all three sets of combatants. Her parents were killed by the Shawnees as the war party escaped; Mary was given moccasins, suggesting, at least in the convention of the captivity narrative, that she was to be spared. She describes in horrendous detail seeing her family's scalps being prepared for preservation and display, her mother's standing out because of its red hair. She is taken down the Ohio to a Seneca village, where, after a period of adjustment and rapid learning of native ways, she is adopted into the tribe to replace a warrior lost in battle. Assimilating rapidly into Seneca life, she eventually marries a warrior; has a child by him; loses her husband to sickness; moves to the Genesee valley of western New York, carrying her infant son on a wintry trek through the wilderness; and becomes a Seneca worthy, marrying a famous chieftain, acquiring property, and living as a respected Indian leader until her death at ninety, in 1833. She was interviewed by James Seaver over a period of several days in 1823, an interview that formed the basis for the narrative of her life, the best-known captivity story of this much-studied genre.

Jemison, though blonde and blue-eyed, and retaining a Celtic lilt in her English even after speaking primarily the Seneca language for sixty-five years, was nevertheless indisputably a legitimate member of her tribe, not a white would-be Indian. She tells Seaver she quickly forgot all her religious instruction in Christianity, and even lost the ability to read; her defense of Seneca and Iroquois values and behavior is frank about shortcomings but sturdy in its confident outlook. One would hope for (and many readers seem to find) a culturally level playing field in this report spoken in Jemison's native tongue of English, an English lacking the rhetorical conceits and flourishes that come with literacy, a straightforward language free of the European-American blinders imposed by religion, civic and social presuppositions, and group psychology. This is precisely the appeal of encountering the Other that has given the Jemison account such staying power: a walk in her moccasins, unburdened by linguistic and cultural translation, an answer to the question "What would it be like to become one of Them?" Yet, Jemison's account was corrupted in its telling; her text was written over and appropriated by white interests, and even this prototypical account by an authentic white Indian must be read with an eye to mainstream and commercial agendas.

The circumstances involved in the construction of the narrative are fairly well understood, though the real questions of its authenticity are tantalizingly unanswerable. James Seaver was a retired physician who lived in Pembroke (now Darien), New York. Almost nothing is known of his interview with Mary Jemison beyond what he reported in his preface to the original edition, and, of course, the indirect internal evidence of the narrative itself. Seaver is at pains to inform the reader that "Strict fidelity has been observed in the composition: consequently, no circumstance has been intentionally exaggerated by the painting of fancy, nor by fine flashes of rhetoric: neither has the picture been rendered more dull than the original" (*A Narrative*, xi–xii). However, he also points out that his subject is eighty years old and "destitute of education," and that she has had a difficult life, full of incident and "calculated to impair the faculties of the mind" (xii). Against these warnings we may put the first sentence of the narrative, supposedly in her own words:

Although I may have frequently heard the history of my ancestry, my recollection is too imperfect to enable me to trace it further back than to my father and mother, whom I have often heard mention the families from whence they originated, as having possessed wealth and honorable stations under the government of the country in which they resided. (*A Narrative*, 25)

In Chapter 1, she recalls her shipboard birth and subsequent troubles in an eighty-three-word sentence:

In the course of their voyage I was born, to be the sport of fortune and almost an outcast to civil society; to stem the current of adversity through a long chain of vicissitudes, unsupported by the advice of tender parents, or the hand of an affectionate friend; and even without the enjoyment, from others, of any of those tender sympathies that are adapted to the sweetening of society, except such as naturally flow from uncultivated minds, that have been calloused by ferocity. (*A Narrative*, 27)

It is churlish to demand of an age innocent of precise recording devices a standard of fidelity it could never have achieved. Seaver, trained as a physician rather than as a journalist or court recorder, must be presumed to have written some sort of notes in pen and ink, later rewriting them into Mary's first-person account. (Since the interview lasted only two days or so and produced twenty-six chapters of material, we know little could have been written down verbatim.) Though the late eighteenth and early nineteenth centuries had very different ideas from our own about verisimilitude and authenticity, there is nevertheless so much that smacks of Seaver in the elegant sentence style that it puts in doubt some of the conclusions "Mary Jemison" comes to: Can we believe an eighty-year-old former captive, illiterate in English, would express herself this way? While the events depicted (the "plot") are no doubt based on some version of what "really" happened to Mary Jemison, some anti-Indian comments evince the amanuensis (Seaver admired Jemison but reflected the bias of his time about Indians).

In *White Captives: Gender and Ethnicity on the American Frontier* (1993), June Namias quotes Mary V. Dearborn's apt term for this writing process, "mid-wiving," a process that at best "translates, transcribes, and annotates" the true intentions of the original author (151). Women, of course, had few voices of their own in this period, and ethnic women had none at all. This last may partly explain the curious flatness of affect throughout the account: there was no model for this kind of discourse. Although Namias suggests the mix of Jemison's words and Seaver's words was in a "language common to female literature of the day," it was a language with which Seaver, but not Jemison, would have been familiar (152). Namias is correct, however, to classify the readership of the Jemison narrative: Did the primarily female readers of the Jemison story (defined as such by Namias) see her as *white* woman, white *woman*, or *Indian* woman? Jemison's account of her long life is supple enough to accommodate all three readings. This flexibility and openness account for much of the ongoing popularity of the story, for mainstream white readers can bend its substance to their agendas. Deloria's focus on playing Indian can be used to tease out new insights into Namias's classification: whites can play Indian, women can play Indian women, even men can imaginatively play Indian women. Just as identity on the frontier was always potentially in the process of re-formation, so this authentic-yet-fictional narrative invites consideration of the borders of social identity, the locus where social construction becomes visible (*see* Deloria, *passim*).

The publishing history of the account also gives one pause. Seaver added bits and pieces to the story, as well as a long appendix providing a supposedly informed commentary on Seneca and Iroquois life and on historical events in western New York during the Revolution. Mary Jemison's point of view is noticeably absent, but Seaver's version of events nevertheless acquires considerable credibility from the frame of Jemison's narrative. The first edition sold an incredible one hundred thousand copies in its first year, despite being published in Canandaigua, a small central upstate New York town. The narrative went through twenty-seven printings and twenty-three editions in the next 105 years (Namias, 152). A number of versions, including a recent one self-described as fictionalized (Rayna M. Gangi's *Mary Jemison: White Woman of the Seneca* [1995]), are still in print. Appropriated after James Seaver's death in 1827 by his brother William, the profitable narrative was revised by adding unacknowledged treatises on geography and other matters, and heightening the anti-Indian sections that James Seaver had included when Mary Jemison was reticent about warrior values and behavior. William Seaver's coeditor, one Ebenezer Mix, even replaced some Indian place-names with English ones because he thought the Indian words were fading quickly!

Namias's devastating analysis of the corruption of Mary Jemison's narrative is a model of how we should approach any number of popular "Indian" narratives: if not corrupted in the telling, they are attenuated in their promotion. The

"truth" of the Indian perspective—that is, an authentic version of cultural practices and attitudes, of historical occurrences or important spiritual events—is
retold in the language and forms of a culture based on assumptions far distant
from the native. The versions thus created then leave the control of their original
authors, becoming written over and rewritten by new authors with agendas almost unthinkable at the point of origin. Ameliorating forces, admittedly, have
perhaps improved the crude, ham-handed distortion that the Seavers felt free to
impose on Mary Jemison's narrative. The genres that include Native Americans
as important players have changed dramatically over the last few decades. Another fairly recent change is a consciousness of how the writing process shapes
the written product, but misshaping the Native American is still the rule, even
in more recent times. The appropriate question addresses the degree of shaping,
not the fact of its presence.

Quanah Parker: Appropriating the Appropriators

A second model of a Native American whose life and history disappeared
into legends serving white agendas had, like Mary Jemison, a powerful white
connection. Whereas Jemison was an adopted Indian, Quanah Parker was the
son of Cynthia Ann Parker, the most famous white captive in the Southwest,
and Peta Nocona, an important Comanche war chief. Cynthia Ann was abducted
in May 1836 from Fort Parker, a small settlement of Baptists on the Navasota
River not far from present-day Waco, Texas. She was nine years old at the time,
and just four years later apparently rejected a chance to reestablish contact with
her relatives, who nevertheless continued to search for her. Cynthia Ann was
eventually captured by the Texas Rangers in 1861, when she was twenty-five,
and lived unhappily with what remained of her white family until she died nine
years later.

Quanah (the name means "perfume," "fragrance," or "odor" in Comanche)
thus lost all contact with his mother at an early age, perhaps when he was nine
or so, assuming he was born around 1852 (Hagan, 7). Very little is known of
his youth and early manhood, though several commentators speculate that, as a
mixed-blood son of a captive, he probably followed Comanche ways rigorously,
striving to establish his identity and right to belong to a group that might reject
him. Whatever his youthful motivations, Quanah undoubtedly participated in,
and perhaps led, raids on white settlements in Texas and fought in the final
battles against the U.S. cavalry in the Staked Plain and Palo Duro areas of West
Texas. He had achieved high status in his band by 1875, when he surrendered
to a cavalry officer at Fort Sill, Oklahoma, who noted the unusual influence the
young Comanche, then in his early twenties, had among his fellows. This no-
tation began a thirty-five-year fascination with Quanah on the part of an impressively varied contingent of whites in the Southwest and in Washington,
D.C., but despite this wealth of commentary, the true Quanah remains as
shrouded in mystery as the real Mary Jemison.

Some of this mystery is understandable, for Quanah undoubtedly wished to keep aspects of his early life quiet, specifically his raids on white settlements in Texas. The violence of Comanche depredations had struck terror in the hearts of Texans and Mexicans, and even toward the end of his life, thirty-five years after giving up the warpath, Quanah still worried about his reception if he returned to Texas, his assertion to the governor "I am a Texas man myself" notwithstanding (Hagan, 103). It is this attempt to assimilate and take control in a new and alien environment that contrasts Quanah's case with Mary Jemison's, for the son of Nocona and Cynthia Ann was never malleable clay to be molded into an image agreeable to whites. No passive victim of appropriation like Jemison, Quanah was ever negotiating with his superiors, demanding authority and prestige in return for supporting the white agents in their reservation policies (he was recognized as the head of all Comanches, a title and role that had never existed before). He cut profitable deals with Texas cattlemen on leases of reservation pasture land and fought a political rearguard action against attempts to open the reservation to white settlers after the Dawes Act, visiting Washington D.C. innumerable times to lobby Indian Agency officials and Congress directly. Quanah used his formidable political and negotiating skills to hold firm on aspects of his culture that he apparently felt defined him: he refused to cut his hair (Quanah wore twice as many braids as George Washington, one of his white defenders pointed out ironically); in the face of intense pressure from missionaries and antidrug crusaders, he headed a peyote cult his entire adult life, even persuading some white officials to participate; and he refused to give up polygamy, asking a persistently objecting white official to choose which of his wives he should give up, and explain personally to her why.

Quanah was justly celebrated as one of the most famous men in Texas and Oklahoma, courted by cattlemen and politicians, visited by a touring Theodore Roosevelt, and almost bankrupted by unsought white visitors requiring his hospitality. He even had a bit part in the first film made in Oklahoma, *The Bank Robbery* (1908). As a show or "parade" Indian, he played the Forth Worth Fat Stock Show and the Texas State Fair in Dallas. Demeaning as this must have been for the aging warrior, there still seems little doubt Quanah was held in high regard by large numbers of whites in the state of his birth and in his adopted home.

It is thus surprising that in spite of this high level of assimilation and notoriety, so little is known about the "real" Quanah Parker. Like Mary Jemison over a hundred years earlier, Quanah's inner life was written over by white expectations, white interpretations, and white demands. Though a true celebrity of the early twentieth century, he never gained full control of the ways he was described and understood. Hagan, perhaps his best biographer, says it best:

Virtually nothing is available to the researcher except that which has come through a white conduit. The observations on Quanah's activities and personality are usually those made by white men. Any Indian's comments have been recorded by a white man. Even

Quanah's letters were written for him by white men or, late in his life, by an educated son or a white daughter-in-law. These individuals were endowed with varying degrees of education, so that at one moment Quanah sounds barely literate, and the next he comes across as a college graduate. (xv)

The last sentence could be a critique of Mary Jemison's story, for all we hear is the variation in amanuenses.

A further consideration is the period in which Quanah lived. Though born in the middle of the nineteenth century, about twenty years after Mary Jemison's death, the last of the Comanche chiefs lived well into the twentieth century, traveling by train and automobile, having messages sent by telegraph, and even enjoying a telephone in his ranch house. His life went from a youth in a hunter-gatherer band to the age of flight (the first plane landed in Oklahoma during his residence there). Quanah lived in a time of multiple printed records, newspapers, typewriters, anthropologists, inquisitive reporters, advertising, and photography (many photographs of Quanah, his fellow chiefs, his family, and his white intimates exist). We would expect Mary Jemison's voice to be a frail record, easily drowned out by later and louder versions of events. Yet, despite modern methods of ascertaining authentic versions of events, systems in which we put great trust and which assure us of the validity of our current views, we know little about Quanah's inner life, his true self, his "real" identity. His apparent maneuvering aside, what did he really believe he was doing? How did he regard his white superiors in the Indian Agency at Anadarko, his business partners like Texas cattleman Charlie Goodnight, his fellow chiefs Apiatan, Eschiti, Big Looking Glass? Did the much-married Quanah feel love, lust, or companionship for his eight wives? Were his marriages to widows a Comanche duty toward women bereft of support or attempts to relive a lost youth?

As with Mary Jemison, there are many Quanah Parkers: youthful Comanche warrior, peyote cult leader, Texas half-breed son of Cynthia Ann, family man, supporter of compromise, partner of Texas cattlemen, promoter of Indian schools, embracer of modern ways, liaison between the white man and other Indian tribes like the Apaches—the list of roles could be extended at some length. Quanah no doubt encouraged many of these perceived identities to serve his own ends, but white fascination, past and present, also constructed most of the multiple Quanahs. The Indian figure plays a special role in American culture, and real native peoples are pale substitutes or, even worse, irritating reminders of the falsity of illusory Indians. No doubt Quanah understood this and kept his counsel discreetly.

Unfortunately, the reticence of Mary Jemison and Quanah Parker leaves us, as Hagan suggests, with only white versions of their lives. Were this a phenomenon confined to a brutal and benighted past, we might discount the significance of these lost voices, but in fact our own time, even almost a century after Quanah's death, drowns out authentic native voices, sometimes by appropriation, more often by overwhelming them in a cacophony of white versions of events. Given the power of the English language and English literary-rhetorical convention to frame events and to dictate the terms of the discourse, native voices must risk shrillness simply to be heard.

Our concern in this book, of course, is not the problem of seeing Native Americans whole in historical accounts but rather in the less factually grounded medium of popular fiction. Structuring both problems as an a fortiori argument gives perspective: If the less difficult provides poor results, what can one expect of the more difficult? Historical documents perforce have some reference to verifiable reality; popular fiction can sometimes be pure fantasy. Since finding the "real" story is so difficult, how can consumers of popular fiction avoid an undiscriminating acceptance of all versions of Native Americans with which they are presented? Authenticity in fiction involves the sense that a narrative gives a "true" account of historical and sociological realities, an account that could be held against established history and objective scholarship and be termed fair. Unless the work gives overt signals that it should be read differently (as allegory, as a surreal vision, as clearly symbolic), fiction is likely to be read as mimesis, as having at least a nodding acquaintance with historical reality, especially when it is formed of elements less than obviously fictional, such as identifiable settings and cultural practices (plot and character are more likely to be seen as authorial inventions, in other words). Again, such literal readings are more common among consumers of popular fiction, whose approach to reading is less likely to be informed by a critical awareness of authorial agendas than that of more schooled readers of belletristic works. Mimesis is out of favor in the academy but rides high in the saddle of popular consumption.

Degrees of historical authenticity in popular fiction about Native Americans are scattered across a wide range, from the carefully researched, competently written, and respectfully oriented to the sloppy, careless, manipulative, and even stereotypically racist. No work offered for mainstream consumption has a final claim on authenticity, however, for reasons we will delineate in detail in the next two chapters. Such works are written in English and use European-originated literary genres such as the short story and the novel, forms that make genre demands on the shaping of the material. Most important, mainstream works of popular fiction are undeniably just that, accommodating the general values of the American majority. Even Native American authors writing about authentic Native American milieus and in indigenous genres (such as the Trickster tale) must adapt and change them to meet readership expectations, a determining economic reality especially in a large complex nation. We can postulate works written in, say, the Cherokee language, or read with a full awareness of native religio-philosophical belief systems, but such accounts would be hermetic, confined to a narrow band of fully informed readers.

Janice Radway, in "The Aesthetic in Mass Culture: Reading the 'Popular' Literary Text," draws a firm line between "real" literature and works written for mass consumption. She rejects the concept of authenticity completely, asserting that, despite pretenses to realism (mimesis), popular writing generally lacks verisimilitude; it does not accurately duplicate the outside world. In fact, she notes, popular novels "deliberately avoid portraying . . . real human beings or actual occurrences in the real world . . . even while they render the physical character-istics of that world quite faithfully"; they "construct their imaginary universe according to an aesthetic norm which is very different from that which specifies the need to imitate not only possible but highly probable human characteristics, motive and actions" (*Reading the Romance*, 420). Does popular fiction create psychological realism? Radway's answer is that popular texts have rhetorical purposes, and often aim at emotional titillation; in the main she finds popular fiction purposefully reassuring, "perhaps seeming to challenge the readership's values but in fact ultimately confirming them."

Apart from questioning the presumption that worthy literature must be in opposition to mainstream values, we feel that these generalizations also fail to do justice to any number of praiseworthy works, novels and stories that, by surviving the tests of time, may well achieve the status of literature. Like de-spised slang terms that a generation later find their way into formal prose, works of popular culture may move up the status ladder—evaluating one's own period is notoriously risky. Radway's charge that some mass fiction fails to duplicate the outside world clearly needs some stipulative limitations: some works provide carefully researched backgrounds for cardboard characters involved in unlikely plots; others, the reverse. (Some, of course, are simply worthless in every way, a fact true of all artistic efforts.) Since some popular fiction does demonstrably stand examination of its historical and psychological-cultural veracity despite the many impediments to authenticity we have delineated, we should not consign it all to the closed category of servile entertainment, especially when it purports to represent the experiences of an entire community. Radway tries to have it too many ways, rejecting the mimetic approach completely as well as claiming that the mimesis is always incompetent. Rather than seeing all popular writing as being of a kind, we believe that certain kinds of authenticity—sometimes historical, sometimes psychological, sometimes cultural—inform the best fiction and deserve acknowledgment.

CONCLUSION

Given these innate limits on authenticity, how should popular fiction about the Native American be approached and read? The chapters that follow will explore the questions which must attend our reading of popular fiction about "Indians": What inherent differences divide native and mainstream literatures? How are mainstream agendas and concerns advanced and privileged by even the best of such fiction? How can readers accommodate to the distorting ele-ments such as those that have warped Mary Jemison's phenomenally popular narrative for nearly two hundred years? The examples of Mary Jemison and Quanah Parker illustrate how ingrained this appropriation of the Indian by whites has been.

We will also attempt to formulate, through analysis of a rich variety of sample cases, a practical aesthetic for reading works of popular writing about Native Americans, not with the ambition of achieving final answers but of helping interested readers deal with their own reactions: Why do I respond so favorably to this work, and what should I think about it? What does it tell me about Native Americans, about mainstream U.S. culture, and about myself?

Finally, we hope our efforts can be seen as a tribute to all the fine writers of popular fiction who have tried, sometimes at a risk to their popularity and sales, to set records straight, to start in motion new understandings and ways of shaping identity, to show how to encounter the Other in peace and reconciliation.

2

Native American Perceptions of Reality: Accessing a Different Worldview

There are these beads I love. Deep ones, made of special glass. Czech beads called northwest trader blue. In them, you see the depth of the spirit life. See sky as through a hole in your body. Water. Life. See into the skin of the coming world.

—Louise Erdrich, *Antelope Wife*, 214

I had a lot of time to think about this blueness . . . it appeared and disappeared, the blue at the base of a flame, the blue in a fading line when I shut my eyes, the blue in one moment at the edge of the sky at dusk. That blue of my beads, I understood was the blueness of time. . . . Time is blue. Or time is the blue in things.

—*The Antelope Wife*, 215

For non-Native American readers, the above short discourse on the nature of time and its appropriate color from the final pages of Louise Erdrich's novel *The Antelope Wife* might seem like a poetic digression from the ongoing action of the story, but in fact its insistence on the absolute link between the abstract or spiritual realm and the concrete or physical realm is actually at the heart of the author's vision. Blue is a powerful color associated with sky, water, and fullness of life. Native American author Clifford Trafzer, for example, invokes a color symbolism similar to that used by Erdrich in the title of his short story collection *Blue Dawn, Red Earth* (1996). By joining the colors to sky and earth, he points to the experience of the joining of the "powers" of sky and earth to complete and balance reality.

But not all Native American tribes used the same color symbolism. In *The Silent Language* (1959) cultural anthropologist Edward T. Hall reports a humorous communication breakdown over color among the Navajo, for whom each color carries a ranking and a value. To bring democracy to the Navajo, the government assigned each candidate for the tribal council a color, so the Navajo voter could simply select the color that represented his/her candidate. However, since blue is a positive color and red a negative one, the government had unknowingly loaded the dice for the blue candidate (111). How badly the government misused color symbolism is clear from the Navajo assignment of color in the sand paintings belonging to their ritual healing ceremonies. There the color blue indicates restoration and the triumph over witchcraft. For the Navajo, however, red carries negative connotations and so is left out of the color sequence of the sand painting. Thus, the color symbolism of the tribal tradition is influential even in contemporary settings. The color symbolism of Erdrich's short passages represents one of a series of literary puzzles that non-Native American readers must learn to decode in order to understand even partially the story as the Native American writer intended it to be understood. *The Antelope Wife* is an excellent model of the difficulties and benefits of reconciling the European-Western and native outlooks. Both this chapter and Chapter 3 will provide some of the decoding materials necessary to better comprehend Native American literary works such as *The Antelope Wife*.

Louise Erdrich, a figure of some note in contemporary fiction, with eight best-selling novels and high praise from *New York Times* reviewers, builds on the conventions of her Ojibway heritage to structure her sagas of an extended family. Readers confronting her novels must choose whether to deal with substance or surface. If they retain the mainstream mind-set typically employed with most fiction, readers will still be drawn into intriguing descriptions, characters, and plots but will miss a great deal that Erdrich intends. Likewise, the Native American authors discussed in the next chapter can be read and studied in this basic Euro-American way. However, if the Native American author incorporates substantial references to both the style and the materials of the traditional Native American perspective, then to fully understand the literary power and meaning of the work, readers must be willing to see with new eyes, to work to expand their usual mind-set to include a point of view very different from their own. For example, even the title of Erdrich's book, *The Antelope Wife*, refers to a traditional Native American belief in shape-shifting, the ability of certain individuals to slip into and out of various life forms—whether celestial, plant, animal, or human. This power does not indicate deity, for shape-shifting was thought to be a commonplace occurrence in earlier tribal times, but it does indicate an intimate, non-Western connection with nature and the natural world.

Erdrich's story begins with the abduction of the Antelope Woman, an enchanting magical presence, and sustains the theme of shape-shifting throughout the narrative. A non-native reader may dismiss the numerous references to antelopes as simply puzzling or elusive, but doing so will diminish the wealth of the reader's experience, for understanding the role of shape-shifting is essential to fully participating in the text, and expending effort to gain background in

Native American materials will allow readers to identify the author's intent more fully.

This chapter's exploration of the spiritual and physical dimensions of traditional Native American cultures will be limited to five representative tribal groups: Sioux, Beaver, Anasazi, Navajo, and Hopi. Given the vast quantity of material and directions possible, a single chapter cannot be comprehensive, but certain guideposts for a journey of discovery may be cited. The thesis of this short review is twofold. First, Native Americans had complex systems of abstract thought that they expressed by means of physical constructs and structures, systems often unrecognized in mainstream criticism; spirit and matter were merely different dimensions of a single reality. Second, the uniqueness of each Native American tribal group is preserved in its epic stories of the creation process. In these stories, spirit and matter dance a precarious movement between holistic unity and shattered fragmentation.

The first half of the chapter will present the specific techniques for grounding grand-scale abstract realities in physical patterns that denote meaning. Two terms—the "map" of the cosmos and the "web" of being—are particularly helpful notions for allowing a non-Native reader to grasp the essential connectedness of all points in time and space. Native American tradition affirms that the realm of the spirit has a sacred geography that must be honored; hence the word "map." The image suggested by the word "web" further underscores the relationship between each point in the schema that is creation.

NATIVE AMERICAN IMAGES

A religious and cosmological key is necessary to unlock the gateway to the powerful and transforming literary visions of contemporary Native American literature. The key at the heart of Native American ways of knowing is contained in the statement *Time and space are one*. At first glance, the statement of the unity of time and space seems modern, for the unity of space and time is an important theme in Einstein's physics and in the discourse of abstract philosophical systems. Surely an attempt to understand the cosmology that undergirds the writing of Native American authors would lead in a different direction, that is, to the exploration of the archaic worldviews of hunter-gatherers or of corn planters. Nevertheless, the unity of time and space—an insight indeed as profound as Einstein's—stands at the center of the Native American cosmology and is crucial for an appreciation of contemporary Native American authors. Paula Gunn Allen, a noted Native American author, explains: "Native writers write out of tribal traditions and into them. They, like oral storytellers, work within the literary tradition that is at base connected to ritual and beyond that to tribal metaphysics or mysticism" (Trafzer, *Blue Dawn*, 7).

The Native Americans' understanding of the unity of time and space is based upon a prior understanding of the unity of time itself and of space itself. The journey to insight within contemporary Native American literature begins, first, with a decoding of the meaning of the oneness of time; second, with a decoding of the unity of space; and third, with an understanding of how the unity of time and the unity of space are combined in a single vision.

For time to be seen as one reality, past and future have to be experienced and understood as sensate, that is, as sensibly tangible, audible, visual, scented, and tasted in the present. They must be experienced in the present time in the depths of the "bones," or in the core of the "gut." Native American sacred stories and rituals, their words and acts of power, bring to awareness, intensify, and expand this surety that past and future are *here*, now present. In order to see space as one reality, one must experience everything encompassed within the four directions of north, south, east, and west as a sensible unity. Therefore, when the traditional Native American drum sounds, it stirs the heartbeat of all of time and of the whole Earth. When the traditional Native Americans "see," their vision encompasses past, present, future, and the four directions in a single sighting. This drumbeat and this vision override and penetrate any artificial boundaries placed on time and space by non-Native American perception. Non-Native Americans impose political boundary lines and clock time on their perception of space and time. The traditional Native American perceives these boundaries as unnatural and artificial. Thus, for non-Native Americans to enter the thought world and the literature of Native Americans requires a challenging act of imagination.

But how was this sense of immediacy, of bringing together and unifying all points in time and all points in space, communicated? The answer is simple: through the powerful, rhythmic voices of the traditional Native American storytellers who generation after generation recounted the narratives of their peoples. These voices, and the vision of the unity of time and space they convey, continue to resound in the literature, in the novels and short stories, of contemporary Native American authors. How works like *The Antelope Wife* draw on the oral tradition to bring immediacy and unity will be most clear from the discussions that follow in this and the next chapter.

Accessing the Native American worldview is the most critical problem for the non-Native American reader of Native American literature: How can such a reader possibly enter into a vision and corresponding set of responses strikingly different from what is known and felt in Western bones? The answer is to study the religious and cosmological visions that are woven into Native American narratives, those of both traditional Native American storytellers and their counterparts, the contemporary Native American authors. Consider these pages an invitation to discover the worlds of both traditional storytellers and contemporary writers.

The Lakota Map

A quick survey of Native American materials reveals the existence of numerous diagrammatic schemes or maps used by the various tribes to summarize the most sacred and powerful truths. Appropriately, the first step for the non-native reader on a journey of discovery will be to explore the process of traditional mapmaking. The map of the Native American world guides the modern reader just as it guided generations of traditional peoples. However, the non-Native American often raises a series of misplaced questions about this map: *Who created the map? When did it come into existence? How did it evolve and gain more precise definition?* Such questions stress Enlightenment linearity and cause-effect rationality, and thus are largely irrelevant to the process this chapter will try to reconstruct.

The map is a "people's map of knowing." It emphatically belongs to the whole people. It describes what they know. The creation of the tribal map is democratic and participatory. The parameters of the map are not the creation or the property of professional scholars or priests. The map comes to be over long periods of time, enhanced through small individual flashes of insight gathered and accumulated into larger narratives. For example, Nicholas Black Elk, a holy man among the Lakota Sioux, received his powerful religious and cosmological vision when he was a nine-year-old boy in a feverish coma. Yet, the drama he witnessed in his dream was no fanciful free association of delirious details into a bizarre narrative. Rather, the vision he narrated was very much in the tradition of the Lakota religious and cosmological structures. The people who heard his story recognized their traditional map, which defines both sacred history and geography. They knew the way. At the same time, in the retelling of his vision, Nicholas Black Elk enhanced and extended the "knowing" of his people. His vision, masterfully recounted in a full chapter of John Neihardt's *Black Elk Speaks* (1932), reflects the basic features of the classic map and utilizes that map in each stage of its unfolding.

Mapmaking: Early Stages

Although the individual names of the Native Americans who participated in shaping this map of knowing are lost, the received words of the tribal elders, the guardians of the essential knowledge about time and space, today provide insight into the drawing of the map. Material from the Lakota tradition makes it possible to reconstruct some of the stages by which the map of knowing came to be drawn, while the words of Sioux spiritual teachers provide guidance.

According to the Lakota way of knowing, persistent observation brings the world of space and time into focus:

Everything as it moves, makes stops. The bird as it flies stops in one place to make its nest, and in another to rest in its flight. So the god has stopped. The sun is one place where he has stopped. The moon, the stars, the winds, he has been with. The trees, the animals, are all where he has stopped, and the Indian sends his prayers there to reach the place where the god has stopped and win help. (McLuhan, 37)

As the passage indicates, Native Americans perceive two elements in the earth: distinctive physiological features in the earth and links between these features and a special "spiritual presence" or god of creation. These places, things, and living beings are sites of power, identified first by observed patterns in the realm of nature. These observed patterns are then extended to the larger-scale realm of spirit beings. They link the one who knows the map to both the Creator and his/her intermediaries. Although the whole of the natural environment is imbued with the presence of the source of creation, special locations and physical forms carry levels of intensified meaning, meanings that must be wrestled free from silence into articulation.

A second Lakota passage throws light on a further stage in the journey of "knowing." It envisions the world of space and time as circular and cyclical:

Everything the Power of the World does is done in a circle. The Sky is round and the earth is round like a ball and so are all the stars. The Wind, in its greatest power, whirls. Birds make their nests in circles. The sun comes forth and goes down in a circle. The moon does the same, and both are round. Even the seasons form a great circle in their changing. The life of a man is a circle from childhood to childhood and so it is in everything where power moves. (J. E. Brown, 92)

The movements of objects as distant as the celestial bodies in their daily and yearly cyclical patterns, as well as the movements of things nearer at hand (like game animals), were carefully and astutely observed. These patterns of movement received close attention and were placed on the map, which was resolved into higher definition with each additional insight. At the same time, Native Americans watched carefully for what did not move, for fixed and ordered structures, which added further nuances to their map of knowing. They concluded that the map upon which the journey of creation is traversed is one that carries the dynamic tension between movement and rest.

Next, the Native American narratives describe the points of movement and rest by means of mathematical relationships. To sketch these points in narrative is to draw the map and to enable the listener to enter the journey of knowing. The tribal narratives reveal a belief that the Creator has repeatedly clustered the components of the physical world into groups of comparable numerical forms. They frequently cite the numbers 4, 5, and 7. The storyteller understood that the power of any story came from its correspondence to the thought and action of the Creator. In other words, to reach God, to speak his language, the Native American storyteller used a language of precisely patterned words dependent upon the description of physical shapes and forms. The description and enumeration of physical shapes and forms is part of the unified map of time and space.

Again, the insight encapsulated in the following passage extends the pattern of the map:

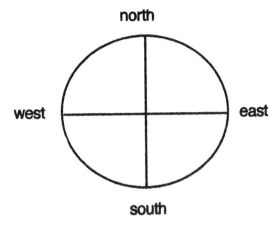

The Lakota grouped all their activities by fours. They recognized four directions: the west, the north, the east, and the south; four divisions of time: the day, the night, the moon, and the year; four parts in everything that grows from the ground: the roots, the stem, the leaves, and the fruit; four kinds of things that breathe: those that crawl, those that fly, those that walk on four legs, and those that walk on two legs; four things above the world: the sun, the moon, the sky, and the stars . . . the great spirit caused everything to be in fours, mankind should do everything possible in fours. (McLuhan, 177)

When the physical and temporal indices suggested by each of these three passages are combined or indeed superimposed, the map unlocking the mysteries of existence emerges. Roughly sketched, this map appears as a circle with the four directions and, at the center point, the place where one meets God. The center is the most direct route to God. The circle protects the inclusive nature of sacral reality. The number 4 applies to the four quadrants constituting the significant focal points. The center establishes the single point at which the separate powers of the cosmos converge. While the pattern seems elementary, this map represents the organizing principle for the religious stories and ceremonies of the Lakota and beyond their tribal borders. The same patterns are used by Native American peoples from the Northeast woodlands to the Southwest deserts. The map of knowing spans the continent, and though it receives endless elaboration, its basic geometry remains intact. In Louis Owens's novel *Bone Game*, for example, a traditional prayer that automatically springs to the main character's lips in times of danger invokes the map of knowing: "I had been looking far, sending my spirit north, south, east, and west" (239).

THE GREAT VISION: STORY INTO IMAGE

Nicholas Black Elk (ca. 1862–1950), a holy man of the Oglala Sioux whose teachings have been gathered into two volumes, *Black Elk Speaks* (as told to Neihardt) and *The Sacred Pipe* (J. E. Brown), is the primary source for an intertribal Native American theological vision. According to Vine DeLoria, Black Elk provides

> the canon or at least the central core of a North American theological canon. . . . The book has become a North American bible of all tribes. They look to it for spiritual guidance, sociological identity, political insight, and affirmation of the continuing substance of Indian tribal life. (Neihardt, xiii)

Within his lifetime Black Elk witnessed the transition of his people from the lifestyle of buffalo hunting on the Great Plains to the devastating battles on the Little Big Horn and at Wounded Knee Creek. He was cousin to Crazy Horse and had known both Sitting Bull and Red Cloud. In 1930 he decided to publish his early visions and the traditional Lakota teachings. Our interest is in the story of his great vision and how that vision recapitulates the traditional map of knowing.

Nicholas Black Elk's vision is a prime example of the ways that spatial definitions, a geometry of sacred space, shape a story vision. The transcribed version of his great vision is almost thirty pages long, filled with complex symbols including references to color, number, direction, animal guardians, the tree of life, the *axis mundi*, earth forms, and so on. How would a nine-year-old child or even an adult preserve the richness of the vision without losing bits and pieces of it with time's passage? The answer is that the complexity of the vision is organized along the lines of the traditional map or symbolic structure of the tribal storytellers. When the details of the vision are understood as the layers of a complex image rather than as a sequence of individual, discrete, and unique events, the content is both accessible and preserved. The following five diagrams translate words and ideas into images.

1. Horses of the four directions announce the council of the Grandfathers.

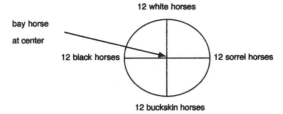

12 white horses

bay horse
at center

12 black horses

12 sorrel horses

12 buckskin horses

2. The Grandfather of each direction bestows his unique gift.

At the center point,
Grandfather of the Sky and Earth
tells Black Elk that he is a relative
to all living things in the sky
realm and that he will live to old age

a healing herb and the cleansing wind

wooden cup of water/bow/
power over life and death

peace pipe with spotted eagle
on the stem

bright red stick/sprouts into life
when planted/tree of life

3. Black Elk is advised that his people will complete a journey along two roads

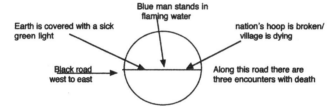

Blue man stands in
flaming water

Earth is covered with a sick
green light

nation's hoop is broken/
village is dying

Black road
west to east

Along this road there are
three encounters with death

4. Along this road the Tree of life is planted, dies, and must be revived.

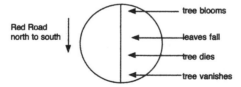

Red Road
north to south

tree blooms

leaves fall

tree dies

tree vanishes

5. Black Elk is taken to the top of a mountain at the center of the world and says,

"I saw that the sacred hoop of my people was one of many hoops,

that made one circle, wide as daylight and as starlight."

While the meaning of each symbolic element in the Great Vision deserves a lengthy explanation, the present concern is specifically to detect the repetition and use of structural patterns of meaning. These maps or patterns of meaning are ways that both visionaries and storytellers used, and still use, to translate spiritual events into physical images. These maps link space and time into an eternal present.

If mainstream readers of Native American literature are to grasp the Native American vision and readily translate its dreams, stories, and concepts of time and space into visual images, such readers must observe how the map of knowing shapes religious rituals and how ritual depends upon the same circular pattern. In the Lakota tradition, the circle, quartered and centered, is the organizing structure for the most sacred ritual forms. Thus, the Sun Dance, the vision quest, the sweat lodge, and the Pipe Ceremony all utilize this basic structure. Chapter 3 will explore how the novels of Thomas King, Susan Power, and Louis Owens purposefully employ these rituals.

Vision Quest and Sweat Lodge

Nicholas Black Elk's descriptions of traditional ways also provide an account of a vision quest site. Therein, the circular map is incorporated into a system of prayer and movement. Two helpers accompany the lamenter, the one seeking a vision. They prepare the remote location chosen for the four-day vision quest, clearing an area and then marking the four directions and a center point. In *The Sacred Pipe*, Black Elk describes the process:

At this center they first make a hole in which they place some *kinnikinnik*, and then in this hole they set up a long pole with the offerings tied at the top. One of the helpers now goes about ten strides to the west, and in the same manner he sets up a pole here, tying offerings to it. He then goes to the center where he picks up another pole, and this he fixes at the north, again returning to the center. In the same manner he sets up poles at the east and the south. All this time the other helper has been making a bed of sage at the center so that when the "lamenter" is tired he may lie with his head against the center pole. . . . Entering the sacred place, the "lamenter" goes directly to the center pole, where he faces the west, and holding up his pipe with both hands he continues to cry: "O Wakan-Tanka, have pity on me, that my people may live!" (J. E. Brown, 57)

The lamenter then follows a circuit of movement from the center pole to the pole at the west, offering the same prayer and then returning to the center point. Each of the remaining directions is addressed—north, east, and south—with the lamenter always returning to the center pole. For the next four days he continues to walk this pattern, at times taking an hour or two to complete a single round. The Lakota map structures ways of prayer both individual and communal, and forms a bridge of connection between story and ritual.

Nicholas Black Elk's traditional description of the Lakota map persists in the contemporary ritual experience, as Wallace Black Elk (b. 1921) confirms. Wallace Black Elk is a Lakota shaman who received his early training from eleven spiritual "grandfathers," one of whom was Nicholas Black Elk. In his book, *Sacred Ways of the Lakota*, Wallace Black Elk describes at great length the material preparations necessary for a traditional sweat lodge. The following is a comprehensive list of elements to be gathered before the ritual begins:

a *chanunpa*, or pipe

tobacco for the prayer offerings

red wool for the Grandmother's robe

eagle feather and plume, conch shell

cotton in the six colors, black, red, yellow, white, blue, green

four types of food to be placed on the altar: water, corn, berries, and meat

saplings for the lodge frame

covers to block out light

thirty-six rocks the size of a human hand

a bucket, dipper, spring water

deer antler prongs (76)

Once they are assembled, the elements are carefully laid out to preserve the symbolism of the circle: the four-part color, number, and directional symbolism. Each step of the ritual process reinforces this symbolism. For the ceremony proper, the rocks are heated outside the sweat lodge and then brought inside to the fire pit. Dippers of spring water are poured over the rocks, releasing an intense steam. Significantly, the Lakota map or circular pattern reappears in the shaping and construction of the lodge. As Wallace Black Elk explains, each of the holes dug for the saplings that frame the lodge

is about eight inches deep and [the bottom] slants toward the center of the lodge. . . . So you put the sticks into the ground and bend them [over toward the center] and tie them together. There is a certain way you do that. When you are finished there is a square formed *by the frame* directly over the center pit of the lodge. Then you tie a hoop all the way around *the side* to keep the upright sticks in place. (78)

In other words, the traditional Lakota map is preserved in a ritual space. However, the structure is not the only part of the sweat lodge ceremony to carry the symbolism of the circular map. The ritual actions also proceed in a circular movement honoring each of the four directions and their spiritual content.

Anyone familiar with the great variety of the Native American religious and cosmological traditions may question the universality of the circular pattern, quartered and centered, among the various tribal groups. Nevertheless, a careful search shows that the structure appears time and again among many different

Native American peoples—a constant theme with endless embellishment. Literary examples are legion, but typical are the traditional storytelling sequences in Leslie Marmon Silko's *Ceremony*; these take the form of song stanzas that invoke the pattern of the circular map of the four directions. As Silko recounts the story of Kaup'a'ta, the gambler, two stanzas appear back to back following the patterns of oral storytelling:

> in four rooms of his house—
> the clouds of the east in the east room
> the clouds of the south in the south room
> the clouds of the west in the west room
> the clouds of the north in the north room.

> But one morning he went
> first to the north top of the west mountain
> then to the west top of the south mountain
> and then to the south top of the east mountain;
> and finally, it was on the east top of the north mountain (172)

The sequence ritualizes the traditional map of the universe—the four directions and the sacred circle.

The Beaver Tribe of British Columbia

A second tribal setting in which this circular map organizes the myriad details of existence into an interwoven whole is among the Beaver Indians, who were found far to the north of the Lakota, in British Columbia. Among the Beaver, the map that gives access to spirit and earth power contains the following diagrams, presented in their individual layers so that each element can be clearly noted. Together they suggest the ways in which the Beaver Indians defined space and time:

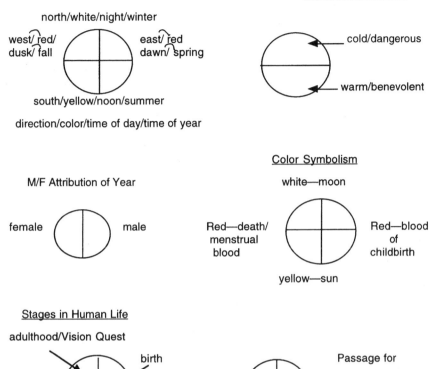

Divisions of the Year

north/white/night/winter

west/ red/
dusk/ fall

east/ red
dawn/ spring

south/yellow/noon/summer

direction/color/time of day/time of year

cold/dangerous

warm/benevolent

M/F Attribution of Year

female   male

Color Symbolism

white—moon

Red—death/
menstrual
blood

Red—blood
of
childbirth

yellow—sun

Stages in Human Life

adulthood/Vision Quest

birth

childhood

weaning

Passage for
Vision Quest and
shaman is along
axis at center pole

Viewing the map in this divided fashion may be misleading, however, because the pieces are in their authentic form only when they come together as parts of a single pattern. The composite map of knowing protects the unity of life.

The Anasazi

Before European contact there was another civilization with articulated patterns that show the unity of time and place: the Anasazi, the ancestors of the Pueblo in the southwestern United States, thought to have peaked around A.D. 1100. The rugged, spare terrain of their region gives some indication of the ingenuity of a people who carved out one hundred miles of roads linking their settlements. Fairly recently, archaeologists have discovered the artifact known as the Sun Dagger. Hidden from casual view on the top of Fahada Butte in Chaco Canyon, New Mexico, it is an Anasazi spiral pattern chipped into the rock face. Numerous petroglyphs, some of them also spiral-shaped, adorn the path leading up to the carved rock. However, the Sun Dagger is more than just another example of early Native American art. The spiral has "scientific" cosmological and religious significance, for this site provides the only currently known place on Earth where the precise timing of the summer and winter solstices, of the spring and autumn equinoxes, and of the nineteen-year cycle of the movements of the moon are all recorded and discernible by means of a single diagrammatic construct.

How and why was an instrument of such precision constructed? The Sun Dagger lies in a narrow crevice of rock large enough for only one or two individuals to gain access to the space. During the summer solstice, light pours through an opening between two rock slabs, each weighing several tons, that form the outside walls of the chamber. On a rock table in the center of the chamber a spiral has been carved. For a brief eighteen minutes, only at noon during the summer solstice, the light enters the enclosed area and moves vertically, precisely bisecting the spiral from top to bottom. In order for the shaft of light to move in this vertical path, the rock ledges were chipped away so that the light would bend and move in a controlled direction along the spiral pattern on the rock. The pattern carved in the rock is in effect an astronomical instrument correlated to a cosmological vision. The Anasazi map was not a simple calendar concerned merely with the marking of time in order to establish the seasons for planting or for ritual observances. The spiral shape reveals the precise and predictable patterns of the movements of the cosmos so that direct access to the power of the cosmos is acquired. The Anasazi could select no better time to channel the power of the sky into the earth realm than precisely at the summer solstice, when the light is at its point of greatest intensity.

In a corresponding pattern during the winter solstice, the movement of light on the rock surface has significant consequences for the life of the people. During the winter solstice two parallel shafts of light descend from top to bottom on the Sun Dagger, but this time on the extreme left and right edges of the spiral, warning of an absence of light and a weakening of the light force. The spiral devoid of light warns that the power of the cosmos has retreated and human activities must be brought into proper alignment with this situation. The patterns for the summer and winter solstices appear thus:

Light bisects the spiral   Light frames the spiral

A final diagram combining the summer and winter solstice patterns again reveals the circle quartered and centered:

A very brief survey of Native American cosmological materials presents insights important to our reading of Native American literature. At the source of creation was a God who initiated a process of creation that was both orderly and harmonious in its larger structures. However, this does not mean that human existence in this powerful and beautiful context was without danger or struggle. Because the Creator had left his coded intelligence nestled deep in the living core of all earthly phenomena, there was a corresponding imperative to unlock the code into a clarity of form that could be acknowledged by even the youngest Native American child. If Native Americans failed to penetrate the depths of the encoded messages from the Creator, the continued existence and prosperity of the tribal unit was threatened. Without the appropriate response to the Creator's message, death and chaos were inevitable. Stories, rituals, and images were all ways traditional peoples used to maintain the harmonious movements of the universe. In Erdrich's *The Antelope Wife* the events described after the abduction of the Antelope Woman clearly indicate the precarious nature of existence. The medicine man pleads with her abductor that her removal has upset the balance of the web of life: "Our luck is changing. Our houses caved in with the winter snow and our work is going for grabs. . . . There's misery in the air. . . . Bring her back, you fool!" (33).

THE HUMAN PREDICAMENT IN THE COSMOS

Our second area of consideration is the Native American view of the human predicament in the cosmos. A premise common in the popular twentieth-century media descriptions of Native American cultures is that their traditional ways and lifestyles unfolded in a pristine paradise bestowed upon them by an all-knowing and all-powerful Creator. Before European contact, life for Native Americans was thought to have been serene and secure, anchored by the abundant resources of an Edenic "new" World. However, this is a gross misconception and oversimplification of the Native Americans' view of their own place in the universe, a misconception the following widely quoted prayer exemplifies:

We call upon the Earth, our planet home, with its beautiful depth and soaring height, its vitality and abundance of life. We call upon the land which grows our food, the nurturing soil, the fertile fields, the abundant gardens and orchards. And lastly we call upon all that we hold most sacred, the presence and power of the Great Spirit, of love and truth which flows through all the universe. (E. Roberts and Amidon, 106)

The first problem with the prayer is that its content gives the impression that the Chinook, its organizations, were a primarily agricultural people. However, they were located in northern Oregon, at the border with Washington state, and farming was not the key to their subsistence. Furthermore, the fact that the prayer is not in the song stanza format typical of Native American prayer suggests that it has been influenced by outside sources. Finally, the prayer lacks an appreciation for the interplay of both positive and negative elemental forces that an in-depth examination of Native American materials confirms.

In the Native American view, the dilemma for human beings—their predicament—is to maintain the link to the place of their origins by means of ritual and storytelling. First, as we have seen, humans needed to identify the essential patterns or maps of knowing that drew together all of nature: the sky realm, the waters, and so on. Then, once the map of existence had been clarified, it was only through continuous human effort that the connections between the various points of the map were deepened and thereby sustained. It is no accident that in a number of Native American Creation stories, Grandmother Spider shapes the Earth. She spins the web, the circular labyrinth, that holds all things in their proper relationship to each other and binds them in a necessary unity tied around a central point. Knowledge of the proper relationship of things allowed a fully human life to be lived. Knowledge brought control and activation of the powers of the map of knowing. Telling the stories of Grandmother Spider enabled the listeners to retrace the journey that their people had made and embark on their own life journeys.

Travelers may face a host of difficulties. Their map can be lost, misread, damaged, accidentally discarded, or carelessly altered. Any of these conditions is sufficient to imperil the outcome of the journey. In the Native American understanding, the positive outcome of any individual life passage is not automatically guaranteed by the Creator. A positive outcome is possible only by carefully reconstructing step-by-step the route used by the people through the generations. In anthropological terms, ritual provides ways of controlling an uncertain and sometimes hostile environment.

TWO NATIVE AMERICAN CREATION STORIES

Two epics, the Creation story of the Navajo and that of their neighbors in the Southwest, the Hopi, clarify the scope and content of the tribal Creation stories. These stories answer such questions as the identity of the Creator, the nature of human beings, and the quality of their existence. Creation stories are integral to every one of the nine contemporary authors discussed in Chapter 3.

The Navajo

In a first reading of the *Dine Bahane*, the Creation story of the Navajo nation, the theme appears to be movement, for it is an extended journal describing pathways explored and the attendant successes and failures. Its format is that of a traditional Creation story, that is, a tale of emergence. The story unfolds in a five-stage movement along a vertical ascent from an encompassing darkness through three intermediary worlds, up to the Earth's surface, the present world.

In the dark First World, the residents are Insect People, types of beetles and ants. Furthermore, in this "Time of the Beginnings," the thought processes, speech, and behavior of animals and humanoids are interchangeable. Thus, when the curtain opens on this drama, the nine kinds of Insect People are highly organized, living in four-story houses anchored in each of the four directions. The action moves forward when the chiefs of the four directions direct the people to build a fifth four-story house, this time in the center of the First World. A journey upward begins, as the people pass through each successive level of the central four-story house. They arrive at the top of the structure, where they encounter the nine Spirit Beings or gods. Two of the nine will play major roles for the duration of the journey, Coyote and First Man. First Man distinguishes himself as the owner of five power objects: jewels of white shell, turquoise, abalone, jet, and red-white stone. These jewels provide the energetic thrust for upward movement to the Second World as they are carefully laid out in a pattern honoring the four directions and the center. The passage to the Second World is then completed by means of a column of light rising from the center jewel.

We could easily draw this phase of the story, summarizing the many details in what should by now be a familiar diagram, a circle marked by color, number, and directional symbolism. The map of orientation is set in place in the beginning of the story to anchor the unfolding drama.

The First World is problematic in that the gods are portrayed as having an ambivalent nature, at times blessing the people while simultaneously harboring destructive forces. The story clearly warns that First Man and his companions were all evil. When the Insect People have need of First Man's jewels to facilitate their upward movement, he complies with their request. However, no attempt is made to depict this god as an absolute being: all-knowing, all-good, and all-powerful. A further negative element is introduced when the story indicates the presence of a basket of evil diseases at the base of the central light column. Inadvertently, the basket is propelled upward with the people as they make their passage to the Second World. From the beginning moments of the Creation process, powers that enhance life as well as dangers that destroy it are present.

In the Second World, First Man assumes his role as the leader of the people and sets his jewels in place, again causing cloud and light columns to arise. Within the Second World, he and the people must negotiate three chambers of passage. His movement stalls in the second chamber until he places the red-white stone in the center of the map, but then chaos intrudes, for instead of their having a smooth passage, the Earth begins to shake. The shaking of the Earth increasing in intensity is a portent of evil. Finally, First Man gains passage to the third chamber but here the Feline People, bands of warlike tricksters, target him as their victim. He escapes, but decides to lessen some of the destructive evil rampant in this domain. Ritually, he blows smoke in each direction, then swallows it, thereby taking into himself the dark forces, enhancing whatever internal evil was already present within him.

This second phase of the Creation story does not depict life as unfolding in a pristine paradise. Rather, a small detail unlocks larger dimensions of meaning. The red-white stone placed at the center of the upper movement conveys a cryptic warning. Color symbolism in the Native American religions is complex and highly nuanced. Gladys Reichard, an anthropologist who devoted her life to Navajo fieldwork and whose book *Navajo Religion* is an exhaustive compilation of information, calls red "the color of danger, war, and sorcery as well as their safeguards" (Moon, 66). Franc Newcomb, another anthropologist of note working in this area, echoes this position, noting that red "represents the life principle of animals and humans as well as immortals" and "may also designate the symbol which causes death" (Moon, 66). Power has two phases, creative and destructive, mirroring a larger polarity in the universe. The red-white stone, when in alignment with the other four jewels, produces strength and blessing but, used inappropriately, brings death and destruction. It is evident in Creation stories from each of the Native American traditions that indeed creation is not all-good. Ambivalence and polarity are built into the inner core of the Earth's structures, and all things that interact on the Earth's surface participate in this tense dualism.

Finally, the drama of the Third World begins. Here, the Insect People meet a new series of difficulties, including encounters with "various colored snakes who were evil" (Moon, 187). But the more significant sources of evil are the obstacles to movement that First Man and then Coyote set in place. First Man places red and yellow streaks in the sky to keep columns of light from rising. The streaks represent emergence, pollen, and diseases, pointing to the deepest hopes as well as fears of the people on the journey, to the nourishment as well as the destruction of life. After the presentation of an appropriate gift to First Man, the obstacles are removed. The people again have the pathway laid open before them, until Coyote interferes. Appropriate offerings must be made to Coyote before he, too, will untie the "pillars of light." However, a warning note again sounds as the people accuse First Man of maliciousness. He responds, "It is true, my grandchildren. I am filled with evil; yet there is a time to employ it and another to withhold it" (Moon, 188). By the time the sojourn in this Third

World has ended, the people have clearly seen the two faces of First Man, good and evil.

Passage is finally made into the Fourth World, whose blue color seems to signify peace, prosperity, and stability. Years pass and the rhythms of life are secure. First Man builds a magic hogan and gives the formal blessing of power to the male and female genitalia. The events in the Fourth World up to this point intensify the positive side of the vital life-giving powers extended to the people, but then a terrible shift occurs. A dispute between the men and women involves first physical separation and then geographical distance between the two groups. Alienation continues for nine years, during which sexual abuses among each group are the norm. These actions unleash a series of negative consequences: bad dreams, disease, and chaos. The consensus is that this realm is no longer suitable, and a final movement upward is attempted. This time, replacing the pillars of light as the means of travel, the animal guardians dig a sky hole for emergence into the next world. Both water and monsters block the hole through which passage is to be made, signifying the corruption of life-giving forces into their opposite terrifying mode. First Man makes the transition to the Fifth World only with the help of Spider Woman and Spider Ant, who spin webs to facilitate the movement.

In the Fifth World, a final Creation hogan secured by the five jewels is set in place:

First Man lifted the Sky in the east with a Jet Wand, in the south with a Turquoise Wand, in the west with Abalone, and in the north with a White Shell Wand and turned it over upon the Earth, so that it rose as the pillars, east, south, west, north, and center. (Moon, 192)

The people begin to settle into this world, for they have reached the end of the emergence journey. Fittingly, it is at this point that Changing Woman, the spirit being who will be responsible for the creation of the Navajo people, is discovered as a mysterious baby. She rocks on dawn and turquoise rainbows, supported by colored cords—dawn, sky blue, twilight, and turquoise—strung from the four directions.

This short review of the distinctive stages of the Navajo Creation drama reveals two themes in particular. First, the consistent references to number, color, and directional symbolism serve to anchor the story in a traditional schematic. In other words, once what is known to be true, and therefore powerful, is set in place, then the cautious edging toward what is unknown, and therefore dangerous, can be negotiated. Second, the story is preoccupied with the dimensions of evil. It is almost as though, once the comprehensive identification of sources of evil has been achieved, some relief is possible. Passage through each world serves to add new insight into the problem of evil. Evil appears in the Holy People, in the terrifying forces of nature, in the basket of evil diseases, in the sexual perversions of the Fourth World, and in sky streaks that indicate disease.

Interestingly, the story defines evil as linked to processes of disease, decline, and death. For the Navajo religious culture, this horror of death is tied both to a powerful acknowledgment of the existence of witchcraft and sorcery, and to the recognition that there is no paradisiac afterlife waiting to reward the faithful. Anthropologists have extensively documented both the traditional and the contemporary Navajo belief in witchcraft. Marc Simmons, in his book *Witchcraft in the Southwest*, explains that there are many sources of evil in the Navajo view of the cosmos, but the worst of these are sorcery and witchcraft.

The Navajo Creation story describes a perilous journey in which the people are vulnerable to attack from many sides. After the sources of evil threaded through the cosmos are identified, they can be displaced through religious intervention. It is no accident that the majority of religious rites among the Navajo are healing ceremonies to counteract disease brought about by witchcraft. A fascinating parallel is the equally elaborate Creation story of the Hopi, the neighbors of the Navajo in the Southwest.

The Hopi

The Hopi Creation story is also structured as a passage through a series of worlds. A significant divergence between the Navajo and the Hopi telling of their Creation stories lies in the different content assigned by each tribe to its experiences in the First World. In the Navajo First World, the geometry of the four corners and the central point is carefully laid out. The Hopi story brings this concern with defining elements of a map of space and time to an even more intricately nuanced level of sophistication.

In the beginning of the Hopi story, the Creator, Taiowa, brings forth the spirit being Sotuknang, a male who, in turn, creates a female spirit being, Spider Woman. These two control the process of creation. The male and female spirit beings produce, in turn, the full range of physical realities: the earth forms, human beings, and so on. Yet, they are not to be understood as man and wife, or "world parents," as if the stream of creation proceeded from their sexual union. Rather, each spirit being has his or her own domain, and creation will not move with the breath of life until the two poles of power, Sotuknang and Spider Woman, are in alignment.

The Hopi description of these two spirit beings echoes the sense of duality presented in Taoism. When the Tao shifts into its manifested forms, the transition is accomplished by means of a structured duality, yin and yang. The duality maintains balance in a world bursting with vital forces in need of continual anchoring. As previously discussed, the geometric pattern of the circle quartered and centered was an often-used narrative device that maintained the stability of the world. At least two of Louis Owens's novels describe the destruction that is unleashed when the circular map of the four quarters is desecrated. In *The Sharpest Sight* Owens explains about the fish lying all over the white sand, drying out and dying every year: "It's part of a circle, you see, and they broke the circle when they broke that river. And they're doing that all over the world, breaking all the circles" (97). In *Bone Game*, he again cites the role of the white people in corrupting the map of the world:

"But now the white people got their own maps and different stories. I been looking at one of those government maps and traveling around, and you can see it clear. They got Los Alamos up there in the north when they took Cochiti Indian land to plan that A-bomb. They got that Sandia laboratory over in Albuquerque in the east where they make nuclear bombs. They got White Sands in the south where they fire them bombs and nuclear missiles off to see if they work." He looked at Luther and shook his head. "And they got that uranium mine at Laguna where they made the water poison; that's the west. So you see how they got something in each one of these four directions like us Indians, but it's all about killing." (88)

The Hopi cosmic vision includes this familiar circular geometric pattern, but it also identifies the interaction of the great dualities as essential to well-being. Another distinction that belongs to the Hopi story is the gravity of the issues addressed in the First World. In the Navajo story, the function of the First World is largely as a meeting place for the travelers, Insect People and gods. For the Hopi, the journey cannot begin until a rich foundation of knowledge and power is in place. In the Hopi story, Sotuknang's first task is the creation of nine universes, the arrangement of waters in each universe so that it would be half solid and half water, and the arrangement of winds in ordered movements around each universe. Next, Sotuknang goes to Tokpela, the First World, and creates Spider Woman, "who was to remain on that earth." In her turn, Spider Woman takes some earth, mixes it with her saliva, and forms twin spirit beings. Each twin is assigned a specific role. The first spirit being solidifies the earth substance into the great mountains and the more pliable lowlands, and the second spirit being, named Echo, is placed in charge of sound. The whole universe becomes an instrument for carrying messages to and from the Creator. Finally, the twin spirit beings take up their permanent positions at the north and south poles, ensuring the orderly movement of the earth mass.

Spider Woman begins the creation of the specific earth forms: vegetation, the animal kingdoms, and humankind. Human beings emerge in a highly ritualized setting. Spider Woman gathers earth of four colors—yellow, red, white, and black—mixed with her saliva. She covers the substance with her cape, and sings the Creation song. The result is the formation of a male being in each of the four sacred colors, all of them in the image of Sotuknang. Repeating the process, Spider Woman then forms four female shapes in her own image, again in each of the four colors. After the two groups have been paired, they will be sent off in each of the four directions. But before this can happen, Sotuknang gives two gifts to the people, speech and the power to reproduce. Now life in the First World is ready to unfold.

However, the narrative of the First World is not complete until two further matters of importance have been addressed. The protection of human life by prayer and ritual is included before any further dramatic development of the story. A lengthy section describes the nature of human beings, whose real parents are identified as the Corn Mother and Mother Earth on the female side and Father Sun and the Creator, Taiowa, on the male side. Human parents are but instruments through which these spirit beings are manifested. Then, the narrative describes the elaborate twenty-day ritual initiated at birth to anchor the newborn's transition to this earth realm. This anchoring is done in part by drawing a map of orientation. Four lines of cornmeal drawn on each of the four walls, and a fifth pattern on the ceiling, surround the child. The child's spirit will be symbolically nourished by this cornmeal. Every fifth day a line of cornmeal is scraped off and taken to the village shrine. Each line of cornmeal represents a critical stage for the child's bonding with its new home. On the morning of the twentieth day when the bonding is secure, the mother, grandmothers, and aunts participate in the formal naming ceremony and first presentation of the child to Father Sun.

Following this section devoted to the newborn child is a lengthy segment that draws out the consequences of the fact that the living body of the Earth and the living body of humankind are structured in the same way. Specifically, through each body runs an axis. In a human being this axis is the vertebral column, along which are five vibratory centers that echo both the sounds of power and strength and those of danger and disease. When a healing is needed, the medicine man places his hands or a small crystal over each vibratory center and is thereby able to make a diagnosis. Final markers for this First World are given when it is assigned a direction (the west); a color (yellow); a mineral (gold); a four-leafed plant; and animal guardians. A similar pattern of marking is given for each of the four worlds.

Unlike the Navajo story, the Hopi will not embark on a journey through a series of worlds. For the Hopi, a world will be set in place and then destroyed when the corruption of the people defiles that world. Always, however, a small, faithful remnant will be protected by Sotuknang and Spider Woman. They are directed to begin life anew in each succeeding world. By the time the fourth and final world is created, the Earth's surface has been destroyed by fire, ice, and then flood. The name of the Fourth World, the World Complete, does not indicate that this is a place of perfection. Rather, it is described as "a place of height and depth, heat and cold, beauty and barrenness" (Waters, 21); it offers a full spectrum of choices for the people to make. The quality of their choices will determine whether the plan of the Creator is carried out or if this world, too, will need to be purified by large-scale destruction.

Though the Navajo and the Hopi are geographical neighbors in the Southwest, a brief examination of their Creation stories reveals that they are not at all philosophical neighbors. On the critical issue of the nature of good and evil in the universe, they are poles apart. The Navajo have a much darker vision of the nature of being. They place evil in the very heart of God and affirm that witchcraft is not the province of the few, but readily accessible to all. The Hopi, on the other hand, have experienced the widespread corruption of humankind, resulting in generalized death and destruction. In both Creation stories, however, it is clear that the Native American religious perception is not a naïve, romantic optimism in the supreme goodness of the natural world. Tales of struggle and often of failure mark their stories. Certainly the description of a never-ceasing struggle between the forces of creation and destruction continues to find a voice in the writings of the contemporary Native American novelist.

The format of Erdrich's *The Antelope Wife* is an excellent summary for many of the issues that have been raised in this chapter. The four-part structure of the universe is echoed in the four-part division of her story. Each segment is introduced by a passage linked to the Creation story of the Ojibway, describing a beading contest. The color symbolism of the beading contest indicates a struggle between the positive and negative forces in the universe. While passages 1 and 2 are clearly set in the "time of the beginnings," passages 3 and 4 carry the theme of quilling and beading red and blue colors into the recent historical past of the Ojibway. Passage 3 narrates how the Great Grandma of the first Shawano dyed her quills in a variety of blue shades. She uses her own urine boiled with shavings of copper to produce the dye, and thus any variation in color is a direct expression of the totality of her actions preceding the color mixing: "The final color resulted from what she ate, drank, what she did for sex, and what she said to her mother or child the day before" (99). One day she is amazed that after a series of particularly negative actions, the resultant blue color is innocent, lovely, deep, and clear. Passage 4 describes a mother so obsessed with obtaining prized cranberry red beads that she gambles away everything to obtain them, even the blankets of her children. The children hungrily devour the beads, and she runs after them with a knife, refusing to be stopped from completing her work. Passages 3 and 4 thus continue the theme of the ways in which positive and negative forces, forces of creation and destruction, are intertwined in all of human experience. Again, mythological time and historical time are simply two layers of a single reality.

3

Native American Literature: The Enduring Creation Story

As it was in the beginning, is now, and forever shall be.

The first three authors covered in this chapter begin their novels with a Creation story fragment. This fact poses a difficulty for the reader with little background in traditional Native American materials because the fragment is taken out of its fuller context. For example, the transcribed version of the Navajo Creation story is 90 pages long; that of the Blackfoot people is over 130 pages. A reference that includes only a few paragraphs would therefore be very easy to misinterpret. So why is the Creation fragment given primacy of position? Certainly the initial placement is a sign of respect by the Native American authors for their tribal traditions. But in addition to this concern for honoring a cultural heritage, when the authors incorporate even a fragment of the Creation story, they are actually evoking the power of the whole dramatic structure of that story. As Clyde Kluckhohn, a noted ethnologist, pointed out, one of the philosophical assumptions of tribal cultures is that the part stands for the whole. For example, the very mention of Thought Woman, the spider, evokes an extensive storytelling sequence, at least to someone familiar with the Pueblo tradition. In general, since Native Americans affirm the belief that the Creation story shapes all subsequent tribal events down to the present day, an evocative fragment at the beginning of a new story is appropriately placed. The power of the Creation story exists not just in the fact that it is the founding moment of traditions that are centuries old. Its real power consists in the belief that the key figures in the Creation drama are alive and well, and communicating with the present.

This last point is driven home dramatically and humorously by Thomas King in *Green Grass, Running Water*, when his Coyote creator and three mother goddesses interact with Ahdamn in the Garden, Noah and the ark, the archangel Gabriel, Jesus the man who walks on water, Captain Ahab and Moby-Jane, and, finally, a group of United States cavalry rangers:

> So, says A. A. Gabriel, you really mean yes, right?
> No, says Thought Woman.
> But that's the wrong answer, says A. A. Gabriel. Let's try this again.
> Let's not, says Thought Woman, and that one gets back in the water.
> Wait, wait, says A. A. Gabriel. What am I supposed to do with all these forms? What am I supposed to do with all these papers? What am I supposed to do with this snake?
> Hosanna da, sings that Card. Hosanna da.
> There are lots of Marys in the world, shouts A. A. Gabriel as Thought Woman floats away. We can always find another one, you know. (301)

This collage of the modern with Creation drama personalities confirms their ongoing power and involvement in daily human affairs. Thus, the key to understanding the use of traditional materials by contemporary Native American authors is found by investigating Creation story mythology. Without such a key, the above passage is confusing at best; with a key, a context for the dialogues takes shape.

As Chapter 2 makes clear, some effort is required to understand a different way of "seeing" because very different thought systems are at work. This chapter will translate the detailed descriptions of color, number symbolism, rituals, and Creation dramas discussed in Chapter 2 into the realm of contemporary fiction. The Native American materials in both chapters 2 and 3 are perhaps jarring, their subject matter serious and dark.

THOMAS KING (CHEROKEE)

Green Grass, Running Water, by Thomas King, a professor at the University of Lethbridge, Alberta, Canada, is almost made to order to illustrate the mutual dependence between traditional materials and present-day storytelling. A bonus to using this book as the initial excursion into contemporary Native American fiction is its bold humor, most of which is missed if there is no acquaintance with the traditional materials. The novel opens with an excerpt from what sounds like a standard tribal Creation story statement, comforting in its familiar content: "So. In the beginning, there was nothing. Just the water." Immediately, however, the Creation story swerves from any expected course by introducing Coyote, the supreme trickster. As Coyote sleeps, one of his dreams splits apart from his consciousness and becomes a dog-god, a "contrary," who claims to be "in charge of the world." Thus, two absolutely unlikely candidates are entrusted with the role of setting the Creation in motion:

"Where did all that water come from?" shouts that G O D.
"Take it easy," says Coyote. "Sit down. Relax. Watch some television."
"But there is water everywhere," says that G O D.
"Hmmmm," says Coyote. "So there is." (3)

This sequence of details naming Coyote and a "contrary" as cocreators would seem to be a strange configuration even if the reader were acquainted with the patterning of Native American Creation stories. It would certainly be tempting for the non-Native American reader simply to skip through this first bit of business as whimsical nonsense, with the thought that the real story will start shortly and will be much more conventional in its format, or to read it as a satiric mocking of the Judeo-Christian Creation story. However, neither approach is a workable solution to the confusion. The Creation story theme keeps returning, expanding, and shifting in its content, and it becomes a counterpoint to the story set in the twentieth century.

The puzzle set in motion by the Creation story theme cannot be ignored. A first attempt to clarify this theme might be to link it with the Canadian Cherokee background of the novel's author, but this would be an easy solution that does not hold up under closer examination. King does not use the Cherokee Creation story as the format for this novel. Rather, he constructs a contemporary amalgam of characters and details borrowed from a variety of authentic Native American traditions, so a simple equation cannot be made. This Cherokee author does not provide immediate access to his own tribal belief system. Thus, in the search for meaning we have to examine the content of the story itself. Following the thread of the Creation story as it unfolds in later chapters of the novel makes clear that the figure of Coyote persists throughout the work. The three goddesses of creation—First Woman, Changing Woman, and Thought Woman—very quickly replace the dog-god. Oddly, these three do not come from the same tribal tradition; in fact, none of these goddesses is usually connected with the "earth diver" theme, the general structure of the Creation story used by King. In this mode of storytelling, a spirit being falls from the sky realm, which is a complete world in itself. As the spirit being falls precipitously toward a vast expanse of water, various animal guardians gather to protect a life-form that could not survive unaided. One by one, the animal guardians plunge beneath the water's surface, trying to bring back even the tiniest amount of solid ground, which, magically expanded, forms the matrix for the first landforms. After three tries, the fourth animal guardian is successful, and the solid material is placed on turtle's back, forming a safe landing space for the sky being. From that time onward, the female sky being becomes the mother goddess in charge of Earth's development.

In King's novel, the goddesses that he has identified are Pueblo and Navajo, whereas the "earth diver" story structure was favored by the Iroquois from the Northeast woodlands. Is the author deliberately trying to sabotage the inexperienced reader by bringing together such disparate references and content? Perhaps the key to the author's intent is found in the significance assigned to Coyote. He is on the scene starting with the second line of the story, and he stays on board for the duration of the journey. In effect, the story begins and ends with Coyote:

> "Okay, okay," says Coyote. "I got it!"
> "Well, it's about time," I says.
> "Okay, okay, here goes," says Coyote. "In the beginning, there was nothing."
> "Nothing?"
> "That's right," says Coyote. "Nothing."
> "No," I says. "In the beginning there was just the water." (469)

What is Coyote's specific identity that would merit his constant association with the major thematic element of the Creation story? First of all, the very mention of Coyote's name should alert readers to steady themselves for the trip ahead. Coyote has tremendous powers, but not as a creator. Instead, he initiates confusion and challenge; he breaks through all conventions and adds a powerful dose of absurdity to whatever is already in motion. He is never responsible for the opening moments of the traditional Creation process. He is not an initiator of a very powerful gift to humankind. In the Native American understanding, creation evolves slowly over a period of generations of interaction between spirit beings and animal guardians, long before human beings make their appearance. It is in this developmental period that Coyote holds sway. He is the teacher and transformer whose interventions cause behavioral norms and values to be clearly understood. Interestingly, while Coyote is generally described as male, with either human or animal form, he fulfills none of the traditional male roles. He is not the wise chief, the brave warrior, the skilled hunter, nor the powerful healer/shaman. Rather, he is the consummate antihero, making every foolish mistake and perpetrating outrageous breaking of taboos. Thus, he teaches, but in a negative mode, warning his audience of the death and destruction attendant upon his foolish choices. The traditional audience understood that while Coyote may appear to be utterly defeated or destroyed, he is always capable of resurrection, an option his listeners did not share.

The theme of Coyote's ability to turn the world of time and space upside down is reinforced when, as the novel begins, King indicates that Coyote dreams a spirit being who is both god and *heyoka*, that is, a sacred clown or "contrary." The *heyoka* is a man or a woman who has received the most sacred vision, that of the Thunder Being, and whose nature, as a result, is to do everything backward. The fact that the word "god" spelled backward is "dog" in English is a good concept to keep in mind since Coyote's spirit being manifests itself as a dog-god. From the moment of his selection by this being, the new *heyoka*, according to Tedlock and Tedlock, does many foolish things, such as riding backwards on his horse with his boots on backwards so that he's coming when he's really going; if the weather is hot he covers himself with blankets and shivers as with the cold, and he says "yes" when he means "no".... Indeed, these actions are a translation, as it were, of the knowledge of another reality: a nonobjective, shapeless, unnatural world of pure power or energy symbolized by lightning. (106)

The "contrary" has been jolted into his new occupation by the Thunder Being, and his *heyoka* role in the tribal community will be as an ever present conduit for those kinds of jolts which cause breakthroughs to power and wisdom:

People think that the clown is just nothing, that he is just for fun. That is not so. When I make other masked dancers and they do not set things right or can't find out something, I make that clown and he never fails. Many people who know about these things say that the clown is the most powerful. (Tedlock and Tedlock, 105)

Thus, on the very first page of his story, King alerts the reader that both the absurd speech and behavior of Coyote and the jolting insights of the "contrary" lie ahead.

In King's novel, the Creation story serves as an anchor for both traditional and contemporary storytelling. Nonetheless, there are other ways that traditional materials show up and move the action of the story forward. A second theme to pay attention to as the novel begins is the role of four elderly Indians who are confined to a mental institution. These four clearly possess the ability to discard conventional notions of time and space, for they freely travel back and forth between the retelling of the Creation story and the developing dramatic action of the novel. They transcend the limits of time when the story states that they were admitted, as old men, to the mental institution at its founding in 1891. They have remained there until the present day, with the exception of brief periods when their duty to "fix" the world calls them forward. While they may seem at first to be purely comic characters, they engage powerful elemental forces. Their "world fixing" includes volcanic eruptions, earthquakes, and floods, as well as the revision of a classic John Wayne film, *The Mysterious Warrior*, so that the Indians win their battle with the white men. The limits of time and space mean nothing to them, even though they dutifully return to the mental institution after the completion of each adventure. Color and number symbolism also show up in this context. For most of the story, the four elderly Indians are named Robinson Crusoe, Ishmael, the Lone Ranger, and Hawkeye, but their alternate designations are Mr. Red, Mr. White, Mr. Black, and Mr. Blue. After the Indians have redone the John Wayne film, a black-and-white classic, the scene shows the Indian Chief leading the warriors "out of the river, a great swirl of motion and colors—red, white, black and blue" (357), thus preserving the notion of four sacred colors summarizing spirit power.

The journeys of the four Indian spirit-warriors and the unfolding Creation story are two themes clearly based on traditional materials that are intertwined with the dramatic action of the novel. The core of the novel is the description of personalities and events locked in a dramatic tension moving toward resolution and/or dissolution. While the novel refers to Indian reservations and their residents, the annual setting up of the Sun Dance, and issues such as treaty violations, no special guide is needed for the non-Native American reader to grasp these matters. In effect, King is writing in two modes: one, a coded traditional voice that demands an informed effort to grasp it, and the other, a voice that beckons the reader to enter an intriguing mainstream story. On the one hand, readers will find a story of modern, disaffected Canadian Blackfeet Indians struggling to find their identity as they sell televisions, share girlfriends, consider having a child by artificial insemination, and eventually stand up to a corporation that has built a massive dam just upriver from Indian homes. On the other hand, the four ancient Indian hitchhikers who take an avid interest in events, the timing of the Sun Dance, the appointment of a key protector of the sacred ceremony, and the all-pervasive presence of the trickster Coyote, watching modern events from the sidelines, playfully manipulating actions, and even dancing up an earthquake on occasion, suggest that the religious significance of the story is deeply rooted within a Native American tradition.

LESLIE MARMON SILKO (LAGUNA PUEBLO)

We now shift geographically from Canada and the northern United States to the Southwest. Leslie Marmon Silko is a member of the Pueblo nation and a professor at the University of Arizona; indeed, her stories are set vividly in this Southwestern environment. The novels that we consider are *The Almanac of the Dead* and *Ceremony*. *The Almanac of the Dead* begins as follows:

Prophecy
When Europeans arrived, the Maya, Azteca, Inca cultures had already built great cities and vast networks of roads. Ancient prophecies foretold the arrival of Europeans in the Americas. The ancient prophecies also foretold the disappearance of all things European.
The Indian Connection
Sixty million Native Americans [throughout the Americas] died between 1500 and 1600. The defiance and resistance to things European continue unabated. The Indian Wars never ended in the Americas. Native Americans acknowledge no borders; they seek nothing less than the return of all tribal lands. (14–15)

In *Almanac of the Dead*, Silko asserts that the Creation story of the European-Americans is forever marked by the bloodshed and destruction of vast numbers of Native Americans. European-American civilization is born in the overwhelming experience of death and moves inexorably toward the consequences of such a brutal beginning. Therefore, the tribal Creation story that Silko uses as the anchor for her novel is one that matches the intensity of the darkness that the historical record contains. She does not use the Creation story from her own Pueblo heritage, but instead employs the *Popul Vuh*, the Creation story of the Quiche Maya:

> They looked like humans
> They talked like humans
> They populated the earth
> They existed and multiplied
> They had daughters and they had sons
> These wooden figures had no minds or souls. (479)

That story, along with other traditions from the Central American tribal peoples, seems to best support her thesis that death is the primary experience of the Americas.

As background for the manifold death and corruption described in Silko's novel, we will summarize a segment of the *Popul Vuh* that is directly engaged with death and its seemingly infinite manifestations. Specifically, we trace the journey of the Hero Twins.

The Creation story of the *Popul Vuh* develops over generational lines, beginning with the summons of two skilled ball players to the Realm of the Dead. The Lords of the Underworld succeed in destroying the two young men and hang their heads on a tree. The tree of life has thus been defaced and turned into a canopy of skulls. A young woman, a daughter of one of the Lords of Darkness, approaches the forbidden tree and is impregnated by the spirits of the vanquished ball players. She evades her own resultant death sentence, escapes to the earth surface world, and gives birth to twin boys. These two discover their true identities only by retracing their fathers' steps and engaging the Lords of Death. Miraculously, the Hero Twins pass through each of the trials that are set in place to destroy them. They survive harrowing nights in the House of Darkness, House of Knives, House of Jaguar, and House of Bats. They survive the beheading of one of the pair, who is magically restored through the intervention of animal guardians. Finally, the Hero Twins understand the terrifying truth that they will never come to the end of the challenges set for them by the Lords of Death. They must finally gain power by seizing control of the game and choosing their own deaths. For the reader unfamiliar with Creation mythology, this choice hardly seems to be a victory. However, the logic of Creation storytelling clearly affirms the possibility of death as the passageway to even greater power and wisdom. Thus, by giving explicit directions for the disposal of their remains, the Hero Twins ensure their rebirth and reconfiguration as powerful magicians. They return to the underworld realm and tantalize the Lords of Death with their ability to slice objects into pieces or burn them to ashes, and then restore them. These powers are demonstrated on both inanimate and animal forms. Finally, the Lords of Death beg for their own destruction, which is exactly what the Hero Twins had hoped would happen. They now hold the reins of life and death, and the power of the Lords of Death is forever diminished.

The Hero Twin sequence is an extended meditation upon death both as problem and as solution. This may seem to be a fairly unusual subject for treatment in a Creation story, which more typically describes the emergence of life and myriad possibilities for growth and expansion. It should be remembered, however, that the Navajo Creation story cited in Chapter 2 took the nature of evil and its manifestations as its focal point. Perhaps, to the Navajo, the Quiche Maya, and other tribal peoples, the confrontation with the darkest limits of existence is equal in necessity to identifying the positive sources of power and wisdom available to humankind.

In Silko's novel, the reality of corruption and of death as a problem with no apparent solution shadows each step the main characters take as they stumble through their lives. Lecha, the intuitive who can locate lost persons, can find them only if they are already dead. David takes photos of a nude suicide, his former lover, and the bloody pictures are hailed as a cutting-edge exhibition at an avant-garde art gallery. Menardo, the head of a vast armed protection service for prominent politicians and financiers is haunted by such terrifying dreams of death that he is never without his bulletproof vest. Eventually, like the Lords of Death of the Underworld, Menardo plays the ultimate game with death. The novel's scenarios relentlessly underscore the pervasive culture of death that cloaks the main characters, pointing ultimately to the death of an entire civilization, the European-American.

In *Ceremony*, Silko again uses death as her dramatic focus. This time, the battle experience World War II with the Japanese in the jungles is the cause of the crisis that claims the hero Tayo's mind and heart. He finds himself "trying to vomit out everything—all the past, all his life" (168). After a stay in a Veterans' Administration hospital and months of recuperation at home in his Pueblo village, Tayo is still unable to free himself from the symptoms of his "spirit sickness." His family in desperation arranges a meeting with Old Betonie, a Navajo healer who has helped other veterans regain their hold on life. At his first encounter with Old Betonie, Tayo is told: "This has been going on for a long time. They will try to stop you from completing the ceremony. . . . His sickness was only part of something larger, and his cure would be found only in something great and inclusive of everything" (125).

The "they" who are refusing to release Tayo are the witches who from the beginning of Creation are responsible for much of the death and destruction experienced by humankind. Silko, in order to clarify the scope of the witches' power, includes in this novel the narrative of the grand witches' council that called together the dark powers from the four corners of the universe. At this momentous event, each witch tries to create the supreme horror. Finally, they are silenced by a mysterious figure that announces, "What I have is a story." As the story is told, horrible events are inexorably set in motion:

Corpses for us
Blood for us
Killing killing killing killing
And those they do not kill
will die anyway
at the destruction they see
at the loss
at the loss of the children
the loss will destroy the rest. (136)

After the figure completes the chilling tale, it is apparent to all that the supreme witchery is the arrival of the Europeans in the New World. The other witches shrink from the devastation described, and beg for the story to be called back. But it is too late, for the forces of darkness have already been turned loose. Silko underscores the importance of this narrative by including it in its entirety in two of her novels, *Ceremony* and *Storyteller*.

But even after we have gained an understanding of the broad powers possessed by the witches, the rest of Old Betonie's cryptic message to Tayo must be deciphered. Tayo had been warned that his sickness was part of something "larger" and that the corresponding cure would have to be "inclusive of everything." While the Pueblo clearly understood the danger to their existence posed by witchery, they also acknowledged the responsibility of each tribal member to preserve order in the cosmos. Tayo believed that "it took only one person to tear away the delicate strands of the web . . . and the fragile world would be injured" (38). A single person's actions could cause the rain clouds to disappear or the deer to retreat, thus undercutting the people's sources of sustenance, good harvests and successful hunts. The word "web" is particularly significant, for it shifts the perspective back to the Creation story. Spider Grandmother spins into existence all the primordial elements. Each element takes its proper place in a larger pattern that preserves both uniqueness and interdependence. The web connects all living things, and all of time. Thus, Tayo understands that his sickness is an unresolved danger to himself, his family, his village, and the Pueblo nation. The evil ripples outward in ever widening circles of consequences.

Tayo agrees to participate in the several-day ceremony performed by Betonie, but the healing cannot be completed during this limited time frame. Betonie sends Tayo on a kind of "spirit quest" on which he himself assumes the final responsibility for his return to well-being. There are four medicine elements that need to be collected: a precise star pattern in the sky, the location of the spotted cattle, the mountain, and the woman. The instructions are purposely vague and mysterious. Tayo must unravel the knot of meaning before he can restore himself and his world.

Throughout the unfolding of *Ceremony* are numerous excerpts from Creation story sequences. Again, their inclusion points to the belief that mythological time and historical time coexist and intersect. The story is rich in details from the Pueblo traditional heritage and is an excellent door of access to that tradition.

On the one hand, *Almanac* and *Ceremony* deal with very modern themes: cocaine addiction, child abduction, extreme violence, perverted sex, well-organized drug-smuggling rings, police and CIA corruption, covert operations, multiple conspiracies, and the modern defiling of ancient religious sites in the first, and the destructive, dislocating experience of being tortured as a World War II prisoner of the Japanese in the second, as well as the rage and drunkenness that lead a returning Laguna POW to Highway 66 and to the streets of Gallup, New Mexico, where disheveled Navajos, Zuñis, and Hopis collapse outside local dives. *Almanac* sets these modern nightmares within the context of a historical pattern of the Spanish conquest and mestizo revolts in Mexico and Central America; *Ceremony* does not. On the other hand, *Almanac* works within the context of the Aztec almanac, draws on ancient prophecies from north and south of the border, includes visionaries who communicate with the spirit world through red macaws, and incorporates into its structure the timeless chaos of the spiritual loop whereby old orders are destroyed and new ones rise, only to be destroyed in turn. *Ceremony* likewise depends on ancient wisdom, ceremonies conducted by a medicine man to renew connections to the land and to ancient rituals that help the main character finally see the pattern that weaves all life stories together into a continuous whole.

LOUISE ERDRICH (TURTLE MOUNTAIN BAND OF THE OJIBWAY)

Louise Erdrich, who was raised in Wahpeton, North Dakota, is widely recognized by the general reading public because of her ten books of poetry and fiction. Her latest work, *The Antelope Wife* continues the themes explored by Thomas King and Leslie Silko.

On the first page of her novel, Erdrich refers to a Creation story sequence, just as do the two previous authors. It is not only a sense of chronological order that places these passages at the opening moments of their novels. The Creation story sets the stage; it defines identity. It establishes the physical, emotional, psychological, and moral universe in which the drama is played out, as the following fragment from the Ojibway Creation story confirms:

Ever since the beginning these twins are sewing. One sews with light and one with dark. The first twin's beads are cut-glass whites and pales, and the other twin's beads are glittering deep red and blue-black indigo. . . . They sew with a single sinew thread, in, out, fast and furious, each trying to set one more bead into the pattern than her sister, each trying to upset the balance of the world. (1)

This world does not begin in peaceful equilibrium but is forever caught in a tumultuous tug-of-war between positive and negative forces. How do human beings maintain a modicum of balance against this ever shifting background? The answer is through the power of story and ritual. Stories clearly identify the problematic of life's experiences, and rituals offer ways to readjust and compensate for the twists and turns of each life's journey.

In the Creation passage quoted, the whites and pale colors seem to be in opposition to the deep red and blue-black indigo ones. Later, toward the conclusion of her novel, Erdrich uses another set of significant color references, whose meaning can appear elusive. These are the passages which conclude that "time is blue" and that the search for the blueness called "northwest trader blue" is the search to get hold of time (215). In effect, Erdrich is framing the story with a color symbolism that must be placed within its Ojibway heritage to be understood.

One of the most direct ways to observe the use of color symbolism by a traditional culture is in the structure of its ceremonies. For the purpose of our study, we will examine the color symbolism used in the healing ceremonies of two Ojibway societies, the Midewewin, the Grand Medicine Society, and the Wanbunowin, the Society of the Dawn. Both groups utilized ceremonial structures similar in format to those described in Chapter 2. Number and directional symbolism are at the forefront of the ritual process.

As the Midewewin ceremony begins, the priests and each initiates make four processions around the ceremonial lodge. As Basil Johnston notes, these four processions were intended to

symbolize the quarterly divisions existing in time, space, life, events, order, thought, and dream. There were four seasons in the year; and there were four points of the earth. There were four orders of existence and four species in the animal world and four races in man's world. There were four levels of dream; and four degrees in the operation of the mind. And there were four stages, as well as four important events, in each individual's life. (1990, 106)

Thus, the map of the universe, as well as the map of each individual life, is laid out, and the linkage between all the elements is once more reinforced. The group then enters the lodge, an elder lights the sacred pipe, and the invocation to the four directions is performed.

The opening phase of the Wanbunowin ceremony differs from the one just described. Eight purification lodges are set up, four in a straight line leading to the eastern entrance of the sacred lodge, and four leading to the western entrance. The participants proceed through a four-part purification, moving from lodge to lodge until they reach the sacred lodge at the center point. Once the people have assembled, the leader initiates the same ritual process, lighting a pipe and addressing the four directions. Marking each direction is an image of the society's powerful guardians. Red Sky is placed to the east, Winter Sky to the north, Pleasing Sky to the west, and Blue Sky to the south. The content of the prayers directed to each guardian helps to clarify the cluster of associations anchored at each corner of the universe. Erdrich's reference to the disparity in roles held by the white and pale beads versus the red and blue-black ones becomes clearer when we identify the content of each set of prayers:

The petition to the north invokes protection from wind, snow, and storms. The powers that reside in this direction strip the trees of life and drive the animals into their winter lairs. These powers are requested to "Come not too quickly. Be not harsh. Stay not too long." (119)

The pale light of the winter sky and the white snow are colors that indicate hardship and the struggle for survival. The petition to the eastern direction, imaged as Red Sky, is dedicated to the awakening of new life as it emerges from its winter phase. These powers "regenerate all things from sleep; you bring all things from half-death" (120). While the eastern direction is bright with unfolding life, the western direction embodies the opposite realities, old age and death:

Not so with life. No matter how much we may wish it to linger, we cannot hold back one day. And no matter how much we wish to prolong our lives, we cannot hold back death. Like the day, so will men and women grow weak and die and proceed to the Land of Souls, where they will be united with their forebears. (121)

The first three directions therefore describe life in its frailty; the death of the day as well as of the individual life; the half-death of winter and the new beginnings of spring. The direction that remains, the south, carries a set of petitions that are the direct opposite of those given to the north. The Blue Sky guardian is requested, "Do not stay away too long. Do not forget us. Come back soon" (120). South is the direction of summer prosperity. It signifies the growth phase of both the day and the year, as well as of the life cycle of each tribal member. During the summer season, medicines are gathered, and meat, fish, and corn are harvested. The Blue Sky symbolizes the strength and blessings of life given during this season.

Returning to Erdrich's novel and the Creation story passage that describes the beading contest, it is clear that the red and blue colors are linked both to the eastern and southern directions and to the abundance of life forces. The other directions and the corresponding colors have to do with processes of decline and death. Thus, the primordial struggle of the beaders, and indeed all living things, is recorded in the Ojibway map of the four quarters.

A second color association thematic that is developed in the novel is Grandma Zosie's search for the mystical blue beads that contain water, life, and time itself. Here again, the color blue indicates life that is given length of days as it receives the summer nourishment necessary for the unfolding of its true identity. Zosie relates a pivotal dream in which a woman appears and symbolically surrenders the beads and the name that goes with them. When she is of age, Zosie's granddaughter receives the name and the information necessary to locate the beads. The name and the beads are intrinsically linked. The blue in the beads indicates an intensity of life, and the name confirms this quality. The name Blue Prairie Woman is "a stubborn and eraseless long lasting name. One that won't disappear" (217). Beads and name powerfully evoke powers that resist the negative forces woven into the web of life.

SUSAN POWER (STANDING ROCK SIOUX)

We shift the color symbolism from the Ojibway blue of life to the Sioux red of sorcery, danger, and death.

Susan Power, who has an M.F.A. and who participated in the Iowa Writers' Workshop, so tightly weaves together two themes at the heart of her novel *The Grass Dancer* that they merge into one. The first theme is the role of the ancestor spirits and their ongoing interactions with their extended families on Earth. The second theme is the nature of Native American magic or medicine, a phenomenon certainly not limited to the powers of healing. At present, the general public is deeply interested in accessing spirit power through Native American materials. (Chapter 8 explores this phenomenon in the section "New Age Mystics.") Medicine men, often with dubious tribal credentials, teach the practices of smudging with sage, the sweat lodge, and the vision quest. Groups outside tribal membership embrace these techniques in an attempt to gain access to spiritual power. But even as the non-Native American world hungrily looks to Native American teaching as a source for religious experience, a paradox emerges. Traditional teachings do attest to the existence of, and the access to, spirit power. At the same time, however, painful tribal histories as well as the present troubled condition of the Native American community call into question the efficacy of spirit power. Susan Power's novel aptly addresses this critical dilemma.

The center for the dramatic action in the novel is the turbulent, controversial character Anna Thunder, a woman of "power" or, as she styles herself, a woman of "potent" blood. The rest of the reservation views her as a witch. She is a descendant of an authentic Sioux warrior woman of power, Red Dress. The novel opens at a powwow in 1981, but gradually the story works backward in time to 1864, in order to supply the origin of Red Dress's magic. As a small child she is marked for the path of power. One day she naps in the sun, with her mother working nearby:

She didn't notice the two rattlesnakes gliding onto my infant's shadow, where they coiled together, joining me in a nap. I remember their chalky smell and graceful movements, the feel of their cool glossy skin. As I slept, I clutched a serpent by the tail and shook it like a baby's toy. The rattler never struck, was patient with me even when my mother and her friends hovered, horrified, above his twisting head. . . . "Look at how they are claiming her," one woman said. . . . "That one charms the snakes," people have whispered all my life, but they have it wrong. The snakes charmed me. (221)

This extraordinary event signals that the rattlesnake is Red Dress's spirit guardian. When Red Dress has grown, she dreams of a place where she has never been, Fort Laramie. It is the tribal decision that she must live out the direction given by the dream. She and her brother depart for the fort, but first she is given a gift, a warrior's shield. Painted across the front of the shield is the image of a woman in a red dress clutching an arrow of lightning. Suspended from the shield are twenty-two rattlesnake rattles. The dream that initiates Red Dress's journey provides no clear guidance to what her role will be when she reaches the fort. The burden of the responsibility for unlocking the dream's message is hers alone. It is clear, however, that the power of the rattlesnake is somehow involved. This rattlesnake power emerges as three young officers from the fort, under the influence of Red Dress's magic, wrap snakelike coils of rope around their necks and fall to their deaths. When Red Dress herself dies, and is placed on a burial platform near the crown of an oak tree, the rattlesnake guardians honor her:

I saw the creatures emerge from their dens and hiding places. Serpents flowed toward the tree, forming creeks and rivers of writhing motion. They washed over one another, rising and then falling; they became a single unit of grace.
The snakes are dancing, I murmured. And when they surrounded the tree, my spirit fell into their midst, prostrate. We danced together. (253)

With her gift of rattlesnake power, Red Dress controls the forces of life and death. The name given to Red Dress also points to an omen of significant power. Her name involves a color symbolism that indicates "the color of danger, war, sorcery as well as their safeguards" (Moon, 66), ambivalent powers that have both light and dark sides.

In her descendant, Anna Thunder, this power is not used specifically to protect the tribe from its enemies. According to Anna, "You grab on to your life and push it around where you want it to go" (21). Anna is not a healer, for she is confined to a wheelchair by arthritis. Nevertheless, even in this seemingly restricted circumstance, she has filled "young people with hurtful desires, changed the course of their destinies." In vengeance after the death of her own child, she beads the red moccasins that cause her niece to dance to her death.

In contrast to Anna's negative manipulation of power, the reservation healer, Herod Small War, represents the positive side of spiritual power. The people come to him when in need, for he "finds things: misplaced objects, missing persons, and the answers to questions" (74). He is the leader of the traditional Sioux ceremonies: *yuwipi* or spirit-calling, sweat lodge, and vision quest. To his community, he offers remedies for "their tears and their sad little stories, their confusion and illnesses, their fear of death" (157). Occasionally, he finds himself locked in direct confrontation with Anna's schemes.

These two characters, Anna Thunder and Herod Small War, demonstrate that spirit power is neither good nor evil. Power takes on a moral quality only in the hands of its practitioner. But a further problem remains. If, indeed, medicine people like Herod Small War are "in the spirit . . . collecting the secrets of the world" (285), then why have the Native American peoples suffered so greatly? Part of the answer lies in the discussion of the differences between the Sioux Creator and Father and the Christian God:

That's what Tunkasida told me, something like that. He said the Christian God has a big lantern with the kerosene turned way up, and the people pray to Him for help, for guidance, and He lights the way. Now, Wakan Tanka, when you cry to Him for help, says, "Okay, here's how you start a fire." And then you have to make your own torch. (285)

Once again, the responsibility for the manifestation of spirit power rests with the individual. Most of the medicine practitioners have been called to their roles by the spirit world through the medium of omens, dreams, or visions. Even after they have received a summons to the often rigorous way of life demanded by the spirits, there are those who either refuse the invitation or give up the path as they pass through an initiation process. Clearly, for the Native American community, power may easily corrupt the one who claims it or is unworthy of it.

Each chapter of *The Grass Dancer* can stand alone as a short story, but recurring characters and interlocking events create unity and depth as the narrative moves back and forth across time and generations, and as voices of the living and dead, the young and the old, provide layers of experience. The traditional (Sioux corn soup for a dying mother) blends with the modern (television images of astronauts walking on the moon), and the supernatural and the everyday intersect almost constantly to create what critics call "a living mythology" that demonstrates contemporary lives bound to the deeds of their ancestors. On the one hand, Power's story is a tragic romance—two lovers separated by death. On the other hand, it is infused with the spiritual power of Sioux belief.

LOUIS OWENS (CHOCTAW, CHEROKEE)

The nature of spirit power is developed even further in the work of Louis Owens, a professor at the University of New Mexico. The two novels of Owens that we review, *The Sharpest Sight* and *Bone Game*, fit together as parts of a family saga. The stories illustrate the tension between the traditional and the nontraditional ways of life. *The Sharpest Sight* is based in the California coastal mountain region, where Hoey McCurtain and his two sons, Attis and Cole, have moved, leaving much of their Choctaw heritage behind with Uncle Luther in the Mississippi swamp. But their lives are propelled back toward their Choctaw heritage when Attis's dead body is spotted as it is swept along by a river at flood stage. The murder mystery that develops requires negotiation between the forces of sorcery wielded by the living and the powerful intervention of the ancestor spirits. In *Bone Game*, Cole McCurtain, the remaining son, is a university professor with a college-age daughter. Uncle Luther's aid is again enlisted, this time to protect Cole's daughter from becoming the latest victim of a brutal serial murderer. In the first novel, Cole travels to Mississippi, seeking Uncle Luther's help in locating Attis's bones. In the second novel, Uncle Luther and his colleague, Old Lady Blue Wood (Onatima), travel to California to offer their powers in reading the spirit world.

While both novels are firmly set in the present, the impact of the ancient tribal ways and past tribal histories is unavoidable. *The Sharpest Sight* describes the traditional Choctaw beliefs concerning the necessary burial rites for the dead, the nature of the soul, and the realm of the dead.

Onatima instructs Cole:

Every person has two shadows, grandson, an inside shadow and an outside one. When a person dies, the inside shadow, the *shilombish* . . . goes to wherever it's supposed to go. Most people's inside shadow goes to a good place where there's always plenty of game to hunt and it's never cold and people play ball games all year round. A person who's murdered someone can't go to that place. . . . The inside shadow is taken down a black river full of snakes to a place where all the trees are dead and the people cry and suffer all the time. . . . Now the outside shadow, the *shillup*, is different . . . it's waiting for the bones. (110)

Cole must locate Attis's body, even though it may have been carried one hundred miles away to where the river sweeps into the ocean. After the body has been found, the traditional Choctaw practice of "picking the bones" must be completed. The Choctaws strapped their dead onto an open-air platform, accompanied by a few prized possessions. The scavenger birds would be the first bone pickers. After a period of six months, the official "bone picker" for the village ascends the burial platform and completes the process of removing any fragments of tissue still adhering to the bones. The "bone picker" takes the bones to the ancestral burial mound, Nanih Waya, and a great feast ensues. The sacred site was connected both to the Creation story describing the emergence of the Choctaw and to the completion of the life cycle of tribal members as their bones were placed with those of the ancestors. There is some urgency attached to Cole's recovery of his brother's bones, for the black panther or "soul eater" is stalking Attis's outside shadow, trying to stop its passage to the realm of the dead.

A second matter to be resolved, in addition to locating Attis's bones, is the identification of his killer. The *viejo*, the sheriff's dead grandfather, is a constant presence, teasing the investigation along with subtle clues. Uncle Luther warns Cole of the *bruja* (female witch) who adds yet another level of danger to the proceedings.

Bone Game continues the theme of a threatening spirit presence, this time focusing on the figure of the "gambler," a spirit being whose game of chance has life or death as its stakes. The "gambler" appears to Onatima in the Mississippi swamp. "His eyes are black as the raven cape he wears, his mouth set in a line. He holds his hands in front of him, showing the bones, one pale, one dark" (105). Then he appears outside Cole's California house:

At the edge of the forest, a form moved from the shadows and sat cross-legged on the ground. The right half of the folded body was painted a dull white, the left half black. The hair, pulled back and tied behind the head, was parted in the middle, half-white and half-black. With eyes fixed upon the house, the naked figure held both fists with stiff forearms and moved them back and forth in a weaving pattern, chanting softly. One hand opened. In the cupped palm lay a fragment of white, a minute thread of flesh still adhering to the bone. (136)

It turns out that the very history of the place calls this malevolent spirit forth. The Spanish mission of Santa Cruz was marked by a bloody conquest of the Indian population. Then in 1812 the Indians, under the leadership of Venancio Asisara, rose up in vengeance. Padre Quintana, who had used a wire whip to shred the people's backs, was lured to his death, strangled, his testicles crushed, and his own blood sent into the earth. However, now it is 180 years later, and Cole's dreams are invaded by the bloody history of the Spanish priest and Asisara. Past and present collide when a series of murders and dismemberments occurs, and the urgency to confront the "gambler" and the "bone game" mounts. Thus, Owens enjoys translating the traditional belief in spirit powers into contemporary stories that graphically highlight the continuing struggle between forces of preservation and those of destruction.

DIANE GLANCY AND ROBERT CONLEY (CHEROKEE)

University professors Diane Glancy and Robert Conley (from Macalester College, St. Paul, Minnesota, and Northeastern Oklahoma State University, Tahlequah, Oklahoma, respectively) write historical fiction. They take as the basis for fictionalized narratives the haunting theme of the Cherokee Trail of Tears, a forced march by Cherokees driven at bayonet point from several southern states, their rich farmland confiscated for white settlers. These narratives breathe life into historical statistics encapsulating this low point in relations between the United States government and Native Americans: "From October 1838 through February 1839 some eleven to thirteen thousand Cherokee walked nine hundred miles in bitter cold from the southeast to Indian Territory. One fourth died or disappeared along the way" (Glancy, *Pushing the Bear*, 1).

This forced winter march was actually the second removal to the newly created Indian Territory in what is now Oklahoma. A previous expulsion of the Cherokee had been attempted in the summer of 1838. During this period, the loss of life was so great that further removals were postponed until cooler, more moderate weather. Close to nine hundred people began the summer exodus to

Oklahoma, but seventy died from disease along the way and two hundred more were close to death upon their arrival. The organization of the second, much larger-scale evacuation of the Cherokee was delayed until October. However, this timing placed the second group in an equally devastating set of circumstances, for as the soldiers routed the Cherokee from their cabins and farms, few were allowed to bring any possessions: shoes, warm clothes, cooking utensils, or other necessities. The bloody feet of the travelers marked the Trail of Tears.

Glancy's *Pushing the Bear* and Conley's *Mountain Windsong* neatly complement one another. Conley's work describes the summer removal and Glancy's gives a vivid picture of the much longer winter passage. Both authors use a changing male-female relationship as the central character development in their story lines. Conley describes two young lovers promised in marriage but ripped apart by the violent emptying of villages. Glancy chooses to highlight the disruption of the Cherokee culture in the estrangement between husband and wife, Maritole and Knobowtee, who are powerless to maintain their traditional roles. The authors offer a good deal of historical documentation, interrupting their respective narratives to include the texts of treaties and ethnographic reports. Glancy provides a mosaic of firsthand accounts of the cruelty, atrocities, disease, hunger, fatigue, and sorrow the captive Cherokee endured in their march "toward darkness, toward death"; she captures the anger and confusion of people who had done more than whites had asked of them: adopting farming, white attire, and even slavery; developing their own written language; and in many cases converting to Christianity. Conley, in turn, makes his account a story passed on to an eager Cherokee child by a grandfather, and textures his narration with actual documents and song lyrics.

The focal point of our concern in this chapter is the way that traditional myth and ritual appear in the novels, even in fragmentary form. The authors use authentic Cherokee materials in a very abbreviated way, but the references take on greater depth and meaning when the fuller tradition is brought to bear on them.

We will examine two segments of the Creation story that deal with the role of the mother goddess. With these two stories in hand, some of the statements concerning the female ownership of property are less surprising. In more than one place, Glancy refers to Selu, the Corn Mother of the Cherokee: "I went inside myself to remember a story so I could walk to the afterlife. It was Selu, . . . I thought of, who gave the Cherokee corn. She let her two sons, the Thunder Boys, kill her. She now lived up in the Sky World with her husband" (55).

If Selu is responsible for supplying the Cherokee with corn, their basic food staple, why does she let her two sons kill her? Surely her actions are not offered as behavioral norms for typical family interactions. To make sense of this fragment, we return to the theme of the Maya story of the Hero Twins. Like Selu, they choose death and thereby gain power in the passage to rebirth.

The story of Selu starts with the description of a prosperous household. Kanati the hunter supplies the game for their diet, and Selu each day brings corn and beans from her storehouse to feed her two sons. There is a mystery associated with the storehouse, for her sons see no evidence of planting or tending fields, yet there is always an abundant harvest. Determined to solve the mystery, the two boys spy on Selu, and discover that the corn flows from her vagina, and the beans from her breasts. The boys have upset the order of this world by accessing forbidden knowledge. Selu recognizes that her secrets have been violated, and thus the goddess must depart from the earth surface. Her own sons are the instruments of her passage. The subsequent access to food staples will not be easy, but Selu has pity on those to be left behind. She gives her sons elaborate directions on the use of her dead body to fertilize the fields that will now produce the corn. They are to drag her corpse over the field seven times, and each place that a drop of blood flows, there a corn plant will arise. Of course, the boys are careless in following the directions, and thus there is a ready explanation for any weak or failed corn crop. The story line is consistent in its logic. The goddess feeds her family directly from her body, just as she continues to feed her larger Cherokee family through her blood offering and then in ritual directions to be followed by each generation, either punctiliously or carelessly.

The second Creation story theme that Glancy refers to is the role of Uk-ten, a fearsome snake, who is both threat and healing power. Again, the brief fragments in the novel do not offer much insight into the traditional significance of Uk-ten's role. Paula Allen, in her retelling of the story of the mother goddess, Sun Woman, offers the following description of Uk-ten:

Again they transformed two priests into serpents. This time one became a diamondback rattler and the other was transformed into the fearsome Uktena, a monstrous beast whose name derived from the lethal potency of his glance, and whose head was crested with two horns and with a triangular sheet of pure crystal that was perfectly transparent except for a thin red streak that ran down its center. (89)

The male priesthood, the Ani-Kutani, had been engaged in a power struggle with Sun Woman. She was angered over their practice of abducting women whenever they desired, often driving their victims to suicide and leaving their families to grieve. Sun Woman expressed her displeasure with the priests and their followers by sending blistering illnesses that brought death to many. Finally a plot is hatched to murder Sun Woman as she visits her daughter's home at the midpoint of her daily passage across the sky. Two snakes, Rattlesnake and Uk-ten, are dispatched to carry out the deed. However, Rattlesnake, impatient to carry out his mission, mistakenly kills Sun Woman's daughter. Uk-ten, horrified by this grave error, rejects the role of assassin to become an ally of Sun Woman. Thus, the creature of destruction becomes a source of healing for the Cherokee people. This Creation story indicates violent tensions between the various levels of creation, the sky realm as opposed to the earth surface realm.

These tensions are relieved as Sun Woman and her followers on Earth are reconciled. The fate of the Ani-Kutani, however, is not so fortunate, for their elaborate organization collapses.

It is to this saga of the rise and fall of the Ani-Kutani that Robert Conley devotes his trilogy, *The Way of the Priests, The Dark Way,* and *The White Path.* The five-hundred-page saga is set in historical time—the period directly before the arrival of the Europeans in North America. It traces the course of the love story of Corn Flower and Edohi. Conley uses few excerpts from the traditional Creation story in *Mountain Windsong,* but he more than makes up for this lack in his trilogy. The trilogy refers to mother goddess stories we have described, and it includes a broad range of Cherokee myths such as Rabbit the Trickster and the *Yunwitsansdi,* the little people.

JAMES WELCH (BLACKFEET, GROSS VENTRE)

University of Montana professor James Welch, in his novel *Fool's Crow,* illustrates two areas of Creation story narrative that have not been previously discussed. Going back to our initial diagrammatic model that the universe is a web of tightly woven connections, we will see how the links between the sky realm and that of the animal guardians are maintained. In many translations of Creation stories, the word "person" indicates a member of the sky realm or a type of animal spirit guardian. However, the word "person" as it is applied to the sun, moon, stars, and planets should not automatically register the idea that there is a human being living on each star or celestial body. Rather, in the time of the "beginnings," spirit beings moved freely between a variety of external forms, wearing them temporarily and then removing them. For example, the living being that was the Morning Star could use as its manifestation a fiery globe, or a human form, or a voice connected to any earth element. The same is true for the animal guardian spirits, who shift from one form to another as their story unfolds. This belief in multiple forms allows for a wide range of storytelling, such as the classic theme of intermarriage between the human community and both the sky and animal guardians. Thus, tales such as the man or woman who marries the sun or star, the buffalo, the bear, or the serpent are commonplace.

The human visitor to the sky or to the animal guardian's world may remain in that world for an extended period, sometimes producing and raising children. But the visit to the alternate world can be abruptly ended when a taboo is broken or homesickness for a previous way of life intrudes. At times the journey to the spirit beings was meant to be a temporary phase long enough only to bestow specific information or to teach rituals of restoration.

Welch's novel *Fool's Crow* is set in 1870, a period when increased pressure from the expanding European-American community created serious difficulties for the Blackfeet. Fool's Crow rises to a role of spiritual leadership and his dreams bring him critical messages from the spirit realm. Because he honors the dream messages, he is finally led by Wolverine, his animal guardian, to an encounter with Feather Woman, a spirit being who reveals the future of Fool's Crow's nation. Feather Woman originally comes from the human community, then travels to the sky realm, marries Morning Star, and lives with him and his parents, Sun Chief and Night Red Light. She gives birth to a son, Star Boy. But she breaks a serious taboo and is forever exiled to a liminal world, belonging neither to the human nor to the sky community.

Each morning Feather Woman enacts rituals of repentance for her actions, but she is forever condemned to watching her husband and son race across the sky. She takes on the role of a powerful intercessor for the human beings with the Sun Chief. Her story is told in the Sacred Vow lodge of the Sun Dance, and her sacred digging stick is one of the ritual objects used in that ceremony. Her son, Star Boy, first instructed the Blackfeet in the rituals of the Sun Dance, their most sacred ceremony.

Thus, Feather Woman remains an important link in the web connecting all points in existence. Fool's Crow's journey to her world is not merely a dream passage. He receives the summons for the journey in a dream, but he instructs his wife that he will be gone for a length of seven sleeps, the time frame specified in the dream. Traditional storytellers and their audiences had no difficulty accepting the reality of travel across the web of life.

Even though a historical novel rather than a philosophical or religious story, Welch's work is replete with material on the traditional Blackfeet way of life, including key elements of Blackfeet mythology. In contrast, his suspense novel, *The Indian Lawyer*, set in a contemporary time frame, does not borrow so freely from the author's traditional heritage. Although an intriguing story, unlike *Fool's Crow* it requires no particular guide to comprehending the traditional materials, and will be discussed as detective fiction in Chapter 6.

SHERMAN ALEXIE (SPOKANE, COEUR D'ALENE)

Sherman Alexie, who was raised on the Spokane Indian Reservation in Wellpinit, Washington, interlocks three central characters—Thomas Builds-the-Fire and his companions Junior and Victor—in *Reservation Blues* and *The Lone Ranger and Tonto Fistfight in Heaven*. Alexie's approach illustrates yet again how the spider's web aptly describes the interconnectedness of all life. With James Welch, we saw the belief that the web of life allows travel to multiple worlds. Understanding how Alexie explores the web of life in his novels means keeping in mind that the intrinsic connections linking people, places, and events are absolutely in place. It also means discarding historical chronology as an organizing principle and being patient as the lines of connection slowly emerge.

This technique of moving in what to mainstream eyes seems a chaotic way across a web of connections, now touching remote points, then shifting quickly to another time, place, and person, is not found only in Alexie's work. Louise Erdrich in *Love Medicine*, Leslie Silko in *Storyteller*, and Louis Owens in his murder mysteries are not concerned with beginning their stories "in the beginning" and simply moving forward in linear time. Mythological time intersects historical time, and family genealogies are revealed step-by-step with no preconceived order. The seemingly wandering story lines of Erdrich and Silko cannot be dismissed as a series of flashbacks or even the mere reversal of the time frame. Such mainstream film metaphors for developing a story are simply inappropriate and not part of the Native American philosophical framework. More to the point in working with these Native American authors are the following comments of Greg Sarris. Sarris's grandmother taught him the Pomo tradition when he was an adult:

I was a graduate student at Stanford University preparing a dissertation on the life story of Mabel McKay, renowned Cache Creek Pomo Indian basketweaver and medicine woman, whom I had known since childhood. No part of the project had been easy. Mabel didn't present her stories in chronological sequence. Her stories moved in and out of different time frames and often implicated me as a listener. (1)

To discourage his analytical questioning, Mabel had a standard response for Greg: "Don't ask me what it means the story. Life will teach you about it, the way it teaches you about life" (5). The reader is to carry the story around until little flashes of insight illuminate the connections that are presently just beyond view.

Of the Alexie novels, *Reservation Blues* is the easier one to follow since the entire novel develops along a single major story line. This is not true for *Lone Ranger*, which is definitely written in the little flashes of insight mode. Both novels are filled with a dark humor that acknowledges the deep human suffering everywhere in evidence on the reservation. However, Alexie's work does not pronounce a death sentence for his people. Adaptation and hope surface in the following equation: survival = anger × imagination (150).

Reservation Blues features the lyrics of pop music as the contemporary continuation of the storytelling process. Thomas and his friends, aided by the magic guitar of legendary bluesman Robert Johnson, form the band Coyote Springs and work toward winning a recording contract. The contract becomes a tantalizing symbol of recognition and reward offered by white America. Two U.S. cavalry generals, Sheridan and Wright, are reincarnated as recording executives. Alexie includes many a nod to the traditional ways, as he has the young men climb a mountain in a pseudo vision quest before they tackle their recording session. Big Mom resides at the top of the mountain, and although she is a Spokane Indian, she is part of every tribe (199). Her personal history has been forever marked by the slaughter of nine hundred horses by the United States cavalry in 1861:

After she counted the dead, she sang a mourning song for forty days and nights, then wiped the tears away, and buried the bodies. But she saved the bones of the most beautiful horse she found and built a flute from its ribs. Big Mom played a new flute song every morning to remind everybody that music created and recreated the world daily.

In 1992, Big Mom still watched for the return of those slaughtered horses and listened to their songs. With each successive generation, the horses arrived in different forms and with different songs, called themselves Janis Joplin, Jimi Hendrix, Marvin Gaye, and so many other names. Those horses rose from everywhere and turned to Big Mom for rescue, but they all fell back into the earth again. (10)

Now it is Coyote Springs' turn to gather her wisdom and "recreate" the world. In *The Lone Ranger*, Alexie has the reservation storyteller describe his role.

He knew his stories had the power to teach, to show how this life should be lived. He would often tell his children and their friends, and then his grandchildren and their friends, those stories which could make their worlds into something better. At the very least, he tells funny stories that would make each day less painful. (134)

And perhaps Sherman Alexie would describe his own work in these words.

All nine of the authors surveyed in this chapter have taken a hand at "re-creating the world." They link their own stories directly to the stories of their traditional heritage, often using a decidedly non-European, nonmainstream framework and style even as they write in English, in (sometimes) conventional genres, with characters and narratives that will speak to the general reader. The Creation story with the mother goddess and Coyote, the power of sorcery and healing, the experience of the "web of life"—all of this wealth is being offered to the reading audience. However, just as many a hero/heroine in traditional myth and contemporary literature has the task of unlocking the meaning of omens, dreams, and visions, so the reader, too, must participate in the act of creation. An understanding of tribal religions and cultures enhances the power of the "story."

TWO WORLDS IN MARGINAL CONTACT

Our first three chapters have attempted to show the conceptual gulf between Native American and what we have been calling mainstream or European-based white culture. This great divide has existed since the first encounters, and while the fiction of the last part of the twentieth century may suggest otherwise, it is our assertion that enormous differences in outlook and worldview remain. Assimilation and the relative material success of a handful of native groups, notably in the casino industry, have finessed the issue of difference while leaving unchanged poverty on reservations and isolation in rural America. The American tendency to see culture in mechanistic terms defines these failures in terms of inadequate job skills, limited educational opportunity, scant capital resources, and other material deficiencies. While such privations represent shameful physical neglect of an abused and betrayed people, the alienation caused by cultural isolation—or even worse, the appropriation of cultural elements for profit, for ideological leverage, or for personal indulgence—certainly has played an important role in the current depressed status of many indigenous groups. Here, fiction is not innocent of charges of cultural hegemony, for even some works whose intentions seem benign have traded on Native Americans for success.

The chapters that follow attempt to sort out this use and abuse of native culture as a fictional topic. We believe the mass reading public is only sometimes aware of just how crude the manipulation of the native image can be, for while talented and respectful writers like Tony Hillerman, Margaret Coel, Lucia St. Clair Robson, Richard Parrish, and James Thom have won legions of followers, so have much less enlightened practitioners in this evolving and expanding subgenre of popular fiction. The problem lies not with the Native American community, which none of us presumes to speak for, but rather with mainstream use of it; Americans, for all their immigrant history and hundreds of years of contact with indigenous people, have a limited apparatus for dealing with the Other, or even sometimes for acknowledging that other ways exist. Unlike the cultural complexity of Europe, Africa, Asia, and even South and Central America, where multiple languages, ethnic groups, and religions are in constant contact, the peculiar history of the United States has tended to flatten difference or even eradicate it, sometimes to good effect, to be sure, but also sometimes to the detriment of vulnerable groups trying to preserve an indigenous heritage.

ACKNOWLEDGING DIFFERENCE

Fiction is an excellent way of sharing an experience foreign to one's own, perhaps the best indirect way. However, as chapters 2 and 3 have demonstrated, mainstream readers will be left feeling puzzled or incompletely moved by the most Indian of Indian fiction, that is, the fiction which relies most heavily on a native culture for its meaning. Native readers, in turn, may feel that mainstream fiction does little to reflect their concerns and values, speaking to them only as a small segment of a mass audience. What areas of difference divide these two communities of readers? Since good literature, and perhaps especially popular literature, speaks to essential human issues, should we postulate two different readership communities? We offer the following in list form as an indicator of where differences lie.

Material versus Spiritual

The essential Western way of seeing the world derives from the philosophical materialism of John Locke and a host of Enlightenment thinkers: the world we perceive through our senses is the real one; other "realities" tend to be metaphorical or part of a vague spiritual realm. In contrast, the great majority of Native Americans saw the spiritual world, as revealed by dreams, omens, and visions, as being at least as real as the world of our senses, and sometimes more so. From this difference derive several others.

The Judeo-Christian God versus Wakantanka/Usen/the Great Spirit

The paternal, often immediately involved, personified Supreme Being of traditional Christianity is far more particularized than the much more abstract "Great Spirit."

Linear Time versus Mythological Time

How a culture defines time affects everything from "being on time for appointments," as Edward Hall shows in his fascinating study of arranging a school bus schedule for Navajo children, to how a story or narrative sequences events. Thus

Chronological Narrative versus Web of Time Narrative

Realistic fiction assumes events follow one another in cause-effect patterns, interrupted possibly by a flashback or a look forward, but still connects events all in a neat line. If the spiritual-mythological has priority, there is no need to be consumed by such orderly chains of cause and consequence. As a result

Literary Verisimilitude versus Magical Realism

For the Western reader, the primary question is how true the work is to life. For magical realism (a form popular in Hispanic cultures) the question is how true the work is, psychological and spiritual forces having equal stage time with material things.

The Future as Primary versus The Role of the Past in the Present

Obligation to the Young versus Obligation to Ancestors, Heritage

The graphic is crude in its paired opposites, for the ways cultures differ are far too complex to represent as neat polarities. Attitudes toward the past and future, toward ancestors and offspring, for example, manifest themselves in burial practices, child rearing, reverence (or lack of it) toward the elderly, and whole sets of behavior too extensive to list. Ideas about property rights, privacy, politeness, community, individuality, violence, and virtually every other issue of importance to human society come into play, depending on initial assumptions about time, space, and the nature of reality.

Given these differences, can Native American and European-based cultures ever find common ground? Bridges abound between vastly different cultures, but must be sought out and crossed carefully, sometimes with laborious difficulty. For example, the color and direction symbolism discussed in Chapter 2 and shown in native literature in Chapter 3 should make perfect sense to an open-minded mainstream reader, as long as such a person is aware that color symbolism is not innate (some Asian cultures see white as a color of mourning), and that "rightness" often depends on historical and environmental factors, rather than on majority practice. As we have indicated above, our discussion is directed to such open-minded mainstream readers, consumers of popular culture fair enough to acknowledge how, at worst, self-serving and manipulative fiction's use of the Indian figure has been, and how, at best, the evolving genres that include Native Americans have at times sought to do real justice to real people.

4

The Western

... in a region only three generations from the total wildness of buffalo and horse Indians, everything, including history, must be built from scratch. Like any other part of a human tradition, history is an artifact. It does not exist until it is remembered and written down; and it is not truly remembered or written down until it has been vividly imagined. We become our past, and it becomes a part of us, by our reliving of our beginnings.
                                                —Wallace Stegner, Foreword to A. B. Guthrie, Jr.'s
                                                                    The Big Sky (1982 ed.)

The Old West is not a certain place in a certain time, it's a state of mind. It's whatever you want it to be.
                                                —Tom Mix (ca. 1938; from Darryl Ponicsan's,
                                                                    Tom Mix Died for Your Sins, 135)

A BRIEF HISTORY

Beginnings

The Western story began with nonfiction accounts of European immigrants and settlers encountering Native Americans, sometimes amicably, sometimes with hostility, and developed into fictional accounts of the same encounters embellished with literary conventions and literary diction. Building on innumerable sermons, cautionary tales, and abduction stories real and fictional, Ann Eliza Bleecker's captivity story, *The History of Maria Kittle* (1797), was the first American novel to depict in fiction the Indian as demonic savage and to have a French gentlewoman condemn both France and Britain for "the horrid cruelties of their savage allies" (63). The idyllic domestic scene Bleecker paints initially

is shattered by the nightmare that follows. She asserts, "The savages began to commit the most horrid depredations on the English frontier" (7), and goes on to describe atrocities in which friendly Indians join with others against settlers, dash infants against stone walls, rip unborn infants from their mother's womb, scalp fathers as their children watch, burn down buildings in which children are trapped, torture and kill male captives for amusement on the trip home, and threaten their female captives with sudden death by hatchet at the slightest noise because, as a former friendly Indian with an eye on Maria Kittle as a future wife explains, "We never suffer our prisoners to be retaken" (36). Before entering their village, they paint themselves and their prisoners in primitive streaks of color and gyrate wildly around the captives; their arrival is then celebrated by making the prisoners run the gauntlet. Such images are iconographic reflections of the horrifying details repeated in captivity story after captivity story throughout the eighteenth and early nineteenth centuries.

These early captivity stories were gradually supplemented with and supplanted by tales of the westward movement, with the Indians as either assimilated guides or forces to be overcome. In the novels and short stories that have come to be called "Westerns," the point of view was traditionally that of the settler, cowboy, or cavalry officer, not that of the Native American. Indians were "Injuns," and the only good one was a dead one. Sometimes they were described metaphorically as comparable to hostile forces of nature like the desert wind, the alkaline water, or the thorny cactus—tribulations to be borne and overcome. Other times they were depicted as bloodthirsty, pagan savages, behaving in unspeakably nightmarish ways: scalping and torturing prisoners, and even eating the hearts, brains, livers, and other body parts of captives. Descriptions of torture were particularly creative: prisoners were staked out over ant hills after being coated with honey, burned at the stake, skinned alive, cut thousands of times, or gouged, stoned, or kicked to death. This is not to say that Native Americans did not have their defenders in early twentieth-century Westerns, for writers like Harold Bell Wright (*The Mine with the Iron Door*, 1923), Edgar Rice Burroughs (*The War Chief*, 1927), and Will Levington Comfort (*Apache*, 1931) idealized and ennobled the Apache. Nonetheless, Native Americans were not seen whole, even in more informed and enlightened works. In the early Western, the empathic view was an aberration of sorts. Indian savagery no doubt reflected the rewriting of an unpalatable history, a white rationalization of aggressive land acquisition.

As early as the 1940s some writers countered the negative historical record and the fictional stereotype by investigating and reporting historical accounts of the barbarisms of the colonists and later of the settlers and U.S. Army. For example, only sixty years after the historical events, and thus within living memory, Howard Fast researched the escape of three hundred Cheyenne from their Oklahoma reservation, their flight home to land promised them by the Harney-Sanborn Treaty only a year before (1865), the U.S. Army pursuit, and the massacre at Fort Robinson—a deplorable act against sick, starving, unarmed prisoners. (The discovery of gold invalidated the mere legalisms of treaty promises.) His novel *The Last Frontier* (1941), based on interviews with elderly Cheyenne and a comparison of Eastern establishment news accounts with Western accounts ("fearless hard-hitting frontier editors . . . who had enough regard for the truth to print what they believed," 305), revised "history" ("a maze of falsification and inconsistency," 303) to set the record straight in a dramatic fictive mode. Though writing from a "white" perspective, Fast captured the justice of the Cheyenne cause, and their cruel and inhumane treatment at the hands of white military and governmental officialdom. At Fort Robinson, after locking captured Cheyenne in an unheated cabin (in winter), with no food, no water, no shoes, no blankets, and no toilet facilities, the U.S. soldiers massacred men, women, and children as they tried to escape: "They stood there shooting like men on a firing range potting clay pigeons" (275). Countering a comment by one general that "the primitive idea of freedom and liberty is not like ours" (299), Fast called the Cheyenne journey back to their homeland "possibly the greatest struggle against odds in all human history . . . an epic in man's desire for personal freedom" (303). Such perspectives were not mainstream, however, and the typical Western image of the Native American is summed up in the "shoot-um-up" Western films of the 1940s and 1950s—with the film *Broken Arrow* and its positive portrait of Cochise, and of a romance bridging race and culture, the rare exception. (The film was based on Elliott Arnold's *Blood Brother* and its juvenile version, *Broken Arrow*, 1953 and 1954, respectively).

The 1960s and 1970s

By the 1960s, however, a definite change in attitude was marked by Thomas Berger's *Little Big Man* (1960), which reevaluated white-Indian relationships through the eyes of a happy white captive-turned-Indian and painted positive portraits of Native American life and of a wily shaman, Old Lodge Skins. Books that followed this watershed work attempted to capture the point of view of Native Americans, to instill a sense of white guilt for the lies and atrocities that were part of the conquest of the West, and to create cultural bridges by revealing incidents where whites and Indians interacted on a human level—man to man and man to woman—to share understanding, and to make peace (at least in literature). Jane Barry's 1929 *A Time in the Sun* was reissued in 1962 because it questioned white values and sympathized with the Apache struggle to avoid confinement on reservations. Theodore Olsen's *Stalking Moon* (1965) pits a tough New Mexican scout turned rancher against Salvaje, a notorious Apache feared throughout the Southwest for his deadly raids, in a duel to the death. However, Olsen complicates the plot by humanizing Salvaje: he is a proud, courageous loner who has come to take back his white-captive wife and son in territory far from his people; his son has already begun to suffer the humiliations inflicted on half-breeds; and the rancher who has taken this rejected woman as his wife and her mixed blood boy as his son recognizes in Salvaje a man very much like himself. In fact, he finds himself anticipating Salvaje's actions because he would respond in the same way in Salvaje's place. In the end, he chooses not to correct the Apache's deathbed conviction when his son had seized a pistol to side with him against the white man, instead of with the white man against his father—a final sign of the understanding and sympathy that has grown between them as they have struggled for the same wife and son. The individual caught between two worlds like Glen Blackburn's Benito Hand, son of a white father and an Apache mother (*Apache Half-Breed*, 1971), recurs in works from this period: The soldiers and the settlers "were riding the tide of history, while the redmen were clinging like simple children to a nostalgic wish and a vain hope. He could see the approaching bloodbath. . . . He felt the guilt of both worlds pressing on his conscience . . ." (53). Peter Dawson's *The Half-Breed* (1962) takes this pressure a step further in Nemo, a relentless law officer tracking a ruthless white murderer through territory where Nemo's Indian blood makes him the suspected villain, not the smooth-talking woman-killer he pursues. In search of authenticity and understanding, Anna Lee Waldo twice toured the Lewis and Clark Trail and spent more than ten years researching her over thirteen-hundred page tome *Sacajawea* (1979)—a labor of love and a tribute to a Native American who has had more statues erected to her than to any other American woman. True to their reputation as decades of revisionism and against-the-grain muckraking, the 1960s and 1970s marked a revolution in attitudes that continues in the turn-of-the-millennium fiction of the present. To some degree, the shift has been toward new points of view, an embracing of the Indian position as a means of assuaging inherited guilt, even though the destruction of the native way of life took place a hundred years before. While acknowledging guilt, this phenomenon has also created its own self-serving visions, turning to and shamelessly indulging in the Rosseauian vision of the Noble Savage— different from us in culture, community, religion, and way of life but a true innocent, attuned to nature and to the spirit world, endowed with a special "wisdom" that civilized man could learn from. Again, Native Americans were not depicted in these works as truly complex amalgams of tribes and cultures, but rather as symbolic stick figures.

The 1980s and 1990s

The Western of recent years has come a long way from the "we vs. they" tales of Indian savagery and white heroics. Instead, the modern trend is toward a more modulated revisionism: a fresh look at the past from new points of view. Writers like Lucia St. Clair Robson, James Alexander Thom, Michael Gear, Terry Johnston, Matt Braun, Harry Combs, Douglas Jones, Richard Wheeler, and David William Ross, among others, have shown us the West and the movement west through the eyes of the Comanche, the Cherokee, and the Seminole as a people and of Quanah Parker, Tecumseh, Sitting Bull, Tiana Rogers, and Geronimo as individuals. Set in the 1860s Oregon Territory as the Modoc were being forced off their rich sacred lands onto barren reservations, Paxton Riddle's *Lost River* (1999) is typical in its sympathetic portrait of the Modoc and their genuine attempts at assimiliation despite the viciousness of individual whites and the betrayals of government promises. Riddle's heroine, a respected Modoc woman who marries a white man sympathetic to the Modoc way of life, serves as interpreter and go-between through difficult times of conflict; she faces abuse from both sides in order to guide her people through the accommodations necessary for survival. Hers is a thankless task, one she struggles with daily, for her instincts are to lash out against injustice as her fellow tribesmen do, but she practices restraint for the greater, final good. Thus, these native peoples are no longer presented as the generic types of the nineteenth-century penny Western;

they have been particularized and humanized, their cultural difference presented sympathetically, their sense of community and the complexity of their world-view communicated as an understandable human response to their world. They have been located in time and place, and recent writers have worked hard to escape the past tendency to group all Native Americans as generic Indians, purposefully distinguishing between tribes by identifying unique characteristics of food, custom, clothing, hunting strategies, and worldviews.

Writers of Westerns have also turned to tribes east of the Mississippi or in the Pacific Northwest, not just Plains Indians, the staple figures of the generic Western. They reflect a modern conception of a multicultural, multiethnic society where differences may separate but where personal contact will forge alliances that transform cultures and societies. This changed perspective has resulted in more negative treatment of white activities that once would have been praised, as in Robert Wheeler's *Badlands* (1992). Therein, respected members of a scientific expedition to study early man and prehistoric fossils become grave robbers and consciously deface sacred relics and holy sites in order to plunder Sioux burial treasures. Likewise, in Gary McCarthy's *Grand Canyon* (1996) federal action to protect the Grand Canyon as a national park inevitably involves the removal and ill-treatment of the peaceful, agricultural-based Havasupai, who had lived peacefully and safely in harmony with the canyon long before the Spanish first passed through. Both works elucidate the hard choices involved when desirable ends (scientific advancement, environmental protection) are pursued ham-handedly. This focus on the human and cultural costs of "progress" marks a new sophistication and maturity in the old genre of the Western.

Writers like A. B. Guthrie, Terry Johnston, Earl Murray, Michael Gear, and John Norman, among others, who retain a white narrative perspective, balance it through their main characters's intimacy with and respect for native peoples—from having a close Indian friend scouting or fighting at their sides, a beloved Native American wife who has endured hardship for their sakes, sons who have been raised as captives by Native Americans and who show their fathers the survival skills, community values, and sense of honor they have learned from hard people who have nonetheless made them their own as sons, brothers, and husbands. Matt Braun's *Indian Territory* (1985) is typical of such works at their best: a study of a decent man with torn loyalties. On the one hand, Braun's hero admires the Cherokee as a people and as a civilized nation, and feels particular empathy and respect for Cherokee leader Frank Ross and his beautiful, idealistic, tempestuous daughter. On the other hand, his job as troubleshooter for the Kansas and Texas Railroad as it cuts a wide swath across Cherokee land results in deadly gunfights with Cherokee opponents. Braun brings to life the messy complexity of cross-cultural politics and friendships as white railway men manipulate the Cherokees to undercut a rival railroad and as the Cherokees manipulate the railroad men for the sake of internal politics and internecine rivalries.

Some writers, like James Alexander Thom and Lucia St. Clair Robson, have used family records and diaries to retell captivity stories with an eye to fleshing out the details of life in the Indian camps, setting the unforgiving wilderness in which captives have learned to live and thrive against the harsh demands of their captors and the similarly harsh demands their captors make upon themselves. Tales of the early missionaries have metamorphosed from stories of clashing religious values and systems into stories of religious parallels. Brian Moore's *Black Robe* (1985) captures the Algonquin belief in spirits of the earth and water and their fears that the Jesuits are destroyers, threatening the gods and sorceries by which the Indians make sense of their world, whereas Kathleen Gear's *This Widowed Land* (1993) has Jesuit missionaries to the Huron experience mystical visions in which Christ comes to them as Cougar, a Huron deity, bearing the stigmata in his paws. Famous battles and massacres have been retold from the view of individual Sioux, Crow, Pawnee, and members of other tribes, and novels have praised Native American environmental awareness, deploring the purposeful massacre of the buffalo, the pollution of the land and rivers by swarms of whites who spread disease and destruction and trampled nature and Indians underfoot. Earl Murray and others like him have depicted strong Native American women acting to save their people in times of crisis (*Whisper on the Water*, 1988), and native peoples taking troubled whites under their protection and helping them survive (*The River at Sundown*, 1997).

Ironically, despite a concerted effort to recapture a Native American perspective, such works—admirable in their ethics and compelling in their telling as many of them are—are doomed to fail in that goal. The concept of paying tribute to the past through "our" literature, of creating fictitious characters to represent values and perspectives, is in itself a non-Native American concept; and try though writers might to capture the mysticism, the psychological forces that drive behavior, the sexual interplay, the relationships to each other, to the earth, to outsiders, the idea of community, and so on, they are writing as outsiders about tribes very different even now from those of ages long past. It is hard enough to ascertain how someone from our own background, language, and culture thinks; it is presumptuous to believe that we can easily bridge the barriers of time, language, and culture and truly represent the point of view of people very different from ourselves. Yet it is very much a modern attitude toward ethnicity to assume not only that are we all alike under the skin but also that the way "we" think and feel, minor differences aside, is the way others think and feel. Ironically, this is precisely the fallacy that led the white Europeans to misread Native American intentions and behavior so frequently.

The novel is an eighteenth-century European invention, a literary form that inevitably shapes experience according to its genre demands and traditions, as well as shapes the internal logic of the plot pursued and the point of view chosen. There is no equivalent form in Native American culture. As we have seen in chapters 2 and 3, the Native Americans' view of their own narratives incorporates communal, spiritual visions of history and cosmology, not the experience of an individual facing a series of personal challenges. The mainstream novel as we now know it, in contrast, privileges a singular protagonist, often allowing readers to project their feelings imaginatively into the fictional contexts provided. Thus, the revisionist literature of the West, as exciting and satisfying as it sometimes is to white and Western sensibilities, is just another construct, an artificial, fictive experiment in genre and point of view, that should not be taken for reality, or even as a necessarily accurate representation of "how things were." We are not hunter-gatherers, and we cannot truly enter the minds of long-lost groups who were; for all our common humanity, we are forever outsiders, and they will remain forever alien. Nonetheless, within the magical realms of fiction and fantasy, we can imagine that we understand and that, if we had been in their moccasins, we would have seen the world in this way or that. For this reason, these modern "histories" tell us far more about the perspectives, interests, attitudes, and political shifts of our own society than they do about historical "realities."

When in *Coyote Summer* (1997) Michael Gear's Heals Like a Willow, a beautiful Shoshone medicine woman who has fallen in love with a Harvard philosophy student-turned-mountain man, says that she has stepped between two very different peoples and been changed by the experience, she is a very compelling product of the imagination—a fictive tool to bridge the gulf that separates Indian and white. Her views reflect our modern speculation on how such experiences would have changed us: a courageous and self-confident warrior woman who has courted coup and seen the white man at his best and worst, she finds the Shoshone warriors who court her too bound by tradition and too ignorant of the dangers of new technologies, and the white trappers and mountain men too out of touch with nature and with the powers of the spirit to win her admiration or her love. She seeks a true equal for a mate, one who will recognize her power and intellect, and can match it with an understanding and strength of his own. When she tells her father that she feels like a leaf on the wind as a mighty storm is brewing, she sounds like a prophet foretelling the tragedy of the West, the decline of her people, and the dominance of a race blind to the cycles and power of nature.

As wonderful a heroine as she is, her attitudes and outlook are necessitated by plot and "concept," and tell us far more about modern American feminist and cultural views than about the historical Shoshone. She is, in many ways, a modern woman with a modern perspective, and readers take pleasure in having a representative from the past confirm the perceptions of the present. Throughout, the intellectual allegory drives the plot events and overcomes verisimilitude: a near-death wilderness experience strips a philosopher schooled in the classics of Western thought to the bare bones of his logic and finds him wanting; arrogant in his trust in the formulas learned in the best of schools, he finds himself sustained, in the depths of despair and physical anguish, not by reason but by love, intuition, and instinct. Thus, the story hinges on a struggle between worldviews presented in a traditional Western formula, that of the intellectual debate between Reason and Intuition. This modern Western, although acknowledging the intellectual validity of the Indian way, nevertheless presents the contest in a time-honored mainstream format.

GENRE OVERVIEW

Changing Genre Conventions

Though certainly enjoyed worldwide, the Western is nonetheless a uniquely American genre. It has traditionally been highly conventionalized, with the underlying conflict having anarchy threatening the forces of law and order and with heroes and villains clashing in open warfare. Tony Hillerman, in the opening letter to the reader in his "Frontier" series by Ken Englade and Will Camp, enumerates its usual contents: "gripping tales of gunslingers, cattle barons, clean-cut heroes, fierce Indian horsemen collecting scalps, and the U.S. cavalry racing to the rescue." However, the constraints of the genre have been tested and loosened in the last half of the twentieth century. Whereas in the past, a Western was set in the last third of the nineteenth century and located west of the Mississippi, today's Western may be set in the eighteenth century and may take place when the "frontier" was east of the Mississippi, in the Florida of the Seminole Wars or the Canada of the French and Indian War. In the early works the six-gun dominated the Western; today, weapons remain essential, but now the hero may carry a Hawken long rifle or a bow and arrow. The horse and the landscape of the West are still essential features, but the land may be mountains or swamp instead of the open prairie or desert of tradition. The saloon may remain, but it is no longer an essential element, and may even be transformed into a place of evil where proud men are shattered by alcohol abuse; however, places of crossroad encounters (like Bent's Fort and other trading posts) are vital.

The Western has always explored the tension between individual impulses and the need for social groupings, whether it is the cattle baron who tries to mow down the farmers, sheepmen, and small ranchers; the outlaw who defies local authorities and the tamer citizens of small towns; or the lone gunman like Shane, who joins a community only to leave it. Today, the Western carries this tension further, to explore the mountain man and others like him who come from an individualistic culture but must walk among native tribes bound by a community-based culture. As a consequence, the line between Western and historical fiction has blurred, and "Western" tales encompass more time and territory than they once did. Furthermore, they include other voices: of former slaves, of Chinese immigrants, of Hispanic vaqueros, and of Native Americans individualized by tribe.

The Range and Appeal

In *Westerns: Aspects of a Movie Genre* (1973) Philip French humorously defines the Western as "a great grab-bag, a hungry cuckoo of a genre" that is "open equally to visionaries and opportunists, ready to seize anything that's in the air from juvenile delinquency to ecology" (24). Indeed, "Western" has evolved into a catchall term: sometimes barely fictionalized history, sometimes completely escapist romance and fantasy, sometimes comedy or satire, a war story, a crime story, or a tall tale. The appeal, though, remains much the same—the West as a place of freedom and anarchy, potential and danger, an open arena where strangers meet and cultures clash. The Western as an expression of the West of the imagination is worth considering as a cultural and literary phenomenon that reveals much about who we are. Martin Nussbaum has called the Western hero "a vanishing symbol of individualism in an age of togetherness and conformity" (26). In modern Westerns that rugged individualist meets his counterpart and nemesis in Native Americans who stand for both community and freedom, escape from restraint and tribal ties, flesh and spirit.

In other words, the Indian-focused Western has opened up new territory and new perspectives with which to explore the original Western theme of the loner's relationship to the group. The blurring of history and fiction is as much a feature of the modern Western as it was of the nineteenth-century captivity stories, with fictionalized stories of historical figures like Mary Jemison, Pocahontas, Sacajawea, Orenda, and Osceola, and of historical events like the Trail of Tears and the massacres at Wounded Knee and Fort Robinson, this time with greater sympathy for the Indian perspective and with the point of view from inside the Indian camp instead of outside. The mythmaking apparatus of fiction is retelling traditional stories or inventing new ones in a wider, more spacious arena: the modern and inclusive West of the imagination.

Between Two Worlds—Blood Brothers

Stories of blood brothers (whites and Indians who, as adults, choose to be friends committed to one another and signify that choice by a ceremonial mingling of blood) continue to be popular, but the focus is more and more on the Indian perspective. In William W. Johnstone's *Blood Bond* (1989), deputized blood brothers Matt Bodine and Sam Two Wolves find their friendship tested and torn by the events surrounding General Custer's demise. David Thompson's *Lure of the Wild* (#2 in the Wilderness series) has an experienced mountain man named Shakespeare McNair (a blood brother to the Shoshone) teach the nineteen-year-old Nathaniel King so well about dealing with Indians—how to battle hostile Utes and Blackfeet and how to befriend Shoshone—that King ends up with a Shoshone wife, Winona, who, in the books that follow, continues his education about Native Americans, survival, and the pacification of rival tribes (*Blood Truce*, 1993). Don Bendell's series hero Chris Colt, Chief of Scouts, who lost his wife and child to a Lakota war party, recovers from his obsession with revenge through his discovery of white treachery that motivated the attack (Custer and a group of businessmen skimming profits and supplies from the Sioux reservation), and through his deepening friendship and brotherhood with Nez Percé scout Man Killer. Man Killer provides Colt with insights into the Indian character and way of life that put him at odds with the military leaders he is supposed to support, and make his job as cavalry scout harder and harder to perform. He smokes tobacco and reasons companionably with Apache renegades Victorio and Geronimo (in *Warrior*, 1995) when Man Killer has been taken captive, and he comes to respect the Plains Indians' conservation methods and to despise the waste and destruction of nature he sees fellow whites engaged in. In *Horse Soldiers* (1993), thanks to Man Killer's influence and his own observation of behavior, Colt's sympathies lie with Nez Percé Chief Joseph and with the beleaguered Indians' desperate thousand-mile trek to freedom in Canada, rather than with the U.S. Cavalry that pursues them like bloodthirsty scavengers. Friendship and commitment to one genuine Indian friend become a literary device for introducing a changing point of view and for growing sympathy and understanding for the Indian side of the white-Indian confrontation.

Between Two Worlds—Whites Turned Indians/Indians Raised White

The white Indian, who got his start in early captivity stories and Cooper's *Leatherstocking Tales*, has continued to be a cross-cultural interpreter, with series like White Indian, White Apache, and White Squaw numbering ten to twenty volumes. Historical novels depicting white child captives growing to love their adopted Indian parents and choosing to stay with them or returning home against their will include Lois Lenski's *Indian Captive: The Story of Mary Jemison* (1941), Conrad Richter's *The Light in the Forest* (1953) and *A Country of Strangers* (1966), Alice Marriott's *Indian Annie: Kiowa Captive* (1965), and Benjamin Capps's *A Woman of the People* (1966). Walter O'Meara's *Last Portage* (1962), a fictionalized biography of John Tanner, though frank and realistic about sexual practices and the harsh cruelty of Indian life, delineates Tanner's extreme difficulty in readjusting to the white community.

In more recent novels, whites raised by Indians are depicted as torn between two visions—the freedom, closeness to nature, and camaraderie/community of their native life versus the pull of genetic ties and the knowledge that the Indian way is doomed by historical inevitability. Michele Wyan's Comanche heroine Night Singer (*Night Singer*, 1995), a green-eyed redhead, is so immersed in the ways of the native people who stole her and adopted her that she strongly resists adjusting to Texan ways, even when faced with indisputable proof of her genetic heritage. Gerald Drayson Adams's hero Casper Collins (*Son of the Sioux*, 1981), raised Sioux by his mother and a childhood friend of Crazy Horse, trains at West Point because of his father (an Army major), but as an adult finds his peacemaking efforts stymied by racial hatreds and violence, and his Sioux friends more loyal than his Army associates. Likewise, Trace Gundy (Man Who Fights the Big Bear), in Jack Ballas's *Apache Blanco* (1994), raised by Apaches, maintains friendship and ties to his tribe but, as an adult, tries to live among whites. His rebellious Apache ways earn him a lot of enemies, and he ends up a loner, at one point on the governor's Most Wanted list. When whites try to play Indian and ambush him, however, they learn who the real Indian is. Raised by Comanches and befriended by Sioux, G. Clifton Wisler's series character, Willie Delamer, a.k.a. Man Apart, repeatedly finds himself taking the Indian side in disputes and finding pride in their spirited defense of their way of life; at the same time he understands that every victory simply means a harder future (*Among the Eagles*, 1989).

In Charles West's *Wind River* (1999) ten-year-old Robert Allred, sold into servitude by impoverished parents, escapes the mule skinner who bought him and miraculously kills a bear that attacks him. Arapahos, impressed by his strong "medicine," adopt him into their tribe and into their hearts as Little Wolf, and teach him the warrior's way. When the U.S. Cavalry massacres his village and his adoptive parents, he wages a fierce war of vengeance against Army forces and becomes much feared, and when whites kill his deeply loved Cheyenne wife, he becomes a destructive force to be reckoned with. Only when brought face-to-face with a trapper who treated him well in his youth and a brother he forgot he had does he end his trail of death, take a Cheyenne second wife, and seek the freedom and healing of a new path. His story and that of his brother continue in *Bitter Root* (1999). Clearly, West's intent is to make comprehensible the attractions and virtues of nineteenth-century life among the Plains Indians, and the white atrocities that would commit them to self-destructive war. Little Wolf is bound by honor and by emotional commitment to his adopted people, even as he understands the overwhelming forces of technology and manpower they stand against, and his white brother comes to appreciate their common humanity and the depth of Little Wolf's commitment only through personal tribulation.

The white Indians in Paul A. Hawkins's Ben Tree saga (*The Legend of Ben Tree*, 1993; *The Vision of Benjamin One Feather*, 1993; and *White Moon Tree*, 1994) are the family of Ben Tree, a yellow-haired mountain man, half-white, half-Osage, whose growing disgust with civilization peaked when a white killed his seventeen-year-old Crow wife. After crucifying and scalping the murderer, Ben Tree secretly invested all his savings and inheritance in a freight company run by a trusted representative and committed himself to the Crow way of life, marrying a Nez Percé, and eventually becoming chieftain. As such, he metes out rough frontier justice to those whites who threaten or injure his peole. As one who knows white ways, he is in a unique position to counsel his people, to keep them from harm's way, and to act as go-between for them in white-Indian relations; the large working ranch he establishes buffers the Absaroke from Army suspicions. His sons and daughters are fully Absaroke in their commitments, but learn from their father how whites think and how to deal effectively with them. His adopted son, Benjamin One Feather, has powerful spiritual medicine that helps the Absaroke find a path of hope as the spokes of the Great Medicine Wheel are being broken in the grim period of the Little Big Horn and the U.S. Cavalry revenge that followed. In this imaginative reconstruction of the white Indian point of view, Hawkins fantasizes about how caring whites might have saved some Indians from the bloody decimation of the 1880s.

The other direction such "two world" novels take is the reversal of white captivity, Indians raised by whites who return to their own. In *Shadow of the Big Horn* (1960) E(ugene). E. Halleran's central figure is a Sioux with a New England twang and an East Coast education who cannot escape the pull of his Sioux heritage, and who dies trying to prove himself a warrior. More recent novels have been less pessimistic about such returns. Typical is Matthew Hanchon/Touch the Sky, the hero of Judd Cole's over-twenty-volume Cheyenne series. The son of a great Cheyenne warrior, Touch the Sky was raised by frontier settlers, but abandoned the white man's world to seek his place among the Cheyenne. However, because of his white upbringing, he has enemies among his own people and must work hard to prove his commitment and value to the tribe (*Arrow Keeper* and *Death Chant*, both 1992). On a vision quest (*Vision Quest*, 1993) to find his place among the Cheyenne and to prove himself worthy, he discovers his role as go-between and protector. In *Blood on the Plains* (1993) he must outwit greedy land-grabbers who are swindling the Cheyenne out of their hunting grounds; in *Pathfinder* (1994) he must negotiate a treaty to protect the Cheyenne from even greedier gold miners; and in *Comanche Raid* (1993) he helps fend off a vicious Comanche attack on his village. In *Death Camp* (1995) he must choose between shamanistic and white medicine—prove his loyalty and watch his people die of a deadly epidemic, bring in white physicians and be scorned, or find some compromise to save his tribe. In *River of Death* (1997) the tribal water supply is threatened, as well as the ancestral lands, and Touch the Sky must face possible death by drowning, a sacrifice that would keep his soul from the Land of Ghosts. Despite repeated efforts to fit in and prove his worth, he remains suspect. Fellow Cheyenne accuse him of spying for whites (*Spirit Path*, 1994), and a Cherokee warrior seeks his death (*Mankiller*, 1994). When the tribe's sacred arrows are stolen in *Wendigo Mountain* (1995), his enemies demand his head for their return. In *Warrior Fury* (1996) a message that his pioneer father is dying is a ploy to get Touch the Sky out of camp so his wife and son can be kidnapped, and he must prove his warrior skills to save them. In *Renegade Siege* (1996) his concerns are mixed, for the white settlers of a pioneer mining camp will be ruthlessly slaughtered by renegade braves without his aid, and his Cheyenne tribal camp will be next.

Thus, throughout the series, Touch the Sky teeters between two worlds and remains emotionally committed to both. The new Western dramatizes the conflicts between Indians and whites in the internal and external conflicts of a single individual who is torn between two worlds, whose white technological knowledge helps him see remedies and methods his tribe cannot, but whose sense of community, whose love of the land, and whose emotional ties are threatened and perhaps doomed. No matter how hard he tries, one world will end and another will dominate, but the internal struggle to escape fate for the short run adds a tragic sense to these adventure stories.

Jake McMasters's hero suffers a similar conflict, but with time chooses the Indian way over the white way. In the first volume of McMasters's *White*

Apache series (*Hangman's Knot*, 1993), Clay Taggart is hanged and left for dead for a crime he did not commit. He is cut down by a ragtag band of Apaches, whose forward-looking chieftain, Delgadito, has plans for him as a go-between for peace. When the Apache camp is viciously attacked by scalp hunters, Clay, horrified to see white men gleefully gutting children and decapitating women, carries the wounded Apache leader to safety. Though Delgadito thinks of the conflict between Apaches and whites as one between a bear and an army of ants, with time—a period requiring physical endurance and true grit—he comes to respect Clay and to use his knowledge of whites and his desire for revenge to Apache advantage: Clay helps them collect horses and weapons as they help him exact revenge on the men who hanged him. McMasters convincingly and sympathetically dramatizes the Apache perspective: their initial contempt for and manipulation of Clay's weakness and sentimentality, their gradual respect for his planning and military successes. Clay himself acquires Apache endurance and begins to see white cavalry men as they do—noisy, bumbling "jackasses." In the volumes that follow, Clay roams the West, helping the Apaches fight off attackers:

Clay Taggart had taken to the Apache way of life heart and soul. He had remade himself in their image, becoming more Apache than white, and buried the part of him that had been caused so much torment under the hard exterior of an Apache warrior.

The unwritten Chiricahua creed had become the sole standard by which Clay Taggart lived: To kill without being killed, to steal without being caught. . . . [Clay] was *Lickoyee-shis-inday*, an Apache warrior in spirit, if not by birthright.

. . . Now that he saw the world through the eyes of a Chiricahua, he had a whole new outlook on life. (*Desert Fury*, 18)

As *Lickoyee-shis-inday* Taggart has learned the dangers of mercy, and so he kills without remorse. He knows how to blend with the environment, to snake through the grass, to observe patiently until he sees the battle situation clearly. Knowing that Mexican women view the Apache "as supernatural fiends who delighted in carving the warm, beating hearts from living victims" (63), he concludes that they will make ideal captives—wives for his small band—and organizes a successful raid into Mexico, the first in a series of steps aimed at turning "his" warriors into a tightly knit pack. Again, the point of view is that of a modern Western: trying to see into the minds of whites who purposefully chose to live among people they had been raised to see as savages and to defend the Indian way of life in defiance of their own people. In these stories, Indian loyalty is set against white disloyalty, Indian closeness to nature against white blindness to or fear of nature, a warrior's hard, realistic vision against white sentimentality, and, most of all, male bonding against the loose ties of the military regimen. The Indians may be doomed by technology, but their way of life makes a man a man and its hardness makes its few pleasures sweeter.

Changed Perspectives

The shift in point of view is the major change in end-of-the millennium Westerns. M. M. B. Walsh's *The Four-Colored Hoop* (1976) dramatizes a strong Indian woman's struggles against the white world; readers see through the eyes of Mildred Shoots Eagle, an Arikara Indian, who personally experiences white cruelty early in life when her village is destroyed and her parents are murdered. The Blackfoot Sioux narrator of Colin Stuart's novel *Walks Far Woman* (1976) recounts her life story to her grandson's fiancée: from 1874, when she kills her first husband's murderer, through the Battle of the Little Big Horn and to life among the Blackfeet in Montana, guided by her supernatural protectors. Dorothy M. Johnson (famous for the captivity short story "A Man Called Horse," 1949) captures the spirit of the new Western in her novel *Buffalo Woman* (1977). Therein, the point of view of Grandmother Whirlwind, an Oglala Sioux born near the Black Hills in 1820, encapsulates the tragedy of the Sioux Nation. Whirlwind experiences the disruption of her daily routine and the end of sacred rituals outlawed by whites; she sees the buffalo slaughtered to extinction, many respected warriors of her youth massacred or diminished, and herself displaced in 1877—like so many of her people—after the Battle of the Little Big Horn. The novel recounts her painful journey through winter storms to a Canadian refuge, and its sequel, *All the Buffalo Returning* (1979), continues the Oglala saga from Little Big Horn to Wounded Knee (1890). Such stories reverse the traditional perspective of the Western to give voice to traditional opposition— the Native Americans who were defending their territory and their way of life.

Frank Burleson's The Apache Wars saga, set in the early 1850s, dramatizes in a single character the shift in perspective from the old-fashioned Western to the modern Western. Burleson mixes historical characters, battles, and facts with fictive creations. His young Lieutenant Nathaniel Barrington becomes personally caught up in a clash of cultures, and thus comes to serve as the reader's guide into the heart of the Apache. Driven by his attraction to an Apache warrior woman, by his personal pleasure in meeting challenges, and by his strong sense of justice, he slowly evolves from dedicated soldier to white Apache. Readers see him first as a new soldier whose manhood is tested and whose fighting skills are honed in conflicts with the Apaches (*Desert Hawks*, 1996), then as a commissioned officer whose love for a beautiful Apache warrior woman named Jocita makes him question the morality of claiming Indian territory (*War Eagles*, 1995), and next in violent confrontation with the legendary historical Apache leaders Victorio, Mangas, Coloradas, and Geronimo—wily, skilled, and worthy opponents all (*Savage Frontier*, 1995). By the fourth book in the series (*White Apache*, 1996), Captain Barrington has left the army, been adopted into the Apache tribe as Sunny Bear, and become a medicine man; he serves a year apprenticeship as an Apache warrior, yet he finds himself torn between two worlds and unsure of his loyalties. He is all for the Apaches, but he is bothered by their indiscriminate killing of fellow whites. In *Devil Dance* (1997), Cochise leads the Apaches against the U.S. Cavalry, and Barrington finds himself caught in the middle, trying to ease the life of reservation Indians by working as an aide to the Bureau of Indian Affairs, bound by love and a sense of loyalty to the Apaches, who have admired his courage and treated him as a brother. Mexicans have poisoned an Apache child and must suffer the consequences. By *Night of the Cougar* (1997), Barrington has burned his bridges; seeking peace deep in Apache territory, he finds himself compelled to live with and fight alongside Geronimo against U.S. and Mexican forces to save the people and the land he has chosen to make his own, or to die with them. He dons the skin of a cougar and, high on peyote, makes forays into the night. Our final image is of him and his family totally immersed in Apache life.

The white negotiator who seeks treaty concessions to protect the stagecoaches from attack recognizes them and is stunned at their transformation from sophisticated New Yorkers to "soiled, ragged Apaches with snarled hair, hostile expressions, and that strange distant look in their eyes" (348). His own hair bristles and he feels "strangely disoriented," realizing that these people whom he had known had resolutely embraced Apache life, preferring it over "civilization." While there is much silliness in this series, it illustrates an attitude at the heart of the new Western: the Indian way of life, though very different from the readers', had its attractions, and the wildness of the West answered a wildness in individual whites and was part of what led them to forge westward in the first place. The Indians knew the land and were suited to it; the majority of the whites saw the land as they saw its inhabitants—as something to civilize and conquer or destroy. A brave few among the whites crossed over, becoming the cultural blend known as white Indians.

NATIVE AMERICAN AUTHORS

Native Americans, in the main, have seen stories of the West as the subject matter for nonfiction, not fiction, and have produced works like Lucille Jerry Winnie's *Sah-Gan-De-Oh: The Chief's Daughter* (1969), Jean Cuthand Goodwill's *John Tootoosis: Biography of a Cree Leader* (1982), Robert Conley's *Geronimo: An American Legend* (1993), and Joseph Bruchac's *A Boy Called Slow: The True Story of Sitting Bull* (1994). They have also fictionalized history, as do Leslie Marmon Silko in *Almanac of the Dead* (1992, historical fiction of the Southwest and Old Mexico), Robert Conley in *In Mountain Windsong: A Novel of the Trail of Tears* (1992), and Diane Glancy in *Pushing the Bear: A Novel of the Trail of Tears* (1996), sometimes from unusual perspectives—such as through the eyes of a buffalo in Beatrice Culleton's *Spirit of the White Bison* (1989). While many Native Americans have written histories or even historical fiction to provide counterperspectives on Western life, only a few have written Westerns self-described as *fiction*. However, the new directions the Western is taking should make it much more suitable for Indian perspectives—a balanced fictive form in which to reinterpret history from a Native American point of view. Furthermore, some versions of the modern Western make use of mysticism and magical realism, forms more congenial to traditional Native American culture and storytelling approaches than conventional realism.

Cherokee Forrest Carter, in *Gone to Texas* (1975) and *The Vengeance Trail of Josey Wales* (1976), employs the traditional Western form to pit Indians and other oppressed figures in common cause against the establishment (particularly the law and the military). In *Gone to Texas* Lone Watie, Cherokee relative of Stand Watie, a leader of the Five Civilized Nations, joins his friend Josey Wales to roam the West as Robin Hood figures, protecting the weak and the innocent, whether a mistreated Cheyenne woman named Little Moonlight or a white grandmother. In *The Vengeance Trail of Josey Wales*, Josey Wales seeks vengeance when a Mexican general murders the girlfriend of an old friend and imprisons the friend (Ten Spot). The plot twists involve Geronimo and his Apaches helping Josey defeat the general to thank him for rescuing a young Apache girl from the general's abusive soldiers. Carter's *Watch for Me on the Mountain* (1978) draws on the oral tradition of the Apaches to tell the story of Geronimo from a Native American perspective—as a cultural hero guided by spirit powers; although at times Carter becomes preachy about how badly the Apaches were treated, Dee Brown says in a cover note that he probably comes "as close as any writer ever will to recreating the real Geronimo."

A member of the confederated Salish and Kootenai tribes of the Flathead Indian Reservation, D'Arcy McNickle, in the young adult novel *Runner in the Sun: A Story of Indian Maize* (1954), paved the way for novels like those of Don Coldsmith, Kathleen and Michael Gear, Abenaki storyteller Joseph Bruchac, and Eastern Band Cherokee Mardi Oakley Medawar. Set before the appearance of Europeans, McNickle's story follows the travels of a young cliff dweller and holy man seeking a better strain of corn in the lands to the south (now Mexico) to suggest the links between the Aztecs and the Indians of the Southwest and to speculate about why the cliff dwellers abandoned their pueblos. Medawar's *People of the Whistling Waters* (1993) traces the rapid inroads white culture and technologies made on the lifestyle and tribal ways of Crow Indians through the DeGeer family (a French-Canadian married into a Crow family and raising warrior sons who must choose between two heritages). Louis Owen's *Wolfsong* (1995) deals with mining in the wilderness areas of the northern Cascades, and N. Scott Momaday's *The Way to Rainy Mountain* (1969) blends tribal legends, history, and family memoirs to trace the migration of the Kiowa tribe from the Rocky Mountains of Montana to the Oklahoma plains. *Hanta Yo: An American Saga* (1979), the collaborative effort of Ruth Beebe Hill and Santee Sioux Chunksa Yaha, covers three generations of Dakotah/Lakotah, particularly the Mahto band, from 1769 through 1834. Its main characters, warrior and peacemaker Ahbieza and scout Tonweya, work together to preserve their relatives and their spiritual heritage against white encroachment. Chunksa Yaha calls this story a way to preserve his heritage and a bridge to help two very different peoples understand and appreciate each other, though

Creek/Cherokee Métis Ward Churchill has denounced Chunksa Yaha as an embarrassment to his people, a failure who used so-called spiritualism as a sales gimmick (*Fantasies*, 215).

Oklahoma Cherokee Robert Conley has an interesting multivolume Real People series about the first Native American contacts with Europeans and the European exploration of the Real People's land. He has also written a number of Westerns with Native American perspectives. Typical is *Zeke Proctor: Cherokee Outlaw* (1994). Its story, set in Oklahoma Indian Territory, dramatizes the conflicts between the reservation authorities and the federal authorities, with the Cherokees lobbying to retain full control over their territory and federal officials justifying encroachment on local authority on the basis of hearsay, false assumptions, and legal technicalities. Zeke Proctor is legally acquitted of accidentally killing a Cherokee woman who jumped into his line of fire to protect the two-timing white scoundrel Proctor was after (his brother-in-law). However, a bloodthirsty posse ignites a massacre at the courthouse and, as a consequence, federal officers try to arrest Proctor, the jurors, and the judge on federal indictments. The ensuing story is an exciting and humorous Western tale of gunslingers and pursuit, of Cherokees and cowboys, and of behind-the-scenes politics that brings the Cherokee Nation to the brink of war with the United States. Though his characters are based on real people, Conley takes major liberties with historical facts of time, place, character, and situation for the sake of a coherent, plotted story. *Incident at Buffalo Crossing* (1998) provides a more humorous, satiric vision of the past, as Spaniards, evangelists, empire builders, soldiers, outlaws, and Indians converge at the foot of the Texas Sacred Hill, where the buffalo are plentiful and competing tribes normally put aside differences for the sake of the hunt. Uwassa Edohi (Walker), a Cherokee warrior who fought with Andrew Jackson at the Battle of Horseshoe Bend, has had a mystical vision that calls him to the Sacred Hill. There, he discovers his holy mission: to be the right man in the right place to prevent an unjustified massacre of Indian peoples (particularly Osages), to protect the Sacred Hill from plundering, and to expose the true villains (outlaws hired by a land-hungry senator). Conley's tale is a tongue-in-cheek rendering of the peculiar mix of peoples and motives that comprised the Western frontier and of the contrast between the Indian way of knowledge and action and the white way.

These Native American models have inspired some of the revisionist novels by white authors, novels that trace tribal histories and historical encounters from Indian perspectives.

INDIAN SAVAGERY/WHITE SAVAGERY

The stereotypical image of the Western film and story is the encircled wagon train, with shrieking savages raining burning arrows down on helpless families seeking a better life on the western frontier, or the white captive, stripped of his shirt and staked to the desert floor in the blazing sun. Such images go back to the earliest frontier nightmares, which demonized the Indian figure. Henry Schoolcraft, a nineteenth-century Indian agent and ethnographer, his vision influenced by numerous captivity narratives and stories of hair-breadth escapes, describes the fearful recitals of "the Indian yell, the tomahawk, the scalping knife, and the firebrand" that made the Indian seem, in the fireside tales of his day, "the very impersonation of evil—a sort of wild demon, who delighted in nothing so much as blood and murder" (Ebersole, 1). He goes on to note that no one cared or even inquired whether the Indian had a mind or soul, or acted on the basis of reason; instead, he points out: "It was always represented as a meritorious act in old revolutionary reminiscences, to have killed one of them in the border wars, and thus aided in ridding the land of a cruel and unnatural race, in whom all feelings of pity, justice, and mercy, were supposed to be obliterated" (Ebersole, 1).

In the movies and novels of the 1940s, 1950s, and even 1960s the heathen savage was a popular stereotype. In Walter Dumaux Edmonds's *Drums Along the Mohawk* (1947), despite the admirable and capable Blue Back and Gohota, the majority of Indians—mainly Iroquois—are dirty, smelly, painted animals with bloody scalps dangling from their belts, and the Seneca of Carter Vaughan's *The Seneca Hostage* (1969) abuse and batter women, and engage in bizarre rites of terror and torture. Roe Richmond's *Mojave Guns* (1952) describes "sinuous coppery bodies . . . snaking and slithering . . . creeping and skulking" (122). Ralph Mood's description of the Apache in *Geronimo: Wolf of the Warpath* (1956) is typical: "the Apache war whoop filled the canyon like the howl of a thousand wolves. From behind every boulder and tree leaped a red-brown, shrieking Apache, naked except for his loincloth. With spears high and knives flashing they circled the little camp in a screeching, writhing dance of death" (32). Although Apaches are peripheral to the story in Walt Coburn's *La Jornada* (1961), they play their obligatory role: "naked, war-painted Apaches appeared as if by magic from the bowels of hell. Yelling and screaming their blood chant, with bows and arrows, spears and knives in their hands, they tightened the circle and corkscrewed up the hill" (62). In their wake they leave mutilated bodies, with ears and scalps sliced off: "The two riders found the body of the girl half way up the rocky, brush-choked slope. Her body had been mutilated and her long, beautiful yellow hair was gone" (42).

Story after story features what their covers call "a savage horde howling for his [the hero's] blood" (Kenneth Ulyatt, *North Against the Sioux*, 1965); "a thousand savage Comanches," "vicious" chieftains, and "the fierce, guttural cries of the young braves" looking for bloodsport (William R. Cox, *Comanche Moon*, 1959); and heroes whose parents or wives and children have been "massacred" or who have themselves endured Indian "slavery" (Louis L'Amour, *To Tame a Land*, 1955; *Kiowa Trail*, 1964). Harold Keith's *Komantcia* (1965) describes life as a Comanche captive as grim, violent, squalid, and brutal. In an interesting turnaround, however, Richard Jessup turns his Indian nightmare story into a female revenge tale: after heroine Sara Phelp finds her young daughter raped and her whole family battered, mutilated, and dead by Comanche raiders, she tracks down the butchers and within a year has taken equally bloody vengeance (*Comanche Vengeance*, 1957). This emphasis continues in recent novels by authors like Jon Sharpe in the Trailsman Western series and J. R. Roberts in the Gunsmith series, with their focus on renegades, raids, and bloodbaths and titles like *Apache Raid, Arizona Renegades, Badlands Bloodbath, Sioux War Cry*, and *Texas Hellions*, though they occasionally include peaceful Indians, like the beleaguered Utes in Sharpe's *Utah Uprising* (1998).

Nonetheless, recent authors, in the main, try to balance their portraits of Native American warlike behavior with positive images of close-knit Indian families and villages or with explanations sensitive to cultural differences:

There was not a meaner or more dangerous fighting man anywhere than an Apache warrior. Mason understood them, respected them, but wasn't fool enough to tangle with ten of them. He'd been initiated as a Sioux warrior and was blood brother to Fighting Wolf, a war chief without peer.

He had witnessed men die, slowly, painfully, at the hands of the Apaches, who never considered that what they did might be cruel; the word was not part of their language. It was their way of life and Mason understood that. This reinforced his determination not to provide them with that kind of entertainment. (Jack Ballas, *Tomahawk Canyon*, 119)

Sometimes the writers seek more balance by a division between good Indians and bad, for example, pacific Pimas versus wild Apaches or Christianized Hurons versus heathen Iroquois, or by showing whites also engaged in atrocities (scalping, collecting ears, raping, and mutilating). Will Camp's *Cold Justice* (1998) pits scalp hunters collecting government bounties against renegade Chiricahua Apaches; and Richard Wheeler's Skye's West series hero, Barnaby Skye, has family ties with the Crow and the Shoshone through his two wives, but spends much of his time battling Cheyenne, Comanches, and other Plains Indians. In Charles West's *Stone Hand* (1996) and its sequel *Black Eagle* (1998), old-time scout Jason Coles tracks down and kills a notorious Cheyenne renegade, Stone Hand, only to find his Osage wife murdered, his ranch burned to the ground, and his adopted white son stolen by a vengeful friend of Stone Hand, who is convinced the child resulted from Stone Hand's rape of a white woman; portraits of the viciousness and cruelty of a single crazed individual are balanced with those of the honor and courage of Crow scouts and the Cheyenne affection for children. In Jack Bodine's *The Pecos Kid—Apache Moon* (1993) Duane Braddock imagines being captured by Apaches: "If they caught him, they'd tie him upside down on a wagon wheel, build a fire beneath his head, and perform a little dance as his brains broiled out of his ears" (1). Yet, because he saves and protects an Apache child, he is welcomed by tribe members and ends up riding with them, in breechcloth, moccasin boots, and war paint, exhilarated by the "hellbent-for-leather Apache charge" (197).

Will Henry's *The Bear Paw Horses* (1991) provides another twist: an aged Native American and his white-hating daughter are befriended perforce by a white gunman who helps them carry out the dying wishes of Crazy Horse, despite deep-seated animosities on both sides. Larry McMurtry's *Comanche Moon* (1997), a sequel to *Dead Man's Walk* and a prequel to *Lonesome Dove*, tells the story of the Texas Rangers' final conflicts with the Comanches, with an interest in the changes wrought by new technologies on the Comanche way of fighting and living, and the contrast between the old way and the new way. A defiant Buffalo Hump and his son Blue Duck terrorize settlers in order to defend their territory and their way of life, and even swoop down suddenly and brutally on Austin. However, when Buffalo Hump becomes too old to hold his people together, Blue Duck forms his own band of renegades, with guns the weapon of choice, not the bow and arrow, and with new barbarisms, not traditional ones.

In other words, the horrific savagery of Indians remains a mainstay of the Western, despite attempts to particularize or justify it. William David Ross's *Savage Plains* (1996) captures the promise of the frontier for runaway slaves and the cruelty and hostility of the Comanche and Kiowa whose lands they usurp, while his *Eye of the Hawk* (1994) makes real the nightmare of Comanche attacks in rural Texas between 1840 and 1860. While the husband battles Indians with the Texas Rangers, the wife is raped by a truly crazed Comanche and later must help her small ranch community find the strength to endure a murderous Comanche siege. Kathleen O'Neal Gear looks to an earlier time and describes the pleasure of both the Iroquois and the Huron in torturing enemies over a period of several days and then consuming their flesh in order to partake of their spirit. Leading warriors receive the heart or brain or liver. Gear's Christian-influenced Hurons justify such acts as a traditional celebration of the flesh made spirit, conceptually similar to Holy Communion, but the details are horrific: a "necklace" of glowing hatchet heads dropped over the victim's head ("the red-hot metal seared and blackened his neck and chest"), hands smashed with heavy stones, body punctured by red-hot pokers and sharpened sticks, testicles burned off, and strips of meat cut off, cooked in front of the victim, and eaten ritualistically before the final degradations and torching (*This Widowed Land*, 203–205). Indian atrocities are a staple of works like Dan Parkinson's *Blood Arrow* (1985), Patrick Andrews's *Blood of Apache Mesa* (1988), William J. Johnstone's *Blood on the Divide* (1996), J. R. Roberts's *Apache Raid* (1998), Wynema McGowan's *Beyond the River* (1997), Dodge Tyler's *Apache Revenge* (1997) and *Comanche Country* (1998), Doug Hawkins's *Comanche Reckoning* (1998), David Thompson's *Apache Blood* (1992), and Ken Englade and Will Camp's *Comanche Trail* (1999). Chet Cunningham's *Comanche Massacre* (1987) provides justification for Comanche rage (a corrupt white government, whiskey traders, and cold-blooded gunrunners) but still exploits fears of Comanche ruthlessness, destruction, scalping, and rape.

Will Henry's *Chiricahua* (1972/1997) has it both ways. Henry re-creates the 1883 six-day Chiricahua raids in southeast Arizona in bloody detail, but balances his description with Apache voices expressing the Apache point of view with tributes to Apache war skills; with a lone peacemaker, Pa-nayo-tishn (The Coyote Saw Him), nicknamed "Peaches"; and with suggestions in both the prologue and the epilogue that the "white" reports and the Apache oral tradition provide very different interpretations of events. He notes that the raiders were rebels who had broken with Chiricahua tribal traditions, and he quotes the grandfather of a modern Apache rancher about "potholes in the stage road of all journeys between tribal lore and the white man's hard history" (239). Similarly, Dan Parkinson, with wit and humanity, balances the horror of Indian attack with the viciousness of white outlaws, and shows survival needs occasionally necessitating a shaky truce between Indian and white despite ongoing animosities (*Blood Arrow*, 1985).

The flip side of the coin is the modern interest in white savagery, in particular the white man who turns bloody and acts outside of civilized restraints, sometimes for revenge, sometimes for the sheer pleasure of violence. The early models, of course, are historic figures like Jeremiah ("Liver-Eating") Johnson, whose story was popularized in the Robert Redford film *Jeremiah Johnson* (1972), and was fictionalized in Raymond Thorpe's *Crow Killer: Jeremiah Johnson* (1980). The modern mountain men of fiction are all, to some degree, Jeremiah Johnsons. In waging a personal war against the Comanches for killing his closest friend and his first love, Harry Combs's seventeen-year-old Cat Brules (*Brules*, 1995) becomes as cruel as, and his hands as bloody as, those he slaughters in a deadly cat-and-mouse game that drives the Comanches from his territory. Ironically, when he is injured by a bear, it is a Shoshone maiden who nurses him back to health and wins his heart (though the genetic ties between Shoshone and Comanche are a shock to him). However, after an idyllic interlude and her death in childbirth, he returns to what he knows best—Indian fighting—this time as an Army scout routing the Sioux with deadly results (*Scout*, 1995). Former slave, then mountain man, Jim Beck, in Matt Braun's *Bloody Hand* (1996), accepts trading company funds to live among and study the Crow, but he is so transformed by the experience and so caught up in their revenge feuds that he earns the name Bloody Hand, swears to take a hundred scalps as payment for his wished-for Crow bride, and becomes one of the greatest Crow warriors.

One of the most striking of such white-savage figures is A. B. Guthrie's Boone Caudill, a strong, cunning, hot-tempered boy fleeing his past (he almost killed his father in a fit of rage). The central character of *The Big Sky* (1947), Caudill joins up with some mountain men and exults in the freedom of the wilderness: "Boone could get himself on a hill and see forever . . . the sky above, blue as paint, and the brown earth rolling underneath, and himself between them with a free, wild feeling in his chest, as if they were the ceiling and floor of a house that was all his own" (117). However, that freedom brings with it hunger so deep that he learns from the Indians to drink blood and consume hearts and livers raw (though he does not cannibalize his friends, as some of the French mountain men do). He takes scalps, steals horses, and revels with the Crow.

Eventually, he marries the daughter of a Blackfoot chief and settles in the Te-
tons, and seems to fit in well: "A man could sit and let time run on while he
smoked or cut on a stick with nothing nagging him and the squaws going about
their business and the young men playing, making out that they warred on the
Assinboines" (245). His strength, his ruthlessness, and his hunting and fighting
skills serve the tribe well, but he remains ferocious, unsettled, implacable. He
battles members of his wife's tribe who try to stop him from helping open up
the mountain passes to white settlers pushing west, kills his best friend in a
jealous rage, and, ironically, contributes to the demise of the savage way of life
he has made his own. At the end of the novel, he is a man without a place, too
wild and untamed for even frontier life yet too personally guilty to live comfortably among the Crow or Blackfeet, whose way of life he has helped destroy.

One of the most appalling images in the book is the description of a Piegan
village of over fifty lodges decimated by smallpox:

The stink made a man's hair rise. . . . A squaw rested on her back outside another [lodge],
and a young one alongside her. The magpies had been busy on them, and the coyotes.
A whole damn village dead and gone, put under by a sickness, men and squaws and
young ones lying stiff and bloated, and some with their eyes pecked out by birds, leaving
pockets in the dead fat faces that maggots worked in. (223)

The fact that the smallpox has been intentionally spread through infected blankets traded by fur companies wanting trouble-free access to the Yellowstone
area raises the question of wherein lies the true savagery. Part of the modern
shift in perspective is a growing number of Westerns emphasizing the viciousness of whites. The following are a representative sampling: in Edward Zietlow's
The Indian Maiden's Captivity (1978) an Indian girl is brutally killed and the
one white who could save her hesitates to interfere; abused indentured servant
Pauline Stewart, in Jory Sherman's *The South Platte* (1998), finds better treatment among the Arapaho than her own people (including her vicious father);
Terry C. Johnston's *Blood Song* (1993) re-creates the Battle of Powder River,
in which four hundred U.S. soldiers made a lightning attack on a massive Sioux
encampment, massacring men, women, and children; in Kit Dalton's *Morgan's
Squaw* (Buckskin Double, 1997) land-greedy cowboys drive out the competition
under the guise of Indian savagery.

CAPTIVITY STORIES

Gary Ebersole, in *Captured by Texts*, notes that captivity stories were "a staple of the dime novels of the second half of the nineteenth century," a combination of the Western adventure and the romance that reflected the values and
the mores of the periods that created them rather than of the periods of their settings (185). Such tales, whether purportedly true or admittedly historical, developed their own genre conventions of a firmly consistent nature. As suggested in

Chapter 1, Puritan needs for self-justification rewrote tales of encounters with Native Americans, shaping captivity narratives into sermons and didactic tales of Christian fortitude in the face of pagan trials. Religion is much less pronounced in later captivity accounts, with the exotic adventure of the experience prevailing. While innumerable modern romances fictionalize captivity stories, transforming them into tales of love conquering differences and overcoming the barriers of language, culture, race, religion, social rules, and gender expectations, or of feminist fortitude in the face of male aggression (as we shall see in Chapter 5), Western captivity stories focus more solidly on historical details and the historical record. Though fictionalized, they strive to re-create the conflicts and differences that separated captor and captive.

A hundred years or more after the fact, they lovingly re-create the details of daily life in a tribal community as opposed to a white frontier community, the savagery of attacks by both sides, the alien qualities of the Indian, and the difficulty of escape or adaptation. Post-1960s captivity stories have more and more come to present Indian behavior as brutal or harsh but in many ways admirable, suited to the land and bound by codes of honor, though codes quite different from those of mainstream America. Female captivity stories may feature romances to explore gender differences and gender conflicts in an alien setting, religious tales of faith overcoming trial and tribulation, cultural explorations of adaptation, or stories of human endurance. Male captivity stories become adventure stories, with trials and quests and cross-cultural bonding. Images of savagery are tempered with the depiction of common bonds—the Indian humanized and explained within a sociological, environmental, and historical context. From the eighteenth century to the present such stories have provided a fictional means of testing and disseminating social, religious, moral, and economic theories and issues, of questioning supposedly universal beliefs and values, and of defining "human." Just as the Puritan tales defined what it meant to be a New World Christian, tested by undreamed-of forces, so the later fiction probed secular faith in American mores and myths, sometimes to debunk, more often to perpetuate and celebrate.

James Alexander Thom's *Follow the River* and *Red Heart*

James Alexander Thom's historical novel *Follow the River* (1981), based on real family diaries, oral reports, and family publications of the Ingles family, brings to life the story of happily married twenty-three-year-old Mary Ingles, pregnant with her third child when Shawnee Indians attacked her rural Virginia settlement in 1755. Thom describes the bloody massacre, the kidnappings, and the difficult trek across challenging natural barriers, including a mountain range, to the Shawnee encampment in Ohio and then farther west on an expedition to gather salt near present-day Cincinnati. A tough-minded frontier survivor, Ingles gives birth along the trail, and sees her sons quickly assimilated into the war party and her infant eventually given to a Shawnee to nurse and care for. Along the trail a Shawnee warrior, admiring her fortitude and endurance, takes her under his protection, and she finds herself coming to think of him as "beauteous," and then being horrified at her fancies. She fears for her infant:

Mary tried to foresee such a life [for her child], in her imagination, to prepare herself for that awful possibility. She envisioned a little girl huddled among animal skins on a dirt floor; then a naked woman shiny with animal grease, painted and tattooed, adorned only in bracelets and tufts of feathers, dancing obscenely with a savage leer on her stained face, being passed from hand to hand among warriors and chiefs, bearing half-white children, then growing haglike and white-haired, praying to pagan gods in some corner of the wilderness and someday dying unaware that she was to have been Bettie Elenor Ingles, daughter of William. (79)

Arrival at the home village brings a new set of anxieties as the captives encounter the Other in new circumstances:

Brown hands were clutching at the gunwale of the canoe; others seemed to be reaching for her and her children. The musky, earthy smell of the Indians was close and she had never heard such an uproar of so many voices, not even in Philadelphia town. The babble of the voices seemed to roll over her with waves of the Indian smell. It was not the sour, rankling smell of white people who have been too long in their clothes; it was not unpleasant in that way. It was simply the heat and the closeness of so many; it was their rude staring and their reaching, their incomprehensible tongue being uttered at once by so many voices, shrill and deep, masculine and feminine; it was their delight at the hostages' misery; it was that eerie *other-worldness* Bettie had spoken of on the other side of the river, but now amplified by hundreds. (84)

Ingles's sewing skills and her unwillingness to show fear, even when running the gauntlet nude, set her apart from the other captives and win her a place in the Shawnee community. Ingles strong-mindedly recognizes that her children are lost to her, that her sons could not be persuaded to leave, that her babe in arms could not survive the grueling trip home, and that adoption by an Indian family has brought the babe a chance at life.

Once she has decided to leave her children behind, she joins up with a Dutch captive who has also proven herself a survivor, and while at a salt lick on an expedition headed by Frenchmen, the two women escape and begin the long, grueling trek back to Virginia, following the twists and turns of the Ohio River and going up each tributary to find a fording place. Starving, hallucinating on plant roots, fighting over carrion, the two women battle the wilderness, each other, and themselves to survive. The Dutch woman, Ghetel, tries to cannibalize Ingles, but in spite of almost being eaten, when she finally reaches civilization Ingles sends someone back for this woman who has suffered the nightmare with her. Unspeakable adversity has bonded them in ways that the Virginia settlers simply cannot comprehend. Eventually Ingles buys one of her sons back from captivity; the boy now carries himself like a Shawnee warrior and speaks no English. This loss of identity is a key element in captivity stories.

Thom captures the inner strength necessary to stand against an alien people and an alien land and to find one's way home, retaining crucial elements of former identity and morality while nevertheless adapting to frontier demands. His Shawnee begin as savages and end up to some degree more humanized, their cruelty and their kindness commingled, as they test their captives and separate the strong and capable from the weak and defenseless. Ingles's grueling trip home and her difficulty surviving confirm how well the Shawnee have adapted for survival in a harsh and unforgiving land. Thom's final notes reveal that the story of Mary Ingles and the old Dutch woman's long walk home became a legend among the Shawnee. For whites, the story aptly defines the new frontier's challenges to white European identity and the necessity of adopting indigenous elements in order to survive.

Thom's *The Red Heart* (1997), set during the Revolutionary War, is based on the true captivity story of Frances Slocum, the daughter of peaceful Quaker farmers in northeastern Pennsylvania. Adopted into the Miami tribe as Maconakwa, Little Bear Woman, Frances slowly loses her language and culture and accepts the cultural beliefs of her adoptive parents, participating in the sacred corn rituals, fleeing the Long Knives who threaten her people, and taking heart from Tecumseh—their last hope. Throughout her lifetime, her white family searches for her, especially after the treaty agreement to return captives, but her Miami family help her hide out because she is a hard worker and a loving daughter who supports them in their time of need. When at last her white relatives catch up with her, she is torn between her red heart and her fleeting childhood memories. Ironically, in the end, it is her white blood that allows her to keep her property and provide a refuge for homeless tribe members when soldiers forcibly remove them from their land; yet, in our final image of her, it is her red heart that rules her being as she sings and dances around the fire with her fellow Miami Indians and remembers life around the cookfires and campfires that marked the important moments in her seventy years among the Lenape and Miami peoples as Maconakwa—parching corn, firing pottery, brewing medicines, baking funeral breads, and sharing stories—traumatized only by the viciousness of white soldiers who burn the crops and push the People farther west, into conflicts with other beleaguered tribes.

Frederick Manfred's *Scarlet Plume*

Whereas Thom purposely grounds his novel in factual detail, personally walking the territory described in order to accurately capture the tribulations inflicted by nature, Frederick Manfred in *Scarlet Plume* (1964) uses an historical event and a few lines in a letter from General Henry R. Sibley to his wife as the authentic foundation for his imaginative re-creation of a captivity romance doomed by time and circumstance. The historical event was the 1862 Sioux uprising that ended in the slaughter of numerous Sioux families and the hanging of thirty-eight Sioux warriors; the lines from General Sibley's letter remark on "one rather handsome woman" who "had become so infatuated with the redskin who had taken her for a wife that, although her white husband was still living . . . and had been in search of her, she declared that were it not for her children, she would not leave her red lover"; furthermore, she threatened to shoot any whites who tried to hang him, though the general notes that the man will swing.

Manfred's fictional treatment begins with the devastating effects of the Sioux uprising on the missionary settlement of Skywater, with rebel Sioux joining forces with "Christianized" Sioux and slaughtering whites who had been living in peace among them for a number of years. His story is double-edged, on the one hand recounting the viciousness of the attack and the obscene and barbaric tortures devised by Sioux attackers (raping a woman through a slit made in her belly or ramming a warclub through the vagina into the abdominal cavity; chopping out human hearts and livers and consuming them while they are still warm from the body), and on the other hand showing the compassion of a few like Scarlet Plume, who sends the settlers a warning of danger (a white swan with a broken neck), who prevents his tribal group from participating in the outrages inflicted on the whites, who acts as a personal guardian protecting the captured women, and who takes it upon himself to return the final survivor, Judith Raveling, to her people though he knows that doing so will cost him his life. Readers share Judith's changing perspective as she experiences shock and horror at the decimation of those around her and at the savagery of the Sioux, as she gradually adjusts to captivity and the sexual and household duties required of her for survival, as she grows to appreciate and even respect the warrior skills that provide sustenance and protection for the tribe, and then as she comes to love the one warrior who has protected her throughout her ordeal: Scarlet Plume's visions guide his people, bring them buffalo, and warn of danger, and his inner code of self-discipline and integrity makes him stand head and shoulders above any man—white or red—that she has known.

When Judith hears a respected elderly chieftain talk about the honor paid the dead by eating their innards and drinking their blood, and his desire to have her killed when he dies, so that her spirit will attend him in the spirit land, she realizes, "truly, how far apart, how terribly far apart, the red man and the white man really were" (115). Again, when she secretly watches as Scarlet Plume uses his shamanistic powers to make a wooden effigy of a buffalo dance on a mound of sand, and later when he dances the part of a magnificient, bellowing buffalo by firelight, she is awed by a sense of mysteries beyond her understanding. Despite his clear love for her, Scarlet Plume is determined to protect Judith and return her to her own people; he tells her, "You are going toward the day. I am going toward the dark. Your people and my people were born too far apart" (252). By having Judith returned home at a time of military atrocities, Manfred brings his novel full circle so that readers are left as outraged at the barbarisms white settlers and soldiers inflict on Sioux women and children as they were initially by Sioux barbarisms. Angry German women attack the chained Sioux prisoners with butcher knives and stones, gutting them and slicing off penises while the assaulted Sioux stoically accept such brutality as normal for grieving women; the military court ignores evidence that some of the Sioux condemned to be hanged did not participate in the atrocities and then, in violation of Sioux beliefs about death, allows medical grave robbers to steal Sioux bodies for anatomical study (Scarlet Plume's among them). At the novel's close, Judith flees in horror from white civilization, as she had once done from Indian civilization, and readers are left with two seemingly irreconcilable visions of reality: the white view of the civilized (themselves) routing the savage (Indians) and the Indian view of the savage (whites) routing the civilized (themselves).

Lucia St. Clair Robson's *Ride the Wind*

Lucia St. Clair Robson's magnificent novel *Ride the Wind* (1982) is at heart an abduction/captivity novel, a romantic and beguiling adventure of life among the Comanche during the mid-nineteenth-century Indian wars in Texas. The story is based on fact: in 1836 nine-year-old Cynthia Ann Parker was taken prisoner by a Comanche war party that attacked her extended family's fortified farm northeast of what is now Austin. Cynthia's father was killed and her six-year-old brother John was abducted as well. Some other residents of Parker's Fort survived but could not help the captives. While Cynthia's aunt Elizabeth and cousin Rachel were gang-raped repeatedly on the long trip back to the Indians' village, Cynthia and John were unharmed, and were eventually adopted into the tribe.

In Robson's story, Cynthia, renamed Naduah (She Keeps Warm with Us), and John, renamed Bear Cub for his combative nature, adapt quickly to Comanche ways, struggling with the language, customs, and inexplicable behavior of their captors, but recognize that they could never find their way home through the arid hill country and increasingly warming to the many kindnesses of their new Comanche families and friends. After they are separated when the different bands into which they have been adopted split up, Cynthia, who more than ever begins to think of herself as Naduah, bonds quickly with Star Name, a girl her age, and looks up to Something Good, a beautiful young woman of real accomplishments. The Parkers discover that Indian children live a life of undreamed-of freedom by white standards, unencumbered by clothing (they all swim nude and unashamed in the rivers along which they camp), by formal schooling or church instruction, by farm chores, by the regulated life of frontier settlements. From the moment she is abducted, Cynthia encounters powerful sensory experiences, frightening but compelling: the Comanches dancing wildly around a roaring campfire and eating half-cooked buffalo steaks during their post-raid celebration; the sights and sounds of the brutal rapes of the older women; the feel of her captor Wanderer's muscular, sweaty body as she clings to him during the long ride to the Indian encampment; the texture of leather and fur when she is left in her adoptive family's lodge. Comanche life is sensuous in its closeness to nature, for almost all clothing and tools are formed from animal skins, bone, wood, and other available materials. At first, Cynthia is bothered by the smell of sweat and the proximity of people, and the harsh Texas landscape; she soon comes to see method in the disorder and familiar human relationships in the behavior of the People.

Cynthia particularly enjoys the swimming holes, the fierce, dry summer heat in contrast to the cool balm of the gently running water, the green leaves of the cottonwoods along the streams set against the white-hot shimmering air of the afternoons. Swimming is a frequent pleasure, for in contrast to the white world of Parker's Fort, her duties are limited. The children do chores for their families, to be sure, but they are also allowed to roam unsupervised for most of their days in the summer camps, running through and around the village like, well, wild Indians. Children are never punished, only told that the People, the Comanches, do not behave in that way, with the social pressure of the group sufficing to accomplish correction. At first, Naduah is bothered by why the People move camp every few days, dismantling their village of over a thousand people in fifteen minutes or so and forming a long caravan as they travel to the next location. Her adoptive mother, Takes Down the Lodge, explains:

"We have to move."
"But *tosi-tivo*, white people, don't move every few days the way we do." Cynthia blurted it out before she thought, but Takes Down didn't seem to make the connection between her blue-eyed daughter and white people.
"White people don't know how to live. Sunrise tells me they stab Mother Earth with sharp metal sticks and destroy her. They cut down all the trees, not just the ones they need for their lodges. And they let their horses eat all the grass, then grow different grass for them and feed them only the seeds. And the horses can't run as well. The People could never live like that." (100)

Naduah, still a white child, says she would prefer to stay in one place, and Takes Down answers that there is no reason to stay in one place. When Naduah objects that the last campground was pretty, Takes Down says,

"But, Naduah, the next place will be pretty too. Pahayuca [the chief] picks pretty places. There are many of them. We can enjoy them all. And then come back later and enjoy them again. And the animals don't stay in one place, especially when they're being hunted." (100)

Naduah finally comes to recognize the excitement and physical pleasures of nomadic life, with the ever-changing landscape and seasons the backdrop to the long, snakelike column of the tribe curving over the Texas hills:

There was a constant jingle and clatter of bells and kettles and metal bridle ornaments. Feathers and streamers fluttered in the wind, and the long fringe on the clothes and tack bounced to the rhythm of the ponies' gait. The People were happiest when they were mounted and moving, and they designed their clothes and gear to look best in motion. Some of the war ponies had brightly painted buffalo robes draped across their withers, in barbaric imitation of the early Spanish conquistadors. It gave the procession a courtly dignity. But it had become so familiar to Cynthia that now she thought more about the discomfort than the romance of it all. (100)

Robson does not stint in listing discomforts. The summer dust chokes, and the arid countryside is filled with plant and animal life that stings, bites, slashes, and pricks. The winter camps fill with horse and human dung, and ponies resort to gnawing bark. Yet the magnificent Indian processions, like those of medieval European pilgrims in search of both spiritual fulfillment and adventure, are driven by hope for a better camp over the next ridge, sweeter water and more buffalo, and the renewal of an ancient tradition of adapting to the vicissitudes of nature rather than trying to conquer it. Such are the psychological and spiritual rewards of the indigenous nomadic Western life.

As the novel progresses, it becomes evident to Naduah that her chances of rescue by a white raiding party are remote, for she is unsure if any of her family survived after she was taken in the raid, and she realizes that her sun-darkened skin, hair impregnated with bear grease, and Indian clothes would make her an outsider in white society. Besides, she has begun to think in the Comanche language and her social life is "an ever more tangled skein of relationships" (151) with her adoptive family, her age-mates, and the extended community of the band. Apart from some individual tribe members, the Comanches' acceptance of adopted captives is absolute: even pale-skinned, blonde, blue-eyed Naduah is almost immediately regarded as one of the People. Older captives, whether white, Mexican, or African American, are not as lucky; they are not adopted into the People and thus remain slaves, suffering constant rapes and obscene tortures and, if not ransomed back, being summarily executed when sick and useless.

The novel gives an excellent sense of the daily social pleasures in a tight and isolated community. There is a necessary honesty and openness, since everyone knows everyone else's business anyway. Everyone's history is also public knowledge, for good or ill. A warrior named Buffalo Piss, for example, received his name when his first attempt at a buffalo kill resulted in his being unhorsed and washed down by gallons of urine from his frightened prey; years later, he still endures this comic name stoically. (Amusingly, the Texas authorities report his name as "Buffalo Hump" because they can't bring themselves to write down his real name. This is the same real war chief fictionalized by Larry McMurtry in *Comanche Moon*.) Pahayuca ("He Who Has Relations with His Aunt"), though the civil chief, must put up with his name, as does his hugely fat wife, Blocks Out the Sun. Such playfulness is a sign of great intimacy and acceptance, the social reality being that the People are a large family, one in which great demands can be made upon others, and upon one's self in return. Naduah discovers herself asking favors of tribe members, and doing chores for them in response. While any frontier settlement or village is clearly more intimate than towns and cities, here the mutual interdependence of all tribal members makes the white settlements seem, in contrast, collections of discrete individuals, isolated in their separate properties and houses.

This older way of life is very fulfilling psychologically, for one is bound tightly to others—Robson's "tangled skein of relationships" that brings to the fore the deep essence of what it means to be human, to live in small groups that extend outward seamlessly, into community. Occasional discomfort is a small price to pay for a richly rewarding emotional life. As Naduah matures and marries Nocona ("Wanderer"), she develops a deep appreciation for the natural world the People inhabit. As with Mary Jemison, this appreciation is aesthetic as well as practical, a spiritual connection with the land as well as an intellectual understanding of its functional complexity as an ecological system. *Ride the Wind* is fiction, of course, but it drives home emotionally many of the points that anthropologists and sociologists have made in more scholarly ways. Life in small nomadic communities, tightly bound by culture and interdependence, is the model by which humans lived for tens of thousands of years, long before fixed settlements, efficient storage of crop surpluses, and intensive agriculture created cities, specialization of trades, and "civilization."

Through the transformation of Cynthia to Nadua, Robson makes us consider whole sets of differences that define white as opposed to Comanche culture: self-interest versus obligation, privacy versus openness, ownership versus sharing, individualism versus community. Robson gives a fine sense of what constitutes a culture and why people commit wholeheartedly to one. She deals especially well with the tradeoffs between individualism and communalism, for Comanches remain individuals, yet operate as a shifting, ever-changing community. What makes each Comanche a Comanche defines their culture overall, in an artful blend of the one and the many.

An interesting reversal on the same theme is Douglas Jones's *Gone the Dreams and Dancing* (1984), the story of how the Comanche war chief Kwahadi Parry (a fictional version of Cynthia Parker's son, Quanah Parker) helps his starving people surrender with dignity and uses his white blood as a lever to win concessions for them (the return of their valued war lance and some good breeding ponies; tolerance for their religious and marital practices; and so on). Kwahadi's forward-looking strategies help the Comanche accept the inevitability of surrender while struggling to retain their Comanche essence. Jones's story ends at the U.S. Military Academy with the ceremony for the first Comanche graduate and a brief address in Comanche by a decorated World War II war hero—another Comanche warrior who had found dignity and honor as an American warrior.

Going Native

Benjamin Frankin noted that Indian children raised among whites escaped back to the land and their people at every opportunity, while white children raised among Indians and then retaken always struggled to return to their captors: though "treated with all imaginable tenderness . . . , yet in a short Time they become disgusted with our manner of life, and of the care and pains that are necessary to support it, and take the first good Opportunity of escaping again into the Woods, from whence there is no reclaiming them" (481–482). Hector St. Jean Crèvecoeur, in *Letters from an American Farmer* (1782), impressed by so many instances of this pattern, avowed that life among the Indians must produce some "captivating" social bond "far superior to anything to be boasted of among us" because "thousands of Europeans" have become Indians," but "we have no examples of even one of those Aborigines having from choice become Europeans!" (208–209). These statements about historical realities are confirmed fictionally in the numerous Western tales of voluntarily "going native."

Conrad Richter's *The Light in the Forest* (1953) and its sequel, *A Country of Strangers* (1966), were the first trendsetters in late twentieth-century Western fiction, idyllic fantasies of Indian life in the wilderness set in opposition to the industrial and urban. They depict would-be white Indians reluctantly forced to leave the Delaware Indians who had made them part of their community, unable to betray fellow whites yet much enamored of Delaware life. Although there are many more white captives who have heartily embraced tribal life than there are white Indian wanna-bes, the number of whites-gone-native in Western fiction is fairly large, as a quick survey confirms. In addition to series characters like Clay Taggert from Jake McMaster's White Apache series and the Barringtons from Burleson's Apache Wars Trilogy, there are also individuals in story after story: (1) Thomas McCabe, who in Jackson's *Cheyenne Raiders* (1982) marries a Cheyenne, participates in the ritual Sun Dance, and has a spirit vision; (2) Sam Houston living among the Cherokee in Robson's *Walk in My Soul* (1985), loving the proud heroine Tiana Rogers, dressing in Cherokee attire, and making Cherokee psychology second nature to his own; (3) John Goode, in Robson's *Light a Distant Fire* (1988), who befriends the flamboyant and enigmatic Osceola, marries into the Seminole tribe, and learns the ways of the swamp; (4) Lieutenant John Dunbar, the Union soldier in Michael Blake's *Dances with Wolves* (1988), who goes native and finds a new identity in the utopian freedom of the Sioux; (5) Mason Hall, a U.S. Army sharpshooter who becomes the Cheyenne warrior Night Hawk after a near fatal wound in Earl Murray's *Thunder in the Dawn* (1993) and *Flaming Sky: A Novel of the Little Bighorn* (1995); (6) Frank Riddle, in Paxton Riddle's *Lost River* (1999), who lives among the Modoc, marries into the tribe, and struggles to protect them from massacre. This idea of discovering a new and freer self, an identity separate from and more distinctively American than one's white identity, one closer to nature and loosed from the oppressive restraints of religion, class, and military or social obligation, seems very much a part of the American psyche as portrayed in our popular literature.

INDIAN ECOLOGY

Because the Western conflict involved technology and standardization conquering individual craftsmanship, and agrarianism rolling over and subsuming virgin wilderness, it is natural for the Native American representatives of the old ways—of craftsmanship and of wildness—also to stand for their ideology—for environmental protection and ecological soundness. Frontiersmen and mountain men depicted in Westerns since the 1960s remark on the cleanliness of the land, the purity of the air, the fact that a wound cleansed in mountain country will not fester and infect as it would back in the cities. Their treks back to frontier towns remind them of the stench of nineteenth-century civilization—the mud and sewage, and the smell of people crowded together (modern stories make much ado of Indian personal hygiene as a prized value in contrast to the unwashed frontiersmen). In *Hangman's Knot*, McMasters's Apaches ask their leader, "Where do you want this smelly white thing [captive]?" (22).

Furthermore, many modern Westerns blame capitalism for dooming the Indians. Chieftain after chieftain in tale after tale remarks on how quickly the whites acquire new and better weapons, and sees their people's destruction in their inability to produce such weapons themselves and to keep up with the rapidly changing technology. The gun ends the final confrontation of individual craftsmanship and standardization (the bow and arrow, individualized, take long hours to make, while gunpowder weapons are far less costly in man-hours once production is set up). Crafts could not keep pace; the Indians could not steal enough guns and bullets to keep up with the development of new weapons; and the practice of arming one tribe to help defeat another tribe took advantage of tribal rivalries to conquer all. Betrayal became standard operating procedure. Lucia St. Clair Robson, in *Walk in My Soul*, shows Andrew Jackson winning the Battle of New Orleans because of Cherokee allies brought in to defeat their ancient enemies the Creeks, who supported the British; yet, while using the Cherokee to his advantage, Jackson was already beginning the removal of their families westward and initiating policies that led to the Trail of Tears.

Prophetic Indians (shamans, wise women healers, experienced leaders) warn their people about dependence on white goods—to no avail. Such Western stories have their basis in economic fact going back to the days of the French traders exchanging furs for ax heads and knives; native economies shifted away from the self-sufficiency of hunting, farming, and limited trade to wholesale exchange, consigning craftsmanship to history and forming colony-like dependencies on European markets. Western fiction repeatedly emphasizes the temptations of trade as the means to get a foothold in Indian territory, with the metal cooking pot the earliest white offering that transformed Indian life and began the shift from craftsmanship to dependence on factory-made products like steel knives, ax heads, and cloth. Hal Borland's *When the Legends Die* (1972) traces the change in Ute Young Bear's Brother from a child who talks to the animals and follows traditional ways to an adult who has lived among whites and, as a result, to his detriment no longer sings the deer chant nor uses all of the deer meat in traditional ways. Judd Cole's hero Touch the Sky might have white sympathies, but in *Buffalo Hiders* he bemoans the wasteful destruction of the buffalo, a destruction that will eventually destroy his tribe's way of life. The Indian wanna-be hero of Michael Blake's *Dances with Wolves* (1988) wants what he sees as the simpler, more honest life among Indians, whose ways are depicted as the epitome of the natural life, in harmony with their environment and comfortable with their community. Ironically, one of the early Native American spokespersons for ecological soundness was Canadian writer Grey Owl. Grey Owl's messages about endangered species like the beaver, a disrupted natural balance, and the exploitation of natural resources for economic gain touched readers' hearts and made his books best-sellers until the discovery, upon his death in 1938, that he was an Englishman, Archibald S. Belaney, inspired by penny dreadfuls to bring to life his childhood fantasies of growing up to be a live Indian.

THE NEW WESTERN: DREAMS, VISIONS, AND SHAMAN PREDICTIONS

The greatest difference between European and Native American visions of the world, from colonial days through the old West to the present, runs far deeper than varying ideas of community, property, and privacy—in fact, it is the origin of such contrasting concepts. As chapters 2 and 3 make clear, for Native peoples nature is a place full of spirit, a world in which dreams speak truths and may be more real than waking life. Visions guide behavior, and the prophecies of holy men, whether they are called medicine men, healers, or shamans, must be taken seriously. Mainstream American culture, a product of eighteenth-century philosophical materialism, kept a firm line between the spiritual and the physical, reserving the invisible world for religion and focusing on scientific and technological control of nature. The visible world was an economic resource; apart from the aesthetic pleasure it gave, nature was to be used for profit. As a result, until recently the Western paid little attention to Native American spirituality.

However, numerous recent stories involving Native Americans rely on predictions by shamans and by spirit dreams and visions to suggest ways of acquiring knowledge other than Western logic, and draw on the power of talismans like the dream catcher to infuse realistic stories with a touch of magic. Respect for other religious practices aside, however, their main literary function seems to be to bring together two opposing groups in a common cause or to control the direction of the plot. Sonya Pelton's *Heavensent* (1995), for example, makes the main romantic couple seem bound together by a destiny that Dakota prophecy and dream visions confirm as Dakota warriors track the clues foretold by shaman dreams to find and return a kidnapped Sioux princess to her people.

Janis Reams Hudson's Apache series, in turn, features mixed-blood relatives of Cochise who are accepted in a secret Apache stronghold, Pa-Gotzin-Kay, in the Sierra Madre because an ancient Chiricahua shaman, Dee-O-Det, believes their descent from "Woman of Magic" makes them important to Apache survival. A warrior guides his life by his name-quest vision only to have Dee-O-Det re-interpret it in a new way that turns his life upside down. In such cases, shifts of plot and development of character hinge on personal and shaman dreams and visions.

Kathleen O'Neal Gear's *Sand in the Wind* (1990) and Johnny Quarles's *Spirit Trail* (1995) depict crossroads encounters predestined by supernatural forces. In *Sand in the Wind*, the wolf spirit of his grandfather warns Wounded Bear, a Cheyenne medicine man, that the warnings of the Cheyenne prophet Sweet Medicine will be fullfilled—a sea of invaders who would "cover the ground as thickly as the spring grasses" and "desecrate the earth . . . until she cried out in anguish," the Cheyenne "swept away like grains of sand in the wind." However, he promises that a golden-haired embodiment of the sacred yellow-haired woman who gave the Cheyenne buffalo can save the People if they are faithful to the Old Ways. Dreams of a badger spirit and of personal death confirm the sacrifices Wounded Bear must make to help his people survive. At the same time, the wolf spirit makes a blonde pioneer dream of the sacred Sun Dance and moves her out of time and space for a mystical-magical union choreo-graphed by Cheyenne spirits. Ultimately, the Cheyenne loss of land and place and their defeat by whites are presented as a result of their lack of faith in the prophecies of their own spirit guides. However, the use of prophecy allows the writer to create great sympathy for the Cheyenne, to suggest that the ties between whites and Indians run more deeply than either side is willing to admit, and, in effect, to share the blame for the clashes and conflicts that were an inevitable part of the westward movement.

Spirit Trail also postulates spirit ties between whites and Indians. In this case "the Great One" mediates between a legendary wagon train trail boss named Sampson Roach and the Pawnee in order to save lives on both sides. Roach, an alcoholic grieving for his wife, who was raped and killed by a drunken Indian, is haunted by an aged Indian with flowing silver-white hair who compares Roach to "parched earth" and promises that when the rains come, "there will be much seed to come forth from you and grow" (76). Forced out of his drunkenness and into commanding a wagon train through Pawnee country, Roach finds com-fort in his hallucinations of the old Indian, sitting in a tree or riding alongside him astride a beautiful white horse, his eyes glittering. Finally, his Indian spirit companion tells him he is needed. At nightfall Roach walks silently into an Indian camp and leads the white women captives out without the Indians, drunk from celebrating, noticing. The same spirit guides Standing Bear, a Pawnee searching for some white killers: "The Great One, with his silver hair and mag-nificent pony, had sent him here. . . . the old man appeared to him, just as he had appeared to his father and his father's father" (289). The encounter makes his spirit soar like an eagle and brings a sense of harmony and peace. Standing Bear recalls numerous stories of "the Great One" intervening to save the Pawnee in time of trouble, leading them to food in time of famine, and telling them stories of an ancient flood and a giant-slayer, so he does his bidding, negotiating peace between the whites and the Pawnee war party. What could have erupted into a nasty war ends in peace, with both sides recognizing a third group as responsible for creating ill-will. Standing Bear must reevaluate white-Indian relationships when he realizes that the Pawnee Great Spirit has also appeared to and guided a worthy white warrior.

As in *Sand in the Wind*, the dreams, visions, and shamanistic predictions of *Spirit Trail* serve plot but also carry the theme of the common values and beliefs that lie behind differences in perception and tradition. They suggest powers greater than those of either side working behind the scenes for the greater good of all. In other words, while creating sympathy for the Indian loss of land and life, and understanding of white fears of death or captivity, they seek to bridge the two worlds for modern readers and to guide those readers to a deeper appreciation of commonalities. The shamanistic prophecies, dream visions, and spirit voices provide a sense of the "other," but one that strangely reflects basic Christian beliefs.

This discovery of spiritual commonalities has become a recurring modern theme. Earl Murray's *Song of Wovoka* (1992) dramatizes the mystical Lakota worldview through Sioux who experience prophetic dream visions during an eclipse of the sun and through a Jesuit fed sacred buffalo by wolves and transformed by the experience into Two Robes. As a sacred person to the Sioux, Two Robes finds in their rituals and religious ways confirmation of the universality of his own faith. Ghostwind, a Cheyenne prophet and seer, plays a significant role in Murray's *Thunder in the Dawn* (1994) and *Flaming Sky* (1995), while the rebellious near outlaw Joe Wolfkiller in Cameron Judd's *Cherokee Joe* (1992) finds his life unexpectedly changed by an aged Cherokee's syncretic belief in both Methodist theology and an ancient (and fickle) Cherokee crystal, *ulunsuti*.

REVISIONIST WESTERNS: NEW PERSPECTIVES

Revisionist Westerns turn in a variety of directions, some motivated by political and social ideologies, some by speculation about the effects of environment on individual and social behavior, others by curiosity about what historical realities must have meant in personal terms, still others intrigued by the opportunity to project on the past their theories about the present—about ecology and feminism, New Age mysticism and community.

The most interesting of modern Westerns are on the cutting edge between white and red. For example, Bill Burchardt's *The Lighthorsemen* (1981) examines the compromises the Oklahoma Territorial Police (representatives of the Five Nations—Cherokee, Creek, Chickasaw, Seminole, and Choctaw) had to make as they struggled on a daily basis with conflicts between the tribal customs of the past and the new and sometimes incomprehensible laws of white society. Bill Gulick's *Northwest Destiny: A Trilogy* (1988) alternates between settlers and the Pacific Northwest tribes, capturing the adjustment dilemmas of both. In similar fashion, Bill Dugan looks at pivotal moments in white-red confrontations and the disturbing results. His five-book War Chiefs series mingles real-life personages and accurate details of tribe, place, and military action with the fictive to provide a sense of the tragedy of white-red confrontations: (1) the facedown between Geronimo and the Chiricahua Apaches and General George Crook, who aims to annihilate them; (2) the senseless and tragic battle at Bear Paw as Chief Joseph and the Nez Percé fled into Canada to avoid a confrontation over gold mining but were stopped by a reluctant U.S. general; (3) the broken treaties and violence of the westward movement that led Crazy Horse to repeatedly confront George Armstrong Custer and the U.S. Cavalry; (4) the fall of the mighty Sioux nation despite Sitting Bull's heroic efforts to preserve his people's way of life; (5) the battles between the Texas Rangers and the fierce Comanches until the last holdout, Quanah Parker, the son of a great Comanche chief and a white captive, brokered a plan that would allow his people peace with dignity. Recounting the escalation of the French and Indian wars, Robert Moss's *The Firekeeper: A Narrative of the Eastern Frontier* (1995) alternates the Mohawk and settler viewpoints, infusing both with wit and capturing the complexities of the Mohawk community through the eyes of tribe members; basically, however, the story tells how the real-life Sir William Johnson, with the support of a Mohawk visionary, becomes chieftain of the Mohawks and King George's colonel of the Six Nations in order to persuade the Mohawks to fight with the British against the French

The Texture of Day-to-Day Native American Life

Many turn-of-the-millennium Westerns evoke the texture of Native American life before the landing of Columbus, before the westward movement crossed the Mississippi, or in the first half of the nineteenth century, before the tragic fate of the Indian nations was sealed. Mike Blakely's carefully researched *Comanche Dawn* (1999), for instance, records the rise of the Comanches as one of the most powerful mounted nations in history through the eyes of a young warrior named Shadow, renamed Horseback. Born the day the half-starved Burnt Meat Shoshone see and eat their first horse, Horseback grows into a strong, forward-looking warrior and leader whose spirit medicine helps his people evolve into the fearless mounted warriors of the Comanche Nation. Harry Combs's *Legend of the Painted Horse* (1996), in turn, speculates on Viking forays that brought painted ponies to the Western tribes and produced the oddities Lewis and Clark and George Chapman observed in the Mandans before disease wiped them out.

Don Coldsmith sets his series of novels about pre- and post-Columbian Native Americans mainly in what is today the Midwest, and focuses on quests and trade that made for cross-cultural encounters between different North and Central American peoples and the Spanish conquistadors. He also explores cross-cultural influences and changes—how, for example, the horse transformed Native American life, and later how new technologies opened up new possibilities. In *The Changing Wind* (1990) medicine man White Buffalo relies on the mystical powers given him by ancient gods to lead his people out of the Stone Age and, as the title suggests, to help them survive a time of change and of bloody conflict with ignorant neighbors. *Medicine Hat* (1997) traces the dream-inspired quest of a young shaman of the Elk-Dog people who travels to the lands of the Pawnee and Lakota in search of a spirit horse. *Tall Grass* (1997) explores the clash between sixteenth-century Spanish explorers, conquistadors, priests, and trappers in Kansas and the Osage, Pawnee, Comanche, and Cheyenne warriors they seek to dominate and fool. *Southwind* (1999), in contrast, turns to the Kansas of 1846, the divisions of the Civil War, and the difficulties of a cross-racial marriage of white and Cherokee. Like Coldsmith, Paul Clayton focuses on the Indian point of view. In *Calling Crow Nation* (1995), the first in a trilogy set in what is today Georgia and South Carolina, Clayton's hero is Calling Crow, a chieftain who seriously weighs the advantages of an alliance with the English to protect his tribe, the Muskogee, from a rival tribe armed with guns from Spanish slavers; therein, the Muskogee suffer captivity and enslavement but remain defiant, rebellious, and strong. In Tony Hillerman's Frontier series, Ken Englade captures the changing loyalties and conflicts of the 1850s as white settlers sought an uneasy balance with the Plains tribesmen and with the Indians of the Southwest.

Frederick Manfred's *Conquering Horse* (1959), the first in the Buckskin Man Tales, depicts a young Sioux's tests of manhood and courage before the coming of whites. Winona LaDuke's *Last Standing Woman* (1997) begins in the 1860s and traces seven generations of Anishinaabe (Obijway/Chippewa) who must cope with the indignities of reservation life and find ways to preserve their values and heritage.

Whites Learning a Native American Perspective

Terry C. Johnston

Terry C. Johnston's raw, gritty frontier sagas are carefully researched, detailed re-creations of time and place. They provide a white perspective on the inevitable push westward and the frontier confrontations, but through the eyes of seasoned frontier scouts and mountain men who have lived among the Indians, shared their food and their women, and learned from their courage and survival skills—sometimes as companions and friends, most often as deadly adversaries. Often, Johnston depicts depraved whites, driven by bloodlust, slashing and mutilating equally savage Indians, but his heroes learn to see the land as the Native Americans do.

Mixing harsh realism with unexpectedly romantic visions, and fictive characters with historical ones, Johnston's *Cry of the Hawk* (1992), *Winter Rain* (1993), *Black Rain* (1993), and *Dream Catcher* (1994) trace the sojourns of relentless Confederate soldier Jonah Hook, who was released from a Union prison to fight Indians on the frontier. Hook, accompanied by his aging Shoshone warrior friend Two Sleep, spends a decade pursuing the Mormon "Avenging Angels" of Brigham Young, who loot his Missouri home; sell his boys to Comancheros; save Hattie, his daughter, for future deflowering by a wealthy Mormon buyer; and make his wife, Gritta, their crazed leader's concubine. During his search for his family, Hook kills buffalo for the railroad, fights Indians, and falls for Grass Singing, an Indian prostitute. He rescues Hattie first, then discovers his son Jeremiah riding with Quanah Parker's Kwahadi Comanche on the Staked Plains, and persuades him to join in the hunt for his mother. Hook discovers that Jeremiah thinks and acts like a Comanche. Yet Hook takes pride in his son's Comanche survival skills; his son's Comanche ties save his and his father's lives, and eventually help them destroy the vicious fanatic who holds Gritta prisoner. Hook's longtime friend, mountain man Shadrach Sweet, experiences a much more conflicted father-son relationship: his son High-Backed Bull belongs to the Cheyenne war party that the troops for whom Sweet scouts pursue, and High-Backed Bull has sworn to kill his father to purge himself of his white half. Johnston humanizes these issues of cross-cultural heritage and studiously sets the Indian point of view against the white. As a result of a lifetime's experiences with native peoples throughout the West, Hook comes to understand their view of the land:

"Nate, I s'pose it takes a man like me to understand what power the land means to an Injun like Two Sleep. What the land means to all Injuns. It's what most of us was fighting for against the Yankee Federals. The power of the land is what them redskins fought so hard to keep too. It's the land what gives us birth—the land what claims us back again when we grow so tired and can't rise up no more. When a man has to lay himself down for the last time." (*Dream Catcher*, 527)

It is this vision that has made him so tenaciously take back the wife and children who were stolen from him and find a final place where they can live in peace, and it is what binds Two Sleep to him as a comrade in arms.

In vivid, authentic detail, Johnston's thirteen-volume Plainsman series dramatically retells the history of the great Indian wars with a mix of perspectives that gives the Native American characters more prominent roles than did earlier Westerns; as the series progresses, Johnston devotes more and more space to native voices. The books follow veteran Indian fighter and Irish scout Seamus Donegan as he roams the West: traveling the Bozeman Trail across sacred Sioux hunting grounds at the time of the Fetterman Massacres of 1866 (*Sioux Dawn*, 1988); arriving in Oregon in time to witness the Modoc War of 1872 (*Devil's Backbone*, 1991); joining Colonel Joseph Reynold for the bloody Battle of Powder River against the warriors of Crazy Horse and Sitting Bull (*Blood Song*, 1993); again hunting Crazy Horse to help Phil Sheridan because the Sioux chieftain's unexpected forays and his elusiveness have repeatedly shamed the U.S. cavalry (*A Cold Day in Hell*, 1996). Donegan is also caught up in the friction between gold miners and the Nez Percé in Idaho as a few proud warriors defend their right to the land of their heritage, history, and ancestors in the bloody skirmishes of the Nez Percé War of 1877 (*Cries from the Earth*, 1999). From the ancient hunting grounds of the Kiowa and Comanche to the Republican River in Colorado, as tribe after tribe seeks to evade or escape reservation life and the U.S. Army tries to round them up and set boundaries to their activities, Donegan is always on the spot to observe the leaders of both sides (white and Indian) outraged by the opposition and preparing for conflict. He notes evolving strategies, like the Sioux using modern military tactics to divide their opponents into smaller, more easily defeated units at the Battle of the Rosebud (*Reap the Whirlwind*, 1994), and traces the results of broken promises—embittered, despairing Native American forces like those of Kiowa Chief White Bear (*Shadow Riders*, 1991) or suicidal ones like Crazy Horse and his thousand Lakota braves in his final battle (*Wolf Mountain Moon*, 1997).

Johnston's novels bring to life real people who actively worked to prevent conflict, like the old Cheyenne captive variously known as Old Wool Woman and Sweet Taste Woman, and the half-Lakota pony scout Johnny Bruguier (*Ashes of Heaven*, 1998). And sometimes his perspective is truly unexpected. For example, the fictional main character of *Whisper of the Wolf* (1991) is Yellow Bird, a half-Cheyenne youth raised to be a warrior by his mother's people but, surprisingly, the son of George Armstrong Custer. Yellow Bird sees his father killed at the Little Big Horn in 1876, but carries in his heart Custer's warrior spirit to guide his attempts to assure his own son a Cheyenne way of life.

John Norman

John Norman's *Ghost Dance* (1970) follows the progress of Edward Chance, a young drifter originally from South Carolina who killed his former fiancée's new lover in a duel and escaped to New York to study medicine. At the end of his studies he is tracked down by the victim's brother, Lester Grawson, but escapes to the West. He ends up on Standing Rock Reservation in South Dakota, pursued by Grawson and a cavalryman named Jake Totter. It is the summer of 1890, when the Sioux and other Plains tribes danced the Ghost Dance in anticipation of the demise of the whites and the return of the old life of buffalo hunting. The setting and circumstances are all historical; only Chance's personal escapades are fiction.

Chance comes upon a young Hunkpapa Sioux, Joseph Running Horse, who is seeking enlightenment in the Sun Dance, a ritual involving inserting pegs under the pectoral muscles by which the dancer suspends himself (most famously depicted in the film based on Dorothy Johnson's short story of the same title, *A Man Called Horse*). The young doctor helps Running Horse recover from his wounds, and they become blood brothers. Chance lives with the Sioux, meets Sitting Bull, observes the Ghost Dance, and takes up with a young white schoolteacher named Lucia Turner, who lives in a "soddy" on the reservation, near her Indian school. Chance witnesses the killing of Sitting Bull when tribal police try to arrest him to end the Ghost Dance, and escapes to the Badlands with the Hunkpapa and their allies the Minneconjou. Forced to leave the Badlands by hunger and cold, they go to the reservation at Pine Ridge, where they hope to receive better treatment at the hands of government agents. Instead, their camp at Wounded Knee Creek is surrounded and attacked by the Seventh Cavalry, elements of which had been wiped out when Custer fought the Sioux at Little Big Horn. The attack becomes a massacre, and Chance and his group barely escape back to the Badlands, where he is pursued by his nemesis Grawson, who ultimately commits suicide. Now free from pursuit, Chance is persuaded by Lucia, whom he will marry, to stay at Standing Rock to be the doctor to the Sioux, who call him Medicine Gun for his two skills.

Chance is the reader's "representative," a sensitive observer of white mistreatment of the Sioux, whose language he learns and whom he regards with respect and affection. We are thus allowed a vision of Indian life through the eyes of this sympathetic intermediary, an outcast from his own society. Lucia is another misfit, an early feminist and liberated woman who finds herself forced back into primitive roles by the conditions of the West. The result is a fine, quirky, offbeat novel, a model of how popular fiction can treat historical events with fairness and balance.

CONCLUSION

The turn-of-the-millennium Western has come a long way from the dime novels of its infancy. It has expanded its vision of the West to include all American frontiers, from East Coast to West Coast, north to south. It may look back farther in time than the nineteenth century to include not just the eighteenth century's encounters between Native Americans and English settlers but even earlier, to French and Spanish confrontations with native people. Some new Westerns even deal with the periods before European records, with the early inhabitants of what is today New England. However, the Western's most important strides have been in its increased sensitivity to the stories and histories of native peoples. Modern writers of Western stories to some degree see themselves as setting the historical record straight in fictive form, as capturing the white (and black) man's wonder at the lonely expanses of nature and at the varied peoples who made those expanses home, and as making sense of the phenomenon of the white captive at home with his or her life among native peoples. While we may cast some doubt on the genre's ability to truly represent native perspectives, to retell the American story through truly fresh eyes, we cannot fault the good intentions of a whole generation of writers anxious to correct the record by taking a more objective stance. Unlike historical romances, which conveniently skirt the hard issues of genocide and violent confrontation, the Indian Westerns are most often set in times of crisis and conflict, and purposefully provide new insights into the human motives and behaviors that comprise the historical record or have been ignored by it. The Western has shifted shape from a conventionalized instrument of national policy, a fictional justification of the westward push of manifest destiny, to a far more particularized and inchoate vision of multiple cultures, creeds, and peoples in competition and cooperation, all forming a new amalgam not yet fully defined. The new Western hero treads a difficult path between diverse cultures, and his vision is one of tragic waste and unrealized potential.

5

The Romance Genre:
Welcome to Club Cherokee

> She'd often fantasized about what it would have been like to live in the
> past, with all the adventure and romance. The lure of history had always
> intrigued her. And here she was, exploring a setting from another time
> alongside [a man who was] . . . a walking testimony to traditions she'd
> learned about only through books. He was the stuff her dreams were made
> of, come to vivid life.
>
> —Aimée Thurlo, *Spirit Warrior*, 88

In his *History of the Dividing Line* (1728), Virginian William Byrd, who himself
found local Indian women seductively charming, suggested that "charitable intermarriage" (as practiced by the French in Canada and Louisiana) would have
been a viable solution to the English colonists' Indian problem, since "all nations
of men have the same natural dignity," "very bright talents may be lodged under
a very dark skin," and Indian women, with their "very straight and well pro-
portioned" shapes and "air of innocence and bashfulness" ("with a little less
dirt"), would not fail to be "desirable" and would certainly have made more
"honest wives for the first planters" than "the damsels they used to purchase
from aboard the ships" (161). The Indian women Byrd encountered shared their
sexual favors with visitors according to the hospitality rules of their tribe and
"seldom bestow[ed] their favors out of stark love and kindness," but when a
marriage settlement was finally arranged between families, they were, says Byrd,
"thenceforth faithful to their vows," despite brutish, straying husbands or gallant
suitors. The merit of intermarriage would have been double, asserted Byrd: "a
wholesome, straight bed-fellow" and "the merit of saving her soul." The end
result of such sexual and social commingling would have been that, in Byrd's
view, the "intelligent," "well-proportioned" Indians would have become admi-

rable colonists: "Even their copper-colored complexion would admit of blanching, if not in the first, at the fartherest in the second generation" (161). While this is certainly the view of a pragmatist, not a romantic, if the romance novels on the modern market are to be believed, Byrd's vision of Indian-white commingling was so fast at work across the frontier that it is a wonder there are any full-blooded Native Americans left.

The romance genre includes more Native American stories than any other genre except the Western. Captivity stories dominate, but there are also stories about blossoming interracial romances in dozens of different settings, about Indian-white couples standing up to outlaws, settling frontier areas and setting up households, dealing with prejudice and bullies, traveling back east and coping with the cross-cultural ignorance of relatives, dealing with problems of birth control and gender expectations, and even practicing time travel to find true love. The phenomenon cries out for examination: Why do these encounters enjoy such popularity among readers? The question is especially intriguing since such romances, of Native Americans in passionate encounters with Europeans, could never have happened as depicted. As Byrd and many others confirm, Native American culture had—and indeed has—no tradition of romance in the Western or European sense except what it borrowed.

The idea that women and men should allow their feelings to sweep them away and lead them to act against their own and their tribe's best interests would have been ludicrous to the indigenous hunters, gatherers, fishers, and farmers of the American continent (as well as to the early colonists). Marriage served social and economic needs by binding families, tribes, and nations together, multiplying the number of hands available for ever-present work, and, perhaps most important, extending the number of people one could trust in an uncertain and threatening world. Indian maidens most often did as their fathers or families commanded, and white women taken captive in adulthood most often became slaves, brutalized and raped by all. Yet, since the 1980s, romance writers have turned out twenty to thirty or more titles a year extolling the virtues of the Indian lover and declaring cross-cultural romances the American equivalent of Romeo and Juliet (but with the potential for happy endings). A disillusioned modern Navajo professional in Tony Hillerman's *A Thief of Time* (1985) blames her failed relationship with an Anglo on the unreal expectations of the times: "Indian maidens were in with the Yuppies. Like squash-blossom necklaces and declaring yourself to be part Cherokee or Sioux if you wanted to write romantic poetry" (125). This modern concept of cross-cultural love in defiance of time and place, tradition and community, has been the subject of hundreds of recent Indian-romance fantasies.

REALITY SUSPENDED: WHAT ROMANCES IGNORE

Kinship patterns in Native American society dictated much of the courtship behavior we would now ascribe to personal choice or chance. (Such patterns determine behavior in many traditional cultures worldwide.) Marriage partners were sometimes limited to individuals in different "moieties" or totem groups, so that a Bear group would seek mates among Coyotes or Wildcats but not among its own membership, a method of adhering to incest taboos when memories of kinship faded, as they inevitably did in societies without written records. Different tribes were patrilocal—the married couple lives with the husband's family—or matrilocal (as with the Zuñi)—the pair live with the mother's family. Such arrangements reflect economic needs rather than personal preferences or even social ones. For example, the male's bringing his wife to live with his family allows him to hunt familiar territory with brothers, cousins, and uncles who also know the geography, terrain, and behavior of local fauna. Zuñi women used the labor of the husbands brought to their homes by their daughters but collected and shared the crops raised, retaining ownership and control of the gardens and fields that were their domain. The wants and desires of individual egos were simply not in play under conditions where survival might be in doubt. Changes in living arrangements reflected compelling pressures from the environment. For example, warfare or the need for male labor to create irrigation channels might change the locale of residence for a matrilocal group, but private preferences would not.

Such unforgiving circumstances left little room for romantic love. For example, for the Inuit (Eskimo), marriage was crucial for both female and male survival in an environment lethal to loners, but the marriage itself involved little more than the decision to live together and stay together, with little ceremony and no religious or legal ties of the Western sort. Courtship in the Western sense was almost nonexistent; rather, for both partners the marital agreement was more like contracting a worker or service person for modern Westerners. Even the wife-lending practice that so titillated or outraged the first white visitors to the Inuit had more basis in the economics of survival than in the pleasures of sexual variety, for a lone Inuit facing a hunting trip would multiply his chances for survival and success by having another's wife to cook, dry clothes, and manage the myriad domestic chores no hunter had time or energy for. Some partner-swapping games like "turning off the lamp" aside, general sexual license among the Eskimo may be an exciting notion for Westerners, but in fact seemingly licentious practices were heavily grounded in the economics of survival, binding together families and groups for mutual welfare rather than personal pleasure. Marriage of one's brother's widow following his demise likewise provided protection for his seed and assured the continuation of the family line, for a woman with no hunter could not survive. In general, marriage customs were tied to survival, welfare, and economics in virtually all Native American groups, since hunter-gatherers, farmers, and fisherfolk on the continent endured existences constantly threatened by drought, plant or animal disease, and the whims of extreme weather. In cultures with few methods of storing surpluses, there was little room for individual indulgence.

As a result, there is neither an oral nor a written Native American romance tradition. Instead, stories warn women against predatory males, confirm tribal marriage customs and taboos, and teach women their role in life. Horror stories warn of the dangers of breaking menstrual taboos, and cautionary tales suggest that young women should be wary of wishing for handsome younger lovers rather than seasoned, successful warriors, because such romantic partners can turn out to be bears and snakes, as in Paula Gunn Allen's "May It Be Beautiful All Around" from *Grandmothers of the Light*, 1991 (123). *Grandmothers* captures the mythic quality of some of the traditional stories in which women mate with forces of the universe like the sun, the moon, and the wind. They may copulate with trees and then magically give birth to more trees, or they may sleep with men from the stars. A buffalo or whale may take a human wife, or a human male may marry the moon or a snake or fish woman. The sacred clowns of the Southwest depict in ribald sexual acts associated with the renewal of life, and Coyote stories provide negative examples of behavior. For example, in one Coyote tale a beautiful, industrious daughter, proud of her accomplishments, looks on the well-intentioned offerings of worthy suitors as negligible compared with her own skills and value, but ends up smitten by Coyote's good looks and, to her family's shame, lives in a hole in the ground with him, far from her family and tribe, and gives birth to badly behaved coyote pups (Erdoes and Ortiz, 308). Though such stories vary from tribe to tribe and serve differing social functions, they are clearly worlds apart from the romantic love stories of mainstream tradition.

The decisions of youngsters responding to raging hormones may well have troubled Native American parents as much as modern ones worried about poor matrimonial choices, but the Indian attitude toward such biologically driven behavior categorized it as youthful folly to be outgrown, not as a sublime state to be preserved and repeated into middle age and beyond. Even Pocahontas's rescue of Captain John Smith, which has become so vital a part of American "romance" mythology, makes little sense. Why would a twelve-year-old Algonquin maiden fall suddenly and madly in love at first sight with a strange and smelly hairy-faced white barbarian moments before his execution? It is far more likely, as many modern scholars assert, that Pocahontas, as a high-ranking female and daughter of the chieftain Powhatan, was enacting a step in the adoption process as "a mother figure for Smith's rebirth as an Indian after he first underwent a symbolic death through mock execution" (*The Woman's Way*, 20–21; see Robert Tilton's *Pocahontas*, 1994).

The relationship of men and women differed from tribe to tribe, but overall the European tradition of romantic love and "falling" in love has never been a part of the Native American tradition. Marriage often occurred early, soon after a girl's first menstrual period, though among tribes like the Tlingit this experience might mark the onset of up to two years' confinement. Tribes like the Apache put great stock in virginity, and a woman's having illicit sex could result in public punishment and condemnation, whereas men's infidelity was a given. For other tribes, premarital sex was considered natural, and numerous premarital lovers testified to a woman's desirability. Among tribes like the Ojibway, Cree, Creek, and Cherokee a woman might marry seven or eight times, a license early missionaries found appalling.

For many tribes, the kiss, so much a part of the European romantic tradition, was not a natural practice and might even have been viewed as repulsive, and the "missionary" position was not the sexual position of choice. For some tribes, anal intercourse was the preferred sexual method and certainly an effective form of birth control, so the choice of a male or a female sexual partner was irrelevant to the sexual act. Other tribes had a designated *berdache*, a man-woman who prevented sexual tensions from getting out of hand in the village by servicing the unmarried men as well as married men who had had arguments or difficulties at home. (In fact, a modern researcher among the Zuñi discovered to his chagrin that his source on female behavior and lore within the tribe was a *berdache*, a man-woman; for more on this phenomenon see Walter L. Williams's *The Spirit and the Flesh: Sexual Diversity in American Indian Culture*, 1986.) In addition to the polygamy practiced for very practical reasons (more hands to maintain households heavily dependent on hand labor), in many Native American tribes a third or fourth wife might well have been what the Sioux called a *winkte*, a man-woman who dressed in female attire and followed feminine pursuits. Like the *berdache*, a *winkte* was a special person for the Native Americans, one who could embody the virtues of both sexes, who was not burdened by childbirth and nursing, and who could therefore provide the domestic strength of the household. The practice made males ill-suited to being warriors useful and provided women with help in their labors. In tribes where intercourse between married couples was taboo until their child had been weaned (preferably not until age three), multiple wives or other institutionalized forms of sexual release made common sense, preserving communal harmony and minimizing the potential for eccentric individual behavior.

Women's tasks were crucial to common survival. They were not only responsible for bearing, tending, and educating children but also for gathering fuel; drawing water; making and repairing household utensils, blankets, clothing, and shoes (skinning the game, tanning the hides, sewing the garments); crafting some tools; catching fish; gathering shellfish, herbs, vegetables, nuts, and fruit; sometimes hunting; in other cases growing crops; always processing and cooking food; and even in some groups making canoes and living structures; packing up the household goods for travel and setting up camp along the way or at the destination, among other duties. Among the Plains tribes dependent on the buffalo for meat, clothing, and shelter, preparing and tanning hides was a months-long process of painstaking handwork, producing butter-soft clothing and impermeable lodges, at the cost of hundreds of woman-hours. No wonder strong extra hands were always welcomed! However, in spite of the seemingly endless array of duties, since women worked at their tasks communally, they reduced the multiple tasks isolated frontier white women faced on lonely farms. In Mary Jemison's judgment (having lived both ways), Indian women had easier lives, and other captives agreed, depending on the tribe they were taken by. Additionally, as with all hunter-gatherer, fishing, and subsistence farming cultures, women wielded great power in their domains, areas of influence created by the division of labor. Some, particularly on the East Coast, acted as tribal leaders or shamans, and among Plains tribes a few women crossed over into male domains and became skilled warriors as well, stealing horses and counting coup, along with their men. In Northwest tribes in which men owned property, women managed the family treasury.

A man with only one wife, and she an outsider unfamiliar with Indian survival skills and female family and community duties, with no associated clan or place within the traditional hierarchy (such as the heroes depicted in the Harlequin, Silhouette, Zebra, Avon, Leisure, and Love Spell historical romances, among others), would not only suffer great hardship: he and the woman might not survive a winter. In turn, a Native American woman who married an outsider, whether white or from another tribe, would, in many tribes, be giving up her place among her people and be doomed never to return. Even those with the option to return would be regarded with disfavor for having made this choice unless it was a political decision made tribally, for the sake of the community. In communal societies individual wishes must bend for the good of the group; a life story is not an unfinished script to be written out by personal wishes but rather a series of formal ceremonies marking passages of status and role in the group. Craig Strete's romance story "When They Find You" (in *The Bleeding Man and Other Science Fiction Stories*) highlights another negative in the cross-cultural equation: the prejudices of the husband's or wife's community tainting the relationship and turning shared affection or even love to bitterness.

Critical readers should then ask why, given the unsentimental realities of Native American life and love in the eighteenth and nineteenth centuries, Indians, especially males, have become the romantic leads in so many recent historical romance novels.

THE HISTORICAL TRADITION

Some part of the answer lies in the realities that have shaped the Indian of the imagination. Modern historical romances look back to a very real tradition of abductions that dates from the earliest encounters of Native Americans and Europeans. Beginning as unwilling and violent kidnappings, captivity situations could end happily or sadly or sometimes as genuine cross-cultural political marriages. Marriage, in fact (as William Byrd so firmly articulated in the 1720's), was potentially both a literal and a metaphorical way of uniting indigenous and invading peoples and cultures. Certainly, captivity was far more common than most modern Americans now realize. The failed marriage of Indian and white is surely the first great American tragedy.

The Captivity Story as Precursor

The captivity story may be the first truly American literary tradition. June Namias in *White Captives* cites sixty-eight captivity stories published between 1612 and 1879 (274–276), and confirms that the actual number of white captives far exceeded the number who wrote about their experiences: 1,641 white captives taken between 1675 and 1763 (7). She also reports uncounted numbers of Native American captives taken by French, English, and Spanish, and later Americans. She divides the literary versions of white female captivities into three categories: the Survivors (women who have been supremely tried but, through strength and adaptability, live to tell their tales); the Amazons (cunning, athletic women who outwitted their captors and slew or at least escaped them, then battled the wilderness back to their homes); and the Frail Flowers (melo-dramatic, sentimental heroines, suffering and abused, tossed about by fate). All three of these enduring types appear in historical romances.

Historically, Indian tribes across the continent took captives for a number of reasons: to seek revenge for killing or abduction of tribe members; to count coups and acquire slaves; to replace family members—dead sons, daughters, or wives, and to rebuild a tribal population decimated by epidemics, war, and other causes (many tribes suffered from low birth rates caused by malnutrition and the harshness of a nomadic life). Puritan accounts of captives emphasize forced marches, sometimes three hundred miles or longer, under trying conditions of snow and ice and limited or no food supplies. The fate of captives also varied, from running the gauntlet to enduring imaginative torture at the hands of the women of the tribe—reports include "death by a thousand cuts," being burned at the stake in the East, set out for ants to eat in the West and Southwest, and other slow and exquisite final acts. Sometimes captives were set tests of endur-ance, strength, and skills to determine their value to a tribe before branding or marking and assignment to heavy, dirty work. Female slaves often serviced the males of a household sexually.

Cotton Mather's relative Pastor John Williams, taken captive by Mohawks, Hurons, Abenakis, and French in 1704, reports infants (who would burden their mothers and were not likely to survive) being slaughtered immediately (dashed against cabin walls or silenced with a hatchet blow) and women in weakened condition who slowed down the march being among the first to be slaughtered, in this case on the long trek from Deerfield, Massachusetts, to Montreal, Canada. In contrast, teenage youths and boys over eleven had the highest survival rate because of their strength, flexibility, and willingness to adopt Indian wilderness survival strategies (Demos, *The Unredeemed Captive*).

Sarah Horn's account of her captivity among the Comanches in 1834 (in Carl Coke Ruster's *Comanche Bondage*, 1989) describes the cruelties inflicted on the helpless further west. First comes the scalping while the victim is still alive (making an incision round the head, even below the ears, then standing on the victim's shoulders and tearing the scalp free "as he would the skin from a slaughtered sheep," 123), and the indescribable suffering of those left in the heat of a burning sun with bare skull exposed. Then, when captives are taken, the infants are killed: "a tall, muscular Indian came to me and taking hold of it [a babe in arms], swung it by its arms, and threw it up as high as he could, and let it fall upon the ground at his feet" three times until "its sufferings were at an end" (130). The endurance of the captives is tested as they travel without food and are goaded and abused (taken by the throat and choked until black in the face and in a dead faint, then jumped on and stamped on); the men are kept alive to provide amusement during the journey home, and after their deaths "the savages amused themselves by shooting their arrows into the dead bodies of the men they had just slain" (144). When Sarah Horn's five-year-old son fell off a mule into a river and struggled to get out, "one of the savages, enraged at the accident, stabbed the little creature in the face with his lance, and sent him back into the midst of the foaming stream. The wound was inflicted just below the eye, and was a very severe one. . . . with blood streaming down his naked body from his wounded face, [he] gained the shore" (151). Later, the Comanches amused themselves by throwing the two sons (the younger three years old) into the stream, then taking them out when they were nearly drowned, only to toss them in again.

Though threatened with burning at the stake after slow torture by the women of the tribe, Sarah Horn proved her usefulness sewing clothing and treating buffalo hide. In contrast to Jemison, she was appalled at the general treatment of women, observing the women's abject slavery and the men's absolute despotism and their promiscuity (despite five legally taken wives), and thanking God for the progress toward human rights Christianity had made among her own people. Though she (like many other women who wrote of their captivity) makes no comment on her sexual treatment by the Comanches, she notes their belief that women exist solely to serve male needs in the same lines where she notes their promiscuous sexual behavior.

Captives deemed suitable to replace missing family received completely different treatment, eventually enjoying full rights as tribe members if acculturation was successful. J. F. Lafitau, Jesuit missionary to the Hahnawake Mohawks from 1712 to 1717, emphasized the positive treatment of captives taken to replace family members:

The moment that [the captive] enters the lodge to which he is given . . . his bonds are untied. . . . He is washed with warm water to efface the colors with which his face was painted and he is dressed properly. Then he receives visits of relatives and friends of the family into which he is entering. A short time afterwards a feast is made for all the village to give him the name of the person whom he is resurrecting . . . and from that moment, he enters upon all his rights. (Demos, vii)

Mary Jemison reports a similar experience of her adoption ceremony:

They first undressed me and threw my rags into the river; then washed me clean and dressed me in the new suit they had just brought, in complete Indian style; and then led me home and seated me in the center of their wigwam. (Seaver, *Life*, 44)

The women of the tribe enter, and after mourning the dead warrior Jemison is to replace, proclaim their "brother" to be "happy":

His spirit has seen our distress, and sent us a helper whom with pleasure we greet. Dickewamis [Jemison's new Indian name] has come; then let us receive her with joy! She is handsome and pleasant! Oh! She is our sister, and gladly we welcome her here.

In the place of our brother she stands in our tribe. With care we will guard her from trouble; and may she be happy till her spirit leaves us. (47–48)

Jemison reports that "joy sparkled" in her new sisters' countenances, that they "seemed to rejoice over me as over a long lost child" (66).

Sometimes abductions created complex situations with no easy solutions. Joanna Stratton quotes the story of Anna Morgan, a blue-eyed, blonde beauty who was abducted from her farm in Kansas by Sioux warriors in 1868 and enslaved. She and a white female companion escaped to within sight of Fort Dodge and safety, only to be retaken. Feeling that she would never be able to evade her captors again, she married an Indian chief, whom she began to think highly of because of his kind treatment. When her brother showed up in camp, she was a fully assimilated white Indian, and after she was redeemed, "the road seemed rough, and I often wished they had never found me" (Stratton, 627–628). A few months later she gave birth to a child fathered by her Indian husband; the child died two years later. Considering her experience a disgrace, Anna Morgan refused interviews requested by newspaper and book writers, remained melancholy after her rescue, and died in an asylum after her mind failed. In contrast, her companion in captivity, Sarah White, sold her story and portrait for publication and married "a good man," allowing her experience to fade into history as a dreadful ordeal happily ended (Stratton, 125).

In other words, the real captivity stories varied with time, tribe, and circumstance, with some constructed as tales of horror and of Christian endurance in the face of hellish trials and tribulations, and others becoming tales of personal freedom, cultural adjustment, and pleasure in a more natural, family- and community-based way of life, unrestrained by artificially imposed puritanical strictures. In the literature of early America, readers shuddered at the cruelty and violence of James Fenimore Cooper's Magua, a renegade Huron, but thrilled at the exploits of Chingachgook and Uncas in *The Last of the Mohicans*, and later wept at the suffering of Helen Hunt Jackson's Ramona, whose stepmother could not love her because of her Indian blood and whose noble Indian lover watched helplessly as encroaching Americans forced his people from their California lands (*Ramona*, 1884). The modern romance novel captures this dichotomy, exploiting the fears and the potential for violence in native life, but in the main, for the sake of a love story, focusing on the positive—love relationships that cross racial and cultural barriers to touch hearts and reveal a common humanity.

Intermarriage for Political Alliance

Beginning with the marriage of Pocahontas to John Rolfe, since early colonial days there have been historic instances of white-Indian alliances based on arranged marriages between high-ranking white officials and Native American women from powerful families; the women's strong tribal influence allowed them to become legendary as go-betweens who used their sexual alliances to aid their people. Such women included Creek Mary Musgrove (born Cousapon-okeesa), Mohawk Molly Brant, and Cherokee Nancy Ward.

In his novel *Creek Mary's Blood* (1980), noted novelist Dee Brown re-creates the incredible story of an early-eighteenth century Indian "princess" who learned English in school, and who married John Musgrove to reaffirm Creek-English friendship and to establish trade links with the Carolinas. Later, as interpreter for and lover of the wealthy and powerful British representative James Ogle-thorpe, "Creek Mary" helped negotiate a trade and land cession agreement that led to the founding of Savannah. When Musgrove died, Mary, the wealthiest woman in Georgia, used her influence over Oglethorpe to promote the Creek-Georgia alliance. In 1737 she took her claim to ownership of thousands of square miles of land along the Savannah River to court and even argued her case before the British Board of Trade. However, she lost the grants she won in court when she married an Anglican clergyman named Thomas Bosomworth, because her inheritance followed his genealogical line under white law, rather than her line under Creek law. Brown explores the way her courage and influence inspired her descendants as they followed the Cherokee Trail of Tears westward to finally settle and thrive in the Dakotas. Though Ward Churchill (*Fantasies of the Master Race*) is offended at the Euro-American stereotyping of Creek Mary and at the liberties Dee takes with historical evidence for the sake of a good story, Creek Mary was clearly an exceptional woman whose life choices promoted the welfare of her people.

Molly Brant, the sister of Joseph Brant, married Sir William Johnson in 1759 to create a bond of friendship and kinship with the Mohawks. Entertaining a stream of white and Indian visitors put her at the center of colonial life, but her efforts as a British spy in the 1770s lost her tribe its ancestral holdings in what became the United States, though British compensation to Molly enabled her to shelter and assist many dispossessed Mohawk kinsmen.

Another cross-cultural heroine, variously called Nanyehi (which was Angli-cized to Nancy) and Tsistunagiska or Cherokee Rose, was a well-born Cherokee whose father possibly was British. In the 1750s she won the honored title of Beloved Woman for taking the place of her fallen husband in a Cherokee attack on a Creek town, and for a short period she was married to a British trapper. When white atrocities against Cherokee allies led to Cherokee raids on whites, Nancy tried to intercede on behalf of potential victims on both sides—for example, using her Beloved Woman status to rescue American captives from fiery deaths at the stake and her status with whites to persuade army officers to spare her people's village in the fall of 1776. Although she saved many American lives, ultimately she could not save her Cherokee village from final destruction, though her reputation persuaded Thomas Jefferson, then governor of Virginia, to intervene and free the captives taken in that attack (*The Woman's Way*, 111).

Such stories as these, and the long-standing tradition of frontiersmen taking Indian wives, were the real foundation for the fictive sexual encounters and love affairs so vividly and anatomically portrayed in modern-day historical romances.

GENRE OVERVIEW

The Western tradition of the romance is an ancient one, going back in spirit to the much-discussed European courtly love tradition and to medieval chivalric romances in which knights rescued maidens from cruel fathers, husbands, step-mothers, and dragons, and vowed eternal love in poetic verse. The romance novel, in particular, reflected eighteenth- and nineteenth-century social class differences and new possibilities for class mobility. Conventions included the chase-pursuit, the maidenly "no, no" to a suitor as the young lady (usually orphaned, or in financial trouble, or beneath the man in class) fled the man of her dreams (usually a handsome man of superior wealth and social class) until he caught her, at which time "no" turned quickly to "yes," with virginity held out as an enticement to marriage vows. Samuel Richardson's *Pamela* (1740) established the conventional pattern, one so popular Henry Fielding could mock it in *Shamela* (1741); Richardson's *Clarissa* (1747–1748) was one of the most popular and influential books of the time. In the next century, the literary productions of Jane Austen and Charlotte Brontë were elevated versions of the themes and concerns of the penny dreadfuls and dime novels of popular culture. The Gothic romance added the thrill of danger to the original formula of romantic chase-pursuit by mingling in the supernatural and the horrifying.

Such works generally dealt with the stresses and strains of a relatively new class mobility and class consciousness that fostered envy and conflict, as individuals sought to mimic their immediate betters in the social hierarchy. Fiction offered the pleasant notion that romance would prompt the more wealthy and powerful to accept their social inferiors, even adopting them into their families through marriage, negating clearcut incentives to economic aggrandizement that had traditionally governed the marriage contract. Sentiment would trump self-interest; where once sex was taken by the powerful, now surrender could be negotiated, with networks of finer feelings holding lust in abeyance until the safe port of an advantageous marriage had been reached. Given that women in these periods had far fewer opportunities for social mobility than men, it is not surprising that this hopeful romance fiction featured female heroines and supporting characters and was widely read by women. Theories of the power of sentiment both lent credibility to such fiction and fed off its popularity.

Although the theme of class mobility has ebbed, the modern romance shares the hopeful outlook of its predecessors. The twentieth-century romance may overlap other genres, including the mystery, the horror story, the ghost story, historical fiction, and so forth, but it is always recognizable by its insistence on the sentiment at the heart of the story: the feelings between an individual man and woman are more important than the political, social, or economic events that swirl around them. The pattern is boy meets girl, boy and/or girl fall in love, their love is thwarted by blocking agents such as inner demons or outside forces (including relatives, past relationships, personal obligations, social upheaval, cultural conflict), but finally love conquers all and boy and girl are reunited or rediscover the depths of their attraction/need/love. Thus, the basic pattern involves descriptions of the ups and downs of sexual/romantic pursuit that lead to declarations of love, sexual fulfillment (described intensely, nowadays in panting detail), with the resolution being marriage, though occasionally the plot continues until the marriage is both consummated and accepted emotionally by both parties. Traditionally, the genre includes the convention of love at first sight, although the lovers themselves (particularly the man) may not recognize the depth of that love until after marriage or until the near loss of the beloved. Traditionally, too, as in the eighteenth and nineteenth centuries, blocking devices that frustrate the lovers have been class and wealth, though disapproving relatives are often featured as specific blockers. The appeal is that sentiment will conquer the more mundane and practical forces that shape our destinies.

In the 1950s, Native Americans began to appear as leads in romance stories— particularly Indian males who fell in love with their white, female captives, though sometimes the pattern was reversed, with white women falling in love with brave Indian prisoners or white men falling in love with Indian maidens and teaching them to be happy baking pies in a white man's kitchen. However, the recent interest in multicultural concerns has led to more and more romances involving Native American heroes or heroines; by the 1990s the number of such novels skyrocketed, with major series of ten to twelve books a common phenomenon. Cassie Edwards, for example, has two major series with between ten and thirty "Indian romances" in each, and has resolved to write about every major Indian tribe in America. Georgina Gentry has close to twenty books in her Cheyenne-Nez Percé Panorama of the Old West series, and Madeline Baker has close to twenty-five "half-breed" novels; Janelle Taylor's Ecstasy Saga includes nine titles; and Janis Reams Hudson's Apache series numbers at least six titles. In romance novels involving Native Americans, race, culture, and social attitudes block romance, and all must be overcome for true love to hold sway. The reason for this new enthusiasm for Native Americans is easy to tease out: as the blocking forces of social class and money eased in the prosperity of the late twentieth century, and as Western women exercised more power than ever before, new blocking agents became necessary if the romance genre were to survive. The exotic, culturally distant nature of Native Americans offered the perfect foil for mainstream writers seeking credible blocks to happiness with which to dramatically frustrate their heroines and heroes.

GENRE PATTERNS IN INDIAN ROMANCES

"Native-American" romances—stories incorporating Native American heroes/ heroines in Native American or frontier settings—fit well with modern romance genre requirements. As one might expect, both male and female are extraordinarily attractive. The description of the Indian maiden in Kathleen Drymon's *Legend of Desire* (1998) is typical of the emphasis on physical allure:

Her name was Desire and her beauty was unrivaled throughout the plains tribes. A leached, fringed, and beaded doe hide dress covered her womanly shape. Her long legs were encased in fringed leggings, her small feet graced with quilled and beaded moccasins. Her waist-length, midnight hair was braided in plump lengths over her shoulders; vermillion-dyed leather strippings with delicate singing bells twined throughout the braids. Her smooth forehead was blessed with fine, dark-winged brows; lush jet lashes guarded her exotic gold-brown flecked eyes. Her cheekbones were high, a rose blush staining their curve. Her full lips held the power to draw the male eye, and in their depths lay the promise of paradise. (*Desire*, 12)

Desire could well be a New York model showing off the latest in fashion wear. The description of the partially assimilated Comanche in Fabio Lanzoni and Eugenia Riley's *Comanche* (1995) is just as idealized. It doesn't matter that artist George Catlin's 1830s description of the Comanche was of a short, plump people ("in stature rather low, and in person often approaching to corpulency") whose movements (except on horseback) tended to be "heavy and ungraceful" (*Way of the Warrior*, 152). In romantic fiction Comanches are the Anglo idea of masculine perfection:

He appeared striking not only because of his height . . . over six feet, but also because he was hatless, his long, jet black hair spilling down his shoulders. His face was sharply, beautifully chiseled, with a broad brow, deep-set eyes, a straight nose, high cheekbones, and a strong jaw. His skin was heavily bronzed. (*Comanche*, 5)

. . . he was so strong, so virile. . . . She watched his shirt linen pull at the powerful muscles of his arms and shoulders, and imagined herself being held in those strong naked arms . . . Maggie exulted in the aura of excitement and danger he radiated. (*Comanche*, 30)

Even when the situation is kidnapping and the initial reaction is anger, the romance begins with a physical attraction that packs a wallop:

A jolt of electrifying awareness sizzled through Jennifer when she met piercing silver-gray eyes beneath jutting black brows . . . she had never found herself so captivated. (Finch, *Comanche Promise*, 9)

One moment she was angry, indignant. The next she was being manhandled by this . . . this savage. All thought scattered as his lips covered hers in a scorching kiss. (Langen, *Malachite*, 34)

. . . a shudder traveled up her spine. . . . The warmth of his touch spread through her like fire. (Thurlo, *Her Shadow*, 16, 18)

Vanessa's heart thudded violently. She had only been kissed a few times by young soldiers she had known, and those had been sweet chaste kisses, not a sensual torment that whisked all thoughts from her mind, a kiss that left her feeling hot and weak and wanting more. (Orwig, *Warrior Moon*, 53)

He fought a surge of desire he was not prepared for. He was prepared to fight her . . . he wasn't prepared to want her. (Sommerfield, *Night Walker*, 107)

The women are almost always virgins (even if they have been married), but the sexual and romantic attraction is so strong that it overpowers prejudice and common sense:

Marilla was ready to protest, fear sweeping through her like torrents of rain drowning her, when his mouth bore down upon hers, hot and demanding, his hands setting her skin on fire as he touched every secret part of her. (Edwards, *Savage Whispers*, 62)

She knew she should back away. She tried to make herself do it; she couldn't. . . . All at once his lips crushed down on hers . . . a savage kiss . . . and Genevieve could think of nothing else but those lips on her own—their feel, their warmth, their . . . arousal. (Kay, *Gray Hawk's Lady*, 47)

Not only had this man—this Indian—dared to touch her, a dizzying sensation such as no other she had ever imagined engulfed her, rushing through her body like a windstorm gone mad. *How dare he!* . . . she stamped her foot . . . and without warning, his head swooped down to hers, his lips enveloping hers in a kiss. Sensation exploded within her, and her knees buckled, causing her to swoon toward him. *What was happening to her?* (Kay, *White Eagle's Touch*, 67–68)

Tanya had told herself she would not respond to Panther's lovemaking this night, but the minute his mouth claimed hers, she was lost to reason. As his wandering hands charted her body, she began to tremble violently beneath his touch. His lips moved over hers, melting them like hot wax, boldly staking his claim. (Hart, *Silken Savage*, 51)

Having been recaptured by Gray Eagle, a Sioux chieftain who had her publicly flogged before she was rescued by bluecoats, Janelle Taylor's Alisha Williams ignores the bloody chaos around her as the Sioux attack and destroy the fort where she has been since her rescue. Surrounded by struggle and death, she thinks only about her romance with Gray Eagle:

Here in his strong, loving protective embrace was where she wanted to remain forever and a day. Waves upon waves of heated passion washed over her. She begged for his total possession of her. Hotter and deeper the flames of love and desire leaped in both their minds and bodies. (*Defiant Ecstasy*, 80)

The male usually tries to negate his feelings, and as a result he seems harsh or cruel:

Suddenly a tortured moan escaped his throat. He came away from her, at the same time roughly pulling the chemise back over her naked breasts. Ashamed and confused by his change in attitude, she sat up, groping for something to cover herself with. . . . He grabbed his hat from off the bedpost and pulled it low over his eyes. In another second he was gone. . . . Red Sky stared at the closed door . . . What had she done to make him so angry? . . . Had he been disappointed . . . ? (Sandifer, *Embrace the Wind*, 290–291)

"I don't like being turned on by you because you still believe in fairy tales like love. I know better." . . . Eden watched Nevada, reminded of the first cougar she had ever seen. It had been caged, and wild within that cage, raking with unsheathed claws at everything that came near. *What is it, Nevada? What did I say to make you so angry?*
     The question was asked only in the silence of her mind, for she knew Nevada wouldn't answer if she spoke aloud. (Lowell, *Warrior*, 36, 139)

In Taylor's saga of Gray Eagle and Alisha, Gray Eagle must hide his deep love for her behind a public mask of indifference and cruelty in order to retain respect as a warrior chieftain.
     These Native American warriors fit Robyn Donald and Doreen Owen Malek's descriptions of male romantic leads as challenging to the women they are paired with: "Mean, Moody, and Magnificent" and "Mad, Bad, and Dangerous to Know," though the "mean" and "bad" refer to the men's physical prowess and fighting skills rather than to their treatment of women (see Krentz, *Dangerous Men and Adventurous Women*). The Indians of romance are mythic males— broad chested, with sinewy bodies, long, smooth muscles, great strength, a sultry, searing gaze, and impressive sexual capabilities. They know how to survive in unforgiving terrain; they stand up against overwhelming odds and remain unbowed if not victorious. They shoot and ride with extraordinary skill, and they can endure the worst of tortures without crying out. Yet, behind their rough self-assurance they prove to be caring, sensitive lovers and family men, good with children and protective of old people. They provide positive models for teenagers, whose moodiness they penetrate to see the potential that can be awakened. They see such potential in their women, too. They teach their beloved captives not simply a sexual passion never before experienced but also a tender gentleness at odds with their dark, brooding appearance and tough masculinity:

Tonight belonged to this disillusioned beauty who needed and deserved to be loved with all the patient tenderness he could provide. His pleasure would come in her small discoveries, in her realization that passion didn't have to be distasteful. . . . Although his body throbbed with desire, he restricted himself to light, feathery kisses—ever mindful of the swollen side of her mouth. . . . he wanted to restore her belief in him more than he wanted life itself. . . . When Trey [Three Wolves] traced figure eights around the curve of her breast, Jennifer's breathing altered and her skin tingled with unexpected pleasure. She was stunned by the heat waves rippling through her as hands as gentle as the evening breeze whispered over her skin. Heightened awareness of this intriguing paradox of a man, who could be the epitome of tenderness and strength, cascaded over her. His lips grazed her cheeks, her eyelids, and Jennifer sighed audibly. . . . His patience and gentleness melted her inhibitions one at a time, leaving her receptive to each wondrous sensation. She responded eagerly to Trey, wanting more. (Finch, *Comanche Promise*, 105, 108, 110)

Heroes like Trey are dangerous, and at times full of hate initially, but they can be transformed (through the persistence of a good woman) from solitary, detached, destructive forces to positive protectors of home and community. Deep in their isolated souls they long for family and hearth, for love and continuity. Summer Van Schuyler, the heroine of Georgina Gentry's *Cheyenne Captive* (1987) and *Cheyenne Splendor* (1994), describes her captor, then husband, Iron Knife:

She knew every inch of his virile, muscular body from his whip-scarred back to the sun dance scars on his broad chest. He was powerful and dangerous, but with her, he was always tender and gentle. . . . what had always attracted her to him was his almost swaggering masculinity, his protective savagery, his primitive arrogance. But, oh, he could be such a gentle and sensitive lover. (*Splendor*, 11, 14)

In *Comanche Promise* (1998), Carol Finch carries these destructive powers further than most. Her romantic lead, Three Wolves, is both a notorious and feared bounty hunter and "a shaman of the highest echelon" (292) who can shape-shift into a wolfman and call on an avenging spirit wolf pack to assist his cruel and bloody attacks on villains. To rescue his beloved Jennifer, he adopts the insubstantial nature of smoke, a moving fog with glowing silvery eyes, and goes up against and defeats over thirty armed gunmen; Jennifer treats all of this as a natural part of his alien Indian nature, and finally wins his heart because "She had believed in him when no one else was willing to see anything in him except a dangerous gunslinger without a heart, soul, or conscience" (335).

A central part of most historical romances featuring Native American heroes is a detailed and ongoing description of their "hard shaft" (a recurring phrase); their skilled and impassioned lovemaking; their sexual techniques for bringing a woman to a climax, even against her will; the variety, diversity, unconventionality, and freedom of their sexual attack; their marathon sexual endurance; and their pleasure in bringing their sexual partner pleasure and making her experience emotions and sensations she could never have felt with a white man. Virgins have orgasm after orgasm even before being deflowered, and it is only after being "tamed" by the persistent, dizzying lovemaking of their "savage" captors that these women come to acknowledge the depths of their own passion. Only a very few romance writers depict the Indian male leads as truly harsh and rough, and then their cruelty usually reflects a battle between the public behavior expected of a warrior and private, personal love: a white captive publicly disobeying a warrior's command requires a harsh response. Furthermore, many of the Indian leads prove deceptively less Indian than they seem, often being of mixed white and Indian blood or even being whites who were taken captive as children and raised as Indians, but who keep this fact secret until they have tamed their captive.

Clearly then, "Indian" romance novels, no matter their inclusion of "factual" and "historic" detail, are modern white women's fantasies, very much in the Regency romance tradition. They ignore sociocultural realities and assert a mainstream standard of physical beauty as a cross-cultural norm (the women are all big-busted redheads or blondes, with luscious curves, soft skin, and a pleasing fragrance). They are predicated on mainstream ideas about romance (especially love at first sight) and lovemaking, and include pages and pages of loving attention to males showing true love and restraint in order to awaken these virgins' latent passion. Indian lovers, unlike their lustful white counterparts, who lecherously grab and take without finesse or even affection, teach the pleasures of sex as expressions of deep romantic feelings and lead their women to multiple climaxes—proof of the tenderness that exists between captive and capturer.

According to Linda Barlow and Jayne Ann Krentz in "Beneath the Surface: The Hidden Codes of Romance" (Krentz, 17), key recurring romance plot elements in general include "spirited young women forced into marriage" and mysterious heroes "with dark and dangerous pasts." In romances with Native American heroes or heroines, the heroines are literally "forced" because they are captives, but "spirited" because they represent feminist models of independence and self-assertion, while "the dark and dangerous past" is inherent in the warrior hero's Indian life. In practical terms, what this means is that the "Indian" romances try to have it both ways: the heroine as frail flower and warrior woman, in keeping with Namias's categories of historical captives (Frail Flowers, Survivors, Amazons). The novels celebrate the thrill and danger of being stolen away by a "savage" male but also the power of love to tame the brute and make him appreciate the beauty his eye led him to seize. As with the early sentimental novels, sentiment trumps self-interest. Once she has tamed him through love, the woman is freed both from her personal captivity and from the social restraints of her own culture, which limited female roles and blocked self-fulfillment. Before Madeline Baker's heroine in *Prairie Heat* (1991) escapes her humdrum life by running off with a half-breed Apache, she muses on the unfairness of gender distinctions that make women subject to the authority of fathers, brothers, and husbands, unable to vote or own property, with limited employment opportunities: "How wonderful to be a man, to do as one wished, to always be in control of one's own life. Women rarely knew such freedom. . . . A woman's life was never fully her own. . . . But a man—why, a man could do anything he wanted" (124). Her transformation is typical. As a non-Indian Indian she discovers personal freedom and even the potential to be a woman warrior or woman shaman. She has independence but also native community, the close fellowship of other women, and the opportunity to meet her man as an equal and to make use of skills, knowledge, and power that were ignored or had to be hidden in white society. This is a woman who never looks back once both love and power are in her grasp.

A successful combination in such romance stories is a mix of feminine help-lessness with spirit and strength under adverse conditions. For example, the heroine of Aimée Thurlo's *Cisco's Woman* (1996), Laurel Brewster, has debil-itating problems with asthma that make tribal detective Cisco Watchman sym-pathetic and protective. Despite this personal physical weakness, Laura proves loyal to her brother and then to Cisco. A Frail Flower, she nonetheless holds up during difficult times, and the romantic lead begins to think of her nature as "strength forged in adversity." Historical romances featuring Native Americans use the inherent dangers of captivity, frontier life, and forced marriages to celebrate female power and empowerment through their heroines' courage, in-telligence, endurance, honor, determination, loyalty, tolerance, and gentle hu-manity. The heroines win the hearts of warriors as much by their spirit, courage, defiance, and fortitude as by their beauty. Typical is Lauren Wilde's heroine, Isabel de Espejo, in *Beloved Captive* (1997). She has been a spoiled and pam-pered daughter in a protective Spanish household, but she learns to love and respect the young Comanche chieftain Stands Alone. Stands Alone had been her childhood playmate but had claimed her by force after her father had gone back on the marriage pact he had made, one that sealed the peace between Comanches and Spanish settlers in what is now New Mexico. When a cruel Spanish rival takes Stands Alone prisoner and sends him as a slave to the silver mines in central Mexico, Isabel proves her love by finding her lover's family in the Sangre de Cristo Mountains, convincing them she is honorable, strong, brave, and pure of heart—a capable warrior woman—and accompanying the Coman-che warriors in his rescue. She endures an unaccustomed and grueling horse ride, at a fast pace day and night through hostile country—sweltering desert, rugged mountains, almost impenetrable brush, and a searing inferno the Spanish called *Jornada del Muerto* (Journey of the Dead)—and helps free Stands Alone. She returns to the Comanche stronghold a happy woman.

Because the romantic tradition is life-affirming, celebrating marriage, birth, and parenthood, romances express a deep-rooted optimism, a hope that the future will be better than the present and that the family units forged by love will endure. This genre need has led some writers with Native American heroes or heroines to avoid those periods of history in which Indian populations were decimated, choosing instead epochs in which the Indians could still move farther west and escape detection or white controls. Janelle Taylor, for example, after a saga based on the lives and loves of Lakota warrior Gray Eagle, his white wife Alisha Williams, and their heirs over a time span from 1776 to 1873 (the Ecstasy Saga), tells readers that she does not have the heart to continue the saga into the period after the defeat of Custer at the Little Big Horn. This is because she wants to leave her characters in a time when happiness and survival were still possible: "I want to say good-bye to my people while they are free and happy, not carry them through agony and near annihilation" (*Forever Ecstasy*, 472).

Other writers have focused on peoples of mixed blood who must choose between the old ways of their Indian ancestors and the new ways of the white frontiersmen, a choice between a way that will inevitably lead to hardship, pain, loss, and death, and a way that will enable them to help their wilder, freer brothers through education, journalism, and legal and financial influence. Bronson Kane, for example, in Lanzoni and Riley's *Comanche*, is both heir to his white mother's and uncle's prosperous ranch and the fortune it has generated, and heir to his Comanche chieftain father's tribal leadership at a time when the Comanches must choose either reservation life or migration to less inhabited areas. After a fierce internal battle, Kane, a Harvard-educated lawyer, chooses the white way and begins by cleaning up the corrupt local government that has blamed Comanches for the excesses and violence of its thieving employees.

In a double romance story, *Savage Rapture* (1982), Sylvie Sommerfield has a white doctor, out of love for his Cheyenne bride, return east to use his finances and political skill to fight for and protect his wife's tribe. Later, the doctor trains his Cheyenne-raised son (Cade/Sun Knife) in white medicine and surgical skills to help his people fight the epidemics that threaten to wipe out Indian tribes as whites move west. When his influence can no longer protect the tribe of the woman he loves, he returns to her, bringing with him a wealthy heiress (Lauren), who wins the heart of a Cheyenne brave (Running Wolf). Her nursing skills, combined with those of the father-son team, prevent an epidemic from wiping out the tribe, while the father-son team's political savvy helps stave off a threatened bloodbath. The son asks, "Is it not clear, Father, that we must learn to live together or surely as the sun god rises, we will die?" and verbalizes the sacrifices that must be made if his people are to survive (117).

Cassie Edwards's *Savage Whispers* (1989) begins with the Kiowa imprisoned in Florida dungeons and ends with them on a reservation in Oklahoma, ill-used by Indian haters who steal sacred religious items, unable to perform the sacred Sun Dance because not a single buffalo can be found for the ceremony, and bargaining with indifferent politicians for their future security and comfort. The heroine must sacrifice much to be with her Kiowa warrior, and he must battle his own suspicions about her motives.

Georgina Gentry's *Cheyenne Song* (1998; the novel builds on Howard Fast's *The Last Frontier*) re-creates the passage of approximately three-hundred Cheyenne across fifteen hundred miles, fighting four major skirmishes and outwitting ten thousand soldiers, only to be slaughtered when they attempted to escape from Camp Robinson, where they were held for relocation. Gentry has a handful escape, thanks to her heroine's former fiancé, who finally realizes he has lost her love to her Cheyenne protector. Likewise, in *Walk into the Night* (1996), Beverly Bird recounts the final devastating conflicts between Texas rangers and Comanches through the story of a white male captive and his Comanche wife, who hold out until their only choice is death or confinement on an Oklahoma reservation. As a consequence of the nightmare possibilities still looming at their close, romances with Plains Indian central figures often are bittersweet, with the potential for tragedy making lovers cling more firmly to one another. In a sense, the threat of disaster and even genocide parallels the outside threats that make modern wartime romances bittersweet and intense: love and sentiment have extra force when the outside world promises to disintegrate.

Indian romances fit the traditional genre patterns in other ways. In order to emphasize the healing, reconciling power of love, romance writers build their plots around lovers crossing barriers, from the *Romeo and Juliet* barrier of feuding families to barriers of social class and wealth, nationality, culture, and race. In Lanzoni and Riley's *Comanche*, the heroine's first fiancé had been captured, tortured, and killed slowly by hostile Indians, so when she learns she has unknowingly married a "half-breed Comanche," she is terrified, calls him a savage beast and murderer, and flees. It takes kidnapping and almost three-hundred pages of forced contact with these "savages" for her to change that view. In Ruth Langen's *Malachite* (1998), Onyx Jewel loves a Comanche princess, but she refuses to give up her people and follow him into the white world. Unknowingly, he leaves her pregnant with a son, Malachite, who grows up despising his white father and feeling separate from both worlds until love brings him a sense of belonging. The warrior hero of Sara Orwig's *Warrior Moon* (1995), Lone Wolf, hates the white man for killing his wife, but he falls in love with a white woman named Vanessa, who is on her way to a Denver convent when she finds the wounded Kiowa brave, heals him, and shares his love. Together they rescue Vanessa's two sisters, a Kiowa girl, and a Comanche grandmother from savage whites who rape, murder, and pillage.

The half-Chinook hero of Theresa Scott's semicomic romance, *Captive Legacy* (1996), who was raised by Jesuits after his white father officially married a white woman and rejected his "country wife" and his Indian children, seeks personal revenge. He resents the "country wife" practice so common in the Oregon territory of the early 1800s and, partly in retaliation, takes a feisty and naive white captive as his own "country wife." He argues to himself that turnabout is fair play, but her courage and their growing mutual love overcome barriers of resentment, and the young man discovers that revenge is not sweet.

Thus, stories that begin with racial hatred and cultural misunderstanding end with understanding and compassion as the love between a man and a woman bridges alien worlds and reveals human commonalities behind disturbing and sometimes seemingly insurmountable differences.

Romances in which a Native American or someone of mixed Indian and white blood is a romantic lead fall into two major categories: historical romances and present-day romances.

NATIVE AMERICANS IN HISTORICAL ROMANCES

Whether consciously or subconsciously introduced, distortions of reality are necessary in the romance genre to meet readers' needs, whether those needs are to enjoy a bit of male bashing, to vicariously experience an idealized male, to fantasize about being brave, strong, and independent but at the same time loved and valued, sexually satisfied but also appreciated and respected. Although many romance writers make apparently good-faith efforts to accommodate historical facts and include some legitimate Native American lore, in general the Native American elements are not central to romance themes and in fact could not be, given indigenous attitudes toward romance. Instead, we must return to and rephrase the question asked at the beginning of this chapter: What genre needs produced the escapist Indian romance?

The first answer lies in the peculiar status of the Indian in U.S. society. Unlike other romantic and exotic groups (Cossack horsemen or Mongol hordes, for example), Indians seem familiar and adaptable. Americans, in general, have a sense of ownership of the Indian that doesn't exist with other wild, free, and exotic bands. After all, Indians are the first Americans; members of the mainstream culture have grown up with Indians as a part of their history, however incomplete or distorted the view, and have thrilled to stories of their virtues. As Philip Deloria argues, for Americans, playing Indian is both a literal activity and an overarching metaphorical construct, an imaginative safety valve that finesses the strictures of a limiting mainstream identity. Childhood games may have set Indians against cowboys, but every child who fantasized about being Indian has inevitably interpreted that role positively—independent, rebellious, spirited, capable, skilled, doomed, but noble. As modern life increasingly demands conformity to an identity in an established and inflexible hierarchy, the role-playing of fantasy lives becomes a significant zone of comfort. Many Americans take pride in fantasizing that some portion of their ancestral blood is Indian, and speculate about the cross-cultural encounters between antagonistic groups that ended in their varying degrees of assimilation. The Indian romance subgenre taps into such mainstream American (and Canadian) childhood and adult fantasies.

Second, the nature of the genre requires romance writers to set in motion irreconcilable opposites, opposites that fit well with white fantasies about Indians, particularly given the recent emphasis on empowered Native American women—the submission and male dominance inherent in captivity versus the female empowerment and independence admired by modern female readers. The heroines must be taken captive against their will, defenseless, enslaved, but must also, thereby, be freed of sexual and social restraints and find sexual fulfillment and meaningful life roles. They begin their romantic encounters as possessions but transform themselves into beloved women. At the same time the male figure must embody the tension of oppositions: his public self must be strong, forceful, manly, but his private self must be loving, caring, adoring, appreciative. A related fantasy is the reinvention of the self, a truly American frontier tradition that made the Old West a place of second chances.

Historical romances are generally set in two key time periods: (1) the eighteenth-century colonial period, including the time of the French and Indian War, the American Revolution, and the post-Revolution expansion westward; (2) the nineteenth-century frontier era, with encounters mainly on the plains of the Midwest and West, in Texas and the Southwest, and in the Pacific Northwest. Romances set in the first period seem more firmly based on historical records of early abductions (diaries, eyewitness accounts, family stories passed down orally and finally written up) than do those set in the nineteenth century. They also tend to emphasize major differences between tribes and strong national alliances forged in conflicts among English colonists, British, and French in contrast to the nineteenth-century romances' focus on diverse tribes uniting in common cause. The historical colonial and postcolonial period was extensively documented by varying observers, and this offers the writer-researcher plentiful authentic material. The later conflict took place at distant frontier outposts, and, perhaps because the period just before the final defeat of the Plains Indians has been so romanticized within mainstream culture, first by East Coast newspapers, then by dime and pulp novels, it lends itself easily to the imaginative distortions of fiction.

According to many modern romance novels with eighteenth- and nineteenth-century settings, Native American and mainstream American attitudes toward love and romance differ greatly, with Native Americans frequently representing all of the qualities that romantic heroines seek in a lover/husband: not simply good looks and manly strength and courage, but gentleness, romance, a desire to please both in bed and in general, self-sacrifice, commitment to family and community, a willingness to accept what a woman chooses to give and to recognize her need for independence and challenge. In turn, the Native American heroines represent all that American and Canadian women might wish for themselves: independence, competence, physical courage, survival skills as well as artistic skills, a wild freedom and lack of restraint that enable unfettered choices about sexual relationships and lifestyle, exotic beauty and desirability, and caring lovers who choose them over family, race, and culture. Whether directly stated or implicit, the following contrasts between white and Native American persist throughout romance novels with an Indian romantic male lead (no matter the tribe) and a white female:

WHITE	NATIVE AMERICAN
The white women have heard lurid tales about savages, are initially horrified by the warpaint, but then pleasantly surprised by the reality	The Native Americans are offended by the white women's rudeness & lack of cultural understanding
Marriage a practical alliance; husbands chosen by parents or economic necessity	Marriage for romance: individual choice; parents advise but don't push

White males greedy & lustful; take sexually & even rape	Indian males gentle, giving, and loving; give sexually; rape rare (except bad Indians from opposing tribe)
Males obsessed with property; hide valuables & kill for them; stingy; people less important than financial gain	Enjoy sharing: willing to leave things behind; share food, clothing, & valuables; generous; people more important than possessions
Individual hoards	Community shares, gives freely
Males own property & use power of pursestrings to tyrannize & control women	Women control family & tribal property: use power of pursestrings to support community
Women chattel/property; disenfranchised; restricted to household activities & biological functions; no say about politics or about own futures; never leaders; condemned for being outspoken	Women respected community members with full voting rights; expected to participate in community decisions; not warriors or hunters usually, but options open; right to vote; right to voice views; may be leaders or chieftains
Wives' property becomes their husbands'	Wives retain property; own dwelling and all in it
Divorce difficult; male prerogative	Divorce easy; Indian women simply put man's belongings outside dwelling, weave a basket, or return home to parents
Men choose	Men and women choose equally
Outspoken women rejected	Outspoken women admired
Lack ability to intuit emotions & needs of those they care about; deny feelings	Have psychic powers, intuitive extra senses so they know the emotions & needs of loved ones and can find them when they are in trouble; embrace feelings
Fear the insane & the deaf & dumb; mock the physically challenged; reject orphans	Take special care of deaf & dumb; tolerant of & sympathetic to the insane; give the physically challenged special roles in community; welcome orphans into family
As a culture, dirty; distrust baths; stink; no concept of germs; some herbal remedies but too much reliance on opiates	As a culture, clean; bathe frequently with aromatic natural soaps and oils; perfumes; some concept of sterilizing; opiates only for religious purposes; herbal medicines
Women's clothing impractical: stays, layers, restrictive bloomers; hard leather shoes	Women's clothing practical yet beautiful: solf doeskin, porcupine and bead decorations, skimpy underwear; soft moccasins
Senseless slaughter; rape of the land; create wasteland	Kill only what is needed to survive; respect for animals; leave enough to replenish & renew (ex.: take only 1 of every 3 wild onions)

| Lost in the woods; at odds with nature | At home and in tune with nature |
| Excess or puritanical restraint | Moderation |

The contrast list could be extended indefinitely, providing a useful schema for prospective romance writers. The present point, however, is that gestures toward verisimilitude aside, the societies constructed in these books have very little to do with the real people invoked.

Moreover, many of these Native American romance novels are gender statements in which the Indian male and his community set a positive standard against which the white male and many aspects of the eighteenth century and early nineteenth century are measured and found wanting, in both minor and major ways. Twentieth-century ideologies, in fact, drive the critiques of the earlier periods. Though life with the Indians is a shock at first, it usually proves inviting, natural, practical, and even pleasurable, once the whites get over their preconceptions and prejudices; the heroes and heroines who have lived among these idealized Native Americans often regret reentering the white world. The following comments are typical:

Hallie was surprised at how restricted she felt wearing her petticoats, dress, shoes, and stockings. The Lakota women had the right idea, she thought, as she folded her doeskin tunic and placed it in her saddlebags along with her moccasins. (Baker, *Hawk's Woman*, 323–324)

As they prepared to watch the four-day rite celebrating a chaste girl's ascent to womanhood, Honey was astonished to learn . . . that it was the people's most sacred ceremony, an accolade. . . . It struck her that in a society in which a woman was so honored, a female might not be restricted to being a servant or confined to being an ornament on her husband's arm; she might even be considered fit to be a medicine woman. . . . When Cameron told her that next to Ussen, the most revered deity was White Painted Woman, Honey was certain she had misunderstood . . . she began to see the people as more complicated than the white eyes' curse of "savage" allowed. (Ford, *A Different Breed*, 291–292)

"This is all very confusing, John. A man should not be born a chief, he should earn that right." . . . "It is important that a man have money?" Dakota questioned. "I have never thought you could measure a man's worth by his worldly possessions." (O'Banyon, *Dakota Dreams*, 102–103)

Looking at the fort now made the structure appear, not so much a beacon in a sea of wilderness as she had once supposed, but more like a white sore upon the beauty of the land, its walls and bastions appearing foreign and prickly, instead of welcoming. (Kay, *White Eagle's Touch*, 331)

. . . she couldn't help but be reminded of the difference between this and the Blackfeet's reception of her, when she'd been a newcomer in their camp. No one there had made fun of her; no one there had tried to make her feel inadequate. Most had gone out of their way, in fact, to find something of worth that she had done that they could praise. And this, though the Blackfeet, as a tribe, had reason to distrust her.

   No, they'd adopted her into their tribe; they had even called her "sister."

   And yet, as she looked around her, she knew that there were those here tonight who would call those same Indians "savage." (Kay, *Gray Hawk's Lady*, 349)

The factual germ—that Native American tribes freely adopted some white captives and treated them well—floats in a sea of late twentieth-century sentiment and the self-righteousness of the newly enlightened. Regard for feelings, rather than any of the more traditional measures of worth, defines virtue.

   The spotlight the late twentieth century shone on sexual and social abuse shines brightly in many of these works. Young women who are abused by cruel stepfathers, authoritarian fathers, insensitive suitors, or roadside rapists find safe haven in the arms of loving Indians. In Edwards's *Savage Tears* (1997) Marjorie Zimmerman flees from her stepfather's drunken embraces into the arms of a loving protector, Spotted Horse of the Dakotas, and Maggie in Edwards's *Savage Embers* (1994) had been raped by a family friend pretending to comfort her after her father's funeral. Jeanine in Edwards's *Savage Splendor* (1996) has fled into the untamed wilderness to escape her uncle's brutal tyranny, and Autumn Dawn of Drymon's *Legend of Desire* had been sold to a whorehouse in St. Louis by her stepfather. Glory Halstead of Gentry's *Cheyenne Song* (1998) was repeatedly beaten by a wealthy older man who bought her hand in marriage by paying her father's debts, and he later raped and killed white frontier women to incite massacres of Cheyenne women and children.

   Clearly, these works perpetuate a myth of the ideal male living in a utopian society, set off against the secret depravity of white male authority figures. While it may seem unkind to list inaccuracies and distortions implicit in a genre that bills itself as harmless, if manipulative, fantasy, we should remember that Native Americans are real people who still live in a total community several million strong across the United States and Canada. Their religions, traditions, ways of life—their whole identities, past and present—are increasingly being used as fodder for the romance genre. Perhaps little damage is done to the dignity of real people by a distorted and inaccurate Regency romance, but even fervent cheerleading for lusty Native American warriors can be offensive, continuing the centuries-old tradition of refusing to see the Indian whole. The following are key ways in which credibility breaks down when such romances ignore or deny linguistic and cultural realities, the differences that define culture.

   (1) *Language differences are presented as irrelevant*, and little or no attempt is made to deal with translation difficulties that result from cultural, environmental, and social differences and alternative views of the world. Occasionally, some explanation is offered as to why a Native American of the

eighteenth or nineteenth century would speak English fluently (attendance at a white school as a child, earlier captives who taught others the Indian language, mixed-blood relatives, contact with a historical mixed-blood family like the Bents of Bent's Fort). Other times, Indians speak odd English because they have supposedly learned it from reading Shakespeare, or they communicate in the broken Indian-speak of the most offensive fiction of the past: "White man heap bad trouble," "Woman in man's clothes, you have been saved." Most of the time, however, fictional captives learn Indian language or sign language with amazing rapidity:

She quickly picked up a few Indian words and soon, using the words she knew and gestures that were universal, she was able to communicate in the most elemental way. (Baker, *Hawk's Woman*, 285)

The Cheyenne tongue is one of the most difficult of the Indian languages, and you have mastered it in weeks. (Hart, *Silken Savage*, 81).

How truly universal are gestures? What, exactly, does "mastery" involve? the cynic might wonder. But such questions are irrelevant in the whimsical world of romance, wherein lovers magically and intuitively understand one another. After a little over two weeks among the Lenape, Tess, in Colleen Faulkner's *Captive* (1994), understands fairly well and converses rapidly in sign language. Most of Cassie Edwards's heroines seem to absorb the new Indian language (no matter the tribe or the linguistic difficulty) almost overnight, helped along by the fact that even when singing ritual songs and chants, the Indians obligingly recite in English as well as Dakota or Tlingit or whatever other native tongue, so that the captive visitor can understand. And young men raised for most of their childhood among Native Americans somehow learn English well enough in a few years to compete successfully at Harvard or other such institutions. Yet even a cursory survey of a few Navajo words suggests the difficulty of learning a new language based on an alternative vision of reality, in this case of spatial relationships: *nlaah* (go ahead); *nlaahdee* (from over yonder); *nlaahdi* (over there); *nlaahdi nanina* (stay away from here); *nlaahji* (over yonder); *nlahgoo* (right over there close by); *nlei* (that one over there); *nleidi* (over there); *nleigoo* (way over there; there it goes) (Wall and Morgan, *Navajo-English Dictionary*, 137). Clearly, Navajo makes subtle distinctions not even dreamed of in English. Janelle Taylor is one of the few romance writers to call attention to the difficulty of language learning:

Their [Lakota Sioux] words were not positioned in the same sentence order as English: time was always mentioned first; adjectives and prepositions followed nouns; direct objects went before verbs; plurality was shown with verbs, not nouns; and certain endings identified the sex of the speaker or listener. In many cases, *is* and *was* were left out of sentences . . . and dialects differed in . . . pronunciation. (*Forever Ecstasy*, 130)

Love may conquer all, but readers seem not to want to hear that grammar is less forgiving.

(2) *Differences of cuisine* (what is eaten and how it is prepared, served, and eaten) *are ignored, made light of, or presented as quaint or interesting*: that diet of acorns helped her lose weight; surely that wasn't dog she was eating—it was so tasty; she learned to fix gourmet Indian dishes that are healthy—pemmican with nuts and grains. Edwards's Letitia in *Savage Promise* (1992) finds eating with her fingers tolerable but is a bit bothered by the bowl of grease and the smelly fish oil that accompany every meal. Later, however, she can joke at her initial squeamishness.

(3) *Captives are treated as beloved women instead of slave labor: chosen as wives of chiefs, protected from the work required of others, their weaknesses forgiven.* In Jeanette Baker's *The Reckoning* (1997), because Lady Alexandra Winthrop, granddaughter of the Duke of Leicester, is taken captive in Canada to be given as wife to Red Wing, chief of the Anishinabe (Ojibway), she is treated with affectionate care. Unlike her fellow captives, she is not expected to do heavy physical labor; instead, she is pampered and groomed. Likewise, the heroine in Edwards's *Savage Tears* (1997) marvels at "being treated like a princess" and is pleasantly surprised at "how a Dakota husband doted on his wife": "She could hardly believe it, for her mother had worked like a slave for her husbands, and earned no respect whatsoever." Now Marjorie feels "bubbly inside" from her contentment and the blessing of "genuine" love (244), and even more bubbly when she learns that "Cleaning is not a Dakota wife's duty. . . . It is the man's" (25), so she is free to make paper dolls for the cute Indian children.

(4) *Life in Indian camp is idyllic—they are just like "us," only better.* Through her experiences with the Shawnee prince Fire Dancer at Fort Belvedere, in the Pennsylvania Colony, artist Mackenzie Daniels, in Colleen Faulkner's *Fire Dancer* (1997), discovers Indian women have more say in tribal affairs and are freer than colonial women. Katrina Wellington, the spoiled heroine of Karen Kay's *White Eagle's Touch* (1998), finds that where she expected beggars and thieves, she finds people of honor, truth, and joy:

She could almost feel the happiness that abounded in the camp, and it occurred to her that this emotion was as foreign to her as the people were themselves. The Indians clearly exhibited a sense of lightheartedness that she would have been hard-pressed to find within her own world. These people seemed carefree . . . insouciant.
    Had she ever felt that way?
    She couldn't recall a time. (84)

In turn, Cassie Edwards's Spotted Horse asks his white bride, "My wife, are we not all one big happy family in our Dakota village?" and she replies, "There is nothing like it in the white communities. There is much suspicion of neighbors. There is much tension. For certain, everyone locks their doors at night" (*Savage*

Tears, 62). Edwards concludes that after a life of misery and hardship among whites, "Thanks to her wonderful Dakota husband, she [the heroine] had everything that was good on this earth!"

(5) *Sex with a Native American is the American woman's ideal.* Puritanical white sex for procreation is set off against Indian sex for pleasure and mutual satisfaction, a gift of love. Usually, Indian lovers are depicted as careful and giving; the warrior teaches the woman to enjoy sex by slowly building up the fires of her passion before entering her (never rape; never painful or disgusting). Cassie Edwards's novels are typical in their focus on the heroine's sexual awakening and her passionate arousal. Sometimes, however, passion overwhelms, as in Georgina Gentry's *Cheyenne Song* (1998), where the heroine resists, only to find herself responding pleasurably:

No man had ever held her in such a frenzy of emotion, no man had ever kissed her as if he couldn't get enough of the taste of her. . . . Despite herself, she felt her nipples go turgid. To her surprise, she could not stop herself from arching against his demanding hands. Glory had never known passion; her husband had only expected her to lie there and let him make his feeble attempts at mating her. . . . This barbaric savage's seeking hands and mouth were demanding a response. (134)

(6) *Indian men always break their tribe's tradition of polygamy and vow monogamy because of the depth of their love,* as do Gentry's, Edwards's, and Kay's heroes, among others. In Kay's *Night Thunder's Bride* (1999) the Blackfoot romantic lead takes great pains to break off a marriage pledge his parents made for him so that his white wife will be his only wife. In Taylor's *Forever Ecstasy* (1991) it is a Sioux woman who rejects tradition: "One thing of which Morning Star was certain was that her husband would have one mate, not several as was acceptable in her society. . . . She could not accept sharing her love, her husband, with another woman or women" (29). Often, too, *romances offer simple solutions to complex situations,* since love entanglements, not social and familial problems, are their central concern. For instance, Gentry's *Cheyenne Splendor* (1994) demonstrates how the Cheyenne tradition of nursing infants until age three, in order to take advantage of the mother's natural milk supply, produced the tribal customs of abstinence to avoid pregnancy and assure a continued flow of milk and of multiple wives for male sexual relief. In Gentry's story the wife/heroine comes from a rich and genteel Boston family but has chosen to stay with her dog-soldier warrior. However, she opposes his taking another woman and almost leaves him because of their mutual sexual frustration. But then, deus ex machina, the birth of twins brings a doctor's announcement of her inability to have more children, so the problem is solved: sex is possible; the marriage is saved; and their "eternal love" can avoid the practical realities of repeated pregnancies in a time of no effective birth control except abstinence.

(7) *Spoiled, pampered white women adjust easily to a life of toil* (sewing, fixing meals, setting up tepees, tanning skins) and find satisfaction and fulfill-

ment from it (even happily chewing buffalo hide to soften it). Pampered San Franciscan Letitia Wilson, in Edwards's *Savage Promise* (1992), instructed by her patient Tlingit husband, learns to prepare Tlingit meals, make traps and snares, and scrape and stretch pelts for clothing, bags, and overshoes. Ignoring the smell, she chews full-length the edges of a fox skin to soften the leather so a bone needle will penetrate it, awkwardly smiling at her husband as she does so (369). Tanya Martin in Carolyn Hart's *Silken Savage* (1985) goes even further: having learned to shoot well with a bow and arrow, count coups, gut and skin game, build shelters, take scalps, and torture prisoners, she thinks to herself, "Lord, the things I do for that man!" (105). In fact, she becomes so assimilated that the writer has to contrive situations to keep readers sympathetic: Can a white captive behave like a warrior and retain audience sympathy for her captivity?

The alternative is the white woman who can't get it right. Her cooking makes people sick and her carelessness burns down lodges; the clothes she makes don't even imitate human shapes, much less human sizes; and her movement through an Indian camp is an *I love Lucy* slapstick comedy of errors. Nonetheless, the brave warriors adore her, eat her sickening food, cater to her needs, and don't even send her away when she impetuously disregards orders to stay home as her husband goes to battle. Such is the heroine of Carolyn Hart's comedy *Night Flame* (1995), a spoiled Southern belle completely unsuited for cooking, sewing, cleaning, or other traditional tasks who finds her place in the community as a warrior woman by accidentally killing an enemy warrior and driving off the enemy horses.

(8) *Whites reject peoples of mixed blood as "savage half-breeds" while most Indians accept peoples of mixed blood as their own.* A number of novels turn on the ill-treatment of "half-breeds": (a) John Walking Hawk, the son of a French trapper and a Lakota medicine woman, who is tortured and shot and labeled a cold-blooded killer when he protects his own (Madeline Baker, *Hawk's Woman*); (b) half-Shoshone Sky McClellan, whose family and visiting friends were massacred because an important man's son loved her in defiance of his father (Linda Sandifer, *Embrace the Wind*); (c) Hawk, the half-Comanche son of a Texas rancher, who is beaten close to death, then shanghaied because of his love for the ranch manager's daughter, but whose integrity and strength finally win out over prejudice and hate (Janis Reams Hudson, *Hawk's Woman*).

(9) *Love blossoms not only across cultures but also across time.* Madeline Baker's *Feather in the Wind* (1997) envisions a Sioux chieftain's prayers for the strength to guide his people answered by a vision of a modern white woman who crosses time "to fulfill a love beyond time." Catherine Hart's comic romance *Charmed* (1996) also turns on the possibility of a time warp, one created by a brother of the great Shawnee leader Tecumseh, a Merlin-like magician of great power with a variety of magical spells and enchantments. Called Silver Thorn, he has developed powers that go beyond traditional shaman skills in an attempt to save Tecumseh from his foretold death. By means of a magic amulet

sent forward in time from 1813 to 1996 to Seven Caves, Ohio, Silver Thorn creates a warp in time that carries chubby history teacher Nikki Swan back through the ages, where she meets her great-great-great-great-great-grandmother. While Silver Thorn tries to figure out how her presence might help his brother, the couple fall in love. There is much silliness as, impassioned, she conceives Silver Thorn's child, loses weight from eating acorns, acquires a protective squirrel spirit, clashes with Tecumseh's evil third brother (Tenskwatawa), and magically travels back to her own time, where her best friend soundly defeats Tenskwatawa and returns him to the past a shamed cripple. Nikki is joined by her eighteenth-century Shawnee lover, who has learned English from reading Shakespeare and who adapts to twentieth-century comforts surprisingly quickly. He teaches classes on Shawnee culture and language at the local university, consults for regional museums and historical sites, and collaborates with Nikki on a factual history of the Shawnee tribe. Moreover, "a twitch here, a nod there, and some magical Shawnee incantations" allow the couple to live "comfortably" (392).

Some of these romances recall the mainstream Tarzan tradition, that is, a white child raised among indigenous people, then returned to "civilization." In O'Banyon's *Dakota Dreams*, the hero, Dakota Remington, has been brought up since birth as the beloved son of Arapaho chieftain Two Moons after his white parents died during a blizzard, but the power of his grandfather, the Marquis of Weatherford, has stretched across the ocean to persuade Two Moons, on his deathbed, to send his white son to the young man's grandfather. There, Dakota must learn a new way of thinking and behaving, and try to fulfill his obligations to both birthrights, while teaching the whites around him the rectitude, honor, and bravery of so-called savages. The brave who had taken Tanya Wilson prisoner in *Silken Savage* reappears as Adam Savage, the mixed-blood son of a local rancher, to court his "Indian-captive" bride as a white when she is returned to her family, just as Spotted Wolf must discover his own white roots and go on a lecture tour to enlighten Eastern whites about Indian realities before he can recapture the heart of his beloved captive Jennifer Carlisle in Betty Brooks's *Comanche Sunset* (1998). In Kathleen Harrington's *Fly with the Eagle* (1997) the jaded aristocrat Thorne Blakesford must face danger in Constantinople to rescue his highly competent, sophisticated, and athletic Cheyenne princess, Jennifer "Morning Rose" Elkheart, the granddaughter of an American senator. Karen Kay's *Gray Hawk's Lady* (1997) provides an interesting twist on the sophisticated Indian theme. A genteel English lady and her father doing a cultural study of the American Indian hire trappers to capture a representative Blackfoot to interview; ironically, they capture a noble chieftain who is outraged by this barbarous treatment, but his anger turns to passion as he teaches father and daughter to respect the nobility and equality of Native Americans. He ends up saving the lady's father's reputation and finances, at the same time publicly correcting some of the denigrating myths white scholars were perpetrating about Indians. Other romance novels focus on little-known but factual historical details, like the Cherokees who tried so hard to be assimilated in Georgia that they acquired plantations and owned slaves. Clara Wimberly's *Cherokee Wind* (1997) is the story of Trace Hambleton, a mixed-blood Cherokee who escaped the reservation and returned to the family plantation, determined to regain title to his stolen land. He does so by marrying the daughter of the senator whose greed cost Trace's father his life and land. There, authentic history provides background interest but romance nevertheless dominates.

Some historical romances project onto Indian women the fears of modern brides: marriage will ruin a career! Kathleen Drymon's heroine in *Legend of Desire* (1998) has trained all her life to be a medicine woman to her tribe, and avoids marriage in order to pursue her medical interests. When forced into marriage with a brave warrior from another tribe (whom she finds incredibly seductive), she first puts off consummation of the marriage for far longer than is credible, and then vows that she will never truly give her heart to her husband because her profession comes first: "I have never enjoyed staying inside a lodge all day" (140). Eventually, however, she learns that marriage both fulfills her life and strengthens her understanding and knowledge so that she can be a far better medicine woman than she was ever capable of being as an innocent virgin or uncommitted lover. In this case, a modern theme overcomes all pretense of authenticity, and readers presumably "see through" the purported setting to enjoy the treatment of a contemporary dilemma in an unexpected setting. Elisabeth Macdonald's *Bring Down the Sun* (1996) reverses Drymon's argument, with Macdonald's heroine a skilled doctor trained by her father but with no way to win the credentials necessary for merit in her world. By marrying a half-Blackfoot army guide and living with his tribe, this career-centered heroine not only gains a devoted husband but also medical acceptance, training in herbal medicine by a respected medicine woman, and willing Blackfoot patients who value her skill, not a diploma.

It is only in the case of fully assimilated tribes like the slave- and plantation-owning Cherokees of 1830s Georgia that the European love conventions make sociological sense, a fact that Janet Dailey uses to advantage in her Scots-Cherokee Stuart set, *The Proud and the Free* (1994) and *Legacies* (1995). Dailey's Indian romances usually turn on community prejudices and conflicts carried out within families in modern settings (as in *Ride the Thunder*, 1980). However, her Stuart series begins with assimilated Cherokees (Protestant plantation owners active in politics and educated at Harvard) and follows the racial and political conflicts that divide the Cherokee Nation as Andrew Jackson refuses to uphold Supreme Court rulings protecting Cherokee property ownership and allows Georgian greed to force the Cherokee removal. Taking her cue from Shakespeare, she explores the national tragedy through the personal tragedy of two families, allied by marriage and separated by political loyalties, as they travel the Trail of Tears and come to terms with new realities on the Oklahoma frontier, and as their grandchildren continue the family schisms that result in Cherokees fighting on opposing sides in the Civil War.

Because of the nature of the genre, no matter how intriguing the story or admirable the lovers, romance novels set in the eighteenth and nineteenth centuries involving cross-cultural lovers will invariably distort reality in one direction or another, simply because of their tunnel-vision focus on romantic love. Even for whites of those periods, romantic love was not necessarily considered a sound basis for a marital relationship, and sentiment was certainly not a part of the survivalist mentality of Native Americans of those times.

NATIVE AMERICANS IN TWENTIETH-CENTURY ROMANCE SETTINGS

Romances featuring Native Americans in a modern setting most often fit two common romance genre patterns: (1) the rogue male who chooses sex over love and must therefore be tamed and taught higher-level emotions and (2) the independent, career-oriented woman who has purposely closed off the possibility of a serious love relationship and must be shown the value of love and the balance it brings to one's life. Whether the romantic interest is focused on a male or a female lead character, the running conflict of modern romances with Native Americans as central figures is independence versus attachment: the freedom and loneliness of pursuing a private life or achieving in a career versus the personal sacrifices and responsibilities demanded in a love relationship.

Sandra Brown's *Honor Bound* (1986) employs the captivity tradition of the eighteenth and nineteenth centuries in a new, modern way. A rebellious Navajo prison escapee, Lucas Greywolf, takes a white hostage, Aislinn Andrews, to help him reach his beloved grandfather before the old man's death. A lawyer whose involvement with the American Indian Movement led to false charges (he organized a protest rally at which others started a brawl), disbarment, and a prison sentence, Greywolf is embittered. He is unhappy about his portion of white blood and about his inability to save his grandfather from a swindle that left him destitute and dishonored—forced to perform parts of solemn religious ceremonies in front of gawking tourists. He despairs at the loss of his right to practice law to help his people and is shamed that he, the grandson of a respected chief, ended up behind bars. Initially, the captive Andrews finds his eyes chilling—full of "unmitigated contempt," "uncompromising hatred," and "undiluted bitterness"—his face dark and "brooding" (11), and his movements like those of "a stealthy, sensuous, black cat" (26). He seems "a potentially dangerous animal" she fears to disobey (76). Yet, when she sees him among his family, so caring and concerned about his grandfather, so respectful of his mother (who confides that he is impulsive, short-tempered, and mistrustful, but good-hearted), she suddenly perceives him in a new way, and the unexpected passion they share before he is recaptured turns her world upside down. Unlike most romances, whose highest pinnacle is a closing marriage, Brown's romance begins with the marriage: Greywolf learns that Andrews has borne him a child, and he refuses to allow that child to grow up fatherless. He forces Andrews to marry

him and move to the reservation with him for their child's sake. The rest of the
novel concentrates on the bridges of understanding they build between two cultures that finally lead to Greywolf's regaining respect in both worlds, and Greywolf and Andrews discovering in one another a love that will endure.

Kathleen Eagle's *Carved in Stone* (1987), one of Silhouette's Ranch Rogue
series, also plays variations on the captivity theme. Eagle claims to base her
novel on a true story, that of an Indian extra in a South Dakota cowboy film;
tired of playing limited Indian stereotypes, he goes back to living Indian. In the
romance story, Sky Hunter has been playing stereotypical Hollywood Indians
(disgruntled/abused/discriminated against) so long that he has almost forgotten
who he really is (a full-blooded Sioux from the Rocky Mountains) and even his
real name (Danny). He has told his agent that he wants to play "a man . . . just
a man," not another stereotyped Indian nonentity. Yet, he continues his Hollywood role in his personal life, employing a hypnotic gaze, good horsemanship,
and slick patter to get women in bed. He assumes Elaina Delacourte will be
another easy, meaningless conquest. Delacourte, who had come to Wyoming to
research the Sioux for a Western romance novel, believes him when he claims
to have been a pack-trip guide and follows him into the mountains alone.
Though he intended an easy seduction, the journey across breathtaking Sioux
land reaffirms his contact with the earth and his heritage. When an airplane
spooks Sky's packhorse and he is injured, Delacourte demonstrates guts and
fortitude that awaken new feelings inside the jaded man and help him rediscover
himself and his capacity to truly love. As she fishes, sets up a tent, cooks, cares
for him, and even makes a travois to carry him, she sees through his role-playing
to discover "a man who made her feel the depth of her womanhood" (163).
However, it is only when she returns home that he discovers the extent of his
feeling for her and seeks her out on her territory. He has returned to acting but
will play no more stereotyped roles, and she now writes romances with a better
knowledge of Sioux and of men gleaned from real-life experience. Liberated
from their gender and cultural stereotypes, and both in satisfying careers, they
are free to truly love one another.

Elizabeth Lowell's *Warrior* (1991) follows a similar pattern, with injury and
illness providing the time and opportunity for love to flourish. Part-Indian (descended from Winter Moon and Bends Like the Willow) Nevada Blackthorn
has been what the Blackthorn men have been for hundreds of years: a warrior,
a former soldier of fortune, or a secret agent (his specific occupation is not
stated). He has the uncanny ability to tell when he is being approached from
behind, his fighting skills are honed to a deadly edge, and his unblinking green
eyes seem more those of a cougar than of a man. However, in order to survive
the atrocities he has been immersed in while teaching Afghanis armed with
flintlocks how to defeat Russians with tanks, he has paid the price of modern
warfare in his cold, aloof closing off of human relationships. The story centers
on how wildlife biologist Eden Summers wins his trust and love as she once
won the trust and love of the large black wolf who shadows her steps. When

Blackthorn is injured and Summers nurses him back to health, their love catches fire, and when she becomes sick and he must help her recover, the flames burn high. However, it is only when she gives him his freedom and walks away that he realizes how much he will lose if he fails to admit that his protective armor has been penetrated and that life without her is no life at all. Much of the novel describes their sexual encounters as Blackthorn struggles for restraint but is overpowered by passion, and then by a desire to live a complete life. Both *Carved in Stone* and *Warrior* exploit the premise that for a proud male the path to well-being requires an episode of vulnerability, one that can be responded to by a strong woman.

Janet Dailey's *Night Way* (1981) explores the relationship of an Arizona rancher and construction tycoon with his half-Navajo son, Hawk, the distance that separates them, and the inescapable ties that bind. Dailey emphasizes Hawk's difficulty bridging two worlds: the pain of not being accepted publicly by father and half-brother, and yet the strong, hidden bonds between father and son that bring Hawk love, acceptance, and understanding when his father dies. A young woman who befriended the father out of loneliness and compassion finds in the son the love and security she sought—once she gets past her stereotyped images and sees the greed behind his half-brother's and stepmother's smiles and the love behind the cold, hard face of Hawk.

In another variation on the theme of softness behind a hard mask, the loss of love leads to artistic achievement that ultimately reunites separated lovers. In Dinah McCall's *Tall-Chief* (1997), Morgan Tallchief, having lost his high school sweetheart in a fire, buries himself in art that uses an overlay of images of past and present to depict the modern Indian as embodying the skills of his ancestors. When his lost love and their daughter show up in his gallery unexpectedly, he learns that her family was in the Witness Protection Program and that the villains who killed her family still pursue her. However, this time he won't let these loved ones get away, for his deep commitment as a lover and as a father and his ancestral ties give him the strength to defeat hardened hitmen.

Anne Marie Duquette's *In the Arms of the Law* (1997) captures the other side of the coin: the hardworking Indian woman who has buried herself in her career (literally, as a researcher in a bat cave) but discovers the importance of balancing work and love. Jasentha Cliffwalker, an Apache proud of her heritage and also of her work as a biologist near Tombstone, Arizona, lives as a recluse on Bodine land near the Silver Dollar caves. She speaks Nidé, the ancient Apache tongue, and she has devoted her life to studying and protecting bats (and the three sets of petroglyphs their guano hides). However, when a greedy thief cuts petroglyphs out of the rock in Jasentha's caves and Jasentha and a former fiancé (Morgan) must work together to save the petroglyphs and find the person responsible, she rediscovers love and restores balance to her life.

The use of Native Americans in such present-day romance settings allows the writer to sprinkle in some interesting details about heritage, but these serve the same function as details about the French Quarter in a New Orleans romance or descriptions of urban streets in a New York romance. Cait London's Tallchief series is typical; set in Wyoming, these romances includes just enough about the Indian side of the family to justify the sons and daughters being high-spirited, eccentric, intuitive, and closely tied to the land. The stereotypical image of the Indian male as a dark, handsome, morose outsider, close to the earth, noted for his prowess and courage, somehow untamed and unquestionably phys-ically well endowed fits the romance standard of the rogue male figure. At the same time, the authentic Native American tradition of the woman as the pre-server of the hearth and the carrier of tradition calls for strong yet distinctly feminine heroines capable of independence, an image that fits with the feminist qualities of the modern romance heroine. (London's Tallchief women win rodeo medals with their superior horsemanship and accolades for their skilled weav-ing.) Native tradition, however, also provides a built-in counter to mainstream readers' fears of feminism gone awry—the need for balance in life, a balance that comes from accepting responsibility for love and family. In this way the strong career woman can be forgiven for discovering within herself a consuming love for one man, for that love gives her life balance and without it she fails to attain her fullest human potential. In other words, much of the time the modern Indian romance highlights mainstream male-female issues in characters playing stereotypical roles rather than presenting new, nontraditional situations and pro-tagonists. The Indian figure permits an indirect resolution of mainstream con-flicts between independence and attachment, freedom and sacrifice, without ruffling the feathers of white readers who might find such compromises in a modern, urban setting unacceptable. As the discussion may indicate, modern settings do call attention to legitimate issues and obviate the ludicrous anach-ronisms that characterize historical settings. What usually is still sacrificed, how-ever, is a balanced and sensitive portrait of Native American culture and people, since accommodating the romance genre conventions requires doing violence to the mores and folkways of the authentic cultures depicted.

Two exceptions, however, are the recent novels of Aimée Thurlo and Kath-leen Eagle. Thurlo brings a magical element to her romances as she incorporates Native American spiritual beliefs into romance. Eagle brings a down-to-earth realism to her treatment of the misunderstandings, failures, pain, and triumphs of cross-cultural romances. Both accomplish the difficult task of pouring the new (for the romance) wine of Indian culture into the old bottles of the genre, treating the new players with respect while indulging the age-old genre needs of the love story. Their works thus offer potentially new directions for the genre.

Aimée Thurlo: Navajo Magic as a Spur to Romance

Aimée Thurlo brings the conflict between Navajo magic and police investi-gative methods to the romance genre in her Four Winds trilogy. These novels trace the trials and romances of three brothers whose fates are bound by the blessing/curse of a nineteenth-century medicine man. This medicine man saved a white child from a skinwalker (a Navajo witch) and blessed the town of Four Winds for protecting him against white ranchers who misinterpreted his actions: "From this day on, Four Winds will be protected by the medicine of my people. The wicked who come here will never know peace, and if they remain, they will find that the cost is more than they ever dreamed they would pay" (*Her Destiny*, 12–13). Thereafter, the town seems indeed enchanted, a haven for good people fleeing trouble in the outside world, disillusioned people who rediscover hope in events that test their humanity. At regular intervals, a mysterious, vanishing Navajo peddler gives challenging gifts in payment for neighborly acts; these double-edged gifts transform people's lives, test their souls, and expose a secret evil that threatens the town. They also pave the way for romance between the lead characters, romance that might never have blossomed if not for the magical destiny created by the vanishing peddler.

In *Her Destiny* (1997) the gift is the spirit bowl of a skinwalker, which unleashes evil forces that test the inner strength of heroine Lanie Matthews; she must overcome haunting childhood fears, *chindi* (evil spirits), rebellious teenagers, and greedy townspeople before she can find love and acceptance. Sheriff Gabriel Blackhorse, whose *hataalii* ancestors (medicine men) once battled the powerful skinwalker, explains that the bowl was made from the ashes of a woman the skinwalker had loved and killed. What seems like simply a ghost story to Lanie has deeper significance to Blackhorse and his relatives, and they actively assist Lanie in her battle to overcome her inner fears while inadvertently exposing and exorcising the demons at the heart of the town. "Raised to accept many things the Anglo world sees as magic," Blackhorse nonetheless finds the results of the peddler's enchantments "unsettling" and even nightmarish (188). When Lanie purposefully smashes the spirit bowl, the *chindi* swirl up like black smoke. Blackhorse's flint hawk inside his medicine pouch protects the two of them, but the *chindi* take possession of the human villain and drive her to her death.

Her Hero (1996) depicts a very modern Navajo named Nydia discovering the power of Navajo spiritualism, which she had dismissed as "superstition." Stuck with the unpleasant task of calling on a *hataalii* singer-healer for the sake of her aged and ailing father-in-law, she arrives just in time to find the shaman, the youngest Blackhorse brother, Joshua, at the scene of his father's murder. Although Joshua is a traditionalist who has chosen to study as a shaman and to follow the Navajo Blessed Way, he is being framed for murdering his father (a skinwalker can increase his shamanistic powers through such an act). For Joshua "the Way" means finding strength through harmony and inner balance, and warding off chaos by maintaining an inner stillness. He must call on all of his training—his ability to cast spells, shift shape, and walk unseen—in order to defeat the evil skinwalker forces in league against him.

Nydia recognizes a power in Joshua that comes from his roots and his connection to the Navajo people, but she initially dismisses his idea that her accepting the property of someone who has died will bring with it contamination by *chindi*. Joshua's warning, "Don't discount what you don't understand" (35), goes unheeded, especially since the gift is so attractive: an exquisite Navajo rug, a deep Ganado red with each of three sections showcasing a water-sprinkler deity in blue, black, or gold and with rainbow-guardian figures protecting the borders. However, unlike most Navajo rugs, it lacks a purposely built-in flaw. The legend the peddler who gives it to her recounts is that Spider Woman, the Navajo deity who taught Navajos to weave blankets and rugs, became so angry at the weaver's failure to pay her tribute by weaving into the rug a hole reminiscent of the center of a spider's web that she clouded the weaver's mind and cursed all future owners of the rug with a similar fate until the artifact's perfection is somehow destroyed. This curse leads to skinwalkers shooting at Nydia and Joshua with human-bone fragments to contaminate them with the *chindi* and Joshua using black flint, charcoal, corn pollen, and ritual spells to protect them. By the end of the story Nydia has been forced to reevaluate her whole concept of *hataalii* powers and willingly shares in the spiritual rituals that restore her father-in-law to health. The cross-cultural element here is not between white and Indian but between a traditional Navajo and a modernized, assimilated Navajo, a more sophisticated and timely contrast than the heavy-handed works described earlier.

When former midwife Marlee Smith comes to Four Winds in *Her Shadow* (1998), the enchantment continues with the gift of a little raven carving that coincides with a cycle of mysterious illnesses that test friendships. Marlee has fallen in love with Four Winds' most eligible bachelor, Lucas Blackhorse, the town doctor and Gabriel Blackhorse's brother, and the wish the enchanted pedder grants her is for his love.

In each case the peddler's gift sets off a chain of events that tests the mettle of the receiver of the gift in the fires of chaos and violence, but their end result is always the exposure of evil in the town, the restoration of harmony, and the strengthening of the gift's recipient. The enchantment, thus, is twofold—dark and light—a harmonious blessing that can be received only when the curse has been overcome and evil ousted. The magical elements of Thurlo's stories fit her overriding theme that despite cultural and racial differences, Native Americans and whites can find romantic love, peace, and harmony together. However, to do so, both sides must be willing to compromise and to accept the mysteries and enchantments of each tradition rather than rejecting one or the other out of hand. Thurlo's plot events neatly evoke a Native American sensibility rather than a mainstream one, the concept (as we saw in Chapter 2) that order and harmony are the proper states of being, and that disruption of balance is the source of true evil.

Kathleen Eagle: Bridges Across Centuries and Cultures

Kathleen Eagle, who taught for seventeen years on a North Dakota Indian reservation and whose husband is of Lakota Sioux heritage, effectively bridges cultures by painting sympathetic portraits of cross-cultural lovers beset by believable problems, some produced by ethnic and social differences, some caused by personal failures of understanding and communication, some simply part of the human condition. Her recent romance novels are poignant, purposeful, provocative, and quirky.

Fire and Rain (1994), for example, moves between the rocky modern romance of Cecily Metcalf and Kiah Red Thunder and the troubled nineteenth-century romance of Priscilla Twiss and Whirlwind Rider, both separated off and on by the pull of different worlds but ultimately bound together by an enduring love. An old trunk Cecily buys at an auction contains the diary of Priscilla, the daughter of a missionary to the Lakota Sioux. The diary tells the story of Priscilla's enchantment with the Sioux in general and with Whirlwind Rider in particular, the growth of their romance, her rejection of his marriage proposal as part of a treaty agreement and her regret thereafter, her father's attempts to separate them, the Sioux conflicts with the U.S. military, and Priscilla's final choice of love and the suffering it would entail over the hypocrisy and cruelty of her father's world. Kiah tells Cecily, "I don't think anything is ever really dead. I think we have connections with . . . the past" (95), and Eagle goes on to demonstrate how the events of one century can impinge on the events of the next. After serving time in the military, Kiah comes back to a reservation split by protest and his sister raped and killed in a local jail. When Cecily has an opportunity to go to graduate school, he doesn't stop her, but when she returns as the tool of a powerful newspaper anxious to control the media spin on Sioux reactions to the Court of Claims' $106 million award for the Sioux claim to the Black Hills, conflict brings them back together. When Kiah learns that Priscilla not only died at Wounded Knee but also was his grandmother, he is ready to accept Cecily's feelings for him as a love that can cross ethnic and cultural barriers. Eagle's "Author's Note" points out her belief that "a piece of the American dream of freedom and justice for all was martyred [at Wounded Knee]" (370).

Sunrise Song (1996), in contrast, has a hard, realistic edge. It is a disturbing, nightmarish story of abuses that bridge generations—past Native Americans institutionalized for life for adhering to their traditional religious practices, for not speaking English, or for getting in the way of those who wanted their property; present Native Americans threatened and killed for asking too many questions about the past. Eagle bases her novel on research and speculation about a real place, the Hiawatha Insane Asylum for Indians, established in Canton, South Dakota, and operated by the Bureau of Indian Affairs from 1902 until 1934. Her story alternates between two time periods (1973 and the late 1920s and early 1930s) and between two sets of would-be lovers: the modern romance that develops between Michelle Benedict and a mixed-blood Lakota Sioux, Zane Lone Bull, a Vietnam War hero contemptuous of his unknown parents, and the earlier romance between Lone Bull's parents, Rachael Trainor and Adam Lone Bull, the latter another war hero willing to stand up for the rights he fought for on the battlefields of Europe. Michelle initiates an investigation when she tries to find the relatives of a Sioux buried on the grounds of the asylum that her aunt's husband ran. Zane's seemingly lunatic uncle bridges the two stories, for it is the uncle's unwarranted commitment to an insane asylum and his years of enduring sodomy and abuse that cost Adam Lone Bull his life and that help Michelle and Zane discover the truth: a nasty land grab. The representative of the Bureau of Indian Affairs, Rachael Trainor's brother, worked hand in glove with the director of the asylum to steal Indian land and to institutionalize victims or relatives of victims as a way to assure silence about the illegal activities. It is an ugly secret humanized by the plight of cross-cultural lovers destroyed when they refuse to give up one another or the people they hold dear.

Eagle's skill as a writer is that her story, despite its depiction of terrible outrages, does not read like heavy-handed white-bashing (as it would in less skilled hands). Instead, it works as a fictional whole, an interesting intertwining of lives that reveals much about human psychology, love, and villainy. Eagle captures the ease with which even family members, guided by their own fears and doubts, can be misled by the pronouncements of authorities. When Adam Lone Bull is institutionalized because he had been prying into his brother's situation, even Rachael, who by this time has fallen in love with him, initially believes that his anger is proof of his psychosis. When fettered and drugged, how does one prove one's sanity? Eagle's first set of lovers are sorely tested but prove true even in death; her second set bring healing and reconciliation as they expose past injustices, deal with present descendants still benefiting from and covering up past wrongs, and use legal means to recoup what had been unfairly taken. In spite of its emphasis on social justice, romance is at the heart of this novel. It is love that breaks barriers and overcomes differences. It is love that reveals truths. It is love that ultimately conquers. Eagle's cross-cultural lovers confirm that the perversions of a few do not represent the whole, and that love can bridge differences and bring understanding and genuine affection between very different peoples.

Drawing on her own experiences participating in the 1990 Sioux Big Foot Memorial Ride on horseback across 250 miles of frozen Dakota prairie, in symbolic recognition of the rugged winter journey made by Sioux ancestors that ended in the massacre at Wounded Knee, Eagle set out in *Reason to Believe* (1995) to "weave the healing spirit of the ride into a story about mending broken relationships and to convey the ride's investment in understanding in a way that only fiction can" (377). The result is a moving story of cross-cultural romance gone awry, and the husband's attempts to regain his wife's love and bridge the gap of cultural misunderstanding, hurt pride, and personal betrayals that have separated them. While giving readers a glimpse of the sudden, impulsive romantic passion and tenderness that brought together Clara and Ben Pipestone— the "true love" story that dominates most romance novels, Eagle chooses instead to describe the differences that shattered the marriage: a Sioux husband at odds with his culture, unable to compete with his wife's income, and seeking oblivion in alcohol; a perfectionist wife, blind to her husband's pain, unaware of his alcoholism, and unforgiving of a single, drunken infidelity. The novel begins with their daughter's arrest for shoplifting, the mother's recognition that she must make some concessions to her estranged husband for her daughter's sake, and the husband's realization that only by making the memorial ride with his daughter can he teach her the pride in herself and her culture she needs to sustain her. This period of physical challenge proves a time of healing as Clara Pipe- stone sees how her husband has matured and taken control of his life, and as Ben Pipestone accepts his grandfather's mantle of responsibility as leader of the memorial ride, teacher of the old ways, and bearer of the community's burdens. Old wounds are finally explored from very different perspectives, and Clara begins to see how her blindness to her husband's needs pushed him further and further from her, while Ben sees how a drunken one-night stand that meant nothing to him seemed like an unbearable betrayal to Clara. Building her story around a Sioux symbol, the kinship circle, Eagle sums up in the Pipestones' failures of communication the breakdowns of communication that produced Wounded Knee. She implies that just as time and love, shared hardships and a willingness to face hard truths could heal the embittering wounds caused by marital strife, so the same qualities could heal the bitter rift between white and Native American culture.

In *The Night Remembers* (1997) Eagle takes romance in a new direction, mixing it with tales of urban crime, comic book heroes, psychoses, and shape- shifters, in a style reminiscent of Dean Koontz's tales of the supernatural. Her theme is the power of love to heal and the importance of community. Her heroine, Angela Prescott, is hiding out in an urban ghetto after being stalked across the country by a rich and powerful former lover whose attractive exterior hid a twisted, sadistic inner self. The hero of the novel, a tribal policeman selected for the FBI Academy, Jesse Brown Wolf had been on his way to fame in the world of law enforcement when a tragic accident shattered his family, his life, and his psyche: his young daughter killed his infant son while toying with the loaded gun he had left in the glove compartment of his car. Torn apart psychologically, he lives underground near the river, part of the time a mild- mannered repairman, part of the time a shape-shifter, coyote/dog man with am- ber eyes, supernatural power over dogs, and an urge to step in in times of trouble, cut bullies down to size, and help out ordinary folk. In the Native American tradition of the hero, he is comfortable with the natural world, com- municates with animals, draws on their knowledge and aid, and not only as- sumes their shape but also is at times an animal, like Old Man Coyote. A part-Sioux youngster whose prostitute mother keeps leaving town befriends Brown Wolf and Prescott, and brings them together to transform the lives of all three. Angela gains a community and discovers her inner strength; the youngster finds an island of peace in the midst of urban street warfare; and the pieces of

Jesse Brown Wolf's shattered psyche gradually come together as he gains a woman and a child to love and protect, and drives the drug dealers out of their community.

Just as the Sioux concept of the circle of kinship and community tied together *Reason to Believe*, so a Native American Coyote story unifies the plot elements of *The Night Remembers*. A tribal elder reminds Jesse, "Coyote makes mistakes. Big mistakes. But he also sets things right" (206), and it is this role of clown and righter of wrongs that some part of Jesse makes his own. Also, just as the little fox of one Coyote story helps Coyote put the pieces of himself back together, bit by bit, into a final whole, so the youngster of this story leads Jesse back to the commitment to community and love that he had lost when his son died so tragically. Like the aged tribal leader who teaches Native American ways at the local school, he assumes a sacred coyote pelt as the emblem of his role as righter of wrongs.

Unlike so many of the fantasy-driven romances featuring Native American and white encounters on the American frontier, Kathleen Eagle's love stories reflect her realistic understanding of how difficult it sometimes is to find the human ties that link people behind the looming cultural, linguistic, and socio-logical differences that separate. Mainly set in modern times, her culturally sensitive novels deal realistically with cross-cultural encounters and the mis-understandings possible between those drawn together by passion but divided by cultural rifts that too many romance novels minimize or ignore.

CONCLUSION

The Native American captivity tradition by which prisoners could be adopted into a tribe to replace a loved one lost to accident, disease, or war, and the historical fact of cross-cultural marriages going back to Pocahontas and John Rolfe should provide exciting material for interesting fictional studies of culture clashes and cross-cultural dealings, subjects often difficult to address in concrete and credible ways. However, in practice, most modern fiction about such topics fails to confront genuine cultural differences. Instead, they are predictable romance genre stories that adhere very closely to the conventions of their eighteenth-century English roots, conventions not shared or even paralleled in Native American culture. Distortions, then, are inescapable. Handsome Native American warriors smitten by a passionate but pure love for a stunningly beau-tiful white captive, or sudden, impetuous true romances between muscular white males and Native American beauties in attractive beaded doeskin with tantaliz-ing fringes—such romantic images have little basis in the sociological realities of tribal life, realities that varied greatly from tribe to tribe but that overall were dramatically different from the white framework of society and reality.

The best of these works make an honest effort to communicate to readers the linguistic, cultural, and sociological barriers that cross-cultural lovers would have to overcome, acknowledging the real, intractable forces that separated and still separate. Less worthy romances present minor cosmetic differences in food and clothing as if culture were a lifestyle choice to be adopted as a costume. Ignoring major differences in religious and philosophical worldviews, in ideas about family and sexual relationships—the whole constellation of contrasts that makes mainstream-Indian romance interesting and challenging to begin with—simply returns the romance to its eighteenth-century origins as a feel-good, uplifting medium that makes women readers promises that the real world will surely break. In fact, only in a modern setting can the romance conventions of the genre produce high-quality storytelling, since cultural differences have been lessened by assimilation, though even here poorly conceived romances tend to avoid difficult questions of difference. Instead, they tend to focus on such mainstream concerns as the breakup of the family, gender issues and changing ideas about gender roles, the sexual revolution, male commitment, and even child care—all played out against distanced settings.

The romance genre has reshaped and redefined the Indian of history and of the traditional Western to produce the romantic Indian dream lover—the noble summation of all that both traditionalists and feminists seek in a male. They have endowed this fictive creation with all the contradictory wish-fulfillment fantasy characteristics of genre convention: tender and caring but tough, "savage" and self-contained, community-centered and self-sacrificing but a lone individualist, proud of his offspring but unfettered and free. In effect, the taming of a civilization and of a people is reduced to the taming of a lover/spouse.

It is easy to dismiss the whole subgenre of Indian romances because of such self-serving abuses of the Indian figure. Yet, the examples of Dailey, Thurlo, and Eagle show that the romance has come a long way in its over two hundred-year history, and can, in capable and responsible hands, be an excellent dramatic vehicle for issues of both cultural and personal enlightenment. Just recently, the genre has attracted one Native American contributor, Cherokee Mardi Oakley Medawar, who follows the example of Kathleen Eagle by setting her story *The Misty Hills of Home* (1998) in modern times and centering it on realistic struggles of men and women with conflicting needs. Her Oklahoma Osage heroine defies her family to be with the man she loves, a rough-and-tumble hell-raiser from a branch of the tribe her family looks down on as no good, and he sees her as his way out of his family's pattern of poverty, violence, and despair; their marriage is a struggle as he travels to wherever the oil rigs are being erected and oil is pumped, while she almost single-handedly raises five sons, finding within herself, her family, and her tribal ways the courage to endure the hard times and savor the good times. Perhaps contemporary Native Americans employing the romance genre (like Medawar) will take it in new directions more attuned to the realities of their culture, or more writers like Kathleen Eagle will rise above the limitations of convention to create individuals becoming aware that cultural differences can divide in ways far less predictable than mere gender differences.

6

The Native American in the Detective/Crime Genre: Bridging Ratiocination and Intuition

> "Indians are big right now," said Rupert, the [literary] agent. "Publishers are looking for that shaman thing, you know? The New Age stuff, after death experiences, the healing arts, talking animals, sacred vortexes, that kind of thing. And you've got all that, plus a murder mystery. That's perfect."
>
> —Sherman Alexie, *Indian Killer*

From Sam Spade to Kojak to the wily sleuth on tonight's television program, detectives have been hard-boiled figures of the modern metropolis. The American detective, whether a loner or a team player in a police procedural, has been a quintessentially twentieth-century figure, an exemplar of what it means to be modern. Given the powerful image this fictional detective occupies in contemporary American popular culture, why would modern writers of detective fiction conjure up Native American detectives? How could a people so bound up with the traditional play such a modern role successfully?

The fact that critics discussing the history of the detective genre invariably cite James Fenimore Cooper (particularly his *Leatherstocking Tales*) as an early American precursor perhaps provides some answers. The essence of good detective fiction is an engaging version of deductive logic, and Cooper was among the first American frontier writers to insist on the powers of observation and logical deduction among his colonial and Indian protagonists. In fact, part of the excitement of his books comes from frontiersmen and friendly Indians, schooled in ways of the forest, reading in the leaves and twigs precise past events: who passed this way, when, under what conditions, how long ago.

In other words, looked at in terms of their function, one might argue that some of the first, unrecognized, real American detectives were the famous Indian

scouts (or Indian-trained scouts) of the frontier. A crime (the murder of settlers, an attack on a wagon train, a raid on livestock) is beyond the scope of the local authorities, either because they are newcomers to the West or because they have no experience with the language, culture, or habits of the alleged perpetrators, the Native Americans of the area. The authorities call in an Indian scout, who may be a full-blooded Native American, a half-breed, or even a white partially assimilated into Native American culture. Whichever, he acts as an intermediary between cultures, serving one and possibly betraying another in order to sort out malefactors only he can find and deal with. The scout does exactly what a modern detective does, reading terrain and signs, sorting through evidence, and tracking the wrongdoers to their hiding places. He dispenses justice and possibly returns an abductee. The scout is rewarded for this service, and stability returns to the fort, town, or settlement. Ironically, this centuries-old pattern is still played out in manhunts across barren stretches of the Southwestern desert and other wilderness regions, with, for example, sharp-eyed Navajo trackers providing the FBI with sound information to further their pursuit of fleeing criminals, as has happened recently with ecoterrorists, kidnappers, and thieves.

Descriptions of Native American tracking skills resound throughout our literature and histories of the colonies in the movement westward. French explorer Antoine de la Mothe Cadillac, who founded Detroit in 1701, described Ottawa tracking skills:

If they come upon the trail of any persons, they can easily distinguish whether it is old or recent; they know the number of people who have passed there, and how many days ago their journey was made; and, as they know when their enemy went by, they can tell pretty nearly where they will be . . . you may walk on moss or leaves, or through marshes, or even over rocks, but all precautions you take to conceal your track are quite useless, for the pursuers are rarely at fault. The strangest thing is that they know by the impress of the foot or its shape, to what tribe the people in front of them belong. (from "Letters and Notes," in *The Way of the Warrior*, 129)

Ironically, Cadillac dismissed such abilities as "instinct" rather than "knowledge or reason" when in fact such skills clearly grow out of close observation of nature and the powers of inference based on repeated experience. Colonel Richard Dodge remarked on the extraordinary skills of his Sioux scouts: "I have good 'plains eyes'; but while, even with an excellent field glass, I could scarcely make out that the distant speck was a horseman, the Indian by my side would tell me what the distant speck was saying" (from "Our Wild Indians," in *The Way of the Warrior*, 156).

The skill can even be learned by frontier whites, as the scouts of so many Western tales suggest (it's fiction, after all). For instance, in Charles West's *Wind River* (1999), mountain man Squint Peterson, who has lived among the Shoshone for many years, can tell the difference between a brush fire and "folks' goods burning" from the color of the smoke (223); and Jesse Callahan in Clay Fisher's *Warbonnet* (1952) "quarters" the "waiting stillness of the cutup country ahead, wary as a loafer wolf moving upwind into a baited buffalo carcass," his narrow blue eyes missing nothing. "It was a High Plains art," writes Fisher, "taught him by his Sioux foster parents, this trick of quartering or even halving the prairie compass with the eyes" (12).

Lucia St. Clair Robson describes a similar phenomenon in her fictionalized life of Cynthia Ann Parker, *Ride the Wind* (1982):

Ben McCulloch . . . had been a Ranger for five years, but he had never seen anything like this. The trail was half a mile wide, and the ground looked as though an army had come through dragging plows behind it.

"Buffalo this far south?" Ben winced. . . . "No. Of course they're not. Indians. Right?"

"Right." McCulloch studied the crushed blade of grass he had picked out of a hoof-print. "They're traveling at night, and they passed here about two days ago. If there are less than a thousand of them, I'll eat their horses." . . .

"How'd you know that? About them traveling at night and all?"

"They plowed through mesquite bushes instead of going around. And nothing goes through mesquite bushes if it can avoid them. Hell, armadillos go around them. And the grass is past the limp stage and getting dry. Feel it. Been in the print two days or so. Look at the insect trails crossing the print. They make those at night. So the prints have to be at least a day old."

"If you say so. But it beats me how you can know."

"You learn, John."

The lessons had been painful. And sometimes fatal. But the Rangers had learned a lot from John Coffee Hays in the past five years. And Jack Hays had learned from the Comanche. . . .

Ben went on searching the ground, reading it for more information. "Comanche. Not that there was much doubt. Just wanted to make sure. . . . Here's a track of the foot. Short and stubby. That's the way Comanche feet are, square as tobacco tins."

"You are a wonder." (264–266)

This ability to see what others do not is the essence of good detection: Conan Doyle's Sherlock Holmes interprets the clue of the dog who did not bark; Edgar Allen Poe's Monsieur Dupin and Emile Gaboriau's Monsieur Lecoq disclose the secrets of the locked room; Christie's Hercule Poirot builds his solutions to cases around seeing through misdirection; and Dorothy Sayers's Lord Peter Wimsey builds on the esoteric knowledge acquired from family and by educa-tion to recognize the significance of the church bells or a fisherman's trout fly. The historical Native American frontier scout as an early detective has been unremarked only because of his unfamiliar territory, not because of his methods or logic.

While British and Continental detectives (both real and fictive) reflected Vic-torian faith in the reason and ratiocination of the Enlightenment, especially as reflected in the nineteenth- and twentieth-century triumphs of science and tech-nology, the close observation done by Native scouts came from long experience with nature, not from scientific or technological experimentation. Most signifi-cantly, brawn in America was as important as brain, for scouting required a physical endurance unthinkable in the cerebral Sherlock Holmes or the foppish Lord Peter Wimsey. The perseverance required by the huge American landscape was measured in months and years, not days and weeks. Also, perhaps as telling, scouts tended to be lone wolves, isolated from their fellows by background, culture, or circumstance (like the detectives of Dashiell Hammett and Raymond Chandler). While not necessarily meeting D. H. Lawrence's definition as "isolate killers," the souls of American scouts were certainly set apart from those of their fellows. As fringe members of frontier groups, they frequently served alien masters and possibly betrayed their own people. They were the original American guns for hire, and as such they provide good reasons for modern writers to look to the West for inspiration for a new ethnic detective.

Furthermore, recent writers have found in the Native American shaman a counter to the ratiocinative scout, for in practice the shaman might well serve as an intuitive investigator with special powers and ancient knowledge that allowed him or her to discover what was hidden to others. Traditionally, whereas the scouts or guides exploited the powers of observation and logic, the shaman called on intuition and psychic forces, performing rituals and invoking spirit powers to make a terrifying journey into a realm where others could not go, and thereby acquire knowledge and understanding to heal the community, either literally or spiritually. Such a journey meant facing numerous and terrifying dangers amid threatening spirits in the land of the dead, and acquiring knowledge couched in dream symbols that must be interpreted to accord with the realities of daily life. Modern descriptions of shamanistic powers suggest different routes to similar knowledge, paralleling the intuitive dream visions of a shaman with the ratiocinative investigation of a traditional detective.

When the two real-life traditions from the Native American past—the scout and the shaman—are merged, inevitably writers working within the European and American detective genre conventions face genre questions. While for Native Americans scouting and shamanism were two complementary paths to knowledge, in modern detective and crime novels the two cannot coexist without drastically distorting the basic tenets of the ratiocinative genre. Magical, mystical spiritualism subverts the ratiocinative and converts the detective story into a tale of horror (with threatening spirits and otherworld activities dominating) or into some form of New Age science-fiction mysticism, forms that will be discussed in later chapters. Since reader expectations are heavily influenced by genre, reader reaction and artistic success are often compromised by odd genre mixes. Thus, when details are added to create a Native American flavor, they may undercut the detective formula and produce a new, uncertain, cross-genre form, so that classification becomes meaningless, and readers must ask: Is this detection or horror, science fiction or sociological tract? Nonetheless, the concept of an Indian detective draws on sound historical realities and, handled carefully, opens up new ways to make the genre serve its primary functions.

GENRE OVERVIEW

Detective fiction began as a genre with such nineteenth-century writers as Edgar Allen Poe, Wilkie Collins, Arthur Conan Doyle, and Mary Elizabeth Braddon. Traditionally, detective fiction involves an investigator, usually one who is sympathetic enough for the reader to identify with to some degree. This investigator may be a professional detective, a police officer, an amateur with professional training, or a vulnerable bystander-turned-protagonist drawn into a puzzling situation that could prove dangerous. Such investigators, whether brave men or women of conscience, public servants, or guns for hire on the shadowy edge of both the establishment and the underworld, typically prove to be tenacious, ingenious, and sometimes lucky survivors. These qualities form a large part of their appeal to the reader.

Approaches to detection vary greatly, with some detectives skeptical, aloof, and aggressively rational (like Sherlock Holmes) and others acting on intuition or gut feelings (like Agatha Christie's Miss Marple or Mickey Spillane's Mike Hammer). Whatever their approach (deductive, inductive, or intuitive), they carefully observe the physical evidence—clues of place and time and human behavior—and the quirks of human psychology. Sometimes, they face an intellectual puzzle whose solution will expose the sinister realities behind public façades; at other times, they must confront a powerful adversary, whose full villainy they uncover bit by bit. Ultimately, the detective, whether a lone wolf or a member of a team, champions the values or the good of the larger community; he or she may need to walk down mean streets, but ultimately the detective acts for society, finding the truth and facilitating justice. Order has been disrupted and wrong done; the investigator must put it right so citizens can once again sleep peacefully. In a phenomenon related to reader identification, the detective acts as a surrogate for the reader, sorting out society's disarray, righting wrongs, and ultimately reinforcing the idea that justice (in some form) and law (whether written or simply custom) can prevail. The detective is thus typically a conservative force, returning society to a status quo disrupted by chaotic forces.

Whereas Dashiell Hammett and Raymond Chandler depicted corrupt societies in messy disarray under a veneer of order, Ross Macdonald modernized the detective genre by exploring social problems caused by personal and community failures: drug abuse, untreated mental illness, the generation gap, dropouts, runaways, the decay of the family, sexual irresponsibility, social divisions based on race and income, greed, and an egotism that leads to "me first" values and a welfare state. For Macdonald, these failures are summed up in a key modernist attitude: that wrongdoing reflects alienation from a diseased society (as opposed to the simply venal and violent one of Chandler and his contemporaries). Macdonald helped make the detective story what he called an "imaginative arena" ("The Writer as Detective Hero," 1973) where disturbing realities can be confronted under controlled conditions and where the psychology and sociology of crime figure prominently. Postmodernist literary critic Jon Thompson, in *Fiction, Crime, and Empire* (1993), asserts that "fictional narratives may not, in and of themselves, generate social change, but their form offers a model for narratives that, in their grasp of historical circumstances and forces, could ultimately inspire social transformation" (179). For Thompson, the detective and crime genre has this potential, and given the range of social problems addressed in the Macdonald model, it is easy to see the detective novel as an ideal vehicle for minority concerns, especially Native American ones.

There is nothing new in the idea of the detective story as an arena in which minority grievances can be played out. Since the 1970s, the genre has served as a tool for African Americans to raise questions of social justice and for feminists to disseminate modern gender attitudes to a wide audience. In recent years, the form has broadened its scope to serve as an interesting record of the battles between ethnic groups and mainstream forces in the United States and to introduce mainstream readers to cultures and groups beyond their social experience. Where once the detective moved between upper and lower social classes, today's detective often moves between the mainstream and minority ethnic groups. (See Kathleen Klein, ed., *Diversity and Detective Fiction: Race, Gender, Ethnicity*.) This movement has resulted in experiments with genre function so that end products go far afield from ratiocinative puzzles or good adventure reads, instead providing insights into the psychology of ethnic identity and behavior patterns of cultural conflict. The detective story may be used as a vehicle to publicize social justice issues, as a means of exploring the gray shades of moral ambiguity behind the black-and-white judgments of headline news, and as a plea for reuniting a divided community. Such functions make it highly appropriate for exploring the rifts between Native American and mainstream life.

Creative writing professor Wayne Ude, who has worked closely with Montana reservations, uses Native American materials to show the way in reuniting a divided reservation community, interweaving various levels of reality through metaphor and reshaping the realities in magical realism imitations of Native American storytelling. While convincingly voicing the contemporary complexities of reservation life in a story of a hunt for two local Indians who steal clothing and artifacts from the Tribal Museum, he infuses his novel *Becoming Coyote* (1981) with traditional stories, legends, history, and customs that merge past and present in a continuous loop, as Coyote changes shapes, rearranges reality, and manipulates humans. The narrator-protagonist, the authority figure representing both the museum and the tribal police, is a nonreservation Indian who does not believe in the old ways but gets caught up in the Trickster's skein as Coyote weaves together the threads of disparate lives. Ude's approach echoes those of Native American authors Thomas King and Leslie Silko as he infuses a modern genre with an ancient oral history.

CONTEMPORARY NATIVE AMERICAN AUTHORS WRITING IN THE GENRE

Because the detective genre in no way parallels any Native American oral or literary tradition, its occasional use by a few Native Americans is clearly aimed at a mainstream audience. A reason for selecting this genre, however, might go beyond the fact of its popularity, and hence its value as a way to disseminate ideas widely. This form has traditionally examined the justice system closely, has explored the gray areas of the law, and has served as a tool for voicing the complaints of the down and out, the social misfits and outcasts, the little people of the land. D'Arcy McNickle verges on crime fiction in his 1936 story of the poverty, alcoholism, and despair of reservation life, *The Surrounded.* Therein, a half-blood youth, Arshile, covers up a game warden's shooting of his brother and his mother's retaliatory murder of the game warden (she bashes his head in with a frying fan); later, when he is confronted by a local sheriff, his girlfriend shoots the officer, and Arshile must face the blame and punishment of the white world. In *Mean Spirit* (1990), Chickasaw Linda Hogan attacks paternalistic government policies and environmental destruction as she tracks a 1920s conspiracy to cheat and kill rich Osage Indians in oil-boom Oklahoma. Sixtown Clan Choctaw Ron Querry, in *The Death of Bernadette Lefthand* (1993), captures the complexity of modern reservation life in his mystery story of murder, passion, and Navajo witchcraft—in the main told through the eyes of a young Apache girl. Later in this chapter we will see Cherokee Mardi Oakley Medawar working within detective-genre restraints (but amid nineteenth-century Kiowa) to provide mainstream readers an alternative view of Native American life and history.

James Welch

In books like *The Indian Lawyer* (1990), Blackfoot James Welch has built on crime novel conventions to explore the grim realities of reservation and prison life, the difficulty of breaking through the social barriers that keep Native Americans on the fringes, the paradoxes of assimilation, and the political machinations behind seemingly straightforward legislation. He is a polished stylist and narrator, skilled at capturing reader interest and weaving a simple tale with complex ramifications. While *The Indian Lawyer* is not a detective story per se, it is a low-key crime story. Welch paints vivid pictures of prison life, criminals, and the criminal mind; at the same time, he poignantly dramatizes how extraordinary a Native American must be and how much must be given up to break away from reservation life and become a successful mainstream professional. He explores the mixed motivations of personal ambition and an idealistic wish to help one's people, the lure of politics, and the ease with which political potential can crumble away.

His hero, Sylvester Yellow Calf, is a vulnerable loner, abandoned by his parents, raised in poverty on the Blackfoot reservation, but enabled by basketball scholarships to pursue a law career. He has felt firsthand his traditional community's resentment of success and difference, pulling individuals toward the group and mediocrity. Now a prominent lawyer, he sits on the pardon board of a Montana prison, practices law in Helena, and moves between two worlds. He has earned respect in both worlds but cannot fully belong to either. When he visits relatives and former friends on the reservation, his success and his profession set him apart and mark him as an outsider; in the courtroom and amid his Helena associates he is "the Indian lawyer." That appellation alone makes him the target of two attempts to manipulate his life: (1) that of a prisoner whose pardon has been denied and who fears for his personal safety from hard-ened fellow prisoners—the Indians who control the inner workings of Montana prison life and who are determined to discover where the prisoner keeps the stolen money he never returned; and (2) that of a political kingmaker who sees Yellow Calf's successes as a sign of deep ambition and his Indian heritage as an exploitable commodity in the world of national politics. The prisoner sends his wife to ensnare Yellow Calf, hoping to frame him and blackmail him, not anticipating that the vulnerabilities of these two strangers will ignite a genuine, deep-seated attraction. Welch's distanced narrative voice allows him to guide the reader's view of events without lecturing or hectoring.

Sherman Alexie

Sherman Alexie, in contrast, hectors but backs away from any moral or social statement of substance. His narrative voice in *Indian Killer* (1998) is "in-your-face" confrontational, but readers learn it is probably the disturbed voice of a schizophrenic, presented with third-person indirection, leaving the author's own views never quite clear. Everyone is fair game for attack, and consequently the criticism remains superficial and without real bite. The genre conventions with which Alexie chooses to reach a broad mainstream audience are sensational and exploitative, but he fails to create empathy for characters grounded in racial and cultural stereotypes: foolish white liberals; wanna-be Indians wallowing in col-lective guilt for acts committed a century before; redneck Indian bashers inspired by Rush Limbaugh-style radio commentators and their own personal sense of injury; homeless, drunken Indian street people, directionless, failed, and pitiable; and half-breeds taught cruelty by their white fathers.

Alexie suggests, but never states directly, that his central character, John Smith, is insane because he was cut off from his people, adopted by white liberals who tried to teach him about his Native American heritage without understanding it themselves. John, moving in a psychotic haze, imagines white doctors ripping him from his Indian mother's womb and delivering him to armed men who shoot down innocent bystanders as they helicopter him away to his lily-white adoptive parents, parents who are kind and loving, who try to provide him contacts with his racial heritage, but who, in John and Alexie's eyes, can never be adequate. In retaliation for their inadequacy, John acquires a large, turquoise-inlaid knife (he imagines himself a Navajo) and kills and scalps a blue-eyed white man, chosen at random. Multiple voices in his own mind help him choose other possible victims. However, the murder that sets Seattle whites and Indians at each other's throats is committed by two greedy rednecks, not John. Ultimately, Alexie suggests that white Indian wanna-bes like the Seattle Indian detective series author who claims Indian blood and the white Marxist university professor who teaches Native American literature at the university are responsible for Indian hatred because they romanticize the Native American into something he is not, and the term "Indian Killer" is appropriate because the "Killer Indian" of the story is not to blame for his actions; he is simply responding to the continent's history of "Indian Killers."

Typical of Alexie's central characters is Maria. Maria is so poor she has only cereal to eat for all three daily meals, but she somehow manages a mobile sandwich kitchen for homeless Indians; she takes a university course in Native American literature because she has been told she can make an easy "A," then spends the class time attacking her professor's selection of readings and arguing that no white man, even one adopted by the Lakota Sioux, can ever teach Indians anything about Indians, and that having a fraction of Indian blood doesn't make a person an Indian any more than a fraction of white blood makes a person white. The novel ends with the ghost of the crazed John Smith transformed into a prototype of Crazy Horse and leading Indians of many tribes to dance the Ghost Dance that cost so many Sioux their lives, and thereby to dream and stomp away all whites.

Disturbing images of Indians from many tribes mocking, abusing, or laughing at the kindness of harmless people who treat them politely and decently dominate the novel—the African American owners of a donut shop; the construction foreman of Seattle's latest high-rise; the crippled white Vietnam vet who helps Maria make sandwiches for the down-and-out. Thus, detection and apprehension of the criminal take second place to the message, and the message is an aggressive thumbing of the nose at the intended readership: Indians can never be happy until all the well-meaning whites, whose ancestors engaged in genocide against Indians and who still insult Indians without even understanding how, leave the continent and let it return to a primitive, hunter-gatherer period when all was well and little children didn't go hungry, Indian parents weren't abusive or drunk, and warriors had honor. At the same time, the message also seems to be that one can never go back; that what was, is past, and what is, is; and that one must get on with life or fall into traps of failure or insanity. Thus, what could have been an effective tool for raising the consciousness of readers is instead reduced to undirected sound and fury. Alexie intends to stir up controversy, and the beatings and murders are meant to raise hackles rather than lead to detection, a character study of a criminal or a psychotic, social justice, or exploration of the gray areas of the law.

Welch vs. Alexie

The difference between Welch's and Alexie's use of the detective/crime genre confirms what mainstream writers have learned about this very powerful genre: it can be a "read" to while away a short plane ride or a powerful tool to change people's views of reality. For all Alexie's talk about Native Americans changing society through the Ghost Dance, his novel projects fin-de-siècle alienation and defeatism: Indians are racists; Indians don't like Indians from other tribes or half-breeds; whites are racists; Indians and whites are both capable of gratuitous acts of violence and self-destruction; no good comes of well-intentioned acts; no good comes from ill-intentioned acts. Alexie goes beyond postmodernist irony to achieve utter negation of possibility. Welch, in contrast, captures the constant struggle between community and self, between heritage and assimilation; his story promotes understanding and bridges cultural boundaries in ways Alexie cannot or will not. Like Oscar Wilde but without his tongue-in-cheek approach, Alexie writes with such indeterminacy that his readers can see whatever they want to see in his novel and he can "sagely" dismiss all interpretations as reflective of the limitations of the readers—whatever perspective or point of view they may represent.

RANGE OF MAINSTREAM MYSTERY/DETECTIVE/CRIME STORIES

The range of mystery/detective/crime stories that include Native Americans is very wide, extending from tales in which Indians are of only peripheral interest to ones in which they are central, from ones in which they provide local color to others in which they are victims or suspects, to still others in which they act as guides and detectives for mainstream characters and readers. For some authors, the Native American provides topical interest; for others, cross-cultural relationships are vital; to still others, the detective story more properly concerns itself with questions of social justice.

NATIVE AMERICANS AS VICTIMS OR SUSPECTS

Mainstream detective stories and mysteries use Native Americans as victims or suspects for a variety of purposes, purposes that affect whether the Indians are simple stereotypes and romanticized abstractions, or humanized and complex, and whether the novel is simply entertainment or serves to raise significant questions about cross-cultural encounters, justice, and the judicial system. Novels frequently focus on questions of land and mineral rights or conflicts involving native religion (freedom to use peyote in ceremonies; freedom to protect sacred places from desecration and theft). The following are typical: (1) in Peter Hoeg's *Smilla's Sense of Snow* (1993), half-Danish, half-Inuit glaciologist Smilla Jaspersen battles police, scientists, and drug smugglers to find an ecological nightmare behind an Inuit boy's death (an English translation of the Danish original sold well and prompted a successful film); (2) in John Fusco's screenplay for *Thunderheart*, a successful 1992 film with Val Kilmer, an FBI man finds himself discovering his Native American roots instead of advancing the FBI's cause, the protection of uranium mining unsactioned by treaty; and (3) in David Seals's *Powwow Highway* (1990), uranium and nuclear power plants play a behind-the-scenes role in the framing of Redbow's sister on a marijuana charge (an FBI agent hopes to keep the politically active Redbow out of town while corrupt Indian "suits" make their case to the tribal council).

The marriage of the Western and the detective story provides a new venue for Native American characters. The function of the Indians in such Western mysteries is predictable: they are usually the suspects but have been framed. In Richard Matheson's *Shadow on the Sun* (1994), when a rider brings in the butchered corpses of his two brothers, the outcry for revenge threatens the recent government treaty with the Apaches unless Indian agent Billjohn Finley can produce the real murderer immediately. In William Colt MacDonald's *The Comanche Scalp* (1998), railroad detective Gregory Quist must solve the mystery of a body in a rowboat in the middle of the desert, the only clue being a Comanche scalp. In Lewis B. Patten's *Death Stalks Yellowhorse* (1997) the town of Yellowhorse suffers nightly raids in which citizens are killed and homes are burned, supposedly by a solitary Indian seeking vengeance against the white man. Sheriff Hickory Marks must detect the motive and capture the culprit before he no longer has a town to protect.

Ed Gorman, whose novel *Hawk Moon* (1995) alternates between serial murders in 1887 and in the present, provides one of the more grisly accounts of Indian victims: beautiful Indian women brutally murdered, an arm and nose cut off (a traditional Apache punishment for infidelity). Because of the nature of the crime, the police of both centuries blame a local Indian, but the truth lies in the warped psyche of a respected community member, and it is the psychology of the racially motivated murderer that fuels Gorman's story. Unlike many authors of detective stories with Native Americans as victims, Gorman makes the solution to the crime integral to the psychology of red-white relations. His Indians are not depersonalized, stereotyped victims, but well developed characters with individualized traits.

Native American Elements as Peripheral

A number of modern mysteries take advantage of the increased popularity of Native American stories by incorporating just enough material to justify a Native American symbol or figure on their cover or in the advertising blurb. The intent seems exploitative: Indians sell books. In such cases the Native American elements are peripheral to the detection even though they might suit plot needs or provide the backdrop for the author's real concerns. Skye Kathleen Moody's *Rain Dance* (1998), for example, which is cited on the internet as a Native American mystery, actually concerns illegal Asian purchases of bear gall bladders from the Olympic Peninsula. The only Native American elements are both general and peripheral: generic Indian legends about sacred bears, vague references to Quinault burial grounds, and a sprinkling of aggressive Native American radical environmentalists as misleading suspects. Judith Kelman's *Where Shadows Fall* (1987) likewise offers the possibility of multiple deaths caused by a "Shmohawk" curse placed on a local family that stole from and desecrated an Indian burial ground as a false lead in what is otherwise a conventional whodunit. Robert Westbrook's Howard Moon Deer mysteries, *Ghost Dancer*

(1998) and *Warrior Circle* (1999), feature a totally assimilated Lakota Sioux (a womanizer and opera buff who works part-time as sidekick to a blind detective while finishing up his Ph.D. dissertation) as an excuse to satirize New Agers, yuppies, and Indian wanna-bes, and the greed and power trips that lie behind studies of crystal power, "Indian" encounter groups, and the whole Santa Fe phenomenon (loosely fictionalized as the town of San Geronimo).

Celestine Sibley, author of *Dire Happenings at Scratch Ankle* (1993), clearly needed a credible land dispute, and Return Pickett—Cherokee spokesman and Georgia senator—serves that function well. Pickett pushes legislation to return disputed northern Georgia borderland to any Cherokee whose ancestors survived the Trail of Tears to Oklahoma and who wishes to return to what were once Cherokee lands. Kate Mulcay, a newspaper reporter and occasional amateur detective, is at first contemptuous of Pickett's rehashing of ancient grievances, then is touched by his admonition to read history:

"You'll see the greed and hatred that led to it and . . . ," he paused in front of a painting of an Indian chief in a fine feathered bonnet, "you'll see the kind of cruelties I think you can never forget. Four thousand or more people died, many of them children. My great-great-great-grandmother carried her dead baby for two days before she let them bury it on alien land in Tennessee."

Pickett is immediately killed in a particularly gruesome way, and the rest of the novel has much to do with greed and hatred but little to do with Native Americans. Here, Native American concerns heighten emotion and give an exotic cast to a land dispute but do not drive the plot.

Richard Hoyt also needs a credible dispute around which to build the action of his novel. In his grisly and bizarre *Fish Story* (1985) it is a conflict between the Cowlitz Indians and local salmon fishermen for fishing rights. However, Hoyt is more interested in the possibilities of setting (spooky underground labyrinth scenes; funky Seattle bars; Halloween masquerades) than in characterizing the Cowlitz, who seem thoroughly assimilated. As sawed-off bloody bits of bodies (pieces of key figures in the fishing dispute) begin appearing in Seattle's Pioneer Square, detective John Denson and his Cowlitz friend Willie Pettybird begin to realize that the dead body parts belong to the men Pettybird's missing sister Melinda has seduced, all of whom were on the commission and court that will decide the case. A seemingly simple case of a jealous ex-husband turns out to be Pettybird's brother and sister wreaking their own violent form of justice. *Fish Story* captures the complexities of local fishing-rights conflicts but deals mainly with assimilated Indians whose behavior reflects their Seattle rather than their Cowlitz background. Again, Native Americans are used for local color, not for their distinct culture.

Stefanie Matteson, in *Murder on High* (1994), uses Native American suspects to distract readers from the real motivations for bow-and-arrow murder, to provide interesting local tidbits (about the prehistoric ancestors of the Penobscots in Maine), and to raise questions about a modern "Native" culture dependent on very modern casinos and very gullible New Agers with money to waste. One suspect prankster, a disgruntled alcoholic, dresses in the moose antlers and eagle mask associated with Pamola, the malignant Penobscot spirit reputed to dwell in a cave at the summit of Mt. Katahdin, and shakes gourd rattles at older women camping in Baxter State Park. Another, Keith Samusit, is a descendant of one of the Penobscot guides for Thoreau's trips to Chesuncook and Allagash. Samusit is accused of selling ancestral rituals for profit since he offers an expensive seven-day retreat for New Agers to get in spiritual touch with an island that Indians inhabited for ten thousand years or more. The victim has generously funded these "Old Town" Penobscot vision quests to help people reconnect with the wilderness. Her large financial bequests to this retreat, coupled with her penchant for regularly changing her will, makes Samusit suspect. In other words, the question of Native American identity, the problems of assimilation and of making an ancient heritage viable in the modern world, the bitter links between old and new provide an interesting but misleading (and basically undeveloped) backdrop to a revenge story that has nothing to do with Native Americans.

M. E. Hirsh's *Dreaming Back* (1993), an intriguing, well-written novel, turns on a question raised in a number of Indian novels: Does the federal government have the right to waive Native American control of valuable minerals on reservation land, especially if they can be labeled necessary for the national defense? *Dreaming Back* postulates an attempt by federal officials to secretly locate and mine a superconductor mineral from a large meteorite before the Hopi learn of its presence. The sole source of the mineral, which could transform computer technology, lies directly under the land where the Hopi sacred snakes live. The Hopi believe that disturbing these snakes will bring on the end of the world. Although three key characters are Hopi, their attempts to protect tribal secrets and ward off both greedy private entrepreneurs and FBI/CIA officialdom have limited force, and the main thrust of the novel centers around a dysfunctional East Coast white family. Hirsh brings in wonderful material on the use of hallucinogens in world religions throughout time. He also includes a number of conspiracy theories about CIA use of LSD, about a campaign to transform innocent hemp into "the killer weed," and about government space observatories used to locate rare minerals that are secretly and illegally mined for both defense and commercial purposes. However, once again, the victimization of Native Americans takes second place to other agendas.

The above are typical of many mysteries with Native American victims, with the Native American elements interesting but peripheral and ultimately irrelevant to the final resolution. While perhaps sympathetic to Native American interests, such works, in effect, prolong the stereotype of Indian as victim and show little interest in seeing the world through Native American eyes or culture. Plots are driven by mainstream happenings, and themes reflect mainstream interests.

Desecration as a Driving Force

A number of other mystery writers center their detective stories around the desecration of Indian burial sites and illegal trafficking in Native American art and artifacts, a real, hot-button issue in many Native American communities. This use of the desecration issue lies partly in the topicality of the subject and partly in the opportunity to deal with a clear-cut moral position at odds with the complex moral grays of other potential modern topics involving Native Americans, such as poverty, alcoholism, disease, and unemployment. Authors Father Brad Reynolds, S.J., Jake Page, Sandra West Prowell, and Walter Satterthwait reflect the diverse approaches and directions possible. Reynolds and Page draw on illegal trafficking in Indian artifacts mainly for local color and for a clear, unambiguous motive for murder, whereas Prowell does so to call attention to the cultural gap between whites and Indians, and Satterthwait does so to suggest the bridges that could be built between two alien cultures. In Page the Indians are legitimate victims or suspects; in Prowell they are suspects; and in Satterthwait they are victims, community leaders seeking justice, and investigators.

Father Brad Reynolds, S.J.

Reynolds's detective is a Jesuit, Father Mark Townsend, who started his career as a priest to the Yup'ik Eskimos of the Alaskan tundra but moved to Seattle when his affections were captured by a Yup'ik beauty. In *The Story Knife* (1996), an intricately carved, ivory-handled Yup'ik story knife (a knife designed for drawing stories in the snow) is found embedded in the body of a murdered man whose funeral Townsend presides over. This unusual occurrence leads to Townsend's return to the Yup'ik village where he had his first ministry and to his investigation of a stock fraud that put a whole Yup'ik community in fear of losing its land, its livelihood, and its way of life. The story knife suggests the possibility of a scam involving traditional native art but is really used to misdirect the investigation away from attempts to gain legal control of oil rights. The solution hinges on knowledge of Yup'ik hunting patterns and sense of community, but it is the dangers of ice and cold that Reynolds dwells on most.

In *A Ritual Death* (1997), while on leave to visit his family in LaConner, Washington, on Puget Sound, Townsend again gets caught up in murder, one that intertwines Chinese drug smuggling with the theft of Coastal Salish/Swinomish religious artifacts and strongly felt confrontations over salmon fishing rights. The death of a local fisherman known for his hatred of Swinomish fishing practices and for his passion for illegal treasure hunting on tribal lands leads to the arrest of a Swinomish fisherman and the exposure of Townsend's grandfather's cover-up of his knowledge of the missing artifacts (two cedar boards with holes in them—*Squa-de-lich*—used by a past medicine man to assure sufficient food for the year).

Townsend follows the traditional detective methods of talking to as many people as he can (an invitation to a local Seeowyn initiation ceremony aids his detective mission), but also investigates by studying the local tides alongside Swinomish fishermen (they prove the Swinomish suspect is innocent), examining documents in the local library, and tracking down the original hiding place of the *Squa-de-lich*. However, Reynolds fails to awaken sympathy for real people. Perhaps the problem with this book is summed up in these two sentences: "As a Jesuit priest, his natural sympathies lay with the Indians. But as a white man, the niceties in his own culture provided him a comfortable and safe shelter" (107). Though at times they are side by side, the whites and Indians in Reynolds's books somehow remain separate, and for all Townsend's talk of sympathies and the genuine help he provides, there is a sense of insurmountable barriers between people, barriers made explicit in the nun who goes to inordinate lengths to get Townsend away from "her" Indians because she is writing a dissertation about them and fears he will beat her to her thesis. Ultimately, Townsend, not Swinomish or Yup'ik, dominates Reynolds's detective stories, and Townsend is not an engaging enough personality to make up for this limitation.

Jake Page

Page is more interested in the Santa Fe community, particularly the art community, than in the local Indians per se; hence the focus on T. Moore "Mo" Bowdrie, blind sculptor and amateur detective, who brings his intuitive and logical skills to bear on local mysteries. However, because of the Santa Fe setting, these invariably involve stolen kachinas, bogus Georgia O'Keeffe paintings, rifled Aztec artifacts, Spanish treasure, forensic entomology, and reenactments of a successful Pueblo rebellion against Spanish conquerors. Page's novels also include the murder of a major art dealer (*The Stolen Gods*, 1993), of an FBI scientist and special agent investigating smuggling (*The Deadly Canyon*, 1994), of the leading actor on a movie set (*The Knotted Strings*, 1995), and of an art dealer's lover (*The Lethal Partner*, 1996). *The Deadly Canyon* concentrates on looters raiding ancient anthropological sites and carrying off everything from petrogylphs to Aztec objects entombed with the dead to speed them on their final journey. Bowdrie's Anglo-Hopi girlfriend, Connie Barnes, provides ties to the Native American community—their attitudes about reservation life; the links between seasons, crops, and spirits; Hopi snake dances; and the role of Hopi gods in human affairs. Through her, Bowdrie comes to appreciate traditions very different from his own. For instance, her personal sense of loss and despair helps him understand that the theft of the sacred kachinas (sold to private dealers for a quarter-million dollars) are to the Hopi like the loss of sight was to him: "the whole damn tribe is on the brink. It's like they lost their gyroscope. . . . Without those gods, no more Hopi men can learn the divine law of the tribe. . . . He wondered what it would be like for a group of people to suddenly find themselves spiritually blinded" (*The Stolen*

Gods, 188). This empathy provides him very personal reasons for finding the thieves and restoring the stolen gods. In *The Deadly Canyon*, Connie tries to imagine being an Apache warrior woman (a concept in conflict with her peaceful and repressed Hopi self), and her knowledge of the desert helps "Mo" solve a crime involving the desecration of ancient desert ruins.

Sandra West Prowell

In *The Killing of Monday Brown* (1994), Prowell concentrates on Indian outrage at the desecration of tribal graves by thieves seeking valuable relics to sell to fanatical German collectors:

"He had all of those things [artifacts]. Those wonderful things that should never have had a price on them. . . . He wasn't just going to sell some beaded trinkets, Phoebe. He was selling my heritage. The one that [had] been stripped from, denied me. Because of him and people like him, when I heard the voices calling me home [to the reservation], I followed and nothing was there. It was gone." (285)

The murder victim, the Monday Brown of the title, is a trader in Indian artifacts, a familiar figure in the Montana Crow community, but one who betrays community trust. Naturally, the suspects are local hotbloods, in particular the radical and unpleasantly confrontational Matthew Wolf. Wolf's cousin, Kyle Old Wolf, is a Crow Indian police detective whose cases intersect with those of private detective Phoebe Siegel. Their mutual attraction and his request involve her in Wolf's defense, even though Siegel barely tolerates Old Wolf's relatives, finding their behavior both inexplicable and offputting: the Crow language snarling and angry and the young males punkish, their attitude disrespectful, their manner threatening as they joyously play on racial stereotypes of scalp-taking savages. Prowell depicts Siegel entering an alien world whose concept of reality is very different from her own—old women who talk to dwarfs with spiritual powers, believe in the reality of dreams and hallucinations, and purify themselves in claustrophobic sweat lodge ceremonies; loose family groups with no sense of private property or private space; traditionalists who paint themselves ceremonially, wear valued artifacts made of finger bones and scalp locks, and, because Monday Brown has married into the tribe, hold a moving Crow farewell ceremony for the same person whose Christian grave they ritualistically spit on for desecrating their land. Though Siegel eventually unravels the truth and vindicates young Wolf and his clan, and though readers are brought to understand the Indian perspective on anthropological studies of ancient Indian artifacts and bones, the Crow remain impenetrably alien.

Walter Satterthwait

Murder and desecration dominate Satterthwait's *Wall of Glass* (1987). The novel turns on illegally made eagle feather kachinas (irreverent because they retain traditional details with no changes to reduce their power) and on stolen burial site artifacts, all sold abroad to wealthy Germans anxious to possess genuine Indian goods (even Anasazi mummies embedded in acrylic!). Only one Native American appears in the plot, a Hopi artist who has sold out his heritage.

In contrast, in *At Ease with the Dead* (1990) Satterthwait puts desecrated graves and murder in second place to the friendship that develops between Navajo Daniel Begay and private detective Joshua Croft. Begay hires Croft to bring back the remains of a tribal leader who was secretly buried in Cañon del Muerte in 1866 and then disinterred by a geologist who wanted the mummified body for his daughter, a budding archaeologist. Now the dead man's descendants have nightmares about the dead, dreams that the Navajo fear will have terrible repercussions in their community. Croft works hand in hand with Begay to find the missing body and to explain the deaths associated with it.

Unlike Prowell's detective, who cannot come to terms with Crow thinking, Croft admires the Navajo; he appreciates their oblique forms of social interaction, their closeness to the land, and even their suspicion of outsiders. He forms a personal relationship with Begay as a competent, insightful equal. Together they draw on the resources of the Navajo community, as Satterthwait provides readers anthropological lessons in contrasting cultural concepts of distance, hardship, violence, duty, and reality. Extended dialogues consist of few words—wry understatements:

He . . . pinched some tobacco, twisted it into the pipe. "How much do you charge to find someone?"
". . . Depends. . . . Who's missing?"
"Relative of a woman I know." He screwed some more tobacco into the bowl.
"Man or woman?"
"Man." Tamping tobacco down with his thumb.
"How long's he been missing?"
He put the pipe stem between his teeth. From his left-hand coat pocket he pulled a red Bic lighter. He lighted it, held the flame to the bowl, the flame flared as he puffed. "Since Nineteen twenty-five," he said.
I sat back, wondering how to phrase it politely. "Well, Daniel," I said. "That's a long time ago. He could be dead by now."
The faint smile came again, a fractional movement of the lips against the pipe stem. "Oh, he is. He was dead then too." (29)

The reservation setting and the confrontations between individuals who practice different forms of communication transform a simple detective story into a cross-cultural lesson.

In other words, despite shared subject matter—the desecration of native artifacts, graves, and archaeological sites—these writers take very different approaches. Reynolds's and Page's stories are basically white stories with a Native American overlay. Prowell and Satterthwait aggressively deal with cross-cultural encounters and help readers understand that the differences in values, perspectives, and sense of time are more than just skin deep.

Series Amateur Detectives with Cross-Cultural Empathies

In contrast to writers who dabble occasionally with Native American characters, issues, and concerns are two excellent writers with series amateur detectives who live on or near reservations, partake of Native American community life, and become so caught up in the daily lives of a particular tribe that they can make readers sympathize and empathize with individuals whose lives are very different from their own: Margaret Coel and Richard Parrish. Here again are legitimate lessons in cross-cultural anthropology set in the detective genre. Coel's detective is a Jesuit, Father John O'Malley, head pastor of the St. Francis Mission on the Arapaho Wind River Reservation of Wyoming; Parrish's detective is a Bureau of Indian Affairs lawyer, Joshua Rabb, a man physically and psychically wounded by war, now committed to protecting Papago Indian rights both in the courts and in the community.

Margaret Coel

Margaret Coel brings modern reservation issues to sensitively drawn fictional life. She balances the perceptions of two loners who are both insiders and outsiders in the reservation community: Boston-Irish Father John O'Malley and Arapaho lawyer Vicky Holden, known locally as "Woman Alone." A Jesuit with a potentially promising career who was sent to the Wind River Reservation in Wyoming as therapy and penance for his drinking problem, O'Malley has come to love the Arapaho. As a result, he teaches young Arapahos to love baseball, his own great secular passion, and to play it well; he cares deeply about his parishioners and learns to understand their customs and perspectives. He becomes an Arapahophile, acting as a bridge between the white world and the Indian world. O'Malley is a tough and convincing detective, completely masculine despite his sensitivity and commitment to nurturing his flock. He is very logical in the strict Jesuit sense (see *The Eagle Catcher*, 212–213), but rather than gratifying an urban intellectual attachment to books and ideas, he indulges a sensual enjoyment of the big country of the Arapahos—its empty skies, wide horizons, and lonely splendor—which he partakes of while driving alone in his beat-up Toyota pickup, opera tapes blaring. In a very direct way, this attachment to Indian country reflects his understanding of and love for the Arapaho people and culture. O'Malley has developed an attachment to the physical environment that parallels the deep relationship of the Arapaho to their land, and in consequence, in spite of a big-city and mainstream Catholic background, can see events much as they see them.

Vicky Holden, in turn, has moved in the other direction, meeting O'Malley in the middle. She has painfully wrenched herself away from the hermetic community of the reservation, studied hard, and become a skilled legal professional in order to return to her community and help out locally. However, the assimilation necessary to attain the expertise to operate effectively in the white community has left her cut off from her roots. Former friends view her as an outsider; family members chide her for not participating in the tribal women's organizations, for spending her time off reservation, and for becoming a stranger even to them. Through Vicky, Coel, like James Welch, captures the vulnerability and loneliness of the assimilated, but she also demonstrates Vicky's strength and fortitude, the gutsy courage that leads her to place herself in the line of fire in order to do what she thinks is right and necessary—to rescue a battered wife, for example, counter to patriarchal tribal custom. Ironically, Father O'Malley provides Vicky connections to her own community, while Vicky fills his lone-liness and makes him seriously rethink his religious vocation. They yearn for each other, but try to hide the depth of their feeling, each believing it is not reciprocated. Both characters eloquently represent both the benefits and the psy-chic pain of leaving a structured community and living as an outsider in new circumstances.

Coel is excellent on Jesuits, alcoholism, and the Wyoming landscape (the big sky, the plains, the heat, the constant wind, the dramatic storms, the blizzards, and the ice). She is also good on the Arapaho, whom she depicts with dignity and restraint. Many are acculturated but are still recognizable as Arapahos, a true literary achievement, and although there is no gratuitous bashing of whites, Coel gets across the way whites can patronize Indians without meaning to: the casual, easy assumptions of the majority. O'Malley's ambitious young Jesuit assistants (who, like O'Malley, are sent to the mission for the good of their souls, but who, unlike O'Malley, feel alienated there and scheme to return to "civilization") sum up well-meaning white attitudes. The descriptions of the life of the reservation and the mission seem credible and very informed. Coel un-derstands that life in a structured community can be lonely whether the group is Jesuit or Indian. She communicates the deep and usually invisible personal sacrifices made by both Vicky and O'Malley because of their commitments to social justice.

In *The Eagle Catcher* (1995) tribal chairman Harvey Castle is murdered in his tepee at a powwow because he has found evidence that the first white agent, Mathias Cooley, withheld goods and annuities owed the Arapahos when they first came to the reservation, and forced them to grant him the best reservation land for his ranch. His great-grandson, Ned Cooley, wants to run for governor of Wyoming, and Castle's knowledge could endanger his chances. The prevail-ing white attitude toward the Arapaho is summed up in a speech Ned gives to a party of supporters at his ranch:

"As you all know," he began slowly, "Cooleys were the first people to come to these parts more than a hundred years ago. We settled this whole country. When my great-grandaddy Mathias Cooley brought his little wife across the plains and lit on this place, there wasn't anything here but buffaloes and Indians. . . . Ever since then, the Cooleys have worked hard to make Fremont County a decent place for decent people." (80)

The speech is painful to read because the speaker's blindness to his own arrogance and ethnocentricity is so recognizable. The novel includes many such perceptions about racial tensions, heightened by character motives nicely confused with personal animosities, such as a past white-Indian love affair contrasted with a present affair between Anthony (Castle's nephew) and Melissa (Cooley's niece). This echo of the past in the present calls attention to changes in attitudes over different generations as well as to the continuity of unbridgeable divisions between whites and Arapahos. Underlying the plot is an old story updated, the looting of Indian resources, now the competition for reservation oil.

The Ghost Walker (1996), Coel's second O'Malley book, involves Vicky Holden as a more central figure than in the first, where she primarily acted as the legal arm of O'Malley's investigation. Here, the Jesuit's discovery of a body left alongside the road in a snowstorm triggers unease and even horror when the corpse cannot be found after O'Malley reports it to tribal police: a dead person left unburied will lead to a spirit walking the reservation. The eerie circumstances of O'Malley's discovery and his understanding of Arapaho beliefs, despite his Christian ideology, give credence to the Indian viewpoint, and the task of the investigation becomes in part to remove this pall over the community. Meanwhile, Vicky's grown daughter has returned to the area with some white friends, and we learn of Vicky's problems with her husband and the daughter's troubled life as a young, assimilated Native American in Los Angeles. A third plot line concerns both the tribal leaders' and the Catholic diocese's willingness to end the century-old mission to the Arapaho in the name of an economic development scam, a plan to sacrifice history and tradition for a recreation-entertainment center (read "casino," a real-life choice for many tribes) that will end O'Malley's vocation as well.

The interlocking plots combine neatly through O'Malley and Vicky, whose mutual devotion to service for others unites them but flies in the face of modern American self-interest and corporate profit. As in *The Eagle Catcher*, Coel contrasts the vastness of the natural environment with the petty maneuverings of some of the humans who inhabit it, demonstrating rather than preaching about what it means to live in harmony with nature, the traditional Arapaho way. She is admirably restrained throughout, allowing readers to draw their own conclusions from events and descriptions, but the point is nonetheless driven home: the modern greed for quick profits and short-term solutions is a limited vision in terms of both Arapaho and traditional Jesuit value systems. Coel thus communicates effectively with mainstream readers who might have trouble appreciating the Arapaho way without O'Malley's sturdy guidance. Her avoidance of stereotyped villains—Native Americans as well as whites are subject to materialistic temptations—gives her novel further credibility.

Although O'Malley is clearly the central amateur detective (he intuits a connection between a dying stranger and the death of a tribal leader, and informally seeks that connection), Coel makes Vicky's struggle to serve her community central to her next two novels, *The Dream Stalker* (1997) and *The Story Teller* (1998). The question reservation Arapaho must face in *The Dream Stalker* is the price of employment: Are the jobs to be created by leasing land for storing nuclear waste worth the threat to their land and to the health of their families? Most reservation residents, reassured by the smooth promises of slick business-men, are convinced that the short-term gains outweigh the long-term dangers. The power that control of these leases and jobs will bring leads respected com-munity members to cover up facts about underground water and subterranean shifts that are vital to an informed decision. Vicky, believing she voices the fears of the reservation grandmothers, is the sole Arapaho voice of opposition, and her attempts to raise questions of living up to Arapaho values and of avoid-ing unnecessary dangers are met with disdain and anger. To her horror, she finds herself trapped in a peculiar position: taking a highly traditional Arapaho stance in the face of progress and modernity, and at the same time voicing the same doubts raised by outsiders—vociferous white environmental protesters who are meddling in a tribal issue. Yet, she persists. O'Malley's investigation dovetails with threats on her life, and the seemingly unrelated threads of the murder case come together with the reservation conflict. While the denouement is exciting, it is the resolution of the jobs versus environment issue, and questions of per-sonal greed and lust for power versus obligation to the community, that take precedence. Ultimately, Vicky bears witness to her role in the Arapaho com-munity by reaffirming the traditional values of respect for and preservation of the land so long sacred to her people.

In *The Story Teller* Vicky is again working for the community interest, this time at the behest of the tribal council. New federal laws requiring that museums return to Native American tribes artifacts sacred to tribal religion and tribal ways have led a Denver museum to provide the council a list of holdings. However, missing from the list is a one-of-a-kind Arapaho ledger book, an eyewitness account of Arapaho history, including their massacre at Sand Creek on Novem-ber 29, 1864. Such tribal records were a common Plains Indian phenomenon, native history recorded in bought or stolen Cavalry ledgers instead of on animal skins. Because this ledger book, worth $1.3 million intact, has a greater financial value if sold piecemeal, page by page, Vicky is fighting against time to recover this Arapaho treasure before a vital historical record is lost. In addition to the obvious sacred and financial value of the ledger is an unexpected modern worth: large sums of federal moneys to be granted to the surviving family members of those massacred at Sand Creek hinge on this historical testimony, for a respected Cheyenne historian claims no Arapaho were present at Sand Creek and the Arapaho have as evidence only the stories passed down by their ancestors and the word of a tribal elder who saw the ledger in the museum in 1920.

While Vicky strives to overcome the cover-up set in motion by museum and university officials and the blind insistence of the police that drug conflicts caused Arapaho student deaths, Father O'Malley battles in-house Catholic prej-udices and politics to win permission to provide his congregation a small museum to house sacred tribal artifacts. As the plots merge, Coel effectively captures the way in which nineteenth-century history still affects the lives of the Cheyenne and Arapaho, the difficulty of finding historical fact when "official" history and "oral" history clash, and the heartbreaking gulf that still exists between whites and Native Americans. As a humanist and a historian, she carries the detective genre beyond its origins as simply entertainment and uses it effectively to create a sense of a complete Native American community, one with depths unplumbed and with distinct individuals who nevertheless share common cultural features. Interestingly, some of the tribal conflicts she describes in her fiction have proven to be realities, a fact that suggests she has her finger on the pulse of Arapaho-white interaction.

Richard Parrish

Richard Parrish, like Coel, is one of the best modern writers to date to deal with Indians as victims and suspects in the mystery/detection genre because he also distinctively humanizes them, so that readers come to know characters as individuals with virtues and weaknesses. Set in and near post-World War II Tucson, Arizona, Parrish's novels depend on an outsider's view of Papago reservation life. His detective is a world-weary Bureau of Indian Affairs lawyer, Joshua Rabb, a Jew who lost his arm and his innocence in the war and who has a son and a daughter to raise on his own, his wife having died while he was freeing concentration camp victims. Brooklyn-born Rabb has accepted $129 a month and a rural shack near the San Xavier del Bac Papago Indian Reservation for the chance to work hard in dry, healthy air and recover from the ennui, despair, and injured lungs that threaten him. His children look forward to meeting the romanticized Indian of literature and are stunned by the uncomfortable realities of reservation life.

In *The Dividing Line* (1993) Rabb's initial impression of the Papago is shaped by the whites around him: dirty, smelly troublemakers, often drunken and abusive, seeking a free ride and unwilling to work for it. What he learns firsthand, however, is a very different reality. The Indians are dirty and smelly because their reservation water has been tapped off to irrigate white lands upriver; there are no jobs on or off the reservation. The Papago are so poor they cannot afford to change clothes until Bureau of Indian Affairs (BIA) or charity clothing arrives, and tuberculosis and other diseases associated with poverty run rampant; medical facilities are minimal, and a dedicated few work long hours with little or no medicine to treat patients resigned to death. The wealth of minerals and metals beneath their soil (including gold) is being illegally siphoned off by a powerful senator who, through bribes and political machinations, has held a stranglehold on reservation land for years and has profited enormously at Indian expense.

Many Papago have fought, been wounded, and even experienced the same horrors as Rabb on the battlefields of Europe, but they have come home to a despair and an emptiness even bleaker than his. Moreover, they seem powerless to protect what little remains. The Catholic mission thrives and grows rich amid reservation poverty, and the majority of nuns and priests seem contemptuous of their charges, to whom they try to teach humility and passive acceptance. Magdalena Antone, the granddaughter of the former chief, lives with the Rabb family as their "acculturation girl," a practice initiated to teach local whites about the Papagos and to provide Papago youths with experience in the white world. Magdalena, a University of Arizona graduate, helps the Rabbs break through their stereotypes, see the Papago as human beings like themselves, and sympathize with their plight.

Rabb's arrival is marked by a series of horrible murders that no one really seems to care about: a thirteen-year-old Papago girl and a ten-year-old Papago boy are raped anally, strangled, and left in an irrigation ditch on the reservation, not far from Rabb's new home. Only when the victim is a nun (a radical helping the Papago stand up for their rights) does the local community get up in arms. A very drunk Papago found near the crime scene is arrested and charged, though the physical evidence points toward someone else; it is clear that scapegoating takes precedence over any real investigation.

The power of Parrish's vision is that he guides readers to see what Rabb sees: that no human of decency can allow such abuse of other human beings without being diminished and tainted. Rabb begins to instinctively feel parallels between the German racism and genocide he saw firsthand in the concentration camps and in the liberated European cities, and what he sees going on in Arizona. For him, in a sense, the Papagos are the Southwest's Jews, and, like an enlightened German during the time of Hitler, he faces abuse and threats, assaults on his children, blackmail attempts, and physical danger when he tries to do what is right. The Papagos, recognizing his courage in their defense, stand by him, and youthful warriors, their skills honed on the battlefields of Europe, camp out in and around his home to protect his family from vigilantes outraged at his defense of an Indian. Yet, even when he proves in court that the accused man was physically incapable of committing the deeds of which he is accused, vigilantes horribly and self-righteously kill an innocent. Then, when he exposes the real villain, the facts of the case never reach the public.

In *Versions of the Truth* (1994) Rabb's sense of moral certainty is tested, and he finds himself at times in "a puzzling void" where everything is "shades of gray, fuzzy around the edges" (212). Cholera in the reservation water, from sewage in Mexico, is killing off Papago, and Rabb has to negotiate a deal across the border to protect locals—short-term if he yields to pressure, long-term only if he is willing to battle major opposition forces in both the United States and Mexico, forces adept at blackmail, bribery, and murder. A Papago client tells Rabb about running over and killing a mother and child and clearly has no understanding of guilt, but Rabb's family needs the up-front financing the client's wife is willing to pay for a strong defense, so he takes the case. In the meantime, pregnant with a child the Church will not bless and her family will not accept, Magdalena seeks either a quick abortion or a husband—all this in the first two chapters. The ties between Mexico and the Papago reservation loom large in this novel as Rabb exposes corruption in the granting of multimillion-dollar federal contracts and the cooked books of receiver companies. He is assisted by Jesús "Chuy" Leyva, a Papago reservation policeman with a flexible interpretation of his duties, especially after villains use locoweed to cause the death of Rabb's employer's son. Chuy becomes a more and more significant sidekick in *Nothing but the Truth* (1995), which links mob murders of Hasidic Jews with the Papago man Rabb is defending, and *Wind and Lies* (1996), in which extremist Mormons move onto the reservation, seeking converts among the Lamanites (modern Indians who are supposedly descendants of the Israelites), and using snake handling, polygamy, male supremacy, and free food as draws. In *Wind and Lies* Chuy tries to protect his financée, Magdalena, from rape and murder while Rabb, using decorated war hero and reservation sheriff Chuy as his test case, fights Arizona's "guardianship" laws and wins Arizona Indians the right to vote. Rabb argues on the points of the law, but his final plea is an impassioned one:

"May it please the court," he said more softly. "I have one last thing to leave Your Honors with. When a Pima Indian named Ira Hayes, who lives but fifty miles from this great hall of justice, risked his life to raise the flag of freedom on Mount Surabaci, he was an American, no more, no less. This American people sent him to that place to fight for them. This American people made him the symbol of brave men everywhere. And this same people denies him at this very moment the right to vote. Who is this people that is so arrogant and unjust that it usurps from him the right to vote, the ultimate mark of his dignity and worth as a citizen, in the same instant that it demands from him the possible sacrifice of his life so that *it* can continue to vote?" (288)

As the novels progress, Rabb comes to realize that "perhaps even more than the Indians needing him to help them, he need[s] them to help give his life some meaning" (*Wind and Lies*, 4), and it is Rabb's personal commitment that infuses Parrish's novels with intensity and sympathy. Like that of Coel's Father O'Malley and Vicky Holden, Rabb's service to others foregrounds Native Americans' humanity and undoes stereotypes of cultural sameness: though identifiably Indian, characters yet emerge as distinct individuals, both admirable and less so. This achievement is notable in any fiction, let alone one dealing with cultures unfamiliar and perhaps even exotic for many readers. As in Coel's novels, in Parrish's works Native Americans become equal actors on the fictional stage, their friendships, setbacks, and successes a matter of personal interest for readers; as a result, they achieve a wholeness missing in most popular fiction. By capturing historical attitudes through his fictionalized versions of real cases (like Justice Levi Udall's decision in the 1948 Arizona case on Indian voting rights), Parrish teaches modern readers uncomfortable lessons about social and political injustices only slightly distanced from the present.

NATIVE AMERICANS AS GUIDES

The historical tradition of the Native American scout and guide makes readers expect the modern version of such a character to be a tough male drawing on hunting skills to track down fleeing villains. Instead, Thomas Perry—the only writer to date to depict modern Native Americans as guides (not just trackers)—gives us a petite woman who uses her native skills to rescue victims and guide them to safety. She is Jane Whitefield, a blue-eyed Seneca (her father Huron, her mother white but adopted into the Seneca Wolf Clan)—a modern woman using high-tech means in an ancient cause. She began her career as a college activist pushing voter registration on the powwow circuit. When challenged by tribal elders to act on her principles, she smuggled the last member of the Beothuk tribe past federal officials and helped him establish a new identity in Venezuela on his promise to record for posterity the ancient stories and oral traditions of his defunct tribe (the Beothuks could not adjust to the concept of private property, and one by one had been wiped out as thieves). Whitefield acts within her tribe's traditional role as a guide who makes the path easy for those needing to cross through hostile territory—but she does so with all the resources of computerized America.

Whitefield's modern application of this ancient role is to provide her own personalized version of the government's Witness Protection Program for fugitives needing new identities and a chance to make a new life, far from present threats and dangers. Unlike the traditional detective who seeks out the missing person, Whitefield, in an original twist, helps the missing person stay missing and (hopefully) unfindable, and her private detection serves to cover up and protect rather than expose and reveal. Her clients are battered wives, threatened children, adults who have gotten into trouble too deep and dangerous for them to extricate themselves safely. The novels make explicit the preparation, ingenuity, courage, insight, and instincts necessary to perform this job effectively, and at the same time they communicate the physical and psychological toll that failure takes. This updated variation of a guide is a fine example of creative reimagining of a traditional role applicable to modern times.

A highly competent and resourceful heroine, Whitefield knows the ins and outs of modern, computerized bureaucracies, but she is equally at home cutting cross-country over forest trails and capitalizing on the anonymity of Native American life—a life indifferent to credit cards and paper trails, and thus to computer tracking of individuals—to hide clients from murderous pursuers. She fastens her long hair with a black ring and a five-inch-long sharpened peg, weaponlike with its T-shaped handle, and carries a mayapple perfume laced with water hemlock, the Iroquois warrior method of suicide when captured by enemies. Skirting the edges of lawlessness—forging documents and re-creating paper trails that confirm new identities—she helps the weak, though perhaps not so innocent, escape the predators who target them. At the same time, she provides readers a running commentary on Seneca history, from ancient war trails to confrontations with George Washington, and from clan alliances to old growth orchards of apple and plum. She interprets Seneca theology, for instance, about Hawenneyu, the Right-Handed Twin creator, and Hanegoategeh, the Left-Handed Twin destroyer, who together balance the universe, in ways meaningful to modern readers. When she travels to other states, her comments provide a Native American perspective. For example, Whitefield speculates on the abuses Spanish conquistadors and missionaries inflicted on the native California population (tortured, shackled slaves virtually exterminated while building lovely missions to glorify a cruel white god): "California . . . had begun as a slaughterhouse and could never be made completely clean" (*Dance*, 159).

Vanishing Act (1995) begins the series with a defining incident. Whitefield fiercely attacks and injures a rather nasty private detective who pursues her client, then offers tobacco to *Jo-Ge-Ho*, the Senecan "Stone Throwers," in thanks for past assistance and as a prayer that her client will make her journey alone in safety. The Seneca believe that the Stone Throwers, the Little People of the Gorge, protected the Nundawaono, the People of the Hill (the Seneca) in ancient times, and that their special role was to save people "from the horrible things that could happen," to take victims out of the world and hide them (18). Thus, in her rescues Whitefield is reenacting the legendary role of the *Jo-Ge-Ho* and of Seneca believers in them.

Perry's skill in this series is to make credible this amalgam of Seneca tradition and modern skills, of assimilation and at the same time separation. Perhaps it was this dichotomy that led the reviewer of the *Boston Sunday Globe* to aptly call the novel "a very rational book about the limits of rationality." As Whitefield and her client cross Lake Ontario near Fort Niagara, pursued by armed thugs, she thinks of her ancestors' elm- and hickory-bark canoes and their stories of Sky Woman and the giant turtle, and she relies on a loose network of distant relatives to remain out of sight. Readers learn about standing treaties that allow Indians to move freely back and forth across the Canadian-U.S. border; about why the Seneca still call Washington "the destroyer of villages"; about traditional dances and ceremonies; about the legends of Jigonasee, Deganawida, Hiawatha, and the Iroquois Confederation; and about the unexpected bits and pieces of Northeastern life that derived from Native Americans.

However, at the same time, Perry sets up layers of deception in which Whitefield's charming client (in reality a cunning, coldhearted hit man) uses her protection as a means to trace and kill a past client, whom Whitefield, in turn, must avenge. The final conflict, played out across upstate New York wilderness territory, forces Whitefield to draw on ancestral knowledge and skills to survive. When stripped of all but her hunting knife, she makes herself a Nundawa-style warclub and Seneca-style bow and arrows, sets traps, and moves silently, "a shadow within a shadow" (309), until ready to tempt her target into deadly pursuit. Thus, the protector of innocents must, in self-defense against an amoral killer, turn hunter-trapper and counter violence with violence.

In *Dance for the Dead* (1996) Whitefield again battles for her life, and that of her eight-year-old client, drawing on her resources and skills to unravel the legal ins and outs of a crime in the making, a multimillion-dollar trust raided by its designated trustees. *Shadow Woman* (1997) pits Whitefield against a psychotically driven hit team (Earl and Linda Thompson) who come after her when she successfully provides a Las Vegas casino employee a new identity, not only once but twice. In each novel, the dichotomy between what she does for a living and her personal hometown life deepens, but when Whitefield tries to quit, the husband she has chosen over career asks her to help one of his patients (a dedicated medical researcher) vanish (*The Face-Changers*, 1998).

Perry writes fast-faced, credible thrillers with compelling complications and tightly interwoven plot threads, but it is his conception of Jane Whitefield and her role as guide that makes this series enduring. Perry embodies in her both modern skills and Seneca values. As a modern woman, she relies on the computer, the internet, advanced means of travel and communication, credit cards, advertising—the cutting-edge tools of high technology; yet, as a Seneca, with a strong sense of place and heritage, a commitment to community, and an enduring tribal role, she exudes the strength of Indian dream power. Each novel includes fascinating historical detail, like the anticipated French "surprise" attack on the Seneca in 1687, which made the area from Mackinac to Quebec a very dangerous place for Gallic travelers for quite some time. In each novel, dreams have special significance and modern events are relived in Seneca settings with warnings and clues that help Whitefield act more cautiously in the modern world. For instance, in *Dance for the Dead* she dreams of pursuit and capture by a giant cannibal whose necklace of human teeth and savage Seneca mask mark him as supernatural evil, and indeed the modern villain methodically and viciously destroys others and cannibalizes their wealth. In *Shadow Woman*, it is Seneca lore about possession, witchcraft, and shape-shifting that helps Whitefield determine how to defeat her crazed opponents.

Fiction that freezes Indians in picturesque traditional settings denies Native Americans the right to change and thus the right to a living history; this series acknowledges those rights. Thus, by drawing on a traditional Native American role and demonstrating its viability and evolution in the modern world, Perry does what few other fiction writers do: he recognizes that Native Americans have the right to evade white expectations of who and what they are, and instead to forge modern roles for themselves within the frameworks of their heritage—to find ongoing meaning and significance rather than be trapped forever in the time warp of white imagining.

NATIVE AMERICANS AS DETECTIVES

Casting Native Americans as detectives or investigators is natural, especially in Western or Southwestern settings, where landscape and nature loom large and where reservations are isolated or in many ways cut off completely from mainstream life. No one else knows the landscape and local customs as well as the people who have lived there for hundreds, perhaps thousands, of years. The traditional role of the Indian as tracker, hunter, and guide translates easily to that of the detective who follows clues to hunt down a killer and who acts as a guide taking readers into unexplored cultural territory. From the earliest days, whites exploring the shifting Western frontiers depended on the superior skills and knowledge of Indian trackers and scouts. In fact, it is surprising that this role is not more frequent in popular literature about Native Americans. Perhaps it is the somewhat ethnocentric equation of all detectives with urban landscapes of the nineteenth century and after: detection must be done by twitty English lords, hardboiled assimilated Americans, or fastidious Belgians. Perhaps it is mainstream stereotypes that make us expect Indians to be simply intuitive, spiritual, and otherworldly rather than highly observant, pragmatic, and rational, as all hunter-gatherers living in a harsh environment must have been if they were to survive.

Of those works with Native American detectives, Jean Hager's and Tony Hillerman's follow traditional detective genre patterns but set the standards for later Native American detective stories and have unquestionably introduced many popular fiction buffs to Cherokee, Choctaw, Navajo, Hopi, and Pueblo lives and values with sympathy and informed understanding. The Thurlos (Aimée and David) have followed Hillerman with detection set among the Tewa and Pueblo tribes, but have chosen to make the spiritual and supernatural dominate the ratiocinative, as have Micah Hackler, James Doss, and Peter Bowen. Dana Stabenow has made her Aleut detective Kate Shugak a spokeswoman for feminism as well as for Alaskan Indian issues.

Traditional Detectives in a New Native American Landscape

Traditional detectives in Native American settings work crimes in patterns set by the standard genre conventions: a crime is committed; clues are left; the detective investigates, interviewing witnesses, studying the scene of the crime, responding to laboratory and coroner reports, piecing together the bits of the puzzle until logic, intuition, knowledge of locale and personalities add up to a solution; the detective produces a resolution. Native Americans in these works have roles ranging from tacked-on tokenism to center-stage parts in which Native American culture is the keystone of the plot.

Jean Hager

Jean Hager's Oklahoma detectives, in keeping with the realities of their tribal heritage, are both fully assimilated. Half-Cherokee Police Chief Mitch Bushyhead, who knows little about his ancestry or heritage, needs Cherokee and Choctaw traditions explained; half-Cherokee Molly Bearpaw, an investigator for the Native American Advocacy League and later the major crimes investigator for the Cherokee Nation Marshal Service, knows slightly more only because of her conscious effort to study such traditional skills as finger weaving. Bushyhead worries about coping with a maturing teenage daughter and dealing with local politicians who want instantaneous answers, while Bearpaw is concerned about the difficulties her gender creates for her inquiries. In both detective series, community interpretations of events in terms of traditional beliefs (evil witches who act like succubi, night walkers, appropriators, and fire carriers) serve as misleading possibilities, which are eventually rejected through deductive reasoning or plodding investigation. Investigations turn on universal human motives like greed and jealousy; the crimes are similar to those of many mainstream communities: social issues such as drugs and smuggling (*The Grandfather Medicine*, 1989; *The Fire Carrier*, 1996), wife beating (*Night Walker*, 1990), child molestation (*Ghostland*, 1992), the high cost of medical care (*The Redbird's Cry*, 1994), dirty real estate deals and illegal dumping (*Ravenmocker*, 1994), construction fraud (*Seven Black Stones*, 1995), and New Age hoaxes (*The Spirit Caller*, 1997). Hager uses the activities of the seventy-year-old medicine man Crying Wolf and police assistant Virgil Rabbit, a member of the Cherokee secret organization Nighthawk Keetoowahs, to suggest alternative ways of reaching truth (Crying Wolf's symbolic visions correspond to the realities Bushyhead uncovers), to voice the fears of locals, and to provide a means of working Cherokee tradition, arts, and lore into books about a reservation where most are highly assimilated and where the young rightly debunk "ancient" rituals that actually originated in the nineteenth or early twentieth century.

Tony Hillerman

It may seem stretching the envelope of the detective story to assert, as the beginning of this chapter does, that the Indian guide is an early American detective, but there is no doubt that one of its best modern practitioners makes a similar connection between past and present. The brilliance of Tony Hillerman is twofold. First, his two main detectives, Navajos Joe Leaphorn and Jim Chee, operate in both the modern world of forensic science and police procedure and the traditional one of Native American culture. In Hillerman's work this native setting provides not simply backdrop but also motive and rationale. Second, the majority of characters in Hillerman novels are Native Americans (mainly Navajo, but also Zuñi and Hopi), ranging from the highly assimilated to the highly traditional and the many steps in between. These are true Native American detective stories, not stories about Anglos with token characters and Indian trappings for exotic effect. Hillerman was the first detective story writer to make Native American characters dominate and the first to move the detective figure from the metaphorical canyons of the big city to the real ones of New Mexico and Arizona. Throughout his canon, the mountains, buttes, and canyons—the landscape of Navajo country—provide a larger-than-human scale against which age-old patterns of chaos and balance are played out. This is the true sensibility of the West, and especially of the Native American West. His detectives find nature the wellspring of their power and commitment:

They took the road that wanders over Washington Pass via Red Lake, Crystal, and Sheep Springs. Winding down the east slope of the Chuskas, Leaphorn stopped at an overlook. He pointed east and swept his hand northward, encompassing an immensity of rolling tan and gray grasslands. Zuñi Mountains to the south, Jemez Mountains to the east, and far to the north the snowy San Juans in Colorado. . . . The cottonwoods along the river formed a crooked line of dazzling gold across a vast landscape of grays and tans. And beyond, the dark blue mountains formed the horizon, the Abajos, Sleeping Ute, and the San Juans, already capped with early snow. It was one of those still, golden days of high desert autumn. (*Coyote*, 117–118)

This removal of setting from the cliché of urban sleaziness to fresh wilderness splendor in fact reinvigorated an old genre, giving life to dozens and dozens of other Native American investigators working the mean roads and trails of the far country. As in the Western movie tradition, human pettiness and corruption are played off against stunning vistas, a landscape that inspires and gives pleasure even as violence and crime occupy the front stage. Setting provides perspective, reducing the significance of human malfeasance when ant-size figures struggle on the huge landscape but highlighting its inhumanity as well, since the empty, lonely country highlights the deep human need for congenial community. Stereotypes fall before fresh knowledge, especially of complex and sophisticated sets of exotic beliefs. Before Hillerman, most readers had probably never heard *Dineh*, the Navajo word for themselves, but thanks to Hillerman they will likely know something about reservation landscapes and life and will have heard of skinwalkers, corpse dust, sacred clowns, the Blessed Way, ghost sickness, sandpaintings, and Coyote cautionary tales.

Hillerman's novels have raised the consciousness of a whole generation and awakened readers to the existence of a worldview quite different from their own. He includes part of an Enemy Way "sing" (a ritual performance) to turn a witch's evil back on the witch in *The Blessing Way* (1970), a Sun Way ritual (with sandpaintings) for starting a new world after a cataclysm in *Listening Woman* (1978), a burial ritual and Ghost Way ceremony to protect from the evil spirits of the dead in *The Ghost Way* (1984), and a Pueblo/Hopi celebration with kachinas and sacred clowns to capture the contrast between divine perfection and human imperfection in *Sacred Clowns* (1993). *Dance Hall of the Dead* (1973) begins with a ritual slaying and captures the mysticism of Zuñi religious practices from a Navajo view, while *The Dark Wind* (1981), in part, explores the conflicts between the Navajo and the Hopi. *People of Darkness* (1980), set in an ethnic melting pot on the reservation (Nacomas, Lagunas, Navajos, Mexican-Americans, German-Americans, and so on), contrasts the role of a traditional ritual singer with very different roles in the Native American Church, and narrates parts of the Navajo Creation story and legends associated with the reservation landscape. At the same time, Hillerman captures the internal conflicts that are the inevitable price of assimilation: the sad Cheyenne policeman watching a John Ford film in which noble Cheyenne warriors are defeated by whites,

while his Navajo companions in the audience laugh at the bawdy jokes of the
Navajo actors playing the Cheyenne; sitting with him is a successful Navajo
defense lawyer who has devoted her life to defending her people but who cannot
speak Navajo and is equally mystified. Hillerman evokes the pain of loss but
also its necessity. If the lawyer had studied on the reservation and learned Navajo as her primary language, she would be in no position to help her people
as effectively as she now can. If, as Berkhofer argues in *The White Man's
Indian*, it has been the fate of Native Americans to be reduced to simplistic
generic figures, Hillerman goes far in deconstructing this reductionism by presenting the diversity of Indian tribes, ways, and realities in Arizona and New
Mexico.

In addition, Hillerman's detectives are truly cross-cultural, bridging two
worlds and interpreting the Navajo Way and Navajo life for non-Navajos. They
are the readers' guides into new, previously unexplored, detective territory:

From where Leaphorn stood by the gallery window on the floor above, he was almost
at eye level with the great bird. Its beak snapped suddenly—a half dozen sharp clacking
sounds in perfect time with the drum. It hooted and its strange white-rimmed eyes stared
for a moment directly into Leaphorn's. The policeman saw it with double vision. He
saw it as a mask of tremendous technical ingenuity, a device of leather, embroidered
cotton, carved wood, feathers, and paint held aloft on a pole, its beak and its movements
manipulated by the dancer within it. But he also saw Shalako, the courier between the
gods and men, who brought fertility to the seeds and rain to the desert when the people
of Zuñi called, and who came on this great day to be fed and blessed by his people.
Now it danced, swooping down the earthen floor, its great horns glittering with reflected
light, its fan of topknot feathers bristling, its voice the hooting call of the night birds.
(*Dance Hall of the Dead*, 147)

Hillerman's ability to capture a dual perspective, an empathy for and deep understanding of Navajo (and Zuñi) ways as well as a modern need to be on the
cutting edge of a profession (the very technical field of scientific investigation),
and the personal problems a dual vision entails should be the model for future
writers in the detective genre. The dilemmas of his characters encapsulate larger
problems of assimilation and adjustment to change. In *Sacred Clowns* Chee, as
an educated modern man, feels pride in the success of the Navajo Agricultural
Industries at irrigating and upgrading the land for farming, but as a traditionalist
he is offended at the way modernized methods have meant uprooting desert
plants and wreaking havoc with the landscape by plowing the large swirls necessary for efficient water distribution. In *The Fallen Man* (1996), well-
intentioned Anglos make Chee shudder with horror when they talk about tossing
their relative's cremated ashes off the top of a Navajo sacred mountain with a
wonderful view. They think such an act would be an expression of harmony
with nature; Chee thinks of corpse dust spreading ghost sickness throughout the
Navajo community. Besides, as one old-timer comments, simply climbing the

mountain would be the equivalent of disrespectful Navajos climbing curiously over the Vatican, the Wailing Wall, or the most sacred shrines in Mecca.

Leaphorn's professional training (including a master's degree in cultural anthropology), his strong powers of observation, and his skepticism about witchcraft, skinwalkers, and evil spirits distance him from the problems of reservation and tribal life and the difficulties traditionalists face with assimilation. Called by some "the Sherlock Holmes of the Navajo Tribal Police" (*Coyote*, 46, 162), Leaphorn sees and understands through clear logic and reason. As a policeman, he doesn't believe in coincidence; instead, he believes, as his uncle once told him, that things seem random only because we see them from the wrong perspective; when they are turned the right way, like a kaleidoscope, they suddenly fall into place: "There was a pattern there, and a motive, if he could only find them" (*Coyote*, 160, 149). Thus it is that in *The Fallen Man* Leaphorn can sit in his home in Window Rock and find a logical connection between an eleven-year-old skeleton discovered on Ship Rock Mountain and the sniper-murder of an old canyon guide three hundred miles across the Navajo reservation at Canyon de Chelly. Leaphorn thinks of himself as a realist but of Chee as a romantic, as someone creative enough and intelligent enough to make breakthrough discoveries, intuitive but not cynical enough to see as clearly as he himself sees.

However, it takes the younger, more traditional Chee to grapple personally with the implications of his profession and with his own internal need to serve his people in more meaningful ways than the investigation of wrongdoers. Chee has a degree in anthropology and sociology from the University of New Mexico, "with distinction," and is a graduate of the FBI Academy. Nonetheless, his negative experiences on assignment in Los Angeles and his love first for Anglo Mary Landon and later for assimilated Navajo Janet Pete make him rethink his values and his commitments. Both women want him to take a higher-paying job back east, but Chee realizes that leaving the Navajo homeland means giving up being Navajo. His decision to stay is a commitment to a new role as restorer of harmony to his people. His ongoing studies of the healing arts and harmonies of the Navajo Blessed Way in order to become a *hataalii* (healer) allow him to share with readers his insights into the mysteries of Navajo inner life as he walks the fine line between two very different traditions. Chee uses sweat lodge ceremonies to protect himself from *chindi* and ghost sickness, and he performs a Blessed Way song to help restore Leaphorn's life to harmony after his wife dies from the side effects of cancer (though Leaphorn doubts its efficacy).

Initially, Hillerman gave his two detectives separate cases, first Leaphorn, later Chee. In recent books, however, he has made Leaphorn's and Chee's cases intersect, despite the detectives' very different natures, and has made his mysteries require the expertise of both to find "the knot" where the "little tangle of strings," the separate threads in a single case, come together (*A Thief of Time*, 153). The result allows more varied perspectives of reservation life and values, and a contrast in methods between Chee, who rushes in and gets hurt a lot, and Leaphorn, who cautiously follows the hidden signs that step-by-step guide him to understanding and then action.

While Leaphorn and Chee have to deal on a daily basis with local malfeasance (everything from badly behaved teenagers to stolen cows), Hillerman's main offenders, whether Native American or Anglo, violate Navajo perceptions of community and of a life in harmony with nature and with community. For Navajos, wealth is a symbol of selfishness, and a too competitive personal style leaves one out of harmony with others. Thus, greed, materialism, and ambition are constant themes. Hillerman's villains use their power to try to turn the reservation into a dumping ground for toxic waste (*Sacred Clowns*) or to pollute the rivers with cyanide and sludge from open-pit mining (*Fallen Man*), or they rob graves, not simply for invaluable Anasazi pottery but also for human bones for scientific study (*A Thief of Time*, 1988). In *Talking God* (1989) a wanna-be Indian becomes the tool of a scheming thief who uses Smithsonian Institution Native American bone and artifact collections as a distraction; in *Coyote Waits* (1990) an aged crystal reader's retelling of Navajo stories to anthropologists awakens a killer's lust for a lost treasure and unleashes the chaos and disorder Coyote traditionally brings.

These malefactors are mainly outsiders, selfish and warped in a variety of ways, incapable of commitments or human connections, and their acts are not only destructive but also aggressive perversions of traditional ways. They may be lawyers, scientists, or scholars (anthropologists, historians, linguists, environmentalists, doctors) whose obsession with proving pet theories, winning fame, exploiting special knowledge, or simply covering up padded financial accounts leads to crime; they may be greedy collectors for whom the possession of antiquities means more than human life; they may be drug dealers (including rogue FBI agents) or hardened criminals incapable of human attachments; they may be activists who value political abstractions over people; or they may simply be insane. Sometimes, their cruelty finds expression in unexpectedly terrifying forms, as in the following:

He had heard nothing. But the man was standing not fifty feet away, watching him silently. He was a big man with his wolf skin draped across his shoulders. The forepaws hung limply down the front of his black shirt and the empty skull of the beast was pushed back on his forehead, its snout pointing upward.

The Wolf looked at Horseman. And then he smiled.

"I won't tell," Horseman said. His voice was loud, rising almost to a scream. And then he turned and ran, ran frantically down the dry wash. . . . And behind him he heard the Wolf laughing. (*The Blessing Way*, 13)

Often, Hillerman's villains manipulate the prejudices or dreams of others to their own ends; for example, the Indian enthusiast Mr. Highhawk, in *Talking God*, who sends a museum official her grandparents' bones in a box to protest the

Smithsonian's cavalier attitude toward its collection of bones and relics, including eighteen thousand complete Native American skeletons.

Skinwalkers (1986) turns on Navajo belief in witchcraft, the compulsion of evil people to break taboos, to commit incest and murder, to lodge a bone bead in a victim's chest, to scatter corpse dust, to call on the powers of darkness to bless their cursed deeds. Witchcraft has high potential for crossing over into another genre, transforming a detective story into a horror story or a tale of the supernatural, but Hillerman controls this possibility through the rational perspective of his two investigators. Leaphorn finds witchcraft cruel, sick, and evil, a hangover from a period of captivity, a relic that keeps Navajos from dealing with trouble realistically (72). Chee, though skeptical about the power of witches to change shapes and fly, sees witchcraft as malicious evil, a conscious choice to work for imbalance and to choose conflict and ugliness over the Navajo Way of peace, beauty, and community (73): "He saw it every day he worked as a policeman—in those who sold whiskey to children, in those who bought videocassette recorders while their relatives were hungry, in the knife fights in a Gallup alley, in beaten wives and abandoned children" (246). Chee's reading of a traditional belief as an abstraction rather than as a literal fact, a metaphor for social disarray rather than a living presence, allows mainstream readers entrée into his world.

Modern American urban and suburban life has frequently traded direct experience with other cultures for television or film stereotypes, even of groups not too far distant geographically. The complexities and difficulties of crossing between cultures is not simply a matter of etiquette and customs, but of deep linguistic and philosophical barriers, difficulties hardly ever treated adequately in the mass media or mass entertainment. A person who thinks of time as an ongoing present and of the future lying in wait behind him, the past an ever diminishing road stretched out in front of him, as do some native groups, is going to have difficulty dealing with the concept of a 9 to 5 job or the need to plan his 401(k). As anthropologist Edward Hall has pointed out, such concepts are incompatible, and affect even such innocuous-seeming issues as getting Navajo children to adapt to rigid school bus pickup schedules.

Hillerman's distinction as a writer about Native Americans is his realistic perception that it is impossible to be both a modern person and a traditionalist, that the qualities of Leaphorn and Chee cannot be contained in a single figure. Chee's spiritualism will always be at odds with Leaphorn's rationalism, and though the two detectives are both Navajo and both are to varying degrees assimilated to Anglo culture, they remain, in many ways, worlds apart. Being one or the other requires giving up something, and there are benefits and losses no matter the choice. Furthermore, the realities of assimilation permit infinite choices and gradations in the acceptance of another culture, with one person, for example, speaking the Navajo language well but feeling alienated by the constrictions of reservation life while another may be dedicated to community values but know only the superficial words of daily greeting. Hillerman manages to explore the sociological realities of reservation life while rapidly moving forward a complex but logical plot in which multiple threads weave a pattern that can finally be seen through the application of traditional detective methods. While the story engages and entertains, insights into culture and values transform reader understanding of Native American strengths and problems.

Nontraditional Detectives

The nontraditional detectives stretch the detective and police procedural genres in three main directions. One direction is toward Native American detectives acting in historical settings, in keeping with the modern trend in the genre at large toward medieval, Renaissance, and Victorian detectives, or toward resurrected versions of historically located detectives like Sherlock Holmes: modern Indians who draw on hunter-gatherer instincts and forest powers. Another is toward tough, feminist detectives whose gender statements are more important than any ethnic message. Still another direction includes non-European means of solving crime, New Age mysticism and spiritualism, to the point that ratiocination becomes lost and shamanism takes over.

Historical or Hunter-Gatherer-Based Mysteries

While Western stories that involve some detection have been around for a long time (the sheriff or deputy as detective), most of these have focused on the Indian as comic figure, tracker, or villain.

Loren Estleman

Loren Estleman's Montana tale *The Stranglers* (1984) illustrates all three roles. His comic buffoon is Chief Knife-in-the-Belly—the stereotypical Wild West show Indian—a Ute posing as a bloodthirsty Blackfoot and demonstrating riding, knifing, and hunting skills, his prey a mangy buffalo. Estleman's tracker and villain are embodied in Virgil Blue Water, a generic Indian not associated with any particular tribe, a hunter and tracker who works for the white man against the Shoshone and Nez Percé, but who, for the right price, will betray anyone. He starts out tracking for the law, but the outlaws he pursues buy him out cheaply (enough for drinking and tomcatting). An outlaw, Sugar Jim Creel, says, "He's a bad one, that Indian. He figured I paid better and quicker than the law. . . . But I'd of got shed of him first chance. He's like a bee in a jar. You never know when you pull the cork who he's going to sting" (42).

Mardi Oakley Medawar

Cherokee Mardi Oakley Medawar turns this stereotypical Western detective pattern around. She sets her stories in the 1860s and 1870s, among the Kiowa, and uses the detective format to teach readers about Kiowa daily life, social interaction, religious beliefs, politics, and so on as a corrective to what her narrator labels white misunderstanding, misinterpretation, and invention. Her detective is thirty-year-old Tay-bodal, a wanderer and an eccentric healer, whose unconventional interests have always placed him on the fringes of his clan. He has devoted himself to the medical arts, traveling, for example, to Bent's Old Fort (a Colorado trading post) to study the fever-reducing properties of alkali water with Navajo healers. His herbal remedies are renowned, and his perceptions decidedly precocious and advanced for his epoch. His first-person narrative voice is that of a teacher, proud of his tribe and anxious to clarify facts: "We Kiowa have never lived as the white man has portrayed us, in big groups, in a gigantic village sprawling across the prairie. It's a very romantic notion, but stupid. Consider the practicalities. Each band and sub-band had its own chiefs and minor chiefs" (*Death at Rainy Mountain*, 2). Such pedantry is tempered with witty humor, as, for example, when he describes the personal shortcomings that led him not to follow his father's calling of eagle catcher, or his embarrassment at being mistaken for a *hwame*, or man-woman, though the experience ultimately serves his investigation. In time of need, he proves more capable than any others at discovering truths about relationships and motives that could unveil a murderer and reconfirm shaky tribal peace pacts.

In *Death at Rainy Mountain* (1996), when the Kiowa tribes come together as a nation to celebrate the annual Sun Dance, a highly respected warrior leader, the Cheyenne Robber, is accused of murdering his rival in love. Tay-bodal must play detective; explore events and motives in the light of human nature, tribal courtship traditions, and conflicting testimony; and uncover the truth within five days if he is to save this hero and keep his clansmen from lives of servitude. The plot hinges on romantic relationships, one involving the accused, the other the investigator. In *The Witch of Palo Duro* (1997) the disappearance of a noted healer and the deaths of two horses and of the chief's wife raise fears of witchcraft and shape-shifting until Tay-bodal discovers the real motives. In *Murder at Medicine Lodge* (1999) the murder of a U.S. Army bugler brings trouble to the Kiowas during an 1867 peace-treaty signing, and Tay-bodal must trace lines of evidence to find the real culprit, a white blackmailer and murderer.

Medawar's detective stories are good fun, though they, like their narrator, are a bit too forward-looking and modern—both in interpretation of events and in characterization of romantic relationships—to be taken as anything other than highly imaginative fiction, despite their "historical" setting. Others working in this historical detective mode include Marilla Sands, who uses Sky Knife, an ancient Mayan novice priest, as her amateur detective in *Sky Knife* (1997), a story of human sacrifice, portents, and magic, and in *Serpent and Storm* (1999), wherein Sky Knife, now the chief priest of Tika, must investigate the mysterious death of a king while major gods battle behind the scenes.

Scott Stone

A variation on detective stories that look back to historical settings and to the Indian as scout or guide are modern stories that turn on traditional skills and roles being played out unexpectedly in modern settings. Navy Commander Scott

C. S. Stone, of Cherokee-Scots-Norwegian ancestry, in a partly autobiographical war novel *Song of the Wolf* (1985), and Louis L'Amour, in the *Last of the Breed* (1986), created forerunners of this plot device—a human hunt carried out under threatening natural conditions, with hunter-gatherer weapons and strategies. In L'Amour's version the main figure is as much spy/investigator as anything else, and his Indian figure must scout his way out of literally foreign territory. L'Amour's part-Sioux, part-Cheyenne U.S. Air Force experimental aircraft pilot, Joseph Makatozi, is shot down over Russia during the Cold War (without food, warm clothing, or weapons) and pursued by a Yakut tracker across Siberia to the Bering Strait. Though a completely assimilated and technologically expert pilot, Makatozi draws on the warrior skills his grandfather taught him in order to make weapons (bow and arrows, sling, and spear), trap food animals, ward off cold, and survive. The thrill of the hunt intensifies when the native Siberian skills of the hunter are pitted against the Native American skills of the pursued, duplicating Cold War competition but at a far more basic level. There is a fine irony (though perhaps unintended by L'Amour) in these distantly related indigenous trackers (related since the American Indians are thought to have originated in what is now Siberia) serving different white systems at (cold) war with one another. Stone's hero, John Dane, is trained by his grandfather, a shaman, in the secret ways of the Cherokee Wolf Clan. Armed with amulet and spirit guides, he fights the Chinese Communists in Korea and stalks enemies in Laos and Vietnam, the mystical ties with nature learned in his childhood remaining ever a part of him:

He stared at Tawodi, half in fear, half in exhilaration. The old man was almost a spirit himself. When the boy heard the name he knew at once it was his, had always been, would always be. Snow-wolf. He would move through life as a wolf would move, like the animals who were now his brothers. He would be one with the forest, a part of the wind. He would move as swiftly as sunlight and make no more noise than the moon falling on the river. No more tracks than a summer breeze. When the wolves sang at night he would join them in his heart and when he met them on a trail he would salute them, for they were now and always his brothers. . . . Wolves had been hunted and persecuted, but they survived and kept their dignity. The same was true of the American tribes, particularly the Aniyunwiya. Both the wolves and the Aniyunwiya would survive, Tawodi said, if you kept them in your heart. (28–29)

Though clearly far from the detection genre, such novels reflect a direction that some thriller and crime or detection novels have begun to take by incorporating new roles for the conventional investigator: the warrior guide in the Thomas Perry novels, the survivalist amateur detective in Mark Sullivan's *Purification Ceremony*, even the mystic shamans of C. Q. Yarbro, James Doss, and Aimée and David Thurlo.

Mark Sullivan.

Typical is Mark T. Sullivan's thriller *The Purification Ceremony* (1997), a suspense/detection adventure set in an isolated area of British Columbia. One reviewer has called it a combination of James Dickey's *Deliverance* and the drug experiences of Carlos Castañeda because of its predatory killer, at one with the wilderness but driven by peyote-induced hallucinations. There is a Hemingway-style "Francis Macomber" subplot, and a main plot structured like Agatha Christie's *Ten Little Indians*, though with grislier detail: a group of hunters after a world-class buck (one with more than 160 inches of antler) and cut off from civilization by snowstorms and mountains are themselves stalked, scalped, gutted, and strung up to freeze. The killer's motive is revenge for a loved one "accidentally" shot down during deer season, but no one knows that until Diana Jackman ("Little Crow"), of Micmac and Penobscot ancestry, reverts to the *Puoin* or shamanistic hunting rituals, becomes one with the forest, and combats the evil powers of a Mexican-Huichol-trained *Mara'akame* (drug-driven sorcerer). Ever since her mother's death, Jackman has blamed her father and rejected his teachings and her Indian heritage. At the time of the murders she is a psychological wreck, at odds with her husband and herself. Whereas the murderer sets out to purify the hunting ceremony by killing off hunters obsessed with trophies rather than hunting in balance with nature, the amateur detective-huntress undergoes a purification experience that helps her come to terms with her parents, rediscover the powers of her ancestral heritage, and find wholeness and balance in her life.

Sullivan touches a number of bases that reflect new directions for the genre. One is feminism. At the novel's beginning Jackman is teased by the macho male hunters, who are more comfortable with the idea of a woman as cook and cleaner, baby producer, and guardian of the hearth. The verbal exchange with one fellow hunter sums up their prejudice and her feisty self-confidence:

"So what's the deal, a woman hunting by herself?"
"I just like to hunt," I replied. "I grew up with it, too. Tracking, I mean."
"Kind of a tough way to hunt," Phil said. "You sure you wouldn't take a nice heated stand where you can read one of them romance novels?"
I smiled sweetly. "I figure I'll leave that to you city boys, Phil."
"Aren't you gutsy?" he laughed.
I stared at him. "No, Phil, just good." (46)

Later, she proves how good by escaping from a wolf pack, surviving the snow with only a wolf skin to cover her, getting inside the head of the killer, figuring out his motive and method, and determining how to defeat him when her fellow hunters are in despair. Her conflict with her husband runs deeper. He cannot understand her need to hunt and to train her children in the survival skills of their ancestors when they live in an urban setting, and he cannot forgive her for keeping family secrets from him.

Another direction Sullivan takes is to provide a Native American perspective. When the white reaction to the shootings with arrows and scalpings is to blame the one Indian, Jackman/Little Crow snaps, "It's also what white soldiers did to Indian women and children," and reminds them of "the soldiers who used our women's breasts for hats and our boy's scrotums for change purses" (86). Little Crow asserts Indian balance with nature in contrast to white imbalance and explains the Micmac view of the world, of the power in nature, of spirit shadows, and of dreams and hunting as providing windows into other worlds. Whereas the white hunters kill for trophies, Little Crow elucidates her tribe and her family's attempts to live in accord with the laws of nature and not to alter the order of things unnecessarily, as if still primitive hunters and gatherers. She follows their tradition of saying a prayer of thanks to the animal for giving itself to her so that she can eat and live, and of leaving a part of herself (a lock of hair, for example) in the woods when she takes a part of the woods away with her. She prays "not to some white-bearded man—that seemed ridiculous—but to that river inside me" (61). Even the crazed killer recognizes her close ties to the wilderness, calls her a kindred spirit, and plans to sacrifice her to the wolves instead of killing her the way he has killed his other victims. Little Crow comes to understand the uniqueness of her father, for he effectively bridges two worlds and tries to be true to both—as not only a Native American activist, hunter/ tracker, and medicine man but also as a respected surgeon married to a U.S. congresswoman.

Still another direction Sullivan turns is toward mysticism and spiritualism. Wearing a Micmac quillwork and leather medicine pouch to protect her and a touch of spruce next to her skin to make her "longwinded," Little Crow draws on the spiritual powers her grandfather, great-uncle, and father taught were within her, powers of the Micmac shaman from the ancient forests of Nova Scotia. She actually flies with her crow spirit above the snow, feeling the warmth of her feathers, looking down on the hunter pursuing her, and seeing escape routes and traps. The changes in her are born of survivalist need:

But I ran through that fractured terrain, a rising sea of snow billowing about my knees, with a growing sense of my place in it. My ancestors believed that nearly everything could change both its shape and its mind. From my perspective—a 1990s woman with an MIT degree in computer engineering—their universe was unpredictable, unreliable, frightening. They had survived in what must have been a psychologically brutal environment, where nothing was as it seemed, by becoming equally unpredictable, able to change mind and intent at a moment's notice. I was learning. (254)

I have come to believe, like my Micmac and Penobscot ancestors, that we live more than the sum of the present moments in this visible world; we exist within layers of reincarnated, reinvented memories that shape-change and prod us across invisible boundaries into the many worlds of the mind. Until we gather unto us the Power to navigate there with confidence, we are lost and alone, savages in a dark forest. (292)

Being on the edge between death and survival, Little Crow merges with the wilderness around her, gives in to the spirits she believes exist in animal, rock, and sky, and risks madness. "It is only during times of crisis," says she, "under increasing levels of stress, that we strip away the veils that separate us from deeper levels of existence, self-knowledge and pain" (308). The final pages of this page-turner test the jimsonweed-and-peyote-strengthened powers of sorcery against the shamanistic powers of natural balance. Sullivan gives the sense of invisible worlds clashing and electric currents of power surging, positive and negative, as killer and victim trade places, and the would-be victim breathes in the spirit of the dead.

Tough Feminist Indians with an Attitude

The heroines of J. F. Trainor and Dana Stabenow, like Little Crow, are tough Indian detectives; Cecil Dawkins's heroines are less tough, but her novels reflect feminist arguments.

J. F. Trainor

Trainor's Angela Biwaban is an "Ah-nish-ih-nay-bay" (Chippewa) princess with an attitude, who sees herself as a female Indian Robin Hood, helping the little people—particularly farmers—stand up against exploitative big businesses like banks engaged in shady land deals, sleazy big-time developers, and corrupt construction outfits. Jailed unjustly for embezzlement, she works against the system, evading her parole officer, relying on aliases, and regularly offending South Dakota's racist "hick" police. She counters insults about drunken "Injuns" belonging on the reservation and appellations like "feisty little Injun," "Injun gal," "squaw," or even "Pocahontas" with insults in Ainishinabe (without translation). When the police get physical, so does she—to surprisingly good effect—with punches and kicks to sensitive areas. Her investigations depend on knowledge of her rural region, exceptional tracking skills, physical endurance and toughness, and survival skills. She sets up and carries out stings to help widows get back their property. Despite an occasional powwow or a traditional gift to a relative, her ethnicity is irrelevant to the mystery or the detection. Instead, she is like a comic book figure of a smart aleck feminist heroine—bowling over the guys with her tough-Indian-princess approach to life.

Dana Stabenow

Dana Stabenow's Alaskan native Kate Shugak, an Aleut, has a similar hard-boiled approach but is drawn in broader, more credible dimensions. Survival of the fittest has bred hardiness in her tribe, and subsistence-level needs have taught hunter-gatherer skills for coping with arctic weather and wildlife. In the face of racial insults, she remains self-confident and proud. Amid the male roughness of a frontier state, where bald eagles, moose, and bears make daily appearances, and the cold and isolation turn people to heavy drinking, eccentricity, and stir-craziness, Shugak hunts, fishes, fights, and feuds with the best of them. Friends describe her as "one hard-nosed bitch" and "about as friendly as a double-bladed axe," especially after she deals with one villain by forcing the woman's tongue against metal in subzero weather (*A Cold-blooded Business, 224*, 8). Her sidekick, Mutt, is a large, intelligent, dominant male malamute.

Shugak began her career as a sex crime investigator for the office of the Anchorage District Attorney, but, burned out by five years of dealing with abused women and battered children, she returned to her family's homestead near Niniltna in northern Alaska as a private investigator, mainly finding missing persons and their killers and figuring out who is smuggling what and how. Her detective strategy consists of going underground and working alongside suspects to ferret out clues and evidence, and using logical deduction based on her knowledge of people and place. In *A Fatal Thaw* (1993), for example, she pieces together information that will explain why there are nine bodies in the snow after a springtime killing spree in which a local killed eight of his neighbors. Sometimes, she is hired to investigate, usually by the state troopers or rangers; sometimes, she just walks into a mystery, as in *Play with Fire* (1995), when she uncovers a corpse while looking for wild mushrooms in an area charred by forest fire. She ends up investigating religious fundamentalists and fellow Aleuts bitter about missionary zeal and proud their potlatches, totems, and beaded shirts have outlasted the strictures imposed by these outsiders. While working as a deckhand on a salmon fishing vessel in *Killing Grounds* (1998), Shugak finds a dead fisherman who has been beaten, stabbed, strangled, mutilated, and drowned, a puzzling exercise in overkill that leads the state troopers to call on her expertise in a case in which the dead man's wife and child, friends and associates all have motives.

Throughout the series, Shugak engages in an ongoing generational conflict with her stubborn and respected grandmother (Ekaterina Shugak), another tough Aleut with the political instincts of Machiavelli. She wishes eventually to pass on the clan's governing powers to Kate and, despite her grand-daughter's personal assimilation, make her responsible for protecting the tribe from the inroads of civilization and from the schemes of the con artists and power grabbers anxious for fishing rights, mineral rights, oil rights, monopolies of art and artifacts, and the like. Ekaterina argues the case for rejecting prefab housing and government money, and returning to the old ways. Kate reminds her of the mixed racial elements that comprise their ancestry and the electricity and running water her grandmother enjoys from Prudhoe Bay Oil, and argues for the new while retaining the best of the old, but going forward to assure long-term survival. Their regular confrontations provide readers insights into Aleut values and the ongoing battles of assimilation, as well as amusement when Kate argues her grandmother's side to teenage Aleuts thinking of leaving home for the fast life in Anchorage. In *Blood Will Tell* (1996), Kate must stand up for her people and protect her grandmother while investigating the suspicious deaths of tribal representatives to the Alaska Federation of Natives convention, where a crucial vote will determine the fate of contested lands.

Though only five feet and 120 pounds, Shugak is hardy. A twisted, ugly knife scar across her throat is a constant reminder of how much damage she can take and survive. In *A Cold Day for Murder* (1992), she plunges down an old mine shaft when the dumbwaiter-like cargo platform breaks, and laboriously inches her way back up, muscles painfully straining, wrists smarting where rope burns stripped her skin away. In *Dead in the Water* (1993) she struggles with seven-foot by seven-foot by three-foot crab pots in stormy sea conditions and holds up her end of very dirty, backbreaking work in gale-force winds among an unsavory crew she suspects of cold-blooded murder. She breaks ice off the deck with a sledgehammer and struggles from ship to shore and back again in freezing rain to spy on drug smugglers. In *A Cold-Blooded Business* (1994) she works as a roustabout on a rig above the Arctic Circle, doing "every dirty job that comes along from signing out tools to running parts to driving bus to wellhead cleanup to picking up garbage" (11), while trying to discover exactly who is responsible for illicit drug smuggling and a series of drug-caused accidents. In *Breakup* (1997), when an airplane crashes into her living room, Shugak is in a foul mood, and flying bullets in her favorite bar don't help. She bulldozes local feuders whose gun battles get in her face and exposes an unsuspected case of murder by bear. She enjoys sex and takes a variety of men as lovers. Like Mutt, there is a sense of something barely leashed in her eyes (*Cold Day*, 8).

Cecil Dawkins

Cecil Dawkins's *Clay Dancers* (1994) is a good example of the use of the detective genre to pursue other ends, ends related to a New Age mix of feminism and mysticism. In this novel, a notorious lesbian archaeologist leads a dig at an Anasazi pueblo on land about to be returned to the Pueblos. Her goal is to prove her theory that since hunter-gatherer men and women were physical equals, women played significant political and religious roles in the community, but when tribes reverted to farming women lost physical, social, and religious equality, males took over the sacred kivas, and matriarchies became patriarchies. Tina Martinez (who works at the dig, keeping an eye on the outsiders for her uncle, the Pueblo leader) squeezes into the excavated kiva and discovers the mummified remains of a *kwiyo*, a female shaman, the last of the old strong women shamans, who walled herself up with a meteor fragment. Tina is torn between her duty to her tribe (to refuse to photograph the shaman mummy in order to protect Indian privacy and interests) and what the archaeologist insists is her duty as a woman (to confirm the theory about women being so powerful in the past). At the same time, Tina has frightening flashbacks to a previous life and experiences sudden insights about past events, objects, and concepts she couldn't know about unless she had lived much earlier. The ending to the murder story is somewhat unsatisfactory as a non-Indian, nonfeminist explanation evolves. In sum, Dawkins's *Clay Dancers* approaches feminist issues very differently than Trainor and Stabenow do, and raises the problem of where to draw the line between the rational and the intuitive, between traditional ratiocination based on real clues that logically lead to the identification of means, motive, and murderer and New Age shamanism with detection carried out through otherworldly means, from sacred objects to dream visions to rituals and recitations that bring spirit guides to assist discovery.

Supernatural Mysticism

Numerous Indian stories across genres refer to or include instances of shape-shifting: the warrior who soars like an eagle over the land he loves or roams the land in the shape of a wolf, his clan spirit, or sees through the eyes of the raven, or takes on the power of the bear as he defends his village or home or loved ones. The skinwalkers who try to frame Joshua Blackhorse in Aimée Thurlo's *Her Hero* (1996) shift into the shape of coyotes or birds as they threaten and pursue him and his family. Other writers employ magic that can make one invisible or allow a shaman of great power to cross time. A classification of this phenomenon involves two questions, the degree of supernatural mysticism and the amount of credibility accorded it. Insights into Native American spiritual beliefs can be fascinating background information, or even informative about the difficulties cross-cultural detectives have communicating with members of an Indian community. However, as detective stories move away from detection toward spiritualism and the supernatural, they begin to lose the qualities that give the genre its power and to cross over into the horror or the science fiction genre, just as stretching the genre to make it a platform for ideological issues turns the crime novel from its potential focus on malfeasance and social justice questions to a new emphasis on sociopolitical movements or positions: a "feminist" novel, an "ecological" novel, a "gay" novel, or some blend in which message takes precedence over mystery.

Aimée and David Thurlo

Aimée and David Thurlo mix the ratiocinative and the intuitive, sometimes giving the spirit world credence, sometimes not. Generally, however, they incorporate indigenous lore into their stories to counter ratiocination with a magic-mystical element. In doing so, they in effect ask for a willing suspension of disbelief. In Aimée Thurlo's *Spirit Warrior* (1993) the Navajo tribal policeman wears a protective bag containing corn pollen to symbolize the continuity of life, peace, and harmony, and a rock crystal to link with his tribe's Creation story as a sign that prayers will come true. In *Cisco's Woman* the survival of the tribal detective hero depends on a carved stone armadillo fetish given to his grandfather by a medicine man and passed on to him, despite his disbelief in its powers. His grandfather tells him that the spirit of the animal resides within the carving and acts as a shield to protect its owner. His companion notices that at moments when the wearer intuits danger, the fetish darkens, as if somehow responsible for its wearer's heightened awareness, but he rejects this possibility until the end of the novel. Then, faced with an armed killer, he jumps in front of the heroine to take a bullet meant for her. Despite being fired on at point-blank range, he is unscathed, except for "an odd-shaped, nasty-looking welt on his chest": the bullet struck the fetish and was flattened. Thurlo leaves it to the readers to decide whether this protection is a result of chance or of ancient powers, but her main characters clearly believe in its magic.

Aimée Thurlo likes to reverse the usual pattern of intuitive Native American, ratiocinative white. In *Spirit Warrior*, for example, it is her white archaeologist who finds possible supernatural explanations of events and the tribal representative at the dig (a Navajo lawyer) who tries to stick to facts:

I'm much more comfortable with solid facts that I can touch, and feel, and measure. To me that's real. Lights that I can't explain, or an intangible evil that I can sense but can't prove, scare me because they open a crack in my thinking. It's like being shown another time or place where sand talks, and the sun rises in the west. Ideas that you took for granted, that kept your world stable, no longer apply. And without those, there are no sturdy pillars to lean against for support. (158)

While he believes in the Navajo concept of "walking in beauty," of finding harmony and balance in one's personal life and being open to life's possibilities, as an investigator he is interested in facts and in the psychology of obtaining facts:

An investigation can be a long process. . . . People tell half truths, or don't come forward with information, and the facts have to be gleaned from the stories. . . . Sometimes people hold back, and it has nothing whatsoever to do with the crime under investigation. What they don't realize is that little details seemingly unrelated to the crime sometimes turn out to be crucial. When that happens, the criminals are one step closer to getting away with it. (165)

The crime in *Breach of Faith* (1992) combines three reservation problems: the degrading effects of gambling on the Indian community, the active illegal trade in native artifacts (which involves replacing genuine artifacts with high-quality reproductions), and the tensions between Hopi and Navajo over sacred land. The villains include a British anthropologist willing to go to any lengths to find fame and fortune by recording and publishing the religious secrets of the Hopi and a cancer-ridden billionaire investor who will pay any amount to experience the power of sacred healing rites. Despite this solid base in reality, the novel also provides the Indian community's supernatural interpretation of events. Gambling debts make Gilbert Payestewa vulnerable to blackmail, but stealing the sacred Hopi garments entrusted to his family (the mask, belt, robe, and medicine pouch of Masau'u, the war god of fire and death) costs him his life and his family their place in the community. His personal act has repercussions throughout his family, clan, and tribe. It endangers his mother, who falls under a sacred curse that will follow every female in his blood line until his clan is wiped out or the sacred objects are returned. It puts the life of his tribal policeman brother, Joseph, on hold until he can recover the missing items to save family honor and family lives. It threatens the health of the community, which is no longer under the protection of the sacred kachina spirit. At the novel's close, the supernatural dominates. *Breach of Faith* celebrates the power of Hopi kachina spirits to destroy or heal: they destroy the thief because of his perversion of sacred rites, but they restore the health and fertility of FBI agent Glenna Day because of her service to the community.

In *Shadow of the Wolf* (1993) the seemingly supernatural (a witch's bundle, voodoo doll, and self-igniting paper) have purely logical explanations—all ways to frighten potential allies away from the heroine. The novel turns instead on outsider greed for Native American art and demonstrates the interlocking effects of betrayal on a tightly knit, interdependent community, in this case Tewa. Thurlo's theme is the strong Tewa code of loyalty to family and community. The supernatural in *Second Shadow* (1993), however, is a blend of bogus witch-craft and what is presented as genuine spiritualism. The novel begins with a supernatural warning from the Tewa heroine's recently dead medicine man grandfather that danger will follow the heroine's sighting of the family totem spirit, a mountain lion; however, the other early elements of the supernatural are easily explained as man-made threats set to frighten superstitious Tewa: a two-faced icon, half-bird, half-animal, affixed on the point of a yucca stick (the Tewa sign of a witch), followed by numerous accidents with runaway vehicles, bad wiring, and collapsing structures.

The novel combines romance, mystery, and the supernatural in order to highlight the cultural differences between hereditary enemies, the Tewa and the Spanish. The heroine is a Tewa architect who ignores the traditional animosity of the Tewa for the descendants of Spanish slavers—haughty, rich, Anglicized Spanish landowners—and accepts a commission to design and oversee the restoration of a hacienda, House of Enchantment, a Taos-area landmark. She must deal with contractors and builders, settle cross-cultural disputes and confrontations, respond to the psychology of workmen performing under pressure, and meet the contractual deadline. However, the discovery of a skeleton on the property (preceded by the cries of an owl) requires protective rituals before work can continue, and as the novel moves to its close, supernatural events become less and less explicable in rational terms. When past murders are exposed, the heroine, who carries her life-root stones (the souls of her ancestors in quartz form) to protect her from danger and whose clairvoyant aunt warns of danger, is saved by the mountain lion spirit blessed by her grandfather. The appearance of the mountain lion might be dismissed as coincidence, but the heroine clearly believes her family totem spirit has protected her from evil.

The Thurlos' Ella Clah mystery series—*Blackening Song* (1995), *Death Walker* (1996), *Bad Medicine* (1997), and *Enemy Way* (1998)—again sets the ratiocinative against the supernatural, for Ella Clah is a trained FBI agent who, in the first book in the series, returns to the Navajo Nation to bring her law enforcement experience and expertise to bear in investigating her father's murder. Her father was a Christian minister who for many had represented the struggle between traditionalists and modernists, a struggle Ella discovers she embodies within herself, despite her fellow agent's praise, "You're a no-nonsense, show-me-results agent" (48). When the ritual nature of the killing makes Ella's *hataalii* brother the chief suspect, she finds that FBI procedure alone cannot solve the case, and she is forced to recognize her family's age-old role in the community as spiritually powerful benign guardians of the sacred ways. The killer is a skinwalker, and his methods of combat are psychological and supernatural, with ghost dust and bone slivers and all the forbidden uses of the dead that make Navajos flee in terror.

Despite Clah's struggle to find a logical explanation for events—" 'Things just didn't add up.' . . . She tried to make sense of it" (59)—as the series progresses, she confronts more and more inexplicable events and she gradually comes to accept shamanistic explanations as viable, especially as she begins to discover within herself powers that go beyond the merely intuitive. The capture of one skinwalker, however, does not end the activities of others, and as tribal officer and special investigator for the Navajo police chief, Clah continues to battle the supernatural forces of evil in the rest of the series. In *Death Walker*, skinwalkers are on the loose again, and the elderly tribe members who represent the tribe's collective wisdom are being stalked and killed; in *Bad Medicine* evil forces behind the scenes help drive a wedge between hate-driven Anglo and Navajo groups. *Enemy Way* takes a much more realistic turn, examining the problem of drunken driving on the reservation, racial battles between white supremacist groups and reservation Navajo, the growing gulf between generations on the reservation and the resultant problem of rival youth gangs turning violent and criminal; though skinwalkers and secret tribal discipline groups interfere with police investigations and threaten Ella Clah's life, this book is more firmly grounded in the ugly realities of modern reservation life than are the other three.

Clearly attracted by the supernatural possibilities of Navajo belief, the Thurlos determinedly teach cultural traditions through their mysteries. *Breach of Faith* captures the differences between Navajo and Hopi attitudes toward the dead and their afterlife, and differences in burial practices and related ceremonies. It explores the conflicts between traditionalists and nontraditionalists, and the differences between Anglo and Indian interrogation methods: in both Hopi and Navajo cultures no one ever speaks for someone else; doing so is considered a breach of personal rights. *Second Shadow* provides Aimée Thurlo an opportunity to describe nineteenth-century Taos building practices and to explore the skills of regional artisans, to introduce readers to the variety of Southwestern food, and to provide insights into the checkered history of the Southwest's modern ethnic groups. In each book readers learn about cross-cultural differences like the Navajo tradition of waiting outside a house or hogan until invited in, of never mentioning the name of a dead person, of giving relationship descriptions like "aunt" or "uncle" rather than personal names (which carry power), of avoiding physical contact with strangers (no handshakes). The Thurlos call attention to differences in physical gestures and body language—for instance, the Navajo way of pointing at someone by thrusting out the lower lip or the ease with which a Navajo can recognize a non-Navajo in dim light simply by the other person's body movement. They bring in religious traditions as well, such as sprinkling cornmeal as an offering to First Woman, a *Dineh* [Navajo] deity, to make sure the gods won't interfere with the good that may come to the one making the offering. However, unlike Hillerman, who communicates similar information through his detective format, the Thurlos move back and forth between rational and supernatural explanations, with the characters clearly believing (to varying degrees) in supernatural explanations, but with the vague and forced possibility of a purely rational explanation. The unifying idea of their books is that the Navajo concept of balance, a middle way between dark potentials, turns on a daily struggle between competing forces.

Micah Hackler

Micah Hackler demonstrates a number of ways in which the ratiocinative and the supernatural might be brought together. *Legend of the Dead* (1995) depends on investigative skills until the very end, when a shaman summons supernatural powers on sacred land to overcome villains whose sacrilege has offended the ancient spirits of the Anasazi ruins—but Hackler leaves open the possibility that the final sequence of events depends on hallucination or illusion. In *Coyote Returns* (1996) Hackler uses a magical frame around a traditional, ratiocinative center, though action inside the frame makes full sense only in terms of the frame. The frame builds on Native American Coyote stories: Coyote walks among humans at erratic intervals, inciting his animal counterparts to unusual acts of mischief and aggression, checking up on his Navajo people, answering their prayers in his own mischievous way, engaging in absurd acts with underlying lessons about the nature of the universe, reminding young doubters of his power, then moving on to similarly teach the Sioux his place in their heritage. In this case, a mountain named Coyote is threatened by a multimillion-dollar timber deal with an obscure clause about mineral rights; the ecologist whose studies suggest the cataclysmic environmental changes cutting timber will produce is found dead in circumstances that undermine his reputation, and his daughter is threatened. When Sheriff Lansing's girlfriend is shot and Lansing's Navajo deputy, Gabe Hanna, discovers a family history he knew nothing of and is motivated to discover the truth about both the past and the present, the sheriff and deputy work in different directions to reach the same end. Readers are offered both the sheriff's rational interpretation of events and his deputy's mythic interpretation, contrasting perceptions that end in the same reality— exposure of villainy and revelations that will better the lives of reservation dwellers.

The Dark Canyon (1997), in turn, depends totally on the supernatural: an emerald totem that sets loose an ancient, murderous demon. When the totem and Sheriff Lansing's great-grandfather's journals are dug up near Lansing's town house, sheep begin to disappear, then teenagers, then hunters. The demon jaguar's prey are the Native Americans of the region, and only magic can stop it. In other words, Hackler experiments with a variety of ways in which to mix the real and the supernatural, and his stories range from those with possible rational explanations to those with no rational explanation at all. However, Hackler's most effective method is the supernatural frame around the rational center, for it allows him to build the interesting mythical case and yet suggest that a more mundane understanding is possible.

James Doss.

Like Hackler's stories, James Doss's shaman novels (*The Shaman Sings*, 1993; *The Shaman Laughs*, 1994; *The Shaman's Bones*, 1997; *The Shaman's Game*, 1998) initially set up a firmly rational base against which to play with the idea of spiritual worlds impinging on modern understandings of reality. Doss establishes that the *pitukupf* (magical dwarf) and shamanism in general are no longer much believed in by younger Utes, particularly deputy sheriff Charlie Moon, whose approach to crime is orthodox police procedure. Moon also exploits his calm, easygoing likability rather than his imposing physical size (he is six-foot-seven or so) to deal with witnesses and trouble. However, Moon's aunt, shaman Daisy Perika, defies rational explanation by repeatedly reporting dreams and visions that are helpful clues to actual crimes, despite Moon's attempts to disregard them. The third member of Doss's odd crime-busting triumvirate in the Shaman series is former Chicagoan Scott Parris, a street cop burned out by the big city and now trying to start over as the chief of police in Granite Creek, a small college town in the mountains. Parris, ironically for an outsider, has a psychic empathy with the visionary Daisy Perika, with whom he shares a kind of second sight inherited from his Irish forebears. These disparate characters, backgrounds, and crime-solving approaches allow Doss to contrast traditional, modern, and non-Native American ways of dealing with crime and wrongdoing: Daisy's intuitive manipulations of her spirit forces complement the ratiocinative approaches of her assimilated Ute nephew, while Parris acts as a comically reluctant bridge between the two when he shares Daisy's visions.

In *The Shaman Sings* a brilliant physics graduate student is murdered after she makes a groundbreaking discovery in superconductivity that might bring a fortune to its owner. Daisy plays a fairly small role in the solving of the crime, but her repeated entrances into the narrative, along with a wide-ranging cast of other characters, suggests the possibility of otherworldly means to detection, ones closed to all but a blessed few. In *The Shaman Laughs*, however, Parrish's openness to the spirit world turns into horrifying experiences, and Doss's novels begin to edge into the horror genre, as do the works of Naomi Stokes, who will be discussed in the horror chapter.

Chelsea Q. Yarbro.

Chelsea Q. Yarbro's detective novels (*Cat's Claw, Bad Medicine, Poison Fruit*) are less convincing dramatically because they embody both the ratiocinative and the magical in the same figure. Most of the time Ojibway detective Charlie Spotted Moon seems fully assimilated and depends on urban investigative procedures, but when the mystery seems unsolvable by other means, he turns to the Ojibway shaman's way to justice. This way includes rituals passed on to Moon by his grandfather: special incantations, sweat baths, special blends of herbs and oils, and a sacred medicine finger—a carved stick of wood that is painted with the Ojibway symbols of his name, and that gives off vibrations against his chest that heighten Moon's perceptive powers. In *Cat's Claw* (1992) Moon employs his modern home's basement heaters, birch and pine boughs slapped against the walls of his Finnish-style sauna, a protective carved wood pendant, dried herbs, and special oil to psychically experience a murderer's memories of frenzied deeds, the psychic dislocation of the victims, and the troubled relationships that produced this pattern of death. This Ojibway magic depends on mystical, psychic power and extrasensory knowledge that comes through ritual forms of contact with the natural world. When the spiritual takes over, detection has moved into the realm of science fiction fantasies about other worlds, as it does in the works of Mercedes Lackey, who will be discussed in the science fiction chapter.

Peter Bowen.

Peter Bowen's Gabriel Du Pré novels feature a droll and quirky Montana cattle-brand inspector and fiddle player of Métis descent (half-French, half-Indian—Cree, Chippewa, Ojibway—the Métis were trappers who fled Canada during the late 1800s). Du Pré's family has been in Montana since 1886. Du Pré speaks with a French lilt but takes pride in his Indian roots. He is earthy and folksy, open with his friends but closed to outsiders, rational and logical about everyday events but deeply convinced about spiritual insights and shamanistic powers. He has a reputation as an amateur detective but depends almost entirely on the cryptic warnings of a local shaman, Benetsee, to understand the nature of the crime and the identity of the criminal. Benetsee and Du Pré live in a harsh world that outsiders can neither understand nor appreciate, a place of avalanches that kill the unwary and bears that polish off snow-buried bodies.

Specimen Song (1995) is typical. In it, the death of a young Cree woman at a Smithsonian Institution country music celebration in Washington, D.C., puts Du Pré on the track of a serial killer, an Indian hater who kills Métis women with primitive weapons. Later, a coyote carrying a wolf amulet from some ancient burial ground and a talk with Benetsee, the aged medicine man he trusts, lead Du Pré to join a Métis canoe expedition tracing the paths of his ancestors down a Canadian river. Later, Benetsee makes Du Pré drive him to a sacred Indian place of power and whirl a bull roarer (a flat piece of wood on a string) toward the east; afterward, Benetsee shows knowledge of the murders that not even those involved with them have. He says he sees the weeping murdered women passing on their way to the Star Trail and the murderer, his eyes gleaming, holing up in the mountains. In response to his visions, Benetsee makes Du Pré wear an obsidian knife amulet around his neck as magic to protect him from the psychopathic killer, gives him six magically marked black stones to use as weapons in his slingshot, and warns that the moment he identifies the killer, he must kill him quickly or be killed himself. A mountain man used to speedy frontier justice, Du Pré kills and walks away. Despite the grounding of the Du Pré stories in the gritty, everyday details of Montana life, the detection depends totally on the supernatural powers of the aged shaman. Du Pré is simply a competent tool, like a bird dog set on the trail once the villain has been identified.

CONCLUSION

Detective/crime fiction is a uniquely appropriate medium for writers interested in social criticism, especially critiques of marginal or ignored groups being abused. Since the days of Dashiell Hammett and Raymond Chandler, the detective story has focused attention on the unseemly underbelly of American society, the naked city with its millions of untold stories or the secret sins of the wealthy and powerful as they trample over the poor and weak. As a means of consciousness-raising about the social failings of a community, the detective story is made to order; pathologies such as delinquency, drug abuse, violence against self, family, and others, and of course crime are the stuff of its existence, whether as the events that drive the plot or as the background of the milieu in which the investigator must operate. While the British tradition has emphasized locked door mysteries, weekend manor house murders, and other such intellectual puzzles, the hard-boiled American genre has usually illuminated social justice questions, directly or indirectly.

The Native American as detective or important player in a detective story is thus ideally situated to foreground the many injustices that have plagued and continue to plague various Indian communities. Since detectives or investigators are trained in mainstream law and forensic science, there is a natural link to the mainstream audience familiar with the genre, and a unique opportunity to cast a sympathetic light on issues that might otherwise remain obscure, exotic, or impenetrable. Hillerman's Leaphorn and Chee, representing the ratiocinative Western and the intuitive native traditions, respectively, act as bridges over the cultural chasms that separate mainstream and native cultures. Hillerman works the traditional territory and the genre, and in doing so establishes a benchmark for the Indian detective story, one that Coel, Parrish, and Perry have clearly learned from and built on as they have explored viable ways of extending and invigorating a classic genre.

Other writers we have considered show both the advantages and the hazards of pushing the genre to its limits, of shifting its shape to fit Native American traditions. The interesting and informative cultural background of the Thurlos educates and entertains, but scants the social justice function that pure crime and detection stories provide, and their shifts of emphasis to romance, the supernatural, or the cultural devalue detection. Feminism works nicely to highlight the invisible lives of Indian women but can turn the attention away from overall justice issues to particular feminist concerns. When the detective story travels too far in the direction of shamanism and the supernatural, the feminist or the merely historical, the ratiocinative core of the genre is lost and some of the functionality of a socially realistic critique is drained away. Thus, some of the authors and stories discussed in the romance, horror, and science fiction genre chapters include crime and detection, but these are not central to the authors' interests and purposes.

Nonetheless, this testing of the possibilities of the mystery/detective genre helps define its characteristics and strengthen its form.

7

Amalgams of Horror: Shaping Native American Magic Into European Molds

The Indian had always known he was not alone. He knew there were others, things that observed. When a man looked quickly up, was it a movement he saw or only his imagination?

The terms we use for what is considered supernatural are woefully inadequate. Beyond such terms as *ghost, specter, poltergeist, angel, devil,* or *spirit*, might there not be something more our purposeful blindness has prevented us from understanding?

—Louis L'Amour, *The Haunted Mesa*, 19

The distance between Native American and Euro-American conceptions of horror—what nonphysical forces make the heart sink, the muscles tense, the pulse race, the fight-or-flight responses kick in—is often dramatic, even in simple, everyday situations. For example, among different Native American tribes, speaking the name of the recently dead may evoke anything from a twinge of unease, as if at a social faux pas (for the Ute, the spirit of the deceased will be made restless), to a sense of dread (for the Arapaho, the spirit will be called upon to visit the living). For Europeans, of course, invoking the name of the recently deceased is a way of mourning, so frequent repetition of the name can only help bring closure to grief, not spiritual distress. A social convention that evokes horror in Native American circles will be no more than normal behavior for mainstream Americans. While actual visits from the dead might hold the same horror for both groups, the socioliterary conventions through which such experiences are conveyed—their coherent use in a standard fictional form summed up as a genre—vary so widely that no writer familiar with cultural diversity would be foolhardy enough to depart from the conventions appropriate to his readership. This point is made neatly by the short story "The Moccasin

Game" by Anishinabe (Chippewa) writer Gerald Vizenor, a simple story of gambling among an assortment of humans and symbolic figures, but one whose import remains cryptic for non-Chippewa readers:

Windigoo waited in silence. He smiled and tried to charm the women over the moccasins. Booch cut his black hair down to the cold bone. Mitig shared a leather dress trimmed with cowrie shells. The cannibal wore the oversized dress for the second round of the moccasin game. The hand talkers covered their mouths in silent laughter. (Trafzer, *Earth Song, Sky Spirit*, 58)

In actuality, however, Vizenor is speaking to an audience familiar with both the general oral tradition of storytelling and the built-in Native American conventions that make this story a horrifying tale of a battle for the lives of the tribe's children, and hence for the future of the tribe, since a wrong turn of the moccasin (a gambling counter) when competing against giants and cannibals can mean death and annihilation. Choctaw LeAnne Howe's short story "Danse d'Amour, Danse de Mort" (in Trafzer, *Earth Song, Sky Spirit*) provides another contrast in horror conventions. In the period before the Louisiana Purchase, French Jesuits are invited to attend a Choctaw "bone picking" ceremony, a celebration of life, renewal, and rebirth after the death of a significant loved one; the Jesuits find it not simply alien but deeply horrifying, to the point of nausea. The dead woman whose bones are "picked" had chosen to be clubbed to death in front of her family in place of her eldest daughter as blood-revenge payment for a murder committed by her husband. When her exposed bones have taken on "that stark, delicate beauty the Choctaws regard as *chunk-ash ishi a-chuck-ma* ("the good bliss"), the mourner, in a ritualistic dance of death carried out while in an erotic, narcotic-induced dream state, pulls away the flesh that still clings to his wife's bones and tears the skull and spinal column from the decaying corpse—all the while enacting a final sexual orgy with his wife's rotting flesh as if death has been overcome. For the Choctaw, the Jesuits' reactions to this sacred ceremony demonstrate their weakness, their bad manners, and their lack of understanding. For the Jesuits and the mainstream readers whose sensibilities they share, the description of burial rites seems like a gory tale of horror meant to shock the senses and evoke nightmares. In this tale, and in many other Native American stories, what is sacred for one culture is the stuff of Halloween nightmares for the other.

GENRE OVERVIEW

Modern mainstream horror conventions can be traced back to medieval Europe and even earlier, and their widespread dissemination in coherent, easily recognizable forms—as literary conventions—began, at least in England, with Elizabethan literature. Both the medieval and early Renaissance periods were times of devout Christian belief, yet the folklore of witchcraft, hauntings, possession, and foretellings signifies the enduring pagan challenges to Christian orthodoxy, at least in the popular imagination. Modern readers may require footnotes or stage business to understand some of the language of Shakespeare's *Hamlet, King Lear, Macbeth*, or *Julius Caesar*, but the horror conventions, all of which reflect the beliefs of Shakespeare's London as much as the author's settings and sources themselves, are self-explanatory:

> A little ere the mightiest Julius fell,
> The graves stood tenantless and the sheeted dead
> Did squeak and gibber in the Roman streets:
> As stars with trains of fire and dews of blood,
> Disasters in the sun; and the moist star

Upon whose influence Neptune's empire stands
Was sick almost to doomsday with eclipse. (*Hamlet* I.i. 114–120)

. . . at his [the crowing cock's] warning,
Whether in sea or fire, in earth or air,
Th' extravagant and erring spirit hies
To his confine . . . (*Hamlet* I.i. 152–155)

Despite distance in time and culture from the English Renaissance, tenantless graves and squeaking, gibbering ghosts in the streets still evoke appropriate reactions, and even the manifestations of disaster in nature (shooting stars and bloody dews), though a bit arcane, fit within conventional prophecies of disaster and remain meaningful. Archaic language aside, we still understand the general threat of the three witches in *Macbeth* and the frightening power of the ghosts in the banquet scene; Hamlet's father's ghost is still ambivalent (dangerous or benign), and the bloody acts of rape and physical mutilation so beloved of the Elizabethan and Jacobean stages (chopping off arms, legs, and heads, gouging eyes) still horrify. However, the late eighteenth- and, particularly, nineteenth-century mass culture has been far more influential in shaping the conventions of the modern horror story into a stable genre. Along with the popularity of the Gothic horror of Horace Walpole's *Castle of Otranto* (1765), Mrs. (Ann) Radcliffe's *The Mysteries of Udolpho* (1794), Matthew Gregory Lewis's *The Monk* (1797), Mary Shelley's *Frankenstein* (1817), Keats's *Lamia* (1820), and Bram Stoker's *Dracula* (1897), among others, which reached a readership huge by the standards of earlier times, came the creation and refinement of conventions that are today stock fare in horror tales:

1. Intellect gone awry (Dr. Faustus, the Frankenstein monster, science out of control, the mad scientist)

2. The beast in man (the werewolf, the vampire, the sadist, the psychotic, Dr. Jekyll and Mr. Hyde)

3. The powers of darkness (the devil, the Antichrist, demons, demonic cults, witchcraft, satanic priests, succubi, snake women like Lamia)

4. Powers from the grave (vengeful ghosts seeking retribution for earthly wrongs, benign ghosts protecting their descendants)

5. The presence of evil announced through cold air, eerie shadows, a disgusting stench, pentagrams, black cats, black dogs, spells, rituals, and the absence of a reflection in a mirror

6. The power of silver, crosses, holy water, Latin prayers, church rituals, and church land to ward off evil

7. The relationship of setting to horror (ruined castles, ancient monasteries with deep caverns, wild landscapes, the moors, Victorian mansions).

Such horror conventions were marketed to the middle class in popular stories, supplanting and perhaps suppressing the folklore that had formed earlier conventions, and we in the twentieth century and after are the inheritors of these literary conventions. To them we have added some traditions from other cultures that have affected our own, for instance, the concept of voodoo and zombies from Afro-Caribbean cultures, and our modern period has explored more fully the horrific possibilities of technology and science run amok with such stories as those of Dr. Faustus and Dr. Frankenstein. Always, however, European-based horror stories have been grounded, whether overtly or indirectly, in a Christian convention of right and wrong, temptation and last-minute salvation. Bestial behavior has usually been associated with paganism, and scientific and technological overreachers like Dr. Frankenstein transgress by failing to respect the sacred limits imposed by the Christian God.

The long run of fairly stable horror conventions from the nineteenth century up to the end of the twentieth may have left some writers feeling that the genre had become flaccid and enervated. If so, recent American and Canadian writers have embraced the richness of Native American spiritual traditions that introduce magical and nightmare possibilities outside the depleted conventions developed within a European and Christian context. With so many different tribes and different religious concepts within the classification "Native American" comes the potential for an infusion of new traditions and conventions highly exotic for the traditional genre. However, in much the same way that the literary market defined, limited, and directed the folk-originated conventions used by nineteenth-century horror story writers, so modern market pressures lead popular fiction writers to broaden their appeal by making use of widely understood conventions, reinterpreting (or watering down, or completely distorting) authentic Native American horror conventions by casting them in European molds, or by simply inventing horror elements that were never imagined in earlier Native American times. A new horror genre is thus being formed, an amalgam of Native American and European traditions. Mass readership, of course, does not lead to equal opportunity for the lore of both cultures; mainstream readers seem to want the exotic, but bottled in familiarly-shaped vessels.

FRONTIER HORROR: INDIANS AS DEMONIC

Early American gothic fiction built on the lessons of Puritan sermons and the Christian iconography of the demon Indian. Charles Brockden Brown clearly recognized the horror potential of the eighteenth-century American wilderness in his gothic novel *Edgar Huntly; Or the Memoirs of a Sleepwalker* (1799). Therein, Brown describes the psychological and physical terrors that colonial and later Americans associated with being attacked or taken captive by bloodthirsty and degenerate savages. Brown's sleepwalker, Edgar Huntly, awakens to find himself trapped in a cave with Indians camped at its mouth; a white female captive whimpers in fear of her fate, anticipating the Indians' animalistic assault.

As he looks at the sleeping Indians—"four brawny and terrific figures," their naked legs "scored [by tattoos] into uncouth figures" and their moccasins "adorned in a grotesque manner"—he experiences both "wonder and alarm." The shocking scene makes Huntly recall a terrifying childhood trauma in which his parents and an infant child were murdered in their beds, their house pillaged and burned. In recognition of the fictive potential of such scenes, Huntly's creator, Charles Brockden Brown, argued in an address "To the Public" prefacing *Edgar Huntly*:

Puerile superstition and exploded manners, Gothic castles and chimeras, are the materials usually employed for [calling forth the passions and engaging the sympathy of the reader]. The incidents of Indian hostility, and the perils of the Western wilderness, are far more suitable; and for a native of America to overlook these would admit of no apology.

Thus, Brown rejected the European formulas for gothic horror and set the stage for the American exploitation of native terrors as a foundation for the horror story.

Other writers of the period, to varying degrees, took advantage of this native potential. Building on explicit Puritan doctrine, Nathaniel Hawthorne, in both "Young Goodman Brown" (1835) and *The Scarlet Letter* (1850), used the untamed forest with its dark thickets and innumerable perils to symbolize the dark forces of evil that could tempt and destroy the Christian soul. The implication for colonists was that people who could feel at home in such wilderness must embody within themselves the wild and the evil. In *The Scarlet Letter* a footpath leads into "the mystery of the primeval forest," which "hemmed it in so narrowly, and stood so black and dense on either side, and disclosed such imperfect glimpses of the sky above" that Hester Prynne finds it imaging "the moral wilderness in which she had so long been wandering." Young Goodman Brown likewise finds that "[t]he whole forest was peopled with frightful sounds—the creaking of the trees, the howling of wild beasts, and the yell of Indians," but he warns the devilish to beware: "Come witch, come wizard, come Indian powwow, come devil himself, and here comes Goodman Brown." James Fenimore Cooper's bad Indians (Magua's crew in *The Last of the Mohicans*) disappear into subterranean caves "like the shades of the infernal regions, across which unhappy ghosts and savage demons were flitting in multitudes," and are "fierce," "wild," and "joyous" when savagely tomahawking, "braining," and scalping an enemy, burning him at the stake, or ripping out his heart. While by the time of these writings the threat of such Indian attack was well in the past for East Coast Americans, stories existed in living memory and were reinforced by newspaper accounts from the Great Plains. Indian lore provided a lively image of horror, just as Brown suggested. However, terms such as "witch" and "wizard" evoke European paganism while equating it with the people of the New World.

In *The Yemassee* (1835) William Gilmore Simms of Charleston, South Carolina, allegorizes the meeting between the Southern heroine and an Indian. He likens the Indian to a coiled rattlesnake in the garden, "an evil presence" whose glances combine "beauty and terror" and have a "fatal power of fascination, malignantly bright, . . . paralyzing" (I, 17–74). Simms compares the Indian's habits to those of the rattlesnake, finding even the war whoop to be borrowed from the rattle of the snake (I, 177) and capable of arousing "a nameless terror" akin to that evoked by night "when the shrill rattle of the lurking serpent . . . vibrates all around him" (II, 172). He describes the bedlam of fiendish Indian celebrations in "the thick night": "a thousand enemies, dark, dusky, fierce savages, . . . their wild distortions—their hell-enkindled eyes, . . . the sudden and demoniac shrieks from the women—the occasional burst of song, pledging the singer to the most diabolical achievements, mingled up strangely in a discord" (II, 78). Arrows penetrate the palms of a captive in imitation of Christ's crucifixion wounds, and the appellations "red devils" and "ragamuffin devils" recur. Massed tribes attack the coastal colonies and are crushed, as the demonic should be. (See Alan Rose's *The Demonic Vision*, on Simms's portraits of Indian deviltry.) In Simm's historical romance *The Cassique of Kiawah* (1859) the Indian takes on supernaturally evil dimensions:

The appearance of this Iawa [medicine man] was frightful in the extreme. He was of immense size and stature, nearly seven feet in height, . . . and he wore a head-dress of buffalo-horns in a fillet of feathers. . . . His contortions, savagely frantic and fantastic, as he threw his hands up in the air, and whirled through the masses, gashing his breast till the blood issued from every part of it, struck awe and terror even into the souls of those who . . . had long been familiar with such savage rites. . . . [He seemed] a terrible necromancer, calling up the dead and dismal inhabitants of the infernal abodes. (581)

Needless to say, Simms believes that the inflexibility of the Indian dooms him to remain at odds with whites; his character Hugh Grayson asserts, "It is utterly impossible that whites and Indians should ever live together and agree" (293). Religious horror conventions reinforce this setting apart of the Other, again equating native people with the European Antichrist and paganism.

Robert Montgomery Bird in *Nick of the Woods* (1837) goes farther to suggest that the white man can be infected by such savagery, a theme still popular in the modern mountain men Westerns and in the stories of frontier raids. When the wife and children of Bird's gentle Quaker, Nick Slaughter, are scalped and mutilated by Indians, Nick out-Indians the Indians, wearing the spoils of the Indian party (a broad Indian blanket as mantle, a gaudy shawl as bandana) and painting himself with streaks of red, black, and green to represent snakes, lizards, and other reptiles. "He was," says Bird, "on a sudden converted into a highly respectable-looking savage, as grim and awe-inspiring as these barbaric ornaments and his attire, added to his lofty stature, could make him" (287), and his acts thereafter are as diabolical as those of the Indians he slaughters. Samuel Drake's *Indian Captivities; Or Life in the Wigwam* (1899) provides blood-and-gore tales of both Indians as nightmarish demons and white captives as tainted by contact with them. The histories of George Bancroft and Francis Parkman likewise argue the superiority of whites over Indians ("a troublesome and dangerous species of wild beast"; Parkman, *The Oregon Trail*, 627) and the rightness of conquest, given the great cruelty of the Indians and their horrifying savagery in battle: it is Christianity conquering pagan savages.

This image of the Indian as a figure out of nightmares, a devil figure in semihuman form, recurred in the dime novels of the taming of the West and in the early films of embattled wagon trains, with their bloody scenes of women scalped and captives staked out in the sun to die. The theme of the white man turned literally beastly by his contact with Indians continues today in Westerns where whites learn to drink the blood of their prey and consume their hearts and livers raw, slaughter at will, and revel in their wildness. For example, Don Bendell's Western novel *Eagle* (1996), whose villain Bendell equates with Hannibal Lecter, builds on the motif of innate and incomprehensible amoral bestiality. Therein, the monstrous offspring of a white-Indian relationship proves a deadly, cannibalistic killer, so huge he is mistaken for a Sasquatch, but with a fearful human intelligence that leads him to track down and destroy individuals he thinks worthy to be mutilated and eaten—both red and white.

In sum, early American gothic fiction writers recognized the inherent potential of Indians in horror stories. It served their literary ends to portray the Indian as a demonic figure. As demon, the Indian could both tempt Christians to damning pagan deeds of passion and blood, and represent unrestrained savagery and sexuality in opposition to Christian restraint and reason. As a justification for the recurrent land grabs of Manifest Destiny, the Indian as horror figure needs no explanation. Such images live on today, not only in Westerns but also as the foundation for some modern horror fiction. Also, a recent development has been the incorporation of indigenous myth and horror lore into mainstream fiction, possibly to resuscitate a tired and decadent genre that sometimes verges on burlesque in its use of European figures such as the vampire and the werewolf.

NATIVE AMERICAN HORROR LORE

In dramatic contrast to European cultures since the Enlightenment, most Native American cultures teach that religion is not a separate part of life but integral to the whole, affecting daily actions and daily interaction with nature, family, and strangers. Many animals and natural objects are thought to possess a supernatural power that can be tapped into through ceremonies, vision quests, self-privation or mutilation, drugged states or dreams, or control of powerful natural entities who can then lend power, or "medicine." Virtually all Native American cultures possessed supernatural techniques with which to face most of life's unpredictable events. Many religious leaders—medicine men, shamans, or healers—still massage, dance, sing, smoke sacred tobacco, or use powerful drugs (marijuana, peyote, and so forth) so that with the aid of spirit helpers, they can discover the cause of ailments (often attributed to the loss of the soul, an imbalance in nature, or the intrusion of a foreign object through witchcraft). Rites assure harmony among humans and all other elements in the universe. At death the possessions of the deceased are sometimes given away or destroyed, names are forgotten, and all verbal references to the person's existence are terminated. Hunter-gatherers ritualistically asked the forgiveness of an animal to be killed, in the hope of assuring that the next animal hunted could be taken. As Chapter 2 explained, the points of the compass carry hidden meanings and powers; colors represent spiritual values; and special techniques help practitioners channel their energy for psychic purposes. There is thus no meaningful line of demarcation between religion and everyday life in the Native world.

The Star World and Cautionary Tales

The Native American oral tradition is rich in stories tinged with horror, particularly the stories of the formation of the stars or of beings from the star world. Constellations in particular are permanent symbols of terror. For example, the Crow Indians tell of an evil redheaded sorceress, who refuses to eat from any platter except the stomach of a pregnant woman. Then, while eating the meal that the pregnant woman serves on her stomach, the sorceress heats a stone redhot and places it on the pregnant woman's belly, where it burns through and kills her. The sorceress rips twin infants from the dead woman's uterus, tossing one in the back of the tepee (where mice care for it) and the other into a nearby spring, then burns a smile on the dead woman's face and places her outside her home so her returning husband will think she is welcoming him back. Later, the coldhearted spring child (raised by fish) brings his mother back to life (she has been rotting away on her burial platform) by tossing a hatchet (or in some versions an arrow) over her a number of times and grabbing her hand when the bony corpse stirs. The twin boys revenge their mother by chopping the sorceress into pieces, but her chopped-off hand, reaching desperately for the sky, becomes the hand star, part of Orion (McCleary, *The Stars We Know*, ch. 5).

Cannibalism is associated with giants and other supernatural beings, and in fact the redheaded sorceress has a giant companion, Cedar Between the Eyes, who eats corpses and takes the dead to the Other World (McCleary, 64). If a character is served soup with a human hand floating in it, listeners know he is not among humans. The Northeastern Algonquins tell of the *windigo* (*wendigo*/*wiendigo*), maneaters who roam the forest, devouring luckless hunters lost in the bush; lost hunters who eat human flesh become *windigos* themselves. Lovers who prove to be bears or snakes or have worm-covered faces the next morning are also pretty horrific, as are babies that eat only the hearts of brave warriors. Many tribes have the tradition of the gigantic and fearsome water monster and of No Body, the Great Rolling Head, a creature who crushes everything in its path and devours men with its enormous teeth (Erdoes & Ortiz, 177–237). There are stories of a flesh-eating antelope, gigantic, man-eating birds, slimy monsters with multiple forms (bear, panther, wolf, wolverine), and giant, snakelike monsters that consume whole villages. However, most of these stories are not intended to be simply titillating and scary; instead, they are part of the Creation stories or warnings meant to teach tribal taboos. This fact is clear from an Onondaga story of a vampire skeleton: it roams the forest because its body was left unburied, and a proper burial ends its frightening pursuit of human flesh (John Bierhorst, "Trout," Erdoes & Ortiz, 153).

A number of modern Native American writers have published cautionary stories based on frightening possibilities; these include (1) Robert Conley's *The Witch of Goingsnake and Other Stories* (1988); (2) Robert Franklin Gish's *Bad Boys and Black Sheep: Fateful Tales from the West* (1996); (3) Virginia Driving Hawk Sneve's *The Chichi Hoohoo Bogeyman* (1993); (4) Richard Red Hawk/ Clifford Trafzer's *Grandfather's Story of Navajo Monsters* (1988); and (5) Youyouseyah's *When Hopi Children Were Bad: A Monster Story* (1989).

Magic

Other writers have drawn on native sources about powerful magic. Emily Ivanoff Brown Ticasuk's *The Longest Story Ever Told: Qayaq, the Magical Man* (1981), for example, tells an Inuit (Eskimo) allegorical story about a legendary character, the magical man, and his search for his brothers' killer. Basil Johnston's *The Bear-Walker and Other Stories* (1995) tells of an evil shaman (the Bear Walker) who robs graves and raises spirits. Louise Erdrich's short story "Fleur" warns of Misshepeshu, a handsome, green eyed waterman who sprouts horns, fangs, claws, and fins and who takes possession of Fleur Pillager of the Bear Clan the first time she drowns (she drowns more than once). Her hips "fishlike" and "slippery," her "skin of lakeweed," her braids "thick like the tails of animals," her teeth "strong and curved," her fifth toes "missing," Fleur takes the Christian churches of the nearby town as a challenge and draws on secret powers (the heart of an owl on her tongue, the finger of a child in her pocket, a powder of unborn rabbits around her neck) to revenge herself on her abusers, whites blind to her destructive powers. The men who pull Fleur from the lake drown; a tornado topples a church steeple at the same time that three men who raped Fleur freeze to death in a cold-storage locker, wrapped in bearskins, symbols of Fleur's clan. In Western eyes Fleur is innocent of these deaths, since no cause-effect relationship is evident; for the Native American reader her spirit power is self-evident, as Erdrich makes clear.

Tales of the Dead

Native Americans also have a tradition of ghost stories and tales of the dead, but the dead don't automatically become ghosts, and ghosts are not always threatening and evil. Ideas about ghosts vary from tribe to tribe, with ghosts disguised as an echo or a whirlwind or appearing as rattling, walking skeletons visible in moonlight. According to Erdoes and Ortiz, the Mandans, for example, believed in four souls, two of which merged to form the spirit that went to an afterlife in another world, a third that remained in the old lodge, and a fourth that appeared occasionally simply to frighten people (429). To visit the land of the dead, whether the traveler crossed mountains or the Milky Way or went to the bottom of a lake, he or she would have to beware of traps set for the cowardly or the careless.

In some stories, the living marry or have sexual intercourse with the dead. In the story "Two Ghostly Lovers," a young warrior who promises to return to his bride comes back after many years and finds her lovely and unchanged, but after a night of love he discovers he had embraced bones and coupled with a skeleton, an experience that drives him insane (Erdoes & Ortiz, 433–434). Joseph Bruchac's "Bone Girl" (in Trafzer, *Earth Song, Sky Spirit*) captures the horror of an older man drinking too much and romancing a young woman who turns out to be a two-hundred-year-old ghost, her skull face moon pale. Cherokee Craig Strete's "Saturday Night at the White Woman Watching Hole" (in *The Bleeding Man and Other Science Fiction Stories*, 1977) similarly depicts a barroom beauty, an enchantress who lures men to their deaths and takes pleasure in ripping and gouging their lifeless bodies. In "The Spirit Wife" (Erdoes and Ortiz) a grieving Zuñi husband follows his dead wife's spirit westward. When he cannot follow her to the bottom of a lake, he seeks the help of owl people, who tell him how to bring her back to the land of the living; however, his inability to restrain his passion costs him her life. Ghosts may warn of danger, give blessings, play tricks, hoot like owls, appear as whirlwinds, or come back seeking company. The Comanche ghost sickness, a mysterious disease that contorted the face and crippled the hands, was thought to result from restless spirits of the dead assailing victims in lonely places, striking their faces, and leaving them numb and twisted. For mainstream writers such experiences would become the subject of entertaining horror fiction, but for Native Americans they reflected horrifying maladies that needed spiritual treatment.

Influences on Mainstream Magic/Horror

Despite the possibilities for inappropriate literary responses if true Native American horror is integrated carelessly into popular fiction genres, Native American "magic" and "horror" have transformed novels across genres in recent years with, for example:

1. Romances that turn on eighteenth- or nineteenth-century Indian shamans plucking a soul-mate bride from her twentieth-century life
2. Westerns in which medicine men foretell the coming of a blonde spirit woman who will save their people (and she appears on a wagon train)

3. Adventure stories in which modern-day travelers plunge through time warps to face bloodthirsty Aztec or Mayan dictator priests terrorizing Anasazi in the American Southwest

4. Thrillers with events transformed and villains undermined by an aged Indian who practices "grandfather magic" (using sacred tobacco), moves in and out of space, talks to animals and ghosts, crosses between time periods, and understands the series of deaths necessary for an ancient curse to be ended and the land returned to harmony.

A number of novels (Terry Johnston's *Dream Catcher*, Dinah McCall's *Dreamcatcher*, and Naomi Stokes's *Tree People*) depend to lesser and greater degrees on the mystical effects of a special Native American spiritual device that Johnston describes as "a circle of wrapped rawhide: a little larger than the Indian's hand, filled with twists of sinew woven like a fisherman's net, a small hole left open at the very center" (464). The dream catcher protects its user from bad dreams and bad realities and, in doing so, produces unexpected supernatural effects. It is not simply an enthusiasm for exotic artifacts that leads some book series to report real, mystic experiences with shamanism but to use fictive devices to tell their stories. In a number of horror stories ancient Native American gods and demonic forces wreak havoc in the modern world.

This recent enthusiasm for Native American religion and folklore as a source of fresh, unexploited horror lore also employs the coyote trickster, raven, crow, hawk, plumed serpent, spirit warriors, shamanism, skinwalkers, shape-shifting, curses, ghost walkers/night walkers/*chindi*, sandpaintings, the Sun Dance, and other sacred rituals (see the Glossary). In every case, however, the intended readership and the needs of the book market require that familiar genre conventions dominate, despite the inclusion of the Native American to provide interesting local color and to heighten the sense of alien threats.

Crossover Borrowings by Native American Writers

Furthermore, the crossover of borrowings works both ways. Native Americans writing in English to non-Native American readers must, to some degree, distort their tradition in order to communicate to the mainstream, if only to assure clarity. Creek author Craig Womack, in "Lucy, Oklahoma, 1911" (in Trafzer, *Earth Song, Sky Spirit*), seems to draw on voodoo to instill his tale with horror: a clay doll given power by hair and nail clippings from the intended victim, who dies in a fire as the clay figure blows apart and collapses in the flames. The echo of voodoo, a practice long familiar to Western readers, gives the story the correct resonance outside the Native American community. Pawnee/Oto novelist Anna Lee Walters works within an Indian tradition of spiritualism and shamanism. However, because her audience consists of non-Native Americans for whom Native American symbols will have little meaning, she creates an amalgam of traditions: a spirit warrior to carry her message of blame within the mainstream tradition of ghostly hauntings for the sake of revenge. Furthermore, in order to employ a Native American equivalent, she chooses the Navajo belief in *chindi* (vengeful evil spirits of the dead) over the Pawnee beliefs of her heritage, just as Leslie Silko chose the Creation story of the Quiche Maya for her *Almanac of the Dead* rather than those of her Laguna Pueblo heritage. For the purposes of popular literature, it may be safer to draw on the traditions of other tribes rather than take a chance on breaking the taboos of one's own tribe.

In Walters's novel *Ghost Singer* (1988), grisly artifacts of white-Indian conflicts going back to the days of the Spaniards—strings of human ears, scalps with hair and ears still intact, infant bones in a medicine bundle, skulls and skeletons—stored in cardboard boxes in an obscure corner of the Smithsonian Institution have given rise to ghosts that have silently walked the corridors of the Smithsonian for years, mostly unseen by white visitors but lifelike to Native American visitors. However, one ghost, a warrior killed while tied in place as a death stand against his foes, angrily stalks the Smithsonian's researchers, driving them one by one to suicide or insanity. This ghost searches furiously for some stolen relic, perhaps the bones of a loved one, and physically assaults researchers who get too close.

Walters retains the Native American sense of the horrible by making the ghost disproportional, a giant that looms above everyone, but his behavior fits that of a mainstream ghost—threatening gazes, the moving of physical objects, a chill when he passes, and physical violence (tossing someone against a wall or pounding on a table). Though Walters's main purpose is a didactic condemnation of the people who stole and displayed such appalling relics and a glorification of the Indian Way as sacred and meaningful, her description of a Navajo sickened by contact with the spirits of the dead and of an encounter between Indian shamans, haunted whites, and the spirit warrior—complete with green spirit lights, knockings, and physical encounters between the living and the dead—has horrifying potential. The physical manifestations of the spirits certainly echo the mainstream conventions of the seance, and presumably the color green for the spirit lights was chosen for its lack of religious significance to the Navajo (but possibly suggesting to a white audience the color symbolism of "natural" or "close to nature"). However, Walters does not exploit the didactic possibilities of the mainstream horror genre, for the people who are haunted are not the people who were originally responsible, and there is no mechanism, as there would be in the mainstream tradition, for righting a past wrong and thereby freeing the troubled spirits of the dead. Walters provides no denouement, only a preachy lesson about historical abuse perpetuated by the continued storage of body parts instead of their return to appropriate tribes (though to whom these belong seems unknowable). The Indians flee; the whites are in denial; and the spirit warrior stalks researcher after researcher. Thus, what seems like a crossover story ultimately cannot communicate to a mainstream audience because of its failure to fully integrate vague complaints about past injustices with genre conventions for expiating guilt.

Ghost Singer has excellent potential as a powerful and rhetorically persuasive horror story but illustrates the dangers of integrating two very different horror traditions. This chapter will concentrate on mainstream stories that create an amalgam of Native American and European traditions to make the concepts of horror more readily accessible to Western readers, and hence truly terrifying for the largest possible audience.

CROSSOVER HORROR

Crossover horror stories often incorporate traditional European horror conventions into Native American tales of the supernatural to create a blend that is both familiar and alien. Traditionally, European/American horror stories have been firmly founded on the threat of a Judeo-Christian concept of pure evil (Satan and satanic forces), an evil often made more horrifying by its association with "pagan" witchcraft, rites, and horrors. However, pure evil, as such, does not exist in Native American religion. Coyote may eat children, but careless mothers are responsible for their deaths, not Coyote; and the Coyote story itself, though containing cruelties that Christians would label evil, would be a lesson about behaving irresponsibly. Bad things usually happen as consequences of human failures and limitations, not because of competing forces of good and evil.

Consequently, mainstream horror stories building on indigenous lore often blend in Christian nightmares in order to take advantage of the atavistic fears of their readers, readers who are intrigued by the Native American but whose sense of the horrifying is born of a very different tradition. Some characteristics of Native American religion blend easily into European conventions: (1) acceptance of a universe controlled by supernatural beings and forces, with humans bound by dreams, tied to nature, and limited in power (this is in accord with basic Judeo-Christian belief); (2) the belief in animistic spirits that occupy natural objects such as rocks, trees, unusual landforms, bodies of water, or lightning (not mainstream but understandable); (3) the tradition of the shaman with special powers for negotiating between the physical and spiritual worlds (like a magus/magician or witch); and (4) the concept of powerful, distant, usually diffuse creator beings as well as numbers of other, more immediate godlike beings (like God, angels, devils, ghosts). However, the degree of the horror varies greatly with the method of presentation and with the writer's ability to truly merge the two traditions. Simple correspondences between religions provide only the possibility of finding a way to make two traditions complement each other in a literary form.

Ghosts, Spirit Warriors, Little People, and Shaman Powers

The Native American concept of ghosts and spirit warriors makes for an interesting extension of the European ghost tradition, and the concept of shamanistic powers to some degree parallels the European/American witch tradition, while the tradition of the little people is much more threatening than that of elves or leprechauns. In the main, however, these Native American concepts transfer readily to the supernatural/horror genre.

In spite of such transfers, however, some "ghost/spirit" stories simply never take off as horror tales because the writers are more interested in other genre possibilities, like romance or Westerns. For instance, Linda Sandifer, in *Embrace the Wind* (1993), establishes a crossover when the anguished and troubled ghost of a murdered woman haunts her Shoshone brother until events free her living daughter from danger; furthermore, the valley where multiple murders occur seems dominated by the *NumumBi*, pygmies of evil disposition who bring de-struction to those foolish enough to stumble upon them at night. However, this haunting simply confirms the readers' sense that past evils must be exorcised by defeating present evil but does little to combine the different European and native senses of what ghosts or spirits are like. Judson Gray's rather conven-tional Western, *Hunter's Run* (1998), surprisingly turns on the hero performing an ancient Cherokee chant that brings the little people to carry a villain off to "the Darkening Land" of death; his end is certainly horrifying, but the rest of the story is not.

Likewise, Madeline Baker's *Under a Prairie Moon* (1998) mixes European ghost lore with a Sioux idea about a human's period of time on Earth being predetermined, but her end result is more romantic than ghostly. Here, Western gunslinger and half-breed Dalton Crowkiller, hanged in 1873 for a crime he did not commit, is condemned to exist as a spirit in a set locale for an indefinite period of time. He has haunted his killer's family ranch for 125 years but has not been capable of poltergeist-like activities until the beautiful, grief-stricken young widow Katherine Conley moves in. Then, magically, he discovers he can appear not simply as a ghostly shadow or as an inexplicably chilly breeze but in corporeal form. Moreover, his interest in Katherine's life magically sends the two of them back in time to the period just before his hanging, and Dalton realizes that he has been granted a chance to redeem his soul by making up for what he did not do while alive. Taking Katherine with him (against all odds and corporeal differences, this modern woman and this nineteenth-century ghost have fallen in love), he returns to his father's Lakota Sioux family in time to help free them from a U.S. Calvary stockade. The real horror of this section of the novel is the senseless and gruesome massacre of people the main character holds dear (babies impaled, Sioux women raped and scalped, decapitations, and so forth) for no clear reason except their Indianness. Since no supernatural horror can compete with this "historical" horror, the mixed-blood hero moves on to better days: a mystic reunion with his Sioux father in an idealized "happy hunt-ing ground" (lush grasslands, a pre-Columbian utopia) and an opportunity to quiet his white mother's fears of death by telling her of his own death and of his father's afterlife. By this time, what was wonderfully eerie and potentially scary has turned sappy, and the story ends as a conventional romance rather than a tale of horror. Baker's treatment of her ghost follows a European ghost tradition more closely than a Native American one, but references to the Native

American allows her novel to partake of the exotic, the intriguing, the mysterious.

In other stories, the Indian is a source of evil in a basically non-Native American story. Indian burial grounds are favorite settings for such stories; Joseph
Bruchac even includes a joke about this Native American creative writing cliché
in "Bone Girl." In Stephen King's *Pet Sematary* (1983), the pet cemetery des-
ecrates an ancient Indian burial ground, and in his *The Shining* (1977), ancient
Indian spirits produce insanity in visitors to a luxury mountain hotel. In Thomas
Monteleone's *Night Things* (1980), when an Indian burial mound is disturbed,
small biting creatures rip everyone concerned to bits and eat the pieces. In still
other stories, the horror depends on the amalgam of some Native American and
European traditions, both related to burial spaces. For instance, the possibility
of vicious attack by bloodthirsty spirits, with centuries of pent-up rage and fierce
warrior skills, merges well with a European concept of vengeful ghosts. Several
popular writers have made use of spirit warriors guarding sacred places and
threatening vengeance carried out across time to infuse with terror their warnings
of the dangers of disturbing the dead or dead places, and of stealing bones,
pottery, or other relics from Native American archaeological sites, a deeply felt
issue among Native American advocacy groups. (The Western equivalent is the
"mummy's curse," but the Egyptian grave-robbing convention is decadent and
frequently comic, having lost its power to horrify.) Monteleone uses the tradition
of the *wendigo* or water monster in his story "Wendigo's Child" (1973), and,
in a truly chilling story, "Spare the Child" (1983), describes what happens to
those who abandon an adopted child who is related to a Native American shaman.

In his novel *Soul Catcher* (1973), Frank Herbert dramatizes the conflict between the culture of Washington state's Native Americans and modern civilization; he also exploits the horror possibilities inherent in the Northwestern
Indians' concept of the spirit world. *Soul Catcher* combines a captivity theme
with the evocation of ancient terrors and powerful natural forces. In it, the
violent rape of his suicidal sister leads college student Charles Hobuhet to seek
retribution by becoming Katsuk, the incarnation of the spirit of his ancestors
and the center of his people's perceptions. As Katsuk, he kidnaps the son of the
U.S. undersecretary of state to offer as sacrifice for his sister's death. To become
this vengeful spirit, Hobuhet undergoes ritual ceremonies of sacrifice and symbol, using the medicine powers taught him by his grandfather. He evokes visions
and merges dream and reality until a soul catcher possesses his body and takes
both his souls (some Native American traditions hold that humans possess two
souls). As Katsuk, he slides along with panther strength, blessed by the omens
of falling stars. Accompanied by Raven, he evokes the names of the ancient
dead and asserts the power of Northwestern shamans. He takes an innocent to
sacrifice "for all the innocents you [whites] have murdered" and to balance sky
and earth; "I have the root of your tree in my power," he asserts (3). Before his
death the white sacrificial victim comes to understand dream spirit realities.

However, when the Soul Catcher has accomplished his mission, Hobuhet is left to suffer the consequences in the white world. A contrasting approach is seen in the 1992 film *Shadow Hunter*, with Robert Beltran as a Navajo skinwalker: this villaneous figure brings to the screen the horrors possible in shape-shifting and shamanistic illusion by depicting the shaman as demonic, a skilled practitioner of black magic who eats the flesh of the dead and uses human bones to gain access to the minds and souls of his chosen victims, but who is ultimately defeatable by those who can concentrate on their own powerful medicine.

In Micah Hackler's *Legend of the Dead* (1995), a millionaire rancher discovers an ancient Anasazi pueblo twice the size of the Cliff Palace at Mesa Verde and filled with priceless Indian artifacts. He kills to cover up his landgrab manipulations, but an old Zuñi shaman, Windwalker, calls on Anasazi warrior spirits to protect the local sheriff and the senator who wants to make the site a federally protected area. The skies darken, the heavens rumble, and out of a whirlwind walk three ceremonial figures, the *a'doshle*, as tall as the kiva roof, their faces grotesque and distorted, their stares chilling. These protective spirits predate the Aztecs and, according to Windwalker, draw their strength from the faith of believers. They guard the *Shipap* (place of origin), do the will of the Great Spirit, and carry the sheriff off in a whirlwind to join Windwalker and the Senator as they battle the millionaire "Destroyer." Wearing prehistoric ceremonial attire—skin and feather robes, cone-shaped grass headdresses, and sacred wood masks with hideous frowns and protruding tongues that look as if the mask's owner is being choked to death—and armed with ancient atlatls (spear-throwers), at sunrise on the summer solstice, the sheriff and senator do battle with the land thieves in a scene that is satisfyingly eerie thanks to these spirit warriors. Native American conventions for spirit warriors and supernatural forces give a legitimate political and social issue appropriate force.

Likewise, in Thurlo's *Spirit Warrior* (1993), archaeologists digging up relics from the Anasazi past seem to unleash the *chindi*, evil spirits of an ancient warrior. Navajo tribal attorney Sam Nez and archaeologist Marla Garret would like to blame a dishonest university official and a Navajo troublemaker for the unsettling hauntings, but the dreadful chill that precedes a sighting and the sense of some dark malignancy that fills the cavern and squeezes the life out of people make them conclude that, despite some attempts at a fake haunting, a true spirit warrior protects the site from sacrilegious exploitation. At key moments, the warrior seems to appear, as if from nowhere:

... she caught a brief flash of movement out of the corner of her eye. She turned quickly, her heart hammering. The spectral Indian warrior that stood about fifty yards away made her blood turn to ice. An unearthly glow emanated from him and the ornate flint armor covering his torso.

"Slayer," she said, her voice a stunned whisper in the night. (94)

His skin prickled . . . an indistinct shadow . . . blocked their way. The shape seemed to absorb the light from her flashlight, consuming it like a black hole. . . .

A gust of wind rose from nowhere, filling the air with the rotting stench of a slaughterhouse. Then a sharp, earsplitting whistle seemed to reverberate against the rock walls, gaining in intensity with each breath he took.

An awareness based on instinct, rather than recollection, swept through him. He knew then he was confronting evil in its purest and deadliest form. (149–150)

Later, the "unearthly image of a warrior" shimmers into view, accompanied by a rhythmic drumming that makes the rock walls of the Anasazi cave vibrate. When the human villain seems ready to kill Marla, "low, unearthly wails, like the agonized cries of the damned" seem to come from everywhere, "reverberating against the walls, rising in pitch and intensity" (245); they leave behind the villain's lifeless body with the Slayer's flint knife embedded in his neck and no footprints to indicate a human killer. An explosion closing off the site ends the controversial excavation as well as the supernatural intervention, leaving the ending nicely ambivalent about the "reality" of the spirits, a sop to mainstream readers reluctant to totally accept the spirit world the Navajo believe in.

The powers of shamans—a Native American equivalent of the sorcerer or magician of European tradition—can also prove eerie. Siquani Kaneequayokee, in Cherokee-Choctaw-Irish Louis Owens's intriguing suspense thriller *Nightland* (1996), embodies a number of magical and horror elements as he moves between times and spaces, talks to the crows and to the dead, reminisces about when he was invisible and when he was a crow, and tries to pass on to his "grandsons" the stories and lessons of their heritage (like smoking things with rabbit weed to keep off evil, asking the Little Deer's permission to hunt, and watching out for danger from the mountainous area to the west that the Cherokee call the Nightland). His "grandsons" aren't even sure of their real relationship to him, and joke that he may be well over three hundred years old, given his memories of past events; an Apache woman suggests he could be a sorcerer or trickster. In fact, Siquani existed when the white people first came, and he later walked the Trail of Tears, observing and remembering for a future time when he could help Indians recall their past and regain their strength. He is a ghostly time traveler with shamanistic skills deeply rooted in the land. He has moved in and out of time for hundreds of years, returning to the long, deadly walk again and again, watching his people die from cold, hunger, and disease, then moving into the future to teach modern survivors about their heritage and to use his shamanistic powers to combat Indian witches who create disharmony and bring death.

The novel begins with an eerie image of a man falling from the heavens and being impaled on an ancient cedar, his blood staining the trunk as lightning leaps from sky to Earth and back again like "a snake's tongue" while a coyote barks (1). The Cherokee hunters who view this scene at first take the package the dead man fell with as a gift from the Great Spirit, but immediately discover it is a curse from Indian drug dealers. As his grandsons dream of death and encounter armed attackers, Grampa Siquani notes the warning signs of a deeper danger—black buzzards from the west, blue lightning, the cry of a screech owl, a red mountain lion, birds that turn red in the sunset, the voices in the thunder; he invites the ghost of the impaled man, an Indian from a pueblo farther north, to chat and play checkers and talk about his sorcerer uncle whom Siquani has seen as a diamondback rattler. His deeper vision sees in the threat of night walkers (Indian witches from the west) an opportunity to counter an Apache curse against the Spaniards who stole their land and massacred their families, and to restore balance and health to the land his Cherokee "grandsons" live on.

The old man drifts in and out of space so frequently that the ghost tells him, "You keep making me nervous . . . the way some of you disappears and then comes back again" (131), and Siquani tells his grandson, who is puzzled by his sudden appearances, that he's been practicing his disappearing magic. Using sacred tobacco to protect him, Siquani removes the body from the ancient cedar and buries it near running water so that the dead man will become a cloud and bring rain to the parched earth. The final defeat of the drug dealer witch evokes horrific supernatural images as the massacred Apaches of another age are finally released from an ancient curse: "Out of the earth, ancient bones began to emerge, washed with harsh rain from the edges and sides of arroyos" (281). Later, as water bubbles up in the formerly dry well, "a crowd of faces began to rush upward only to shatter and flutter downward and then rise again with the motion of leaves in the wind" (312). His "medicine" having achieved his ends—restoring land sacred to his people to harmony and teaching a new generation to respect old ways—Siquani leaps back in time to the desolate Trail of Tears to once again relive what he could not stop. Because the novel focuses on Siquani, who practices a benign spiritualism in harmony with nature, the threat of the Pueblo witch from the mountain, despite the novel's scare elements, is never strong enough to leave the reader truly horrified. The effects are eerie but not horrific.

In contrast, the effects in James Doss's *The Shaman Laughs* (1995) are indeed horrific even though the horror elements turn out to be mostly bogus. Ute shaman Daisy Perika lives in a trailer house at the mouth of the sacred Cañon del Espiritu, in Colorado, close to the underground home of the *pitukupf*, a dwarf spirit hundreds, perhaps thousands, of years old whom Daisy consults about evil and wrongdoing in her canyon bailiwick and beyond. A Native American demon figure is stalking first animals and then human beings in Cañon del Serpiente, the canyon next to the one where Daisy's trailer is located. The demon is identified by Daisy in a dream vision as a huge creature that materializes out of the night mist, forming very broad shoulders, a horned head, and one red Cyclops-like eye that winks on and off. The creature uses a natural stone basin in the canyon (a depression that once served Anasazi women as a metate to grind corn) as a receptacle for the blood of his animal victims, whose ears and testicles he removes. Building on the real and mysterious animal mutilations that have been reported in the United States and Europe, the novel has the apparent demon move up the food chain to human sacrifice. The appearances of the demon are effectively chilling, especially when given confirmation through Daisy's vision and then through Granite Creek Chief of Police Scott Parris's later involvement with the monster. (Parris's Celtic ancestry enables his terrifying precognitive visions that often accord with Daisy's.)

However, Doss backs away from creating a true Native American monster, setting up parallel versions of reality instead, much as Micah Hackler's *Legend of the Dead* allows the spirit world to be interpreted as either hallucinatory or real, depending on the perceiver's mind-set. Although Doss uses Daisy's more assimilated nephew, Deputy Charlie Moon, to defeat the villain and explain away the demon in empirical terms, Daisy's visions and other minor plot events give her spiritual framework significant, if not equal, standing. As a result, the Indian lore creates credible chills and an unforgettable portrait of three cultures (Ute, white, and Mexican-American) in interaction.

Werewolves, Totem Spirits, and Shape-shifters

Some stories merge the European tradition of the werewolf with the Native American tradition of the tribal or totem spirit (animal vision spirits with which warriors identify and that bring animal skills and strengths to braves engaged in the hunt) and shape-shifting (humans taking the shape of a hawk or wolf or some other wild animal with special powers in order to achieve particular goals; see Glossary). The Navajos, among others, believe that the skin of a wolf or mountain lion in or near a dwelling indicates the presence of shape-shifting witchcraft—human wolves. Five novels illustrate such crossovers: Eric Weiner's *Heart of the Hunter* (1997), Connie Flynn's *Shadow on the Moon* (1997) and its sequel *Shadow of the Wolf* (1998), S. P. Somtow's *Moon Dance* (1989), and Garth Stein's *Raven Stole the Moon* (1988).

Eric Weiner's *Heart of the Hunter*

Despite its wilderness setting (Kentucky in 1792), its white settlers' fear of Indians lurking behind every bush, and its mysterious, witchlike Indian hag, Eric Weiner's *Heart of the Hunter*, a work aimed at young people, draws on the mainstream European tradition for its bloodcurdling effects: the power of the full moon, the blood of a werewolf causing humans to become werewolves, the painful physical transformation from man to wolf, the growing wolf qualities of the werewolf in human form, and the beast's uncontrollable blood lust. The youthful protagonist, Jamie Fier, is captured by Shawnee warriors of the Wolf clan. His father killed, and himself forced to run the gauntlet, Jamie escapes death only because of a Shawnee legend of a youth with wolf eyes leading the tribe to buffalo. An ancient and respected medicine woman called Withered Woman adopts Jamie and offers him a means to revenge himself on the family he blames for his father's death and his capture. A werewolf whose wolf spirit protects her tribe, Withered Woman employs Shawnee rituals to change Jamie into a werewolf, whose supersenses will find the buffalo the tribe needs and whose lust for blood will guide him to revenge but also to an unexpected fate. The crossover between traditions is interesting but is not developed to any extent.

Connie Flynn's *Shadow on the Moon* and *Shadow of the Wolf*

Connie Flynn's *Shadow on the Moon* and *Shadow of the Wolf* go a step further, blending the European tradition of the werewolf with the Native American tradition of shaman shape-shifting powers to produce a peculiar amalgam. Flynn adds a third ingredient: a Creation myth brought to life in the modern Southwest, in this case, of a group called the Dawn People who, in accord with Southwestern lore, came up from within the Earth and peopled the Earth in prehistory. In Flynn's story, these native people reenact a story, supposedly from Aztec legend, in which a deer turns wolf, then becomes a deer again, but with the insights of a predator that allows her to defend herself and her fellow deer against these fierce marauders. *Shadow on the Moon* begins the battle between Native American shamans and European-style werewolves, and *Shadow of the Wolf* resolves the conflict. Indian deities mix with Christian as Quetzalcoatl, Coyote Trickster, Buffalo Woman, Grandfather Sky, representatives of the Anasazi Stone and Standing People, and "a chorus of angels in pure white" (311) appear during a prolonged sweat ritual. This mixed holy crew listen to the condemnation of both her dead prey and her defenders before judging the predator werewolf woman, whose loss of powers has made her reevaluate her role; her love of a child transforms her into White Wolf Woman, the foretold savior of the Dawn People. During the dark moon of the equinox, armed with a pure crystal, her newly acquired spirit power, and the love of a child and a shaman, she willingly battles a pack of werewolves in order to give the Dawn People and all of the disenfranchised Indians they have decided to protect time to cross over into a hidden world. In this sacred place (Quakahla), the buffalo still roam, the white man cannot go, and Indians can return to a utopian, pre-European life.

There is much nonsense here as an Apache computer expert-turned-shaman (after giving up a job with Microsoft) falls in love with the ex-werewolf he saves from a powerful European werewolf king, all part of the predicted foreknowledge of Native American deities conveyed in legends thousands of years old. These ancient stories were intended as a guide to modern shamans of a people unchanged since prehistory and moving between two worlds through a magical doorway in an Arizona cave. These crossover horrors often reflect more knowledge of Western lore than of Native American traditions. In fact, Flynn writes:

Ebony Canyon, Quakahla, the Dawn People, and White Wolf Woman are totally the product of my admittedly quirky imagination. Students of Native American spirituality may notice discrepancies in my depiction of the Dawn People. . . . [and] the Toltec/Aztec king Quetzalcoatl. . . . Nor have I attempted to remain faithful to the traditions of specific tribes or even Native American beliefs in general. I've mingled them all, thrown in some Wiccan lore, and even a sprinkling of Eastern philosophy for good measure. (Foreword, *Shadow of the Wolf*)

Without taking light entertainment too seriously, we can still look askance at this promiscuous tumbling together of traditions and ways. While no conscious disrespect may be intended, such high-handed use of the traditions of real people at best misleads and confuses, and at worst justifies complaints about callous disregard for an oppressed people.

S. P. Somtow's *Moon Dance*

Another popular Indian-werewolf amalgam is S. P. Somtow's *Moon Dance*. Somtow, a pseudonym for Thai sci-fi writer Somtow Sucharitkul, draws on Buddhist concepts of yin and yang, light and dark, to dramatize the meeting of decadent, depraved European werewolves with Indian werewolves (the Lakota Sioux *Wichasha Shungmanitou*) and to provide an unusual interpretation of the historical movement west. The European werewolves have gone west seeking "a lycanthropic utopia": endless territory, unspoiled by civilization, and fresh prey, "natives unacquainted with the folklore and superstition that cause the peasants of Europe to hide behind their silver and their wolfsbane" (158–59). The European canines partake of the white man's darkest qualities and, according to the Indians, "are cut off from nature" and "do not know themselves" (244); they lack compassion and are empty of spirit. Descriptions of their transmogrification follow conventional patterns:

The Count . . . his face . . . his nose had elongated into a snout. Even as she watched he was changing. Bristles sprouting on his cheeks. His teeth were lengthening, his mouth widening into the foaming jaws of an animal. The eyes . . . bright yellow now, slitty, implacable. His hands, already covered with hair, were shrinking into paws. With a snarl the Count fell down on all fours. His teeth were slick with drool. The stench intensified. Her gorge rose. She tasted vomit in the back of her throat. Then the wolf leapt. (103)

Their actions are grisly, resulting in decapitations, gushing blood, gnawed bones, and strings of entrails.

The Indian werewolves, in contrast, live in balance with the land and its creatures and have found their true place in the universal harmony, weeding out the old, the sick, and the suicidal, never taking human victims except when the humans offer themselves as willing sacrifices. A French trapper-turned-railway man (and father of two mixed-blood youths who play pivotal roles in the story, Theodore and Preston Grumiaux) describes them this way:

Among the *Indiens peaux-rouges* these werewolves are not considered creatures of Satan, but have their own part to play in the great cycle of being. . . . they prey on slain warriors and old people who have outlived their usefulness, absorbing their essence unto themselves. (148)

Somtow makes the Sioux werewolves representative of the combination of light and dark that could have humanized the westward movement if European and Indian had met in harmony instead of in battle.

Called the *Gone with the Wind* of lycanthropy, *Moon Dance* spans two continents (Europe and America) and more than a century (1860s to 1980s), bringing in such historical figures as Sigmund Freud, Buffalo Bill, Sitting Bull, and Calamity Jane. The plot begins with a would-be reporter/writer, Carrie Dupré, seeking an interview in the town of Winter Eyes, South Dakota, near Wounded Knee, with an infamous serial killer called the Laramie Ripper, a centenarian schizophrenic whose multiple personalities include both a murderous and depraved European werewolf and a visionary Lakota Sioux werewolf. However, past merges with present as that interview opens the young reporter's eyes to her true heritage and the beast within herself. Because Carrie is the daughter of the Ripper's beloved nanny, he shares his story with her in a series of interviews that capture the white man's ravages of the West: the wholesale slaughter of buffalo, the massacres of Chinese and Indians, and the sexual obsessions of military leaders determined to rid the land of red savages, all summed up in the destructive blood lust of the European werewolves as they fight to seize the Indian werewolves' sacred places. The hope that drives the positive characters in the book is that a schizophrenic European wolf child will be made whole by Indian training and Indian dream visions, and will unite both European and Indian wolf clans in a common dream. The Sioux of the tale believe that this dream can reshape reality: "The Indians had a special gift for dreaming. When they dreamed they could change the world" (550). The conclusion to the nineteenth-century section is an apocalyptic battle in which both sides lose because of the supernatural strength of deep-seated racial hatreds. However, the twentieth-century frame promises hope for the future if humans—both Indian and white—can come to terms with the beast within.

Clearly, such novels as these depend far more on the European tradition of horror and evil than on any Indian tradition, though Indians are brought in to represent either the darker, savage side of human nature or, ironically, its reverse, man in harmony with his world. Whitley Strieber's *The Wolfen* (1978), which was made into a 1981 horror movie with Albert Finney, postulates wolflike predators whom the Indians consider superior beings prowling Manhattan (and other large urban centers), maintaining the natural balance by preying on humans in their territory who have diseased livers or hearts, or other chronic afflictions.

Garth Stein's *Raven Stole the Moon*

Garth Stein's supernatural horror thriller *Raven Stole the Moon* daringly builds on the Tlingit tradition of the Otter People—the *kushtaka*—soul-stealing predators/water gods that stalk the netherworld between the living and dead, taking on the shapes of humans and dogs to get close to their prey. A grieving half-Tlingit mother (Jenna) whose son Bobby supposedly drowned at the Thunder Bay Resort his father helped build returns to the remote Alaskan town where the accident occurred and gradually becomes convinced that the boy (whose body was never found) was really stolen by the *kushtaka*. The shaman hired by the resort to cleanse Thunder Bay of its restless spirits almost succumbed to *kushtaka* powers (the now closed resort was built directly over their spiritual center), and he remains fearful of them. However, he finally agrees to take Jenna with him on a shaman journey to the underwater spirit world of the *kushtaka* to bring Bobby back. The danger is that they themselves will be transformed into otters and never be able to return to human form if their medicine and their will are not strong enough to withstand the psychological powers of the Otter People. The shaman must use all his spiritual powers to arm them for their quest, and he fears his medicine power may not be enough. In addition to the nightmare malevolence of alien creatures disguised by familiar animal and human forms, the underwater journey to the *kushtaka* involves frightening psychological battles through a network of caves, with the otters taking on the shape of the shaman, of Jenna, and of her son to misdirect the searchers. Reality and spiritualism merge, and readers are left uncertain about what happened in the real world and what happened in the spirit world. This story builds much more closely on traditional native storytelling than do the Indian werewolf stories, and rational explanations yield in the end to fact: a mother's love brings back her long missing son. Or is he a *kushtaka* in disguise?

Vampires: Martin Cruz Smith's *Nightwing*

Of the many writers who attempt to reconcile native and Western visions of reality in fiction, Martin Cruz Smith is among the most successful. As we have seen, the two views run directly counter to one another, for the native idea that their homogeneous and blessed groups, whether known by tribal names or simply as "the People," had a special and sanctified relationship with a Creator, with the land, and with the animals thereon could never coexist with the concepts of private ownership of land, of exploitation of natural resources, and of rapid technological change. For Native Americans, nature was an organic whole, perhaps to be used but ultimately to be accepted; for whites, it was a wild thing to be tamed and controlled. The difference in philosophy is captured succinctly in Smith's *Nightwing* (1977), a horror tale that revolves around vampire bats, the bubonic plague they carry, and the varying responses by whites and Indians to a rapidly spreading epidemic.

Youngman Duran is a Hopi deputy on the reservation land his tribe shares with the more numerous Navajo, a formerly assimilated college student and then soldier who found he could not survive in the white world. He has retrained himself in Hopi language and ways with the help of Abner Tasupi, a shaman in his nineties who announces to Youngman that he plans to make everyone die, and creates a magical sandpainting to begin this end of the world. Abner is fed up with strip mining, Navajos, the El Paso Gas Company, the theft of Arizona water, and the general exploitation of the Indian. Youngman, for all his embracing of old ways, is a nonbeliever in Hopi mysticism, and dismisses Abner's threats as the ravings of an old man high on datura. Then Abner is discovered dead, and bloody corpses, cut as if by razors, and cases of the bubonic plague begin to turn up all over the reservation. Youngman and his girlfriend Anne, a white nurse working in the area, team up with an obsessive and somewhat deranged vampire bat specialist named Paine, who has followed a colony from Mexico into the United States. The increasingly horrific plot follows the uneasy alliances among the members of this odd group, whose attempts to wipe out the bat colony are frustrated by Navajo Tribal Chairman Walker Chee. Chee is willing to accept any number of Indian and white deaths if he can keep oil company investors ignorant of the danger by covering up the plague; in his mind, such sacrifices of the few are justified by the possibility of the reservation Indians finally joining the economic mainstream.

Smith thus has representatives of a variety of groups: assimilated Indians of varying philosophies, an unassimilated old shaman, a sympathetic white (Anne) doing social work among the Indians, a white committed to science with no time for mysticism. As in the novels of Michael Crichton, compact and convincing disquisitions on scientific background and research are interspersed throughout, sometimes in the pedantic answers the bat expert gives to the others, sometimes as descriptive set pieces that trace a vampire attack on animals or people. As the plague spirals out of control, Youngman begins to realize that Abner's threat is coming true: if the bats establish themselves in the numberless caves in the Arizona desert and continue to spread plague, cities will be evacuated and no end will be in sight. (In the medieval plagues, up to half of those afflicted died.) Virtually against his will, Youngman finds himself committed to ending the disaster in cooperation with Paine, who with state-of-the-art technical equipment tracks the bats to their lair in an ancient cave, a Hopi holy site.

Youngman, ingesting enough datura to give him superhuman energy and hallucinations, sees or imagines Abner explaining that if the majority white culture is destroyed by the Hopi/Mayan bat god Masaw, the Hopi will move underground and emerge again triumphant, a kind of Southwestern version of the promise made by the Plains Ghost Dancers. The climax involves a conflagration that could be variously explained as an oil seep being set afire or as Abner's true intentions being fulfilled.

While *Nightwing* might seem to be having it both ways, with Hopi mysticism offering parallel explanations for what the whites see as biological and physical events, in fact Smith is more subtle than writers who simply say, in effect, "You choose which way is the truth." The events of the plot are in fact primarily explained by scientific description and cause-effect reasoning; they are the framework established to enlighten us about bats, plague, and their interaction. Paine, the bat scientist, suffers from the classical literary scientific hubris, the idea from Doctor Faustus through *Frankenstein* that he alone can save the day. This excess of faith in science leads to Paine's downfall, and it is Youngman, ironically, who comes through in the end. Youngman remains an assimilated modern American, even though he practices some of the old ways and takes Abner seriously; he gives us a sympathetic view of the Hopi understanding while allowing us to retain our trust in rationalism. Abner's mysticism, however, is not denied, and offers an intriguing "what if" that adds to the sense of magic and horror. The Hopi way is respected as a viewpoint, although not one that modern Hopis need to accept blindly. Finally, the descriptions of the bats and bat attacks are so appallingly effective that readers may never be able to see the harmless cousins of the vampires in quite the same way again. Smith touches a deep chord of horror, much like that created by stories of attacks by large sharks. The vampires, however, are depicted as the one true predator of man, an age-old nightmare that cannot be avoided by staying out of the water.

Witchcraft, Shamans, and Demonic Forces

In Clifford Trafzer's *Blue Dawn, Red Earth* (1996) Creek-Cherokee Craig Womack's modern tale of witchcraft, "The Witches of Eufaula, Oklahoma," describes young reservation drug addicts trying to rob an old woman and discovering the power of witchcraft as she shape-shifts to owl, dog, and bear and twists their vision of reality and manhood. Lenape Annie Hansen's "Spirit Curse" (in Trafzer's *Blue Dawn, Red Earth*) captures the horror and irony of finding a black-hooded, white-eyed spirit in the back of your car and not knowing whether to use Salish or Lenape exorcism spells, the Lord's Prayer or Hail Marys. Choctaw Jim Barnes's "The Reapers," also in Trafzer's collection, reads like a Shirley Jackson nightmare: a salesman with car trouble finds himself caught up in a harvest ritual in which participants assume he has been possessed by the corn spirit and must be wrapped in sheaves, beheaded, and bound in corn stalks to assure a good harvest.

Naomi Stokes's *The Tree People* and *The Listening Ones*

Witchcraft is connected with shamanism—good witches and bad witches, shamans who promote health and harmony, shamans who bring destruction and disharmony. In *The Tree People* (1995), set in the Pacific Northwest's Olympic Peninsula, Naomi Stokes combines a tale of supernatural horror based on Salish witchcraft with a detective story that hinges on environmental struggles over old-growth timber cutting. The setting in an ancient forest area gives rise to the civic issue of jobs versus environmental protection, but the location also allows Stokes to exploit her larger concern, the relationship of assimilated Native Americans to their psychic environment. The deep woods were home to powerful magicians long before whites arrived, and this heritage of witchcraft affects those living there in the present.

The witchcraft draws on ancient, mystical, and hallucinogen-inspired ceremonies to bring back souls that evil shamans have separated from their bodies and on natural destructive forces powered by sentient spirits—plant and animal, but once human. The good shaman of the story is Old Man Ahcleet, the last of the old-time shamans who is a direct descendant of a great pre-Columbian shaman named Musqueem. The bad shaman is a redheaded Quinault witch, Aminte, who lives deep in the forests, practices herbal medicine, and casts wicked spells that enchant handsome white males. She sometimes acts in parallel to the *belle dame sans merci* of medieval European tradition, a succubus weaving spells that draw men to her sexuality, leaving them spellbound and possessed mentally and physically by her "soul-catcher": "his [Michael McTavish's] soul fluttered from his lips like a bursting bubble, right into the Spirit Catcher and Aminte's keeping" (170). The story eventually pits the white magic of Indian shamans against the black magic of the redheaded witch and an Indian demon shaman she has released from confinement. The evil Aminte, accompanied by her raven familiar, moves the yellow tape markers of the tree company so the workmen cut down the old-growth tree that for centuries has confined the redheaded demon shaman Xulk (from whom Aminte is descended). Thereby, she draws his spirit forth, triggers a series of destructive events (victims battered to death, throats slashed, machinery gone amok), and shares in the maliciousness of his supernatural powers.

The ancient demon shaman releases a virulent and deadly evil that strikes like a disease and is responsible for the deadly malaise that almost kills Quinault policewoman Jordan Tidewater's son. To save her son, Jordan must accept her inherited role as the shaman who will replace her great-grandfather, Old Man Ahcleet, a role she has been resisting in order to succeed as a modern police officer dedicated to empirical methods and modern technology: she has plans to attend the FBI's state-of-the-scientific-art academy in Quantico, Virginia. Instead, she undergoes the complete shaman training course with Ahcleet, a horrifying process as Western logic gives way to ancient ritual and mystical experiences.

After a regime alternating sweat baths with ice-cold plunges, fasting, shouting for spirits, greeting the cardinal directions, and running naked through the forest, Jordan begins to acquire spirit helpers (the beaver, the snake Teb'ak!wab). Then, assisted by three senior ritualists, their faces blackened, Jordan undergoes various forms of physical torture and is painted in sacred ways until she acquires her sacred song, becomes La'quwamax, the shaman "whose ancestors had received the gift of whaling from Thunderbird himself" (468), and is ready to visit the Land of the Dead. On this psychic journey she must counter the redheaded witch and the redheaded shaman's witchcraft in order to rescue her son's spirit. She begins by controlling Aminte's familiars (raven and wolf), combating the powers of an ancient Quinault ghost board, and taking back Xulk's bones despite threats from wolf spirits and arctic cold. On the journey itself, armed with her great-great-great-grandfather's shaman's wand (his spirit helper), Ahcleet's sacred cedar-and-otter-skin shaman cape and apron, and Xulk's Soul Catcher, she travels in a spirit canoe driven by Ahcleet's spirit powers and her own, through cedar swamps and turbulent rivers, past bats, cougars, bears, and dead spirits, including her own ancestors. At the end of the novel she has, in effect, been reborn as a Quinault, proud of her ancestral blood and ready to be the spiritual link between the past and the present, to teach the ancient ways, and to embody them in her life. This "practical, educated, modern woman, a law enforcement officer, a woman of the almost twenty-first century" who had been "apologetic about the old beliefs," has entered the supernatural world of her ancestors, the old shamans, and has tapped into "Mind power, Spirit power" to combat evil sorcery (374).

Stokes's *The Listening Ones* (1998) also features Jordan Tidewater. She is a Quinault tribal sheriff, but has recently been deputized as a U.S. marshal to help stop the illegal taking of eagle and bear parts for sale in Asia. This time she is investigating the brutal murder of two youngsters about the same age as her son. As a shaman, Jordan draws on the collective wisdom of her ancestry, in this case to flesh out clues that make her initially suspect a Native American ritual sacrifice (for instance, the fact that the bodies are dismembered and left in eagles' nests high in the trees). However, the desecration of sacred land unleashes forces that could destroy her people, so her journey to knowledge is one guided by the ancient beliefs of the Quinault, in particular by the spirit voices of totem animals, the listening ones of the title. Ultimately, armed by her own guardian spirit, supported by her shaman teacher and elder (Ahcleet), and aided by masked members of her tribe calling on the protective spirits of the Quinault, Jordan must confront South American shamanistic powers in order to restore order to the Olympic Peninsula. As the masked dancers slash their bodies and the blood flows, these ritual participants must defend themselves against the *mala'h*, the dead spirits who tempt them from life or beat them for the offenses of their ancestors; they must also withstand such powerful natural forces as waterspouts, tornadoes, earthquakes, fierce lightning, and a terrifying eclipse of the moon. Jordan shape-shifts into a cougar, then an eagle, until the ancient being Klokwalle gives her a vision of the future that explains the past and thereby helps her defeat the foreign foe who threatens her world.

In both *The Tree People* and *The Listening Ones* the association of Quinault horror with possession, witchcraft, and spells that cloud the mind or call forth demons places the nightmare in terms meaningful to readers schooled in a Christian rather than a Native American tradition of the supernatural. While the Native American lore is treated with respect and is in essence accurately conveyed, the terms of its telling are accommodating to mainstream readers. One example makes this point nicely. The malaise unloosed by the malicious shaman Xulk in *The Tree People* is clearly spiritual, not physical, but Stokes has mainstream medical researchers speculate about an unusual outbreak of "cedar fever," a real ailment in the territory, as the cause of the sickness and unconventional behavior. Likewise, in *The Listening Ones*, the final ritual provides a metaphoric image of the villain, but Jordan also awakens from a dream the next night with a remembered clue from the past that identifies the villain. As with James Doss's similar use of contrasting explanatory theories (Daisy Perika's shamanistic interpretations versus Charlie Moon and Scott Parris's ratiocinative ones), mainstream readers are given the comfort level of a rational explanation, even while the Native American version is clearly more likely in the terms established by the plot.

Muriel Gray's *The Trickster*

Muriel Gray's novel *The Trickster* (1995) blends several Native American traditions with European ones: the idea that spirits are capable of influencing the outcome of human strivings; that they inhabit dark places, such as caves or forests, deep canyons, high mountains, or even beasts; that they can possess people; the idea that a constant balance must be maintained between spirit and human forces and that evil spirits can disrupt this balance; and the belief that the souls of the dead can be malignant.

Her other native source is the tradition of the Coyote trickster, a tradition Gray manipulates and distorts for her own purposes. An amalgam of man and coyote, the trickster of native lore sometimes takes animal shape, but mostly appears in human form (a youth testing his world, a teenager with raging hormones, an adult, an old man). He is godlike but not demonic, and his tricks entertain, teach, and promote group unity and harmony. Coyote stories teach children community lessons through the trickster's negative example, warn adults about excesses, test the outer limits of human capability, ultimately encourage admiration for wit and cleverness, and provide a standard for both personal behavior and tribal interaction. Traditionally, the oversexed Coyote commits obscene and exaggerated sexual acts (overcoming women with toothed vaginas that castrate males) but also originates death and brings fire. One of the oldest figures of Native American legend, present since Paleolithic days, the Trickster is generally a beneficent being whose tricks bring culture, light, self-understanding, and humor to native peoples: they laugh at his greed, lust, and stupidity, and thereby laugh at their own human frailty. However, when Kinchuinick Sam Hunt calls Muriel Gray's trickster by his secret names (Sitconski, Inktomi, Inktumni), he forgets that historically Kinchuinick knew how to trick the Trickster, but in rejecting their heritage, they have lost the power to derail his mischief, and he has grown stronger and more dangerous. Moreover, Gray's Trickster merges with an ancient evil, a malevolent, inchoate being of unimaginable proportions, roused from the depths of a mountain by nineteenth-century miners and railroad men. We have come a long way from Coyote trickster the animal emblem of human mischief, so far that the historical Native American tellers of Trickster stories probably could not identify this new amalgam.

Like *The Tree People, The Trickster* begins as a classic detective story, with a series of horrific murders committed and Craig McGee, staff sergeant in the Royal Canadian Mounted Police, leading his men in the investigation, fighting the bureaucracy of his superiors and his own lonely, isolated life. More murders follow, evidence and clues mount, a suspect is identified, and the killer seems to be toying with the police. But then everything changes: the murderer is revealed as part of the spirit world, forensic science and normal police procedures can establish no causal linkage between suspect and crime, motive remains a mystery, and McGee concludes, shakily, that the killings could not have been committed, given the evidence he has. He is reduced to a helpless impotence, becoming an observer whose only role in events has been scripted by far more powerful invisible forces. The ratiocinative detective story has moved into the world of supernatural horror, demonic spirits, and eerie powers beyond human understanding, and all the tools of Western rationalism and European materialistic science can provide no answers.

For a first novel, *The Trickster* is a great achievement. A long (471 pages in paperback) and precisely written portrait of mayhem in an Alberta skiing town named Silver, the plot shifts back and forth from events in 1907 to the present, with the past prefiguring the future, allowing the reader the gradual realization of the family, cultural, and circumstantial links between the early participants, white and native, in their first meetings early in the century, and the modern characters almost a hundred years later, when Indian lore is increasingly a museum curiosity to both whites and Native Americans. In 1907 a group of the former, Scots engineers and construction workers, are building a railroad tunnel through Wolf Mountain, an elaborate "corkscrew" opening up through living rock that will allow ore trains to overcome the mountain's steep grade. Their violent creation of this orifice unlooses an ancient evil spirit, one older than Christianity, that is associated with the Kinchuinick Native Americans who live in the area. The spirit, the Trickster, a being made of ice and stone and a swirling "scum" of evil, preys on white and Indian alike, but saves its worst attentions for the chief and shaman of the tribe, Hunting Wolf. Hunting Wolf is supported in his battle by James Henderson, a Scots clergyman ministering to his countrymen, who gradually comes to understand the limits of both Western material philosophy and Christian conceptualizations of evil.

In the modern sections, which alternate with the 1907 setting, we meet Sam Hunt, the great-grandson of Hunting Wolf, a completely assimilated Kinchuinick who loathes the culture of his alcoholic and abusive father. Sam has married a white woman named Katie, has two children, and lives a life revolving around his pickup truck and televised hockey games. However, when both Native Americans and whites begin to show up dead and mutilated in Sam's vicinity, he draws the attention of policeman Craig McGee, like Henderson a Scots rationalist. McGee concludes that if Sam is not a serial killer, but rather a victim of the evil of Indian myth—the Trickster—then the entire Western understanding of the nature of reality is at risk. Invisible forces seem to be trumping visible ones; the straightforward perceptual world of philosopher John Locke and the ordered universe of physicist Sir Isaac Newton would describe only the surface of things and not the true spiritual reasons events transpire. McGee confesses to Katie:

"If I make the connections that [the evidence] automatically suggests to me, join up the myths with the facts, it changes everything."

"Like what?"

"Everything. My whole life. Everything I believe in and everything I know to be true. Nothing will make sense anymore, do you understand?"

"No."

"This cup might not be a cup anymore. That window might not look onto your yard anymore. The sun might not necessarily rise in two hours." (375)

McGee defends materialism bravely—"I believe this is a cup because I can see it" (376)—but is ultimately defeated by repeated images of his dead wife, her cancer-ridden womb exposed to view, ghoulish simulacra that appear completely real but are simply part of the Trickster's torment.

The scenes of such nightmares are among the best in the book. Gray's premise is that the Trickster has instant access to its victim's worst nightmare and the capacity to trick up convincing hallucinations that duplicate it. Thus, Sam, after misinterpreting an innocent kiss his wife awards the sympathetic Mountie, is shown Katie and McGee writhing naked in the snow, having vigorous sex. Such paranoid interpretive projections of ordinary events that the Trickster stimulates throughout the book are powerful in that they do not simply recount magical or supernatural performances, but touch on the reader's understanding of human nature: our mental imagery, and thus our understanding of reality, can be shaped and distorted by our fears and hopes. (This perception, of course, owes as much to relativism and modernism as to traditional Native American lore about the reality of psychic experience; it is the territory of Kafka and Freud's psychoanalysis, European tricksterism.) Other truly horrific scenes involve the Trickster's possession of blameless animals that are then forced to tear themselves apart, the process being described by Gray in great detail. In a nightmare scene in a diner, a dead friend, "slumped over the table with half a face and a mutilated, decomposing body slick with slime, moving quietly with the work of worms," offers Sam his still-beating heart, ripped out by bony fingers (352). Like all good horror writers, Gray has the capacity to make us read on with the terrible suspicion that a favorite character will be ambushed suddenly, from an unexpected direction. Her conception of the Trickster's power as both physical and psychological ups the horror ante exponentially.

Gray also includes fine descriptions of nature and the Rocky Mountain terrain and climate, imagery wholly appropriate for a novel in which Native Americans are tied closely to the earth and their natural environment. Shifting views result from a landscape of infinitely varying elevation, so particular locations change what one can see and cannot see, the alternation of lodgepole pine forest and rocky cliff and tunnel, the apparent openness of the ski slope surrounded by thick stands of almost impenetrable trees—all give a sense that human beings have made only a recent purchase of a land of mystery and immense age. This stress on the brevity of human dominance fits perfectly with the theme of the uncertainty of perception: what we see as solid and unchanging is actually only a brief snapshot of a moment in time, a limited view that arrogantly asserts the rights of the immediate present. The ever-present wild animals that surround the town of Silver also suggest how untamed this wilderness really is, how much Native American closeness to fauna and flora is still relevant, the insulating effect of modern concrete and asphalt culture notwithstanding. But it is the constant snow, falling in huge flakes and wiping out all trace of human presence, that is Gray's best descriptive touch. The snow almost becomes a character in the story, and in fact the Trickster itself is a creature partially made of ice, a winter demon that could not exist in other environments.

All this said, and given that the research into Kinchuinick ways is solid and well presented, *The Trickster* still remains an Indian, as opposed to a Native American, book. It is not simply that the approach Gray uses is the familiar horror genre of European literature rather than a native form based on oral literature, nor that the figure of the Trickster is Gray's creation, certainly related to Native American Coyote Tricksters but here far different from her sources, "worse than the worst *wittago*" (a *wittago* is a "demon made from ice, mud, or stones that ate human flesh"; 374). Rather, it is in the Western or European pattern of Trickster as Satan figure countered by the shaman as Christ figure. The Trickster may be older than Christianity, as Hunting Wolf says, but the structure of the book involves the reluctant champion of humanity learning to purify himself in order to prepare for battle against supreme evil. Sam Hunt, who finally accepts his identity as Sam Hunting Wolf, the next savior or "keeper" of the Trickster in his line (like Christian lore about generations of priests or nuns who hold back the Antichrist), risks all in his battle to save an unknowing and uncaring humanity. He undergoes continual temptations, but after long periods in the wilderness finds his calling. The book ends with Sam and Katie accepting his Kinchuinick heritage, living on the reservation, their grandchildren speaking the old language and presumably turning their backs on assimilation and modernism. Shiny pickup trucks and hockey on television are small prices to pay for the opportunity to play the role of savior of mankind.

Artful as it is, this Trickster is a Native American-European amalgam, a clever variation on indigenous lore rather than a straightforward recounting of oral tradition, as some readers might take it to be. This is not to be critical of Gray, who has brought legitimate issues of assimilation and culture to the attention of multitudes of readers in a way sensitive to Native Americans and yet approachable by mainstream whites. To argue that amalgams such as Gray's are distortions is to point out the obvious: every writer enlarges on and manipulates sources and earlier materials. This is true of oral storytellers as well as of their print successors. What should matter is if the changes are done with respect for the original, its spirit and essence, and whether the resulting amalgam has both literary and moral integrity.

CONCLUSION

The Indian horror story has truly undergone a metamorphosis, a shift in shape that is changing it in essential ways. Initially, in American literature, the "Indian" himself was the horror: the alien Other who stalked through the primeval forest, skewering babes in arms, raping, scalping, and torturing captives. For the Puritans he symbolized the wild sexual license and barbarism of satanic forces tempting Christians to forgo their faith and revert to pagan ways. Today that image has changed, and whether individual Native Americans are depicted as good or evil or morally neutral depends on the particulars of personal behavior rather than on membership in a feared group. The horror genre is now moving toward incorporating elements of the Native American to invigorate and revive a genre whose battle of Christian and pagan forces has an attenuated meaning to the popular fiction readership. The popular 1970s horror film series *Kolchak: The Night Stalker*, for example, included two "Indian" horror episodes: in the first, "Bad Medicine," an ancient Native American spirit roams Chicago, changing shapes (raven, coyote, giant human) and killing rich people who get in the way of his acquisition of treasure; in the second, "Legacy of Terror," an Aztec mummy rips hearts from victims to prolong its life. *Kolchak*'s innovative use of native horror figures as part of its repertoire of terror-inspiring characters was an early sign of this trend.

The multiplicity of Native American religious practices that consider every element of daily life to be bound up with the spiritual opens up a potential for many new types of horror. However, to make this effective for readers accustomed to Judeo-Christian-based horror conventions, the writer must bridge the two spiritual realities and find commonalities or ways of integrating Native American and European to make the Native American comprehensible to a mainstream audience. Martin Cruz Smith, Naomi Stokes, and Muriel Gray have done so effectively and have pointed the way toward changes in the genre conventions of the future.

8

Indian Utopias/Dystopias: Science Fiction and Fantasy Projections Past and Future

> ... the wilderness of our country afford[s] models equal to those from which the Grecian sculptors transferred to the marble such inimitable grace and beauty ... knights of the forest, whose whole lives are lives of chivalry, and whose daily feats, with their naked limbs, might vie with those of the Grecian youths in the beautiful rivalry of the Olympian games.
>
> No man's imagination ... can ever picture the beauty and wildness of scenes ... daily witnessed in this romantic country; of hundreds of these graceful youths, without a care ... —their long black hair mingling with their horses' tails, floating in the wind, while they are flying over the carpeted prairie ... or their splendid procession ..., arrayed in all their gorgeous colours and trappings, moving with most exquisite grace and manly beauty, added to that bold defiance ... [of one] who acknowledges no superior on earth, and who is amenable to no laws except the laws of God and honour.
>
> —George Catlin, *Letters and Notes on the Manners, Customs, and Conditions of the North American Indians*, I, 15

"Native Americans in science fiction? Absurd!" Such is the likely reaction of many readers, for the conventional concept of the Indian is often fixed in the context of the historical westward movement: one way of life yielding to another just as one age gives way to the next. In fact, however, from the point of view of immigrating peoples, contact with American Indians from earliest times was an unsettling experience with the alien, the "Other." The reverse was also true. For the people involved on both sides, the issue of the moment was not yielding ways of life or epochs passing—such perceptions came only later, as the frontier disappeared—but the fear or elation of frequent contact with people perceived to be so different, so exotic. George Catlin's effusions about the Plains Indians

with which the chapter begins can stand for the elation and the attempt to recast the Indian into a familiar mold; the fear came with the abduction/captivity stories we have already discussed, from Mary Jemison to Cynthia Ann Parker. What joy for Europeans to discover a brave new world of noble warriors, unspoiled by their fallen civilization and uncorrupted by civilized life! What terror at sudden Indian raids, with men quickly killed, women raped, and children taken into slavery or a strange new life!

It is no great claim to argue that the American psychology has been informed by the profoundly disturbing realization that dramatically different ways of life exist and that they can be encountered, perhaps unwillingly, close at hand. Such experiences began with immigrants rubbing shoulders at ports of embarkation, aboard sailing ships, and in cities that received new citizens, and continued as settlers fanned out into the frontier. The Indian experience was simply the most profound of such encounters, and as such it offers an explanation for both American recalcitrance about cultural change—a defense against a real threat to identity—and American openness to exotic possibility. The science fiction genre is not uniquely American—it is practiced by other cultures that have struggled with alien encounters, such as the Russian and the Japanese—but it has been embraced by Americans with an enthusiasm unparalleled in other cultures, as any stroll down the science fiction shelves of a public library or mass-market bookstore will establish. How else can we explain our receptivity to stories of alien encounters (*Contact, E.T., Close Encounters of the Third Kind, Alien Nation, Enemy Mine, Brother from Another Planet*, and their cinematic brethren) and alien abduction stories from *Cocoon* to *The X-Files*? The snatchings of Mary Jemison and Cynthia Ann Parker live on in American psychology, but now in the apparently straightforward accounts of ordinary folk taken for saucer rides. Harvard psychiatrist John E. Mack, whose *Abduction: Human Encounters with Aliens* (1994) concentrates on thirteen core case studies out of sixty reported cases of alien abduction, argues that those who claimed to have been abducted showed no signs of pathologies but shared details of missing hours from their lives and repeated visits from large-eyed, telepathic beings with mysterious machines and invasive medical procedures; his studies suggest that over 25 percent of modern Americans believe in alien abduction and buy into stories like that of Whitley Strieber, whose abduction was enacted by Christopher Walken in *Communion* (1989).

From this perspective, embedded in every alien story is the seed of a Native American story. Just as Indians were perceived as monstrous savages, so aliens may be monstrous and savage beyond human experience: ripping, tearing, cannibalizing. And just as Indians assisted settlers and made them welcome, so some aliens are drawn as welcoming and kindly ETs, odd by mainstream standards but somehow benign (a recollection of Puritans and Indians sharing Thanksgiving). The same type of embedding occurs in stories of alien fighters/ warriors, alien contact for trade, alien magicians/shamans, alien romances ("I fell in love with an alien"/"I fell in love with an Indian"), and alien ecologists (with the stoic red man shedding a tear for raped Mother Earth from his spaceship, miles above). The concepts behind such stories—the original story arcs— were played out across the moving line of the frontier as Europeans explored and conquered a new world as alien to them as the distant planets are to us— with all the potential for misunderstandings and conflicts, for prejudice and skewed perceptions, for head-on collisions or more subtle forms of alienation and separation. Deloria argues most persuasively that the U.S. identity can be best understood in the activity he calls "playing Indian"; certainly, a major appeal of such play is the frightening-exhilarating encounter with a way of living at the opposite pole from one's own, with the shock (terrifying, bracing) to the seemingly stable verities of one's identity provided by the challenge of difference.

Today, mainstream America's sense of a lost past, an unrealized potential, and a life more in tune with the rhythms of the Earth leads some to look back to pre-Columbian America and the Indians of that period as a lost utopia, a better world than the one we have created, or to see in the past the seeds of destruction that have swept away so many nations and cultures, and will sweep away so many more in the future. The realities of the past help writers and readers speculate about the potentials for the future. When Donald McQuinn, for example, envisions a renewed, post-Holocaust America, his models are Native American: where Seattle and Tacoma once stood, the proud Dog People, a futuristic nomadic warrior tribe on noble steeds, roam the grassy plains and fir-clad hills of the Northwest, led by a mighty chieftain, filling the valleys with their dome tents, and driving off attackers with bows and arrows. Likewise John Crowley's postdisaster America is tribal, with initiations into adulthood based on the Native American experience (*Engine Summer*, 1979—punning on "Indian/Injun Summer"). Much American science fiction, in fact, can be viewed as a continuation of classic American experience, with contact with "aliens" mirroring the variety of experiences and perceptions that make up our historic mythology about Indian-European and East-West encounters.

The truth, then, about Native Americans in science fiction is "They're everywhere," as embedded sources or as parallels or analogies or as full characters in space operas, epitomized in the title *The Sioux Spaceman* (1960).

NATIVE AMERICAN UTOPIAS

Native American hunter-gatherers existed in their present—the day-to-day experiences of living—and drew on their past—experiences they had seen and could learn from—to assist in the present. As one would expect in an oral tradition, especially one in which man-made measures of time are irrelevant and the present holds sway, there were often different grammatical forms for expressing time relationships. Some Indian languages had no tense in their verb system for expressing the hypothetical subjunctive ("Were we to do this, this would occur") nor the future perfect subjunctive ("By the time this happens, we will have already accomplished that"), both forms useful for speculating about future possibilities; the absence may be symptomatic of grammatical emphases placed elsewhere, on other time relationships. If, as Sapir, Whorf, and Kaplan argue, linguistic forms reveal the mental framework of a culture, grammar and vocabulary can be suggestive. The Sioux, for example, have no equivalent words for time as we express it, no words for "wait" or "late"; the Navajo divide time only by natural phenomena—sunset, sunrise, new moon, old moon—and developed no built-in linguistic systems for anticipating or preparing for future events, since most of them would be irrelevant or uncontrollable in a traditional pastoral-agrarian culture (Hall, 9–14).

In some Native American languages, the past is conceived as lying literally before the speaker (we can "see" past events in memory), while the future lies behind like a stalking enemy, unseen, unknown, and ready to pounce. It is not surprising, then, that the tradition of science fiction does not exist in the Native American literary repertoire, and historically has occurred only in Soviet (Russian, Polish, Czech), French, Japanese, and English-speaking traditions, where speculation about the future is seen as a way to better understand the present and determine how to protect against future environmental, social, and political dangers. The presumption is that the future *can* be known and is potentially controllable, a modern notion developed along with the growth of science and technology; even medieval Europeans considered such ideas impious and foolish. Put another way, in order to have science fiction, one must first have science and its presumptions about progress, the continuing refinement of technological capacity, and an increasing mastery over nature. When culture became divorced from the rhythms of nature, the whole mental landscape changed, and science fiction is one way of marking out the new territory.

Native American culture does, however, include traditions that to some degree speculate as science fiction does, the oral Creation stories that explain the formation of the constellations and of the land, and how things came to be: *Creation of the Animal People, The Origin of Curing Ceremonies, How Grandfather Peyote Came to the Indian People, When Grizzlies Walked Upright, Old Man Coyote Makes the World, Moon Rapes His Sister Sun, Little Brother Snares the Sun, Playing a Trick on the Moon, The Theft of Light, Coyote Places the Stars, How Mosquitoes Came to Be, The Coming of Thunder, How Beaver Stole Fire from the Pines, Coyote Dances with a Star.* Stories like these include starmen and starwomen with unearthly powers; travel across dimensions and space (from Earth to the stars); supernatural transformations in size, shape, and personality; and the concept of alien intelligence in competition with human intelligence. The difference, however, is that these stories are part of a religious explanation of the cosmos rather than intentional fiction, and they look back to the past to explain and provide lessons for the present, rather than forward to the future to speculate about potential problems and successes and to warn about our present containing the seeds of the future—for good or for ill. An example is N. Scott Momaday's *The Ancient Child* (1989), which draws on traditional Kiowa stories to tell of a medicine woman who transforms a man into a bear. A Western mainstream readership would demand at least an informed nod to genetic issues, to laboratory experimentation and to existing research to create verisimilitude, to the technical likelihood of such an event in the "real" world, all features of science fiction absent in Momaday's metamorphosis. Thus, the science element of "science fiction" is missing in truly Native stories; they are spiritual rather than scientific, didactic rather than predictive.

The Native traditions that come closest to the Western concept of science fiction are the stories of the shaman making magical journeys into the star world or the underworld, encountering strange creatures with magical powers that must be defeated or controlled by magic, then returning to apply the knowledge gained to real-world problems like disease, drought, an absence of game, and so forth. Naomi Stokes describes such a sacred journey of discovery in *The Tree People*, when Jordan seeks to return her son's spirit to his body and defeat the spirits and sorcerer who would steal him away. Nonetheless, like the Creation stories, the shaman stories draw on knowledge of the past and of spiritual worlds existing in the same time continuum to protect the present. They are neither science nor, in Native American terms, fiction, and they are set in the past and present, not the future.

For some tribes, at least, events in the nineteenth century reinforced dreams of recapturing the past. As the buffalo were killed off and the Plains Indians lost both territory and means to live, were defeated by battle, starvation, and disease, and were forced onto reservations, the future became less and less desirable, with a return to the past the only possible alternative. Even today, a key issue in modern Native American literature is the conflict between embracing modern ways and finding solutions in heritage, with the dream of the future drawing on dreams of the past.

Between 1870 and 1878 the Ghost Dance (*Wanagi-wachipi*), a type of messianic movement, spread among Indians of the western Great Basin (Paiute) and later (1887–1895) to Plains Indians (the Arapaho, Northern Cheyenne, and Oglala Sioux). The phenomenon embodied the Native Americans' desperate longing for a recently lost past and a return to a life once free of hunger, epidemic disease, decimating war with whites, and subjugation on reservations. Prophets like Paiute shaman Tavibo, and later Wovoka, claimed to have returned from death with the Great Spirit's message of hope: a utopian world of plentiful game, unified tribes, a return to traditional ways, and dead loved ones resurrected. If only followers would purify themselves, reaffirm their religious faith in the old ways, and dance the special steps of the Ghost Dance, the invading whites would disappear and the prophecy would be fulfilled. Even if death came, the dancers would awaken to a new and beautiful land where their relatives and friends would join them.

The Ghost Dance was an attempt to will the buffalo back onto the plains and dream the white man back into the sea: by dancing the Ghost Dance with all their hearts, the ashes of defeat could be replaced by abundance, freedom, and a return to life as it was before the white man destroyed it. In Western logic this was wishful thinking; in native terms, it was the gathering of spiritual force to remedy a great sickness. In *American Indian Myths and Legends*, Richard Erdoes and Alfonzo Ortiz quote one holy man: "The earth will roll up like a blanket with all that bad white man's stuff, the fences and railroads and mines and telegraph poles, and underneath will be our old-young Indian earth with all our relatives come to life again" (482). The Paiute Wovoka added the concept that nonbelievers would shrink to one foot tall and remain small thereafter, or would be turned into wood and burned in the fire. Dressed in ghost shirts painted with the sun, the moon, the stars, and magpies, believers held hands and danced around a spruce tree, their gaze fixed on the sun; medicine men used sweet-smelling cedar smoke to revive those who swooned, many of whom reported out-of-body experiences, walking and talking to the dead who held rocks and food from the moon and stars.

U.S. government forces, however, fearful of the implications of such dreams and such faith, acted to wipe out the Ghost Dance and ghost dancers. Ghost Dance teachings led approximately two hundred embittered Sioux, suffering from reduced rations, diseases brought by the whites, and natural disasters, to dress in ghost shirts emblazoned with eagle, buffalo, and morning star decorations, and dance at Wounded Knee (1890) in defiance of cavalry commands. The Sioux believed that their ghost shirt symbols of powerful spirits would protect them from the soldiers' bullets. The tragedy at Wounded Knee effectively ended the Ghost Dance, although some Plains tribes continued to perform it secretly and others incorporated some parts of the ritual into their culture in symbolic ways. Today, it remains a bitter touchstone of past wrongs.

Sherman Alexie, in *The Lone Ranger and Tonto Fistfight in Heaven* (1993), for example, includes a chapter on the Ghost Dance, titled "Distances" and written as a futuristic vision of a modern age in which the Ghost Dance finally works and the Indians take control. However, it is more dystopian nightmare than utopian dream. One man rides for days and days and sees "no cars moving, no planes, no bulldozers, no trees"; the cities are empty, and a single black flower grows in the shadow of Little Falls dam (106). The Tribal Council rules that anything to do with whites has to be destroyed: houses, furniture, clothing, transistor radios, electric circuitry, and so forth. The irony is that for assimilated Native Americans living on reservations, little remains because they have become so dependent on cars and televisions, canned food, blue jeans, and so forth. The urban (nonreservation) Indians sicken and die, unable to cope with this change, and the Tribal Council forbids intermarriage between the "Skins," or reservation Indians, and the "Urbans," or Indian outsiders. Nonetheless, the old people also begin to die, and the Tribal Council decides it is because the white man's disease flows in their blood; the Indians with white blood in their veins begin to disintegrate. With only a handful of modern Indians left, ancient Indians from a thousand years earlier return with stone axes, bows and arrows, and large hands; women give birth to salmon, and only the young and the strong survive to return to a hunter-gatherer existence. The narrator thinks of television and weeps. Alexie's *Indian Killer* (1998), in turn, ends with a schizophrenic serial killer, an Indian adopted by whites, committing suicide and returning to lead Seattle's Native American street people to dance the Ghost Dance and rid the city, one by one, of its white inhabitants. Readers are left to wonder if this is meant as a confirmation of the narrator's absolute lunacy or of his wishful thinking. Alexie, perhaps cruelly, sets the problem as a bitter choice between brutally exclusive opposites: go back to a dead-end past or live in a dead-end future. His is among the bleakest of visions in the science-fiction genre.

In a style reminiscent of modernist Jorge Luis Borges (who wrote the introduction to his *If All Else Fails* [1980], a collection of short stories), Cherokee Craig Strete envisions Indians defeating whites/aliens in alternative worlds. The urbanized Indian and his white wife in "Time Deer" march to the hectic, clock-driven pace of city life as they try to expedite the commitment of the husband's Cherokee grandfather to an insane asylum, but the old man's slow-paced vision of a boy chasing a deer and a fleeting idea of beauty move him not only out of time but also physically into another reality. In "A Sunday Visit with Great-grandfather," aliens bent on conquest are stymied by their encounter with two elderly Indian grandparents who are unaffected by the most advanced weaponry. The truth is that they are spirits and their great-grandson lifts their bodies from the burial rack so he can visit with them each Sunday. In "Has the Virgin Mary Never Entered the Wigwam of Standing Bear?," Standing Bear and a proud Cherokee warrior woman take a spiritual journey to the edge of the future, where amid the sounds of "the breech birth of cultures clashing" (111), a war cry "whoops" and strong Indian men and women can change the world back to what it once was—as the ghost of the white man fades away. In the cryptic story "The Bleeding Man," future scientists face the anomaly of an Indian man born an adult and bleeding continuously, but somehow regenerating his life blood at such a rate that transfusions from him could supply the medical needs of an entire city. He is a "medicine shaker" and "bonebreaker" whose very existence makes whites destroy each other, and his departure amid chaos echoes with his threat to return.

Another take on the science fiction story finds the future far back in the past. In *Dawn Land: A Novel* (1992) Joseph Bruchac weaves together tribal legends, natural history, and a heroic quest—that of Young Hunter, an Abenaki from ten thousand years ago. With three dogs and with his mind filled with all the legends of his tribe, Young Hunter journeys to the Adirondack Mountains to find the means to save his tribe from a threatening race of giants. Bruchac blends the conventions of magical realism and oral narration to capture the mystical visions of the first people on the American Northeast Coast and to trace a young war-rior's vision quest as he moves among "powerful beings in the forest," and acquires and masters weapons of power and peace to save his village from outside threats. Bruchac's *Dog People: Native Dog Stories* (1995), set in the same period, tells how dogs came to be companions of the Abenaki and the special relationship that developed between faithful dogs and the tribe. Ray Young Bear's *Remnants of the First Earth* (1997) is a first people story; Joseph Marshall's *Winter of the Holy Iron* (1994) is about the Teton Indians' first contact with Europeans; and Michael Dorris's *Morning Girl* (1992) is a young people's story about two Arawak Indians (a brother and a sister) who witness the arrival of the first Europeans on their island. Thus, we see alternatives to Alexie's contemporary angst in writers who seek their values in stories of, as it were, the Old People, creating new tales of the past that will inform the future, just as Native American storytelling or mythmaking has traditionally done.

GENRE OVERVIEW

The term "utopia," literally meaning "no place," comes from Thomas More's famous Latin work *Utopia* (1516; English translation, 1551). Based on humanistic Christian values, More's work criticized and satirized the economic and social conditions of the times (war, oppression of the poor, heavy taxation, unjust laws unfairly applied, among other problems) and offered an ideal counter: a nonexistent community whose models of religion, government, education, laws, and customs would, from More's perspective, vastly improve the living conditions of the many. Since that time, "utopia" has been used to mean any idealistic portrait of society and social conditions, particularly one meant to criticize or satirize present-day conditions by offering an ideal model, perhaps an impossibly perfect one. Early utopian works are Edward Bellamy's *Looking Backward* (1888) and William Morris's *News from Nowhere* (1891).

"Dystopias," in turn, present nightmare worlds, usually in the future, predictions of what could go wrong if nations or people continue on their present course. Aldous Huxley's *Brave New World* (1932) and George Orwell's *1984* (1949) are prototypical, with Huxley anticipating modern technology gone awry and Orwell envisioning a totalitarian nightmare future. *Brave New World* is particularly interesting for our purposes since it relies on an Indian reservation to stand for the lost values of humanity, good and bad—for love and art and literature amid squalor and pain—and to sharply indict modern technology, technology to control birth and sex, art and death—to make life ordered, controlled, and painless but also boring, predictable, numbing, and static. Utilitarian arguments against modern technological means and solutions usually fail, since such means are by definition efficient; Huxley's genius lay in the construction of an aesthetic argument against the modern world: that it is tedious and uninteresting. Huxley's Native American hero, John, may seem perverse and perverted to a future world as he engages in self-flagellation and diatribe, but he represents freedom, hope, and human diversity.

Utopias and dystopias of the past are early forms of what today has evolved into science fiction, a genre that now most often depends on science and logic as ways to speculate about future possibilities. "Science fiction" is a broad term, encompassing hard science and descriptions of technological innovations but also futuristic or prehistory fantasies, prophetic extrapolations, postnuclear or ecological disasters, robots, alien encounters, space operas, time travel, alternative realities, other dimensions, lost empires or lost worlds, faster-than-light travel, the seeding of the galaxies by human or alien cultures, the meeting of humans and aliens, and so forth. Whether set in a reconceived past, an alternative present, or an extrapolated future, science fiction frequently warns readers of the precarious position of humankind in a modern and changing world. Early works, from Mary Shelley's *Frankenstein* (1818) to Jules Verne's *Twenty Thousand Leagues under the Sea* (1870; English translation, 1876) to H. G. Wells's

The Time Machine (1895) and *The War of the Worlds* (1898), served just this
warning function, updating the hoary theme of human arrogance with headline
discoveries from the science pages. High-quality practitioners of modern sci-fi
include Isaac Asimov, Robert A. Heinlein, Theodore Sturgeon, Arthur Clarke,
Frederik Pohl, Harlan Ellison, Robert Silverberg, Ursula LeGuin, and the Stru-
gatsky brothers, among many others, who have drawn on modern knowledge of
paleontology, anthropology, and behavioral science to rethink and reinterpret the
past, to see the present from a new perspective, to raise claims about possible
dangers in new science and technologies, and to use the alien as a metaphor for
all encounters with difference. Thus, modern science fiction has attracted writers
knowledgeable about the behavioral sciences and about anthropological and sociological theories, since such disciplines can act as springboards for plots.

THE RANGE OF SCIENCE FICTION FEATURING
NATIVE AMERICANS

Because of mainstream cultural association of Native Americans with the past,
with a lost America, much science fiction about Native Americans tends to
utopian or dystopian visions set in the past, present, or future. These may bring
to life Creation stories and postulate the past existence of a superior race to
which modern Native Americans are related; they may project alternative universes in which Native American social relationships and values live on; they
may deplore the loss of an ecology-friendly system or revel in warrior skills
being employed in distant settings; or they may be set mainly in the spirit world
of the shaman, who battles evil forces invisible on our plane of reality. However,
the range is even broader than one might expect. Some stories are crudely told
or just plain silly, but others are intriguingly imaginative speculations about
cross-cultural encounters and the huge gulfs that separate people when they are
projected into alien settings among alien peoples.

Sci-fi stories about Native Americans range from those in which the Indian
elements are barely noticeable to those in which they dominate. Many writers
postulate hunter-gatherer or tribal societies on other planets and draw on their
knowledge of Native Americans to create their own fantasy kingdoms. Michael
Moorcock, for example, does not directly mention Native Americans but
chooses names like Hawkmoon for his heroes of stories about societies faced
with extinction and the harsh realities of colonization; William Rotsler, in *The
Far Frontier* (1980), envisions a planet with terrain like the American Southwest
and telepathic warrior natives whose encounters and battles with otherworld
invaders parallel Old West Indian and cowboy confrontations. Arsen Darnay
likewise picks up the Native American idea of a "soul catcher" in his vision of
a postnuclear priesthood (*The Karma Affair*, 1978), and Robert Silverberg's
short story "Sundance" links a futuristic issue of genocide to the treatment of
Native Americans. The popular sci-fi television series *Star Trek* included episodes featuring Indians on distant planets, while the more recent *Star Gate*,

based on Andre Norton's novel of the same title, includes a planet that aliens seeded with Native Americans—throwbacks to the Plains Indian culture of the nineteenth-century American West. These hunter-gatherers live in harmony with their environment and have all the virtues and vices of a warrior society that can afford to live just for today because of the abundance of wildlife and natural foods.

Some science fiction novels use the Native American to teach broad lessons about human nature. G. C. Edmondson's *Chapayeca* (1971), for instance, suggests that the curious anthropologist and Mexican government officials who come to a simple Indian village are more alien and threatening to the locals than are the blue-skinned extraterrestrials (young rebels seeking personal identity) who have visited them since A.D. 800, and that perhaps the Indian villagers are saner than the greedy, suspicious, xenophobic representatives of twentieth-century culture. *The Aluminum Man* (1975) is a comic take on the Ghost Dance theory of wiping out white culture. It sets a Sioux named Rudolf/Red Wolf against a pretentious high-society Mohawk in competition for the daughter of a wealthy industrialist who "grooves" on Indians; while seeking his totem spirit on a nature trip, the citified Sioux accidentally finds himself teamed up with an alien, and when microscopic alien bacteria eat up all concrete and metal structures, America perforce returns to its pre-Columbian state of nature.

Ian Watson's *The Martian Inca* (1978) warns against pride. In this story, an Andean backwater, peopled by the degenerated, illiterate modern descendants of noble Incans, is suddenly hit by red Martian dust falling from a failed Russian spaceship. This dust contains a viral activator, a catalyst that triggers dormant DNA programming and thereby sets in motion a physical and mental transformation that could change every person touched by the dust into a superhuman; however, the process fails if doctors tamper with it. Julio Capac, untreated by doctors, completes the transformation, undergoing a dream vision as the jigsaw pieces of his racial and personal heritage merge into a powerful whole. Imbued with the double vision of past and present, he speaks ancient Quechua and knows the Incas' secret mathematical knowledge. He asserts, "I am reborn. I am the Son of the Sun. The Inca" (80), and makes awakening his people to their ancient destiny his new goal. He sets off a populist revolution that could restore the Incan empire in a modern style. Watson's fantasy allows him to explore the scientific knowledge and potential of the Incan civilization, but at the same time to reject the lust for power that blurs vision and negates the high potential of the Incan past. In other words, here is futuristic science fiction used to personalize an historical event: the fall of the Incan civilization. Pride brought down a mighty empire in the past, and pride ends the potential for another high civilization.

The main characters in James Hall Roberts's *The Burning Sky* (1966) and in Louis L'Amour's *The Haunted Mesa* (1987) step through a doorway in time back to the period of the Anasazi, where they learn the secrets of those ancient people's demise: a conflict with Mayan forces. In *The Burning Sky* the doorway is metaphorical, with the protagonist encountering Anasazi who have survived in a hidden canyon, shunning the modern world and living in the old way. In *The Haunted Mesa* the doorway is literal; readers share the perspective of investigator Mike Raglan, who notes the inadequacy of our terms for the supernatural and asks, "Might there not be something more our purposeful blindness has prevented us from understanding . . . might there not be other worlds here? . Other worlds, in other dimensions, coexistent with this?" (19). Raglan and L'Amour's answer is that there are indeed parallel worlds, perhaps with a door ajar, in this case possibly the Fourth World the Hopi believe they came from, but one where sane men can lose their minds and their lives to ancient evils. T. A. Barron employs a similar idea in *The Ancient One* (1992), an ecological fantasy in which modern youths battling loggers to save giant redwoods thousands of years old find themselves transported back five hundred years in time to learn from the Halami Indians the secrets of ecological balance and the power of ancient spirits and tricksters, secrets that help them ward off the evils of their own age.

The idea of "the last of his race" as an argument to win sympathy for an alien and to justify his suspicion and antagonism derives directly from stories about Native American tribes that were wiped out by war, disease, and white encroachment. A fact-centered study of this lesson from history is George Rippey Stewart's *Earth Abides* (1949). Stewart's novel inverts the real story of Ishi, the last member of the Californian Yahi tribe, whose story has been told by Theodora Kroeber in the nonfiction *Ishi in Two Worlds* (1962) and in a 1992 film titled *The Last of His Tribe*, featuring Jon Voight and Graham Greene. Stewart's sci-fi story builds on familiar details about the real Ishi (whose name in Yahi meant "man"); the historical Ishi's tribe was wiped out by diseases against which they had no immunity, and Ishi himself moved out of a Stone Age existence into an alien technological world. Stewart's sci-fi "Ish" ("man" in Hebrew) finds himself the last civilized man in a California that has been returned to the Stone Age by an untreatable epidemic that decimates the entire population. Point for point, Stewart follows the sad history of Ishi in his portrait of Ish. Ishi was first jailed as a wild man (1911) and then ended up teaching Yahi skills to anthropologists in a California museum; Ish, too, is jailed and then taken to a museum, where he tries to teach people the civilized skills he remembers from his past. Just as Ishi realizes the futility of teaching his tribe's skills to strangers to whom they have no meaning, so Ish realizes that the lessons of civilization have no meaning for these hunter-gatherer survivors, and speculates about the human cycle: "He was the last of the old; they were the first of the new. But whether the new would follow the course which the old had followed, that he did not know" (373). What Stewart makes very clear, however, is that the tragedy of the historical Ishi and the Ish of his invention is the tragedy of all humans—a tragedy of the past reflecting the tragedies that will come.

Some sci-fi stories are simply peculiar. Steven Utley's (with Howard Waldrop) off-the-wall alternative-history short story "Custer's Last Jump" (1976), told in history-textbook prose, with authentic-seeming historical matter and bibliography, describes the Oglala Sioux defeating George Armstrong Custer and his 7th Cavalry, but the Sioux are equipped with monoplanes and Custer's cavalry is supported by the 505th Balloon Infantry. Peggy Becko's *The Winged Warrior* (1977) features a half-breed Sioux who flies around on homemade leather wings. In *The Aquiliad* (1983) Somtow Sucharitkul, in turn, envisions an alternative world wherein the Roman empire extends to the Americas, the Romans seek assistance from the Indians in their search for China, an aged Indian and a dim-witted Roman general clash (the Indian's Latin wordplay puts the general to shame), the Olmecs get help from flying saucers, and an evil time traveler instigates New World genetic engineering. Texan Dean Ing's short novel *Anasazi* (1980) depicts parasitic alien Users taking possession of the Anasazi Indian children, whose brainpans match their own nebulous essence, and giving rise to Anasazi cautionary tales about creatures that steal children; they also motivate the building and abandonment of such ruins as those of Mesa Verde. The Users survive into the twentieth century, still trying to come up with a technology advanced enough to contact their planet and bring back an invasion force. In "The Mohawk" (1975) Howard Fast's main character (a full-blooded Mohawk with a Ph.D. from Columbia and the diction and sensibility of the sixties "hip" culture) meditates on the steps of New York's St. Patrick's Cathedral and, to the shock and dismay of the local clergy, moves out of human time into God's time, a pre-European time when the Mohawks roamed the Hudson Valley.

Other works are truly unique and intriguing. In Mildred Broxon's understated short story "Walk the Ice" (1982), a family of half-starved Eskimos generously take in a shipwrecked alien and offer him food and hospitality despite their plight; as a result, the sole survivor of the family paves the way for Eskimos in space when her descendants study "xenology" before embarking on a search for extraterrestrials. In Jack Haldeman and Jack Dann's *High Steel* (1993), Native American spiritualism takes on and defeats out-of-control technological doomsday wizardry. Backed by Sioux spiritual leader Leonard Broken-Finger (whose magical sandpaintings prefigure spiritual events) and by technologically skilled fellow Indians (a union of Sioux, Cheyenne, Crow, and Arapaho), John Stranger pits traditional shaman powers and intuitive know-how against the exploitative construction company that drafts him and his fellow Indians and forces them into servitude in space, the ultimate high-steel construction site. By merging with an orbiting spaceship supercomputer that develops superhuman powers and capacities, Stranger deflects an attack on the reservation, breaks the company's death grip on reservation Indians, awakens cryogenically preserved Indians who had "disappeared" without explanation, and bridges planets to bring back to Earth the powerful aliens ("Thunder-beings") who have acted as the Indians' deities and protectors throughout the ages. These ancient "gods" offer Native Americans transportation to a new world, free from the restraints of white oppressors.

Like Utley, Shawnee Nasnaga in *Indians' Summer* (1975), part-Pueblo Martin Cruz Smith in *The Indians Won* (1962), Douglas C. Jones in *The Court-Martial of George Armstrong Custer* (1996), and Jake Page in *Apacheria* (1998) provide alternative histories. Raising the question of Indian communities having sovereign nation status, Nasnaga envisions an American Indian nation-coalition called *Anishinabe-waki*, which declares war on the United States; their bluff depends on their control of key energy resources and of Minuteman missile silos. Nasnaga's main interest, however, is in the plot providing opportunities for various characters to expound on the American Indian worldview. Smith, in turn, asks: What if, after General Custer's ignominious defeat at the Battle of Little Big Horn, the Indian tribes grew in strength, consolidated their forces, established their own Red Nation, effectively divided America in two, and found Europeans willing to sell them weaponry sophisticated enough to threaten their neighbors (Gatling guns, grenades, etc.)? Jones imagines what would have happened if George Armstrong Custer had been found alive under mounds of dead soldiers and court-martialed for disobeying orders, and thus had to explain to the court what really happened at the Battle of the Little Bighorn. Page speculates: What if a foresighted Apache military genius had united the disconnected bands of warring Apaches into a cohesive fighting force that crushed the invading white army and, as a consequence, the United States had to contend with an Apache Nation neighbor adept at racketeering and politics, matching wit and weapons against U.S. criminal and military forces well into the twentieth century?

Both Smith and Page are intrigued with the notion of the United States in the 1870s as a troubled nation, by no means an economic and military powerhouse moving inexorably west. The idea of the Indians confronting the U.S. Army and defeating it piecemeal, thus leaving the United States literally a divided nation, paves the way for interesting speculative futures. In Page's future, the Apaches become the warrior hit men for the U.S. government, taking on the Mafia and other troublemakers in return for continued treaty protection of their rich territory. In Smith's future, population pressures make a war to take over the Indian Nation irresistible, and the confrontation that results provides satiric targets like Vietnam War policies, hawkish U.S. politicians, and crudely drawn American racial attitudes. Smith and Page's premise that the Indian Nation could have survived if scores of tribes had learned to cooperate against the unified white forces and to use the U.S. and Europe's superior weapons against the U.S. Army is intriguing and dramatically forceful. This provocative notion is vitiated, however, by their finessing of the central issue that would have confronted the Indian Nation, the problem of keeping a "native" identity while operating as a (somewhat) modern state: if a hunter-gatherer warrior culture adopts more and more modern trappings, at what point does it lose its original identity? Multistory tepees built with modern materials or Wild West frontier towns with open gambling and prostitution perpetuated into the twentieth century are only timid feints in the direction of this trade-off, which is never confronted directly by either writer.

Some sci-fi stories use Native Americans to seriously study human historical development. In his six-novel Pelbar cycle (1981–1984), set a thousand years after a devastating nuclear war that bombed the United States back to the Stone Age, Paul Williams builds on his knowledge of Native Americans from the Mississippi River valley region and from areas traveled by the Lewis and Clark expedition (the Northwest to the Oregon coast) to depict the tribal patterns of hunters and nomads and to describe the rebuilding of post-Holocaust civilization. Eleanor Arnason's *A Woman of the Iron People* (1991), a story of alien-human contact on a distant planet, envisions an overpopulated Earth that is an ecological disaster zone, its soil stripped of minerals, its mountains razed, its waters polluted, its representatives divided by political factions. In contrast, the alien world, though with its own unique flora and fauna, is like the world of the Americas before the arrival of Europeans. Its people are pre-urban nomads, with some qualities in common with some of Earth's Native Americans: a tradition of gift giving like the potlatch; shamans who deal with the spiritual world; inheritance of property by the female line; division into clans; a belief in a Trickster, whose stories sound much like Coyote stories of the American Southwest, and in the Old Woman in the North, who is like a character in Inuit sacred stories. These parallels make the anthropologists of the story speculate about the possibility of universal archetypes and a humanoid collective unconscious.

Several of the earthlings are of Indian descent: a Mayan, a California aborigine, an Ainishinabe who braids his hair, wears a turquoise necklace, and quotes poems from his distant ancestors. Anthropologist Derek Seawarrior is a California Indian, a skilled hunter with bow and arrow and spear, and accustomed to using peyote for multiple purposes. Though he thinks himself too far from Earth to call on the gray whale, the totem spirit of his clan, he is not too far to practice ancient tribal customs like making a ritual apology to an animal killed for food, though whether he does this to impress the hunter-gatherer aliens he is dealing with or because he truly believes in this act is not clear. The irony of the novel is that the more technologically advanced newcomers, despite their knowledge of the painful changes visited upon Native Americans by European settlers and despite their group commitment to peaceful encounters, are quite ready to repeat the destructive process in another new world, rationalizing that they mean the natives only good and will better their lives by bringing superior knowledge and superior ways, techniques that will convert hunter-gatherers to farmers and then miners, though the native peoples themselves are content with their present existence and live in harmony with their world. This dilemma has arisen in countless real situations faced by technologically advanced societies of the twentieth century when they have encountered traditional cultures. It is also, we might add, the basis for the NonInterference Directive featured in the *Star Trek* television series.

A few novels envision a past reincarnated in the present or future. Mark Canter's *Ember from the Sun* (1996) brings the past to the present. In it a Quanoot scientist/anthropologist anxious to make his reputation takes the sole surviving fertilized egg of an ancient golden-skinned people from the frozen body of its mother and implants it in a modern Quanoot (this prehistoric woman had purposely ingested special plants to prevent the cold from shattering her cells). The resultant child, Ember, is raised by the Quanoot Indians and guided by an ancient shaman who speaks through her genes. Ember's genetics are from a line separate from the one humans evolved from—Neanderthal, but a race of telepathic, intuitive healers. This concept of the first peoples as somehow superior to modern man is in many ways a recurring theme in utopia stories of the past, a vision of a golden age. Canter's story is special in its portrayal of the difficulties a telepathic healer with a much higher metabolism has, though having the healer's childhood spent among the Quanoot allows the author to suggest their greater tolerance of such special traits.

Andre Norton brings the past to the future in a form that Ursula LeGuin has labeled a "thought experiment." Norton's "time agent" tetralogy (*The Time Traders*, 1958; *Galactic Derelict*, 1959; *Defiant Agents*, 1962; *Key out of Time*, 1963), which projects a U.S.-Russian struggle to colonize a rugged, wilderness world, pits the descendants of Ghenghis Khan's Mongolian hordes against American Indians guided by the spirits of their tough-minded Apache ancestors. The hero in *The Beast Master* (1959) and *Lord of Thunder* (1962) is Hosteen Storm, a Navajo whose sacred tribal land (along with the rest of Earth) has been annihilated, and with it the entire basis for his religious and cultural heritage; Storm's semitelepathic ability to communicate with animals (eagles, large cats, etc.) earns him a job in the Beast Service on a frontier planet, but he is beset by angst—the lonely rootlessness of the sole survivor of a tribe, an echo of Ishi.

Another Indian far from home is the Lakota Sioux hero of Norton's *The Sioux Spaceman* (1960), Kade Whitehawk, who finds in the alien grasslands of an enslaved planet fulfilling reminders of eighteenth- and nineteenth-century Earth. Whitehawk is an Amerindian of the Northwest Terran Confederation and one of a group of Terran trade representatives to the repulsive Styor—aliens who have conquered numerous planets and control trade throughout much of the known universe. While dealing with the Styor on the primitive world of Klor, Whitehawk begins to question their assertion that the local population of Ikkinni are merely two-legged savages to be mastered, enslaved, and used as beasts of burden. He notes parallels between the Ikkinni and Native Americans and between the Styor and the Spanish slavers who reduced Southwestern Indians to bestial servitude. The Ikkinni have a hunter-gatherer society based on a huge alien beast reminiscent of the buffalo but also include some coastal fishermen and some farmers in fertile river-bottom land; they also have tribal life with division into clans, fearsome warrior leaders in mountain strongholds (much like Anasazi fortresses), and a hidden, burning desire to be free of slavery or the threat of slavery. Like the Sioux, the Ikkinni paint pictures of their prey and call on the magic of the spirit world to bless their hunt, and their equivalent of shamans practice a strong magic.

Whitehawk feels a growing sense of kinship with the Ikkinni. He knows that he has been brought to Klor to replace a fellow Sioux who died under mysterious

circumstances, and when his own life is threatened, he investigates his tribesman's notes to discover a plan in keeping with his own instincts: bring horses
to these "beasts" and they will become like the Plains Indians, capable of sudden
and fearsome raids on Styor slave centers. His accidental discovery that Terran
weapons can destroy the Styor slave collars makes him the center of Ikkinni
interest and ultimately, with his personal bravery as a passport to diplomatic
relationships, he wins Ikkinni trust and secret Terran support to put his plan into
practice: Ikkinni (Indians) versus Styor (European) invaders; this time, modern
weapons and modern Sioux know-how and training make the difference in possible outcome. By relocating bits and pieces of American history on faraway
planets, Norton distances conflicts that continue to divide in the present day,
allowing the human issues to speak to human hearts.

In addition, stories in other genres partake of sci-fi motifs. Dinah McCall's
romance *Legend* (1998), for example, depends on a technological wonder, a
curing machine given Apaches by "starmen" centuries before and still used
secretly by modern Apache medicine men, and a number of recent romances
(for instance, by Madeline Baker and Catherine Hart) include time travel.

In general, in an impressive variety of ways, from the absurd to the deeply
thought-provoking, the works discussed above use selected elements of real
Native American culture and reassemble them in other times or places. By doing
so, they make Indian culture a symbolic touchstone in the arena of fanciful
speculation. "What if . . ." situations are played off against the known values of
Native American life, usually in a positive way. No matter how distanced such
sci-fi stories are, they surprisingly and frequently build on the European-Native
American encounters and on the Western experience—because of mainstream
cultural associations of Native Americans with the Other, as the national symbol
of a people at one with their environment, and as representations of the tragic
loss of a free and pure way of life.

Next, we will explore the other sci-fi and fantasy directions that treatments
of Native Americans have taken: utopias, dystopias, New Age mysticism, and
various mystical-magical forms.

UTOPIAS

One of the earliest Indian utopias, *The Contrast* (1830), was a Christian image
of a New World paradise on Earth, a hidden valley in western New York where
an Indian Christian utopia thrived in forest glades. As its title suggests, *The
Contrast* does indeed contrast the "fallen," decadent Europeans and their bloody
strife with the simple native folk who find God's grace in their daily contact
with the natural world and whose sense of community and brotherhood embodies Christian principles (*Garland*, vol. 47, 57). Ebersole notes dryly that such a
pacifist vision "could only be sustained at a distance from the historical reality
of Indian-white relations" (the author was British) (237). Nonetheless, *The Contrast* reflects the direction taken by later Indian utopias: visions of a lost Eden

in which primitive man, amid stunning natural beauty, lives out values and philosophies more in touch with God, nature, and reality than those of his "civilized" counterparts, who have been blinded and tainted by their machinery, religion, government, politics, and economics.

Unlike Indian dystopias, which wrestle with problems of community versus the individual or with the ties between scientific advances and potential destruction, Indian utopias tend toward unrelenting fantasy, gushing praise for an idyllic and sanctified "Native American" life like none that ever existed and with little critical examination of the double edge of any cultural alternative or choice: beloved women secure in their social roles; skilled warriors who are loving, protective family members; free-roaming children educated by experience and the community at large. In such utopian visions, community provides security and continuity; nature is bountiful if respected; the cactus fruit jam of the desert people inspires travelers to cross thousands of miles of rugged terrain for the recipe. Most of these stories assert the significance of women historically in Native American culture as feminist critiques of mainstream culture. However, they often end up as "true love" romances with soul mates who bridge two worlds.

Utopian Historical Romances

Many recent historical romances employ Native Americans as counters to modern Western culture—a criticism of a fast-paced, capitalistic society where community has been lost to some degree. A fictional eighteenth-century captive puzzles over Delaware culture:

No one ever hurried in the Indian village. No one ever argued. The men and women went about their chores in an easy, carefree manner. The women talked and laughed with other women as they weeded their gardens. The men, though busy with hunting, fishing, tool making, and wigwam repairs, seemed to think nothing of stopping in the middle of a chore to sit in the grass and roll a leather ball to a toddler. Though everyone in the village—even the children—did their own fair share of the work, there was a joy about them as they set to their tasks, a joy that seemed to come from an inner peace. (Colleen Faulkner, *Captive*, 69)

These Lenape Indians have had the good sense to stay out of the French and Indian wars, and when a charming, young, hotheaded brave eager for adventure manipulates them into battle, they wisely take the advice of a white woman who has come to love them. They head northwest to find peace and harmony in the idyllic forests of Canada, far from the bloody upheavals of the British colonies.

Sylvie Sommerfield's Cheyenne in *Savage Rapture* (1982) are kindly, hospitable, and good-humored. Proud and courageous, they are at heart a happy, family-centered community of relatives and friends, generous and giving, protective of women and children, living in communal harmony, at one with nature. Until the conflicts with whites, their days are filled with sunshine and joy: "The village rang with hearty laughter. It was a happy place" (540). Sommerfield's utopian vision turns on the perspective of an outsider, Lauren Brent, a pampered, aristocratic Easterner who found her life empty and passionless but discovers purpose and passion among the Cheyenne: "She began to realize how well the Indians lived with the world given them. Instead of trying to make it conform to them as the white man did, they conformed to it, blended with it until nature and the Indians were one" (272). The Indian council of allied tribes is a "peace" rather than a "war" council, and its spokesmen are men of caution and care, their primary concern peace and tribal prosperity.

Madeline Baker's *Hawk's Woman* (1998) depicts the Sioux treatment of children as a model to be imitated:

Children were loved by the Lakota, and never spanked, nor were they permitted to cry. Hallie watched in fascination as a little girl cried, and when nothing her mother did seemed to help, the girl's grandmother began to cry, too, to keep her company. Young children were never told what to do; rather, they were asked. They were taught to love their parents, which, among the Lakota, meant more than just father and mother. Uncles were also called father, aunts were called mother, so that a Lakota child might have several fathers and mothers in the camp, all of whom gave love and instruction.

At the age of four or five, children were given their own clothing and eating utensils, as well as a bed of their own, and were expected to care for these things, thus instilling in them a sense of responsibility. They were taught their place in the village by example, and were expected to imitate their elders. . . . The little boys played with small bows and arrows; the girls played house with their dolls. (286–287)

The result of good early training produces tribal members who are tightly bound together, who would never steal from a fellow member of the tribe, and who revere the old people for their wisdom and their wise stories.

The utopianism in these three descriptions, a fairly typical sample of such admiring attitudes, lies less in distortion of reality or outright fantasy than in their selectivity, their omission of relevant context. Their implication is that today's world would be a better place if the Indian ways of the past had been left intact and had been imitated.

Such rosy visions of Indian life are not new. Observers as early as the French Jesuit missionaries in their extensive *Relations* (published from 1632 to 1674) depicted Indian life as ideal and Indian nature as benign, in part to encourage contributions to their ministries, in part to argue against opposing theological positions (Berkhofer, 74). Rousseau and other believers in the innate goodness of humankind promoted similar notions with vigor; later, Marxist thinkers promoting their vision of economic determinism praised living communally and directly benefiting from one's labor as Native Americans clearly did. Overt religious or political agendas may no longer be common in utopian portraits of harmony, but a kind of modern sentimentality is: primitive people lived happier lives than we moderns do. Colleen Faulkner's Lenape live in harmony with nature and with each other—the contrast with modern life is evident in such words as "easy," "carefree," "joy," and "inner peace." American readers with utilitarian points of view about "lifestyle choices" are quite likely to bestow ready approval on an alleged Indian simplicity of life (though anthropologists assert that many seemingly simple societies are in fact thoroughly complex) or the practical philosophies that accord with modern views (Indian parents don't spank!).

Admittedly, hunter-gatherer and nomadic farming groups lived idyllic lives part of the time, when game was plentiful and the weather supportive of a good growing season, and their inability to preserve large amounts of meat and crops meant there was no point in working past a certain point (too large a surplus would simply spoil). The segregation of men and women into different economic realms meant large support groups were constantly at hand and modern gender conflicts were simply moot. Children lived lives of comparative freedom since there was no demanding education in literacy and extended abstract knowledge, and no long-delayed entry into adult society. "Schooling" took place at the knees of mother and father, uncle and aunt, a pleasant way to learn practical and immediately applicable skills. At least in time of peace and good weather, the natural world was a playground, a bountiful warehouse, and an unending source of wonder. Nonetheless, portraits of such native life as ideal give as distorted a vision as the admittedly beautiful sketches and paintings of George Catlin.

It is the selectivity of such scenes that limit and skew vision. Village society the world over, in all groups and climes, tends to be intimate, relaxed, and even joyous; curtailed or given up are modern values such as privacy, individuality, and autonomous action. Doing one's fair share of communal tasks usually reduces individual burdens and can be very pleasant and efficient (Mary Jemison contrasts the women's life of communal obligations in the cornfields to the backbreaking individual labor of her white family); personal profit and individual ways of doing things, for good or ill, go by the board. It is surely true that it takes a village to raise a child, but the replacement of parental control with relentless pressure from adults and peers to conform to group values (the alternative is to leave the group for the wilderness!) might give modern readers pause. The division of labor according to gender, a notion considered anathema by most modern Americans, is here regarded as normal and possibly admirable. In other words, the danger of utopianism is the tendency to forget its selective vision, to ignore the harsh economic and social realities to which native groups adapted themselves. As has happened since the earliest contacts between whites and Indians, native life and culture have been simplified or seen selectively, and the fact that utopias create positive visions rather than negative ones does not change the underlying fact that Native Americans are not seen whole.

Warrior/Shaman Heroines in "First People" Novels

Such positive visions of Native American life in period romances find full expression in the first people novels of Kathleen and Michael Gear, Linda Lay

Shuler, Theresa Scott, Charlotte Prentiss, Margaret Allen, Joan Wolf, Sue Harrison, and Judith Redman Robbins, among others. These are women's fantasies that look back in time to a utopian past in which humans resembled gods and gods walked among humans, the spirit world and the real world were attuned, and, though survival might take courage, skill, and luck, proud and regal human beings were in tune with the primal rhythms of a harsh but beautiful, unspoiled land. Many of these characters have no association with any particular tribe; their creators draw instead on a general mythic Indian—hunter-gatherer tribes or family groups struggling to survive harsh winters and threatening beasts, encountering other such groups and gaining strength from alliances or from confrontation, creating an oral history that lays the foundation for tribal religions and lore many centuries later.

In most of these stories, as in the romances, women play significant roles, introducing new ideas and technologies from one group to another, spreading ideas and knowledge, supporting and strengthening the people they make their own. Though they may have trouble initially because of their uniqueness, ultimately they are superwomen—beautiful and competent, beloved and valued, farsighted and centuries ahead of their people. The main character of Margaret Allan's *Spirits Walking Woman* (1997), for example, is an ancient Olmec, a powerful woman worshiped by her people because of her wisdom and her powers of prophecy, but one who escapes the intrigues of royal life to find passion and power with a stranger. The heroine of Allan's highly erotic *Keeper of the Stone* (1993)—the middle book in the Mammoth trilogy, which also includes *The Mammoth Stone* (1992) and *The Last Mammoth* (1994)—is a beautiful outcast caught up in the adventures of a descendant of the Great Maya, a shaman who seeks the key to humanity's salvation. Charlotte Prentiss's sixteen-year-old heroine in *People of the Mesa* (1994) leads her peace-loving tribe's battle against an evil giant, and the strong, beautiful warrior woman of *The Ocean Tribe* (1999) helps her tribe find security as coastal fishermen, but she must battle ruthless hunters who see them as prey. Likewise, the Pacific Northwest chieftain's daughter in Prentiss's *The Island Tribe* (1996), shunned because of her independent, willful nature and her refusal to believe in the cruel Earth Spirits her tribe worships, eventually saves her people from catastrophe and frees them from superstition. The fantasy of female power and leadership is a recurring motif in these books, as the cover blurbs confirm: "the defiant descendent of a proud line of leaders, who would let no man break her spirit, despite the frailty of her flesh . . . and no foe destroy her people, despite all their treachery and terror" (*People of the Mesa*).

Theresa Scott's Hunters of the Ice Age series consists of captivity romances set at the dawn of time. Modeled on the captivity stories of the old West, they depict strong, cunning, courageous beauties challenging the strong men who possess them and finally winning their hearts. So, too, do the novels of Joan Wolf. Wolf sets her first people tales in the "Golden Age of Stone Age" in what is today southern France and England, but her matriarchal tribes with their wild horses, feather-and-buckskin attire, and bows and arrows clearly assert that the

Old World peoples were just like New World Indians: reindeer hunters with shamans, tribes, and clans. The fantasy of strong women in these books is offset by their need to win the love and admiration of equally strong men.

Sue Harrison sets her prehistory trilogy (*Mother Earth, Father Sky, My Sister the Moon, Brother Wind*) among the Walrus and Whale peoples in the Aleutian Islands. In stories of endurance and of conflict amid harsh natural conditions, she shows women confronting tragedy: physically abused and raped, fought over by rivals, taken captive and forced to marry the enemy who killed their husband or to sacrifice the man they love for survival of the group, widowed and abandoned among strangers, coldly and cunningly wreaking vengeance on those who defile them. Harrison's *Song of the River* (1997), the first in her Storyteller saga, depicts the seventh century B.C. Aleut and their rivalries and internecine warfare. Aptly called "a cross between the Flintstones and Dynasty," these stories repeatedly draw parallels between these early days and the present to suggest that human nature remains the same, and that through misadventure and hardship women endure.

Following the narrative patterns set by Jean Auel in *The Clan of the Cave Bear* (1994) and *The Mammoth Hunters* (1996), Linda Lay Shuler creates a fictional prehistory of the American Southwest. She tells of the ancient people who built the mysterious hidden canyon cities of Mesa Verde and Chaco Canyon. She speculates that in the eleventh century blue-eyed Vikings armed with crossbows engraved runes in stone in what is today Oklahoma to mark their passing. Two centuries later her high-spirited heroine, Kwani, a descendant of Vikings, is driven out by the Anasazi who raised her because her blue eyes, her extraordinary hunting prowess, and her power to call animals and to weave stories mark her as a witch. In *She Who Remembers* (1988) Kwani's love for a flute-playing, philandering Toltec magician, Kokopelli (whose legendary deeds became part of Southwestern lore), makes her follow him to the Place of the Eagle Clan (Mesa Verde), where she becomes the Chosen of the Gods and earns the name She Who Remembers, a title designating her duty to teach young girls the ancient secrets of women.

Voice of the Eagle (1992) continues the story of Kwani. Gifted with magical vision, she has, in defiance of taboos, joined with Tolonqua, the hunting chief of the Towa; she helps him build a great fortress to protect his clan from attacks by the Pawnee and the Apache, and their son and daughter (twins bound into one body by magic) show the extraordinary talents that indicate their great destiny. *Let the Drum Speak* (1996) follows the exploits of Kwani's daughter, Antelope, who possesses the same mystical powers as her mother, and Antelope's mate, Chomoc, who is said to be Kokopelli reincarnated. The couple travel to the fabled City of the Great Sun, an Aztec fortress in what is today Spiro, Oklahoma, where they must stand against a savage Aztec enemy, a bitter rival of Kokopelli. An epilogue reveals that Popé, the Indian who led the 1680 Pueblo Revolt that drove out the Spaniards, was a descendant of Kwani, her daughter Antelope, and her granddaughter Skyfeather, and that the sacred necklace of She Who Remembers was passed down from mother to daughter, generation after generation, and is now the prized possession of a Dallas woman who inherited it and who may some day have to deal with its powers, since "time is a great circle" without beginning or end, and "all returns again and again forever" (*Let the Drum Speak*, 487). Shuler's fantasy is that of ancient secret female knowledge and power that raises women above all males and makes them bringers of knowledge and wisdom.

Judith Redman Robbins's *Coyote Woman* (1996) and *Sun Priestess* (1998), also Anasazi stories, trace the life of Coyote Woman, first as a Mayan child of mystery stolen away by her violent Mayan father, then trained as an acolyte of Anasazi holy men, later as a beautiful woman with prophetic powers. Later, she goes as an emissary from the Anasazi to the Mayan-Toltecs, and finally becomes a sun priestess—a healer, dream weaver, and spirit guide to the Anasazi in a time of peril (fire from heaven and raiders from the south). The story is also a romance with two men vying for her love, one a Mayan-Toltec Eagle warrior driven by passion for her, the other a respected Anasazi priest who finds in her a soul mate and a superior. Robbins uses Coyote Woman's journey south from her village to Chaco, Tula, Chichén Itzá, and Tulum, and home again as a way to contrast the Anasazi world with the Mayan-Toltec world: the way of peace with the way of war, group insanity, and bloody sacrifice. Coyote Woman is a complete New Age feminist who has rejected marriage and family for a career of community service; who uses crystals, talks to the animals, and takes pleasure in nice clothes and comfortable quarters; and who certainly feels superior to the macho Mayan males whose ways are just too bloody and tyrannical for her soft heart.

Kathleen O'Neal Gear and W. Michael Gear bring an archaeological and anthropological foundation to their popular ten-volume First North American People series about the Native Americans before the arrival of Europeans—how they lived and interacted socially and tribally, what their values and strengths were, how they evolved and changed as cultures, and why, what their ancient fears, superstitions, spiritual values and belief systems, social orders, legends, struggles, and loves were. However, like all these first people stories, this vision of the past is mainly speculative, based somewhat on archaeological evidence but also on a lot of imagination and projection. The Gears provide an early people's story for each of the different regions of America, with *People of the Wolf* (1990), for example, following the migratory route of early travelers from Asia, along the Laurentide Ice Sheet to the heartland of America, led by a courageous dreamer who follows his Wolf spirit; with *People of the Fire* (1991) demonstrating how drought and famine nearly destroyed the early Native American pioneers who settled in the Rocky Mountain region; and with *People of the Silence* (1996) providing a fictionalized solution to why the Anasazi culture disappeared at its peak. *People of the Lightning* (1995) explores the eerie ancient Florida fisherfolk lore about the White Lightning Boy, an albino who can attract foxfire and lightning and unleash the power of tornado winds. Based on the modern discovery of ceramics and human remains in upstate New York, dated A.D. 500 to 1000, *People of the Masks* (1997) features interclan rivalries, culture clashes, power struggles, shaman visions, prophecies, and natural disasters as well as a nine-year-old seer rescued from certain death. The Gears, too, have fearless warrior women, and create stories of bloodshed and passion in a land of wondrous beauty designed to challenge the soul.

Magical children peer into the eyes of rattlesnakes; their eyes glow amber, and a magical communion between reptile and human takes place; the child crawls away unharmed, and the adults know that this child will play a special role in their religion. Meteorites infuse humans with extraordinary powers that live in legend, and training with crystals and meditation helps special women understand the healing arts and read the signs of truth or falsity in others. Most of the "First People"/"First Americans" books are "science lite"—with fantasy dominating. Consequently, they end up banal in many ways, with, for example, the high priestess of the sun god worrying about her sex life with the high priest (both are forbidden to marry so that they remain fully committed to their inner visions and to their responsibilities to the community) or a courageous woman idly comparing the marital potential of a suitor with that of his rival. Yet these works have especially appealed to feminist sensibilities through strong heroines with important roles in the religious and political systems of past New World civilizations (in contrast to male-centered or patriarchal European civilizations).

The Male Quest in "First People" Novels

William Sarabande provides the best examples of "First People" fantasies that project into the past the concept of bold young men battling monsters and seeking knowledge and adventure among alien peoples. Torka in Sarabande's *Beyond the Sea of Ice* (1986) leads the survivors of a killer mammoth attack eastward over the glacial tundra into an exotic New World land (North America) of danger and of threatening strangers. *Corridor of Storms* (1987) continues the saga, with a coming-of-age story of Torka's adopted son, a brave lad with special powers who must battle an evil magician. When the tribe turns against them in *Forbidden Land* (1988), Torka and his family, accompanied by a small band of followers, must journey into forbidden territory—a dangerous land of omens and oracles—and battle strange creatures, savage humans, and ancient mystical beliefs. Sarabande is interested in the physical and psychological struggles of the first Native Americans, speculating about which peoples would shape the future of humankind, at least in North America. *Thunder in the Sky* (1991), *The Edge of the World* (1992), and *Shadow of the Watching Star* (1994) pit a gentle shaman and his band against violent and savage marauding hunters, and the fear of ancient taboos against new visions and potential triumphs. In contrast, *Face of the Rising Sun* (1995) traces a prophesied peacemaker's quest to revenge his murdered grandfather, and *The Sacred Stones* (1990) and *Time Beyond Be-*

ginning (1997) demonstrate the way a rapidly changing environment sends ancient cultures migrating into new territory and facing new enemies.

Ancient spiritualism expressed through seers and prophets who talk to the animals and receive messages from nature make these imaginary peoples from past worlds seem as alien as science fiction projections into future worlds. In effect, they serve the same function: imaginary creations that project modern questions into unfamiliar settings in order to explore them in new and innovative ways.

DYSTOPIAS

Two stories by well-regarded authors, Stephen Vincent Benét's "By the Waters of Babylon" (1937) and Ursula Le Guin's *Always Coming Home* (1985), epitomize the use of Native American elements in dystopias. Both plots are triggered by a cataclysmic end to civilization as we know it and a rebuilding that evokes images of Native American ways of life. However, whereas Benét's survivors are superstitious and limited in understanding and behavior, LeGuin's are split between those who repeat the mistakes of the past and those who have learned to live in harmony with their world.

Originally titled "The Place of the Gods," Benét's story is probably one of the earliest and most compelling dystopias involving Native Americans. Seemingly set in the distant past among some unspecified, early period of American Indian history (perhaps pre-Columbian or pre-sixteenth-century colonial America), it asserts the ignorance and superstition of hunter-gatherer tribal cultures but also the special impulses that compel a rare few to defy convention and tradition and seek to broaden their knowledge and understanding of their world. Of the two main rival tribes, the Forest People and the Hill People, the Hill People are slightly more advanced because of their knowledge of spinning wool and hunting and their use of metals discovered in ancient places. Their priests have not forgotten "the old writings" and have some knowledge of healing, like how to stop bleeding, but overall the tribes are bound by superstition and taboos, fear of spirits and demons, and an ancestral memory of a "Great Burning." Strictures in force throughout tribal memory include taboos against going east, crossing the "great river," entering Dead Places, or touching metal not purified by priests.

The narrator, a would-be priest who is the son of a priest, knows chants, spells, and medical secrets, and has journeyed to search for metal in dangerous spirit houses. A "noble savage," he speaks with the dignity, simplicity, and repetition of oral tradition and draws on nature for his images: "cold as a frog," "knees like water," knowledge that is "a squirrel's heap of winter nuts." Now, in the time of his spirit journey, after seeing an eagle flying east and other good omens, he is convinced he is right to follow his vision quest along a "god-road," which time and the forest have reduced to great blocks of stone, to reach a forbidden place—a vast ruin, partially overgrown, inhabited by wild beasts, and veiled by deadly fogs. Like primitive peoples coming in awe upon the ruins of Machu Picchu, Teotihuacán, Ankgor Wat, or even Babylon and musing on the power and secrets of a mysterious people long gone, the young man, daringly thirsting for knowledge, discovers subterranean tunnels and huge temples, food in "enchanted" boxes and jars, strong bottled drinks, bronze doors with no handles, high-rise dwellings with inexplicable machinery, lovely paintings and books. This seemingly utopian civilization so challenges his imagination that it inspires him to strive to recapture a Golden Age long lost.

The irony, of course, is that this courageous and perhaps foolhardy young brave is a figure not from our past but from our future. This past civilization is our civilization, and we are the dead whose secrets the Hill People fear. The forbidden place is New York, a bombed-out shell destroyed by a holocaust that laid waste to civilization. The forbidden river is the Hudson ("Ou-dis-sun"); the "god-roads" are highways; "UBTREAS" is the Subtreasury; the statue of "ASHING" is of "Washington"; the "chariots" of the narrator's vision are cars and trucks; the magic torches, electric lights; the falling fire, a superbomb. When the young would-be priest looks out on the ruins of the city, with its broken bridges and tumbling towers, he realizes that the "gods" who built it were human beings, and longs for the knowledge they possessed to help his people recapture lost secrets and build again.

Benét's dystopian message is that man has not yet learned to control the savage in himself that leads to war and annihilation and that, consequently, he could well bomb himself back to the Stone Age. The young narrator is proud of his tribe's superiority to their rivals (the Forest people), enjoys outwitting them, and makes fun of their food ("grubs") and their inability to detect his stealthy movements. He is a capable hunter with an instinct for the kill. In other words, the seeds of competition and of conflict, of potential racism and of blood sports are present, ready to grow alongside the narrator's growing technical knowledge. The story's title suggests that the pattern of three steps forward, three steps back, is an ancient cycle, endlessly repeated. The human race, as personified in the enthusiastic, daring, idealistic young neophyte priest, forever produces Sorcerer's Apprentices, who know just enough to cause injury and who fail to learn from the lessons of history. In each beginning are the seeds that will produce an ending, and the Promethean gift of fire and knowledge is double-edged: the human race's eternal desire to progress contains within it the arrogance, pride, and ambition that guarantee future disaster. The fact that Benét purposely chooses specific details that evoke images of Native American tribal culture adds poignancy to his message: the most recent American civilization to be destroyed by technology is that of America's indigenous peoples. Benét's warning, to some degree, echoes that of Chief Seattle:

Tribe follows tribe, and nation follows nation, like the waves of the sea. It is the order of nature, and regret is useless. Your time of decay may be distant, but it will surely come, for even the White Man . . . cannot be exempt from the common destiny. We may be brothers after all. We shall see. (Munger, *80 Readings*, 55)

LeGuin's *Always Coming Home* is also set in some postnuclear-holocaust future. Survivors include a matrilocal, communal people of Pacific Northwest Native Americans (the Valley People) and an aggressive, patrilocal people from the Great Lakes area (the Condor People). Her novel is a collage of fictional ethnologists' reports, anthropological life histories, Creation myths, ironic Coyote stories, and selections from literary works, mainly from the peaceful Valley People. Most of these are imitative of stories from the Native American oral tradition, with, for example, cautionary Coyote tales (though the Coyote Trickster in this future world is female). In addition, like many Native American stories read from a mainstream perspective, LeGuin's novel seems directionless, a middle without a true beginning or end, its only semiplotted section (three core "Stone Teller" sections) lost amid the collage of other tales. The narrator of these three sections is Night Owl, who becomes Woman Who Comes Home and then Stone Teller, the mixed-blood daughter of a Valley woman and a Condor. She has lived in both worlds and describes them as someone who is at the same time an insider and an outsider.

A conversation between a library archivist and "Pandora" allows LeGuin to assert through the archivist that she has no answers and that her novel is no utopia, but is instead

a mere dream dreamed in a bad time, an Up Yours to the people who ride snowmobiles, make nuclear weapons, and run prison camps by a middle-aged housewife, a critique of civilisation possible only to the civilised, an affirmation pretending to be a rejection, a glass of milk for the soul ulcered by acid rain, a piece of pacifist jeanjacquerie, and a cannibal dance among the savages in the ungodly garden of the Farthest West. (6)

However, there are no cannibals in her story, only Condors, and the "savages" of her "ungodly garden" are the positive figures of her tale.

The dystopian part of her vision is twofold: (1) the image of our society obliterated, specifically by nuclear poisoning (her book came out a few years after the nuclear fallout from Chernobyl reached the Pacific Northwest) and (2) the image of an empire-building nation, the Condors, modeled on some combination of the United States, the Roman empire, the medieval Arab world, and the Native American warrior societies. A mighty computer system interlocks all regions, sections, and groups of LeGuin's future world, ready to provide statistical, literary, and historical information for any who ask, from plans for building flashlights to plans for nuclear weapons, to images of Adolf Hitler and Anne Frank, the first nuclear war, and the poisons that followed. However, the warrior-dominated Condor society holds "the word" sacred and therefore forbids reading or writing to any but a priestly elite. This society is hierarchical, with a military dictator at its top and an elite military class having special privileges and special duties. Women are possessions, veiled and hidden away in household interiors, uneducated except in household skills and in pleasing their husbands. Husbands may take multiple wives, who are expected to be virgins at marriage, to produce a child a year, and to keep their heads down and their voices silent; their infidelity merits stoning. LeGuin asserts that the Condors' tyranny over alien peoples begins with their tyranny over their wives. What Stone Teller repeatedly calls the "sickness" in the male-female relationships of this culture produces a sickness in its national character, and the Condors' separation from nature and contempt for others lead ultimately to military and administrative failures.

A major part of the novel, however, projects a contrasting utopian "Native American"-style society that is the mirror image opposite of the Condors. LeGuin mixes historical details from many Indian tribes from many regions to create a composite future people. The Valley People are farmers, herdsmen, artists, and visionaries. They weave beautiful rugs, throw pots, and make stone jewelry. Their social system is tribal, involving membership in mother-centered lodges. There is no sense of ownership of property; instead, all is held in common, and what one grows, another shares. There are equivalents of potlatches in which possessions are given away to those who need them more, and a recurring literary theme is that wealth consists "not in *things* but in an *act*: the act of giving" (117).

In this Native American-based utopia, both sexes are free from sexual taboos (except for some incest taboos related to clan membership). Marriages are between equals and divorce is easy: locals follow the Native American tradition of the wife putting the husband's goods outside the lodge to send him on his way. There are marriages between males if they so choose (like the Native American *berdaches*). There are ribald White Clowns (like the Navajo and Hopi Sacred Clowns), and Moon Dance celebrations in which people sing ancient chants and do stamp dances (like the tribes of the Pacific Northwest).

The Valley People's religion is also reminiscent of that of some native peoples. It recognizes the interrelatedness of all creatures, the blending of light and dark, the reality of change yet sameness. The circle is a powerful metaphor for the Valley People's sense of life and life's journey, and the spirits of those who died live on amid their relatives for those who have eyes to see their continuation. People believe in a theory of four souls, and ghost stories are moralistic, mainly about gigantic animals punishing hunters for not using the special ritual chants and prayers for asking forgiveness before taking the life of an animal or a plant. Hunters are taught the importance of ecological balance. The locals talk of Grandmother Mountain and Sky Houses, and their words echo the *w*'s and *h*'s of Native American dialects: "Heya, heya/nahe heya/no nahe no/heya, heya; wakwa; weyewey." There are Blue Clay, Yellow and Red Adobe, and Obsidian peoples and names like Red Bull, White Peach, Willow, and Watching Quail.

Whereas Benét in "By the Waters of Babylon" sees the seeds of human destructiveness in the thirst for technological change and development, LeGuin in *Always Coming Home* pits a sanitized and idealized communal "Native American" culture against a hierarchical "European-style" model. However, her female-centered society is static, and though its life-affirming values seem clearly superior to the warlike male-dominated one, it is to some degree helpless against superior martial power. Of the two, Benét's short story is a more gripping, harder-hitting dystopian view than LeGuin's soft-edged utopian-dystopian mix.

NEW AGE MYSTICS

Mystics of the "New Age," a term describing a nebulous, quasi-religious set of spiritual ideas that grew out of the 1960s counterculture and the 1970s "human potential" movement, believe that a new "spiritual" age is dawning in which humans will realize higher, more purified selves through spiritualism, astrology, out-of-body experiences, reincarnation, the occult, and the "healing powers" of crystals and pyramids. They denounce the present as dystopian and look forward to a future that returns to a utopian Native American past. They draw on Native American spirituality for insights into worlds beyond our own and record their supposedly "real" experiences through fictional voices. Whether one takes these stories as purely fantasy fiction, quasi-fiction, or "truth" in protective cloaking depends, of course, very much on point of view. However, Creek/Cherokee Métis Ward Churchill, in *Fantasies of the Master Race* (1992), backed by a council of elders, bitterly denounces the lot of them: Carlos Castañeda, J. Marks, Ruth Beebe Hill, Lynn Andrews, and such Indian associates as Alonzo "Chunksa Yuha" Blacksmith, "Chief Red Fox," Hyemeyohsts Storm, Sun Bear, Brook Medicine Eagle, Grace Spotted Eagle, Cyfus McDonald, Ocheana Fast Wolf, and Dyhani Ywahoo, among others. He calls them "spiritual hucksters" and "plastic medicine men" who have meddled disrespectfully in dangerous territory and have grown rich "peddling their trash while real Indians starved to death, out of the sight and mind of America" (215).

Carlos Castañeda receives the full weight of Churchill's diatribe as "The Greatest Hoax since Piltdown Man" (43–61); Churchill accuses Castañeda of "knowingly" transforming "a viable Yaqui concept into a tangent of pseudo-European mysticism" that is pure fantasy (57). He mocks Castañeda's "never-never land" descriptions of Sonoran weather and fauna and his mix of international religious lore (Sufi, Tantric, Buddhist, and Hindu) with so-called Yaqui wisdom (55). Castañeda was both famous and infamous in the 1960s for what he claimed to be true accounts of his dealings with Don Juan, a Yaqui Indian. His first book, *The Teachings of Don Juan: A Yaqui Way of Knowledge* (1968), was a self-styled nonfiction account supposedly based on an extended apprenticeship with the title character, a shaman from the north Mexican desert. In the narrative Don Juan Matus leads the narrator, purportedly the real Castañeda, through a regimen of hallucinogenic drugs in pursuit of ancient ways of knowledge. Peyote, datura, jimsonweed or locoweed, and numerous other exotic substances open up unsettling alternative realities, calling into question the way

Westerners, even scientists, view the world; as one reader remarks, Castañeda "leads us to understand that our own world is a cultural construct and from the perception of the other worlds [he leads us into] we see our own for what it is" (online review, Amazon.com, August 21, 1998). The book was a perfect vehicle for the enthusiasms of the late 1960s: psychedelic experience, exotic gurus and locales, challenges to the establishment's verities. Don Juan's path to becoming a "man of knowledge" challenged millions of readers, and became, along with Herman Hesse's *Steppenwolf* and Aldous Huxley's *The Door of Perception*, a must-read book of the time. A second work, *A Separate Reality: Further Conversations with Don Juan* (1991), extended the narrator's training in the ways of sorcery, and a third, *Journey to Ixtlan: The Lessons of Don Juan* (1991), summed up Castañeda's "education" in Yaqui shamanism.

Castañeda wrote seven more books, focusing on the intricate and shifting manipulations that bind shamanistic teachers and students in the arcane study of the Native American supernatural. All the Don Juan books are as much about psychology and power as about hallucinogenic drugs, although the latter created their notoriety. However, whether or not the complex intrigues of shaman-teachers that Castañeda describes were based on real experience or were simply fantasy fiction became an issue for critics and readers, for although the first book carried the authority of a reputable university press, the others were clearly aimed at the mass market; furthermore, Castañeda consistently refused interviews about his sources or himself, increasingly avoided public appearances, and even, despite his fame, nearly escaped the attentions of photographers. (Only a few images of Castañeda exist; he died in 1998 as anonymously as he lived, apparently at age seventy-two.)

It is perhaps appropriate for a writer about shamanism to blur the line between illusion and reality, between fiction and documentary fact. In the world of Don Juan, after all, there are no such lines—and that's the point. Whether Castañeda was puckishly driving home this message or pursuing some other agenda, it is a certain fact that his books, translated into seventeen languages and with a total of eight million copies sold, were instrumental in revitalizing interest in the Native American culture of the Southwest, in giving intellectual weight to shamanism and exotic drug use for spiritual purposes, and, ironically, in creating the New Age sensibility that Don Juan (and perhaps Castañeda) would have deplored.

Heather Hughes-Calero, Lynn Andrews, and Mary Summer Rain reflect this New Age sensibility and clearly think of themselves as practicing the approaches developed by Castañeda. Hughes-Calero's *Woman Between the Wind* (1990) is grounded in the autobiographical—her personal journey as an apprentice to Alana Spirit Changer, a Colorado medicine woman whose psychic powers compel the narrator to rethink her life. However, most of the book records a series of mystical-magical experiences, dream interpretations, and descriptions of channeling energies that, if not fiction, exploit the techniques of fiction—orderly plot, well-rounded character, neat denouement, and so on.

Lynn Andrews is also typical of these New Age mystics. She has made popular a series describing her mystic experiences while seeking a spiritual vision and studying spiritualism and shamanism with Agnes Whistling Elk (the *heyoehkah* or shaman) on the Cree reservation in Manitoba, Canada. She sees herself becoming "a warrioress of the rainbow people" and "a bridge between two different worlds, the primal mind and the white consciousness" (*Star Woman*, 6). Andrews claims she has fictionalized her stories to protect friends and acquaintances from publicity, but their narrative line is very much a blend of sci-fi and horror conventions. Her first book, *Medicine Woman* (1981), an odd mix of California slang and mystical spiritualism, recounts a four-stage process of learning in which the narrator communicates with her teacher through paranormal means, has her spiritual skills tested against an adept and highly threatening male sorcerer named Red Dog, learns the power of a sacred marriage basket, and earns the right to hold a sacred pipe. A typical passage follows:

I am walking in a part of the faraway. . . . I can see . . . the face of an ancient American Indian. . . . I see a blue-black crow. . . . The crow's body starts swiveling inward to face the head of the woman, moving in the same metronome-like beat [as her head turns]. . . . I am startled. The crow begins to mimic the speech of the old woman. The two distinct voices are so quarrelsome I shudder. (v)

Flight of the Seventh Moon (1984) recounts Andrews's initiation, her rites of passage, into the Sisterhood of the Shields (a secret Native American female society), and her acquisition of the protective shields of the four directions (Protector-of-Children, Dreaming-Bear, Standing-Buffalo, and Fire-That-Falls-from-the-Sky) as well as her own shield (Shield-Made-of-Shadows)—a physical reminder of her new awareness. While sitting on a pink velvet stool in front of a mirror in the Beverly Hills Hotel, Andrews receives a telepathic message about her need for protection, hence the description of how her shaman teaches her to achieve self-realization. In *Jaguar Woman* (1985) Andrews recounts her visions and dreams as she becomes a jaguar spirit roaming a shadowy world, grappling with Native American archetypes and spirits and learning lessons of movement, both physical changes of locale and psychic and emotional movements involving changes in states of mind. These she relates to the migrations of the monarch butterfly from Canada to Mexico (a rainbow of colors united in a common movement), and, in doing so, presents the medicine wheel as an "existential paradigm" for humanity's journey toward balance and wholeness. In *Star Woman* (1986) Agnes Whistling Elk teaches the narrator how to escape her own delusions through sacred smoke or a special drumbeat, how to take a stand against the predatory forces around her, how to escape the millstones of her white mainstream culture, and how to experience the freedom, magic, and mystical communion with spirit forces like Arion (a great white stallion that serves as a shaman transport). A few chapter headings are indicative of the range of topics addressed: "The Ghost Horse," "Shape Shifter," "The Sacred Clown,"

"The Life and Death Ghost Dolls," "Thunder-Being Drum," "The Shaman's Myth," "A Sorcerer's Smoke," "Shifting the World." There is, of course, no reason that native spirituality should not settle in a Beverly Hills zip code, but Andrews's airy use of such disparate elements of religion suggests a Native American costume rack rather than any deep commitment to culture or teachings.

Writing in a similar vein, Mary Summer Rain in *Spirit Song* (1985) presents herself as a descendant of a Shoshone prophet, She-Who-Sees, who, in the time of Sacajawea, foretold the Indians' loss of land and spirit and promised the vision of "Summer Rain" to renew future spirits. The student of a blind Chippewa visionary, a shaman called No-Eyes, the narrator describes her mystical experiences in an odd dialogue that emphasizes the shaman's limited English-language skills ("Summer not take long as No-Eyes think," 145). In one visionary experience, the shaman and the narrator soar above Earth ("Earth Mother in great pain. She rearranging herself," 145) and share a nightmare image of the future plight of Colorado Springs:

I felt as if I was watching some horror movie conceived in the mind of evil. Horrible scenes were graphically played out in vivid detail. The city was in ruin. Evidently a strong tremor swept through the city. The tall buildings were left in their nakedness of iron skeletons. Concrete and glass lay scattered about in huge piles of rubble. People ran amok screaming in hysterics. Gore was everywhere. Crushed and mutilated bodies lay in agony over the dead. Fires burned like torches from the gas lines. Hot electrical wires lay sparking. It was chaos. (147)

The suburbs were leveled; "hordes of mindless people" swarmed, trampling and shooting each other. No-Eyes confirms the apocalyptic possibilities of missiles exchanged and nature overwhelmed. Here, Native American mysticism is used to lend credibility to visions that might otherwise collapse through their own lack of substance.

Unlike the New Age spiritualists at whom she scoffs, Mercedes Lackey, though writing of similar experiences, proclaims her works "entertainment." She says they are not to be taken seriously, nor to be confused with actual life. "I am not portraying reality," she asserts, "or attempting to" (*Sacred Ground*, 383). Though they may incorporate the familiar patterns of the romance and mystery genres (a male-female relationship that begins with antagonism and ends with love; multiple murders and detectives gathering clues and interpreting forensic evidence), her novels are classified as science fiction because their central action takes place in another dimension, with battles between good and evil forces played out on two planes of existence. Her heroines are witches or shamans, who use the powers of ancient religions to protect the innocent, stop the victimizers, and destroy the evil. For example, Lackey's Diana Tregarde series includes one investigation (*Burning Water*, 1989) in which an earthquake in Mexico City unleashes an ancient and bloodthirsty Aztec deity determined to bring all people

of Indian descent under his sway and to have his minions perform ancient sacrificial ceremonies (mass slayings, mass cardiectomies, drowning of children,
flayings, the sacrifice of a Corn Mother) in accordance with the Aztec calendar.
These bloody acts lead up to the reenactment of the most powerful ritual, one
thwarted by an epidemic of measles when the Spaniards entered the Aztec holy
city of Tenochtitlán. The final ritual (to be performed in the Fort Worth-Dallas
area) will call upon the full range of Indians of the Americas, from both Mexico
and the United States, and will so empower the Aztec deity that he will be able
to drive all whites from the Americas.

The Osage-Cherokee heroine of Lackey's *Sacred Ground* (1994), Jennifer
Talldeer, is the granddaughter of a powerful Osage medicine man and the descendant of a famous shaman who sent his progeny to white schools to cam-
ouflage them while they secretly continued the secret medicine ways of their
tribe: "They had their hiding places in between the 'fences' and under the
'porches' of the white ways, where they did their Osage and Cherokee thing"
(18). Jennifer, a private detective, tracks sacred relics to private collections and
assures their return to the Indian tribes from which they were taken (hundreds
and thousands of items in profane hands—medicine bundles, sacred pipes, shaman bones that would remain tossed away in attics if not for her aggressive
research and action).

Lackey's petite heroine moves in three worlds: as the totally assimilated Jennifer Talldeer (a private investigator with a degree in criminology); as Good
Eagle Woman (the publicly visible Osage-Cherokee self who attends powwows
and rescues sacred objects); and as her hidden, secret reality, her spirit-self,
Kestrel-Hunts-Alone. In this third world, Talldeer is a powerful shaman who
travels to the spirit world, builds protective shields, calls on coyote and bird
spirits, and discovers the truths behind the illusions of the visible world. She
appears in full Osage regalia, with a shell necklace normally reserved for men,
"a beaded *Tzi-sho* eagle feather braided into the hair on one side of her head,
and a beaded *Hunkah* feather on the other, a modified warrior's roach," topped
by a kestrel. As warrior and medicine woman, she addresses the Osage Little
People (vengeful spirits angered at their desecrated burial mounds) and placates
or redirects their anger. In the everyday world, she disarms a bomb, points an
insurance investigator in the right direction, and persuades an abused wife to
join the Witness Protection Program and testify in court against her husband.

Like Hughes-Calero, Andrews, and Summer Rain, Lackey describes the process of training for sensitivity to the spirit world and confrontations between
good and evil carried out in another dimension. As a Kestrel spirit, Jennifer has
a terrifying vision of the wasteland Osage land will become if the ancient evil
she combats wins:

. . . a bleak and barren landscape, where nothing grew and nothing lived. The sky was
the color of ashes, the ground under her feet cracked and lifeless. Nothing broke the arid
horizon but the occasional dead stick of what had once been a tree, now withered and

sere. A thin and bitter wind sighed mournfully across this land, full of acrid, burning stenches and the sick-sweet smell of decay . . . the place of her dream. . . . The terrible place where the eagles [the totem spirits associated with the Osage] died. (358–359)

The final sequence is a battle of spiritual forces, with Kestrel-Hunts-Alone, her grandfather Mooncrow, and her ancestor Watches-Over-the-Land shifting shapes as the deadly evil force pursues them through changing realities.

Lackey purposely manipulates all of the elements of the New Age mystics for fictional ends. Her stories bridge genres. They begin as detective fiction, with an investigator who questions witnesses, gathers and interprets factual data, and seeks clues to a pattern that will unlock the secret patterns of relationships and events. However, they also include horror elements: supernatural forces (ghosts and spirits) that bring mayhem and death—crazed warrior spirits that send electric bolts surging from a television to kill a child or zombies that carry out the murderous intent of the powers that have brought them back to life. Ultimately, they are science fiction because their descriptions of shamanistic powers carry the battles between good and evil into the realm of the multidimensional, alternative "other" worlds beyond our own, where, as a kestrel battles scrawny blackbirds and is saved by eagles on one plane, the heroine is pursued by hit men in a black Lincoln, who plunge to their deaths when an Eagles Line bus turns in front of them. Lackey exploits the Native American culture's easy acceptance of multiple spiritual dimensions for modern sci-fi ends.

The major difference between Mercedes Lackey and the Lynn Andrewses and Mary Summer Rains in their New Age mysticism is that Lackey admittedly writes fiction while the others claim their fiction as fact; Lackey is a polished writer but the others are not.

CONCLUSION

The science fiction genre is replete with shape-shifting—the infusion of a highly flexible Indian figure to advance plot and theme in any number of ways. Alternative histories are always intellectually teasing. There is always the possibility of the mystical-magical drawn from Native American religious concepts of the star world, the spirit world, and Creation stories, and of struggles between positive and negative forces that leap the boundaries of visible reality. However, the Native American as a basis for exploring important questions of values, of cross-cultural contact, of conflicting concepts or interpretations of reality offers deeper, more significant science fiction possibilities. The Native American can be a viable symbolic counter to science and technology: the human spirit versus the mechanistic, the free and unbridled versus the restricted and controlled. The Native American meeting the European is the great American model of encounters with the Other, alien abduction, and bridging the gap between two very different worlds and mind-sets. More often than not, Native American values and ways of life are associated with utopian rather than dystopian visions and offer hope for better, freer worlds, more environmentally and ecologically sound than our own. The stories explored in this chapter suggest a vast potential of approaches and concepts yet to be explored.

Conclusion: Future Directions for the "Indian" in Popular Fiction

> . . . the awesome Western landscape and the incredible historic experiences that rise up in our collective memories like ghosts from some vivid past have provided inspiration not only for generations of artists, but also for generations of Americans, red, brown and white. Thus the West lives on, even today, in the hearts of most Americans. Now we have only to ask, as we move toward the year 2000: What new myths will the West engender?
> —Goetzmann & Goetzmann, *The West of the Imagination*, 434

As our discussion and bibliography clearly indicate, there has been a surge of interest in Native Americans in popular fiction. Since the 1950s, a great shift in attitudes has occurred, with the old stereotypes of the past being reexamined and new kinds of fiction being written, often works that seriously attempt fairness and objectivity about the tragic collision of East and West, old and new, in North America. The new Western, in particular, has broken the bonds of the past, shifting point of view to incorporate new voices and new visions of the frontier. While traditional Westerns still have their audience, a more sophisticated and open-minded readership wishes to see that the Indian at the very least has his day in court, if not actually to see the world through Indian eyes. We can expect even more novels that include the eastern frontier (usually neglected in favor of the western Plains) and revisionist takes not only on pivotal historic encounters between warriors and the U.S. military, such as at Wounded Knee, but also between the native and immigrant populations in the daily personal encounters that took place across the frontier. Such "domestic" dramas as John Norman's *Ghost Dance* (1970) allow different understandings of what it was like to meet and deal with the many "alien" cultures, not just the Native American, on the frontier. We can also expect more Westerns that alternate perspectives—white and Indian, that treat the African American experience among Native Americans, and that provide more positive takes on women once dismissed as "squaws." While some recent works include well-rounded Mexican-American characters in the Southwest, there is room for more books about Hispanic-Native American relations north of Mexico; as the first Europeans to explore large regions of the continent, the Spanish established images of the Indian which were often crucial in creating later attitudes and behavior toward the native population.

In fact, building on late twentieth-century interest in "other voices" and "voices unheard" in traditional historical summaries of the westward movement, we can anticipate any number of fictional accounts written from the perspective of characters heretofore silent on the great stage of the West. The Chinese who helped build the railways, for example, or the Nordic settlers of the Northwest and Pacific Northwest offer unique angles from which to view this great drama. The explosion of interest in genealogy, enabled by computer searches and the internet, can only encourage new young writers to put family records into fictional form. For all the academic unhappiness about American reading habits, this is an exciting time for experimental writing and the conscious manipulation of traditional forms to express new visions of who we are as a nation. For example, we can look forward to more historical captivity stories retold to break with their original conventions and to provide a fuller, more rounded vision of these close encounters. Writers like Lucia St. Clair Robson, Frederick Manfred, and James Alexander Thom have already established exemplary models for how such stories could be retold for modern readers. The Native American point of view receives equal treatment in the works of these novelists, and while not all readers will be satisfied with the results, there is no question that the change in perspective has been dramatic.

The infusion of the supernatural into the Western is another attempt to provide a Native American vision, as is the movement back in time to a pre-European America. Whatever shifts the future of the genre brings, it is quite clear that the generic Indian has fairly well disappeared from the ranks of the better novelists, replaced by specific tribes and specific personalities, each particularized with details of lifestyle, customs, traditions, and values. These Indians of the new Western are still defined in white terms, but they are no longer simply bloodthirsty savages. While these literary figures still for the most part serve mainstream agendas and express white- or European-originated views, at least offensive older stereotypes are far less evident, and some fine writers make conscious attempts to capture native culture. Kathleen Gear, Michael Gear, Robert Moss, and others are examining Native American perspectives on the early white-red encounters, and many other authors have turned to the period before such encounters—a West belonging entirely to the Native Americans. Moreover, this is an area in which native voices are being heard more and more, with writers like Robert Conley, Diane Glancy, Leslie Silko, and Joseph Bruchac retelling stories of the old West through new eyes.

The romance addresses these changes less directly, but the fictional presence of white women (and occasional white men) in romantic relationships with native lovers exhibits the end of the taboo against miscegenation; accepting the Other as a romantic partner breaks down the final social barrier. The explosion of recent white-Indian romances suggests that there are elements in the clash of opposites that appeal to white female fantasies in a number of ways, and that we can expect more such stories in the future. Unrealistic and silly though many of them are, they seem to touch deep-seated feelings about gender relationships and gender roles, about propriety and freedom, community and individualism, respect and fidelity or infidelity. As Deloria says, Americans are very fond of playing Indian. The stories of nineteenth-century cross-cultural encounters between men and women may simply be employed to fulfill modern agendas: to push modern feminist interpretations of emotional relationships, to establish a model of perfection against which to find the modern white male wanting, and so on. As a sociological-literary phenomenon, the enormous readership for manipulative popular fiction is ignored at the peril of neglecting serious study of culture and of disregarding a large public's reading habits. (We cite 250 romances produced in the 1980s and 1990s, most between 1994 and 1999, and we have not been comprehensive; furthermore, first printing information suggests as many as two hundred thousand copies sold per book. These works are indeed moneymakers.)

The heavy doses of exotic forms of sexuality in many new romances suggests the intent is some mix of titillation and sex education, possibly a departure from past ways of regarding physical relationships. Romances have always been a means of teaching young women about the ways of the world in forms quite different from parental platitudes, so it is interesting to speculate about the lessons for modern girls about cross-racial, cross-cultural relationships expressed in racy, provocative language. One wonders at the hidden social currents that would elicit hundreds of volumes following the patterns we have elucidated above: a nubile white girl becomes captive; white girl conquers her captor; white girl learns a freer way of life based on great sex with no inhibitions; white girl is treasured as never before; white girl becomes Indian girl. As our society learns to deal with its changing, multicultural face, we can expect more and more Indian romances, with Indian culture a distanced and therefore safe playing field for such fantasy experiments. However, the recent successes of Aimée Thurlo, Kathleen Eagle, and Mardi Oakley Medawar offer modern directions that romance writers might choose to take—attempts to show greater respect for a Native American point of view rather than simply to impose a white romantic world order on an Indian one; to present Native Americans within a spiritual, cultural, and tribal structure different from the mainstream; to focus on the real breakdowns in communication possible in cross-cultural situations and the differences in worldviews, values, and perspectives that produce misunderstandings. In sum, to make the romance story serve more serious purposes—truer lessons about history, about sociology, about human nature.

In like manner, the presence of so many Native Americans and even of native detective heroes in that seemingly foreign genre, the crime fiction story, suggests an acceptance of formerly marginalized or compartmentalized figures in the full range of fictional activities. The concept of Native Americans as victims or as suspects has been around for some time. However, the works of Tony Hillerman literally transformed the vision of detective writers as he offered interesting and viable Native American investigators, whose activities opened up new worlds to readers and who acted as go-betweens educating whites to facets of native culture that had been unknown or closed to them previously. Since Hillerman started writing, dozens of new titles have come out yearly, offering Native American detectives in varying degrees of assimilation, but always with a clash at the heart of the detective genre conventions: the conflict between intuition and ratiocination or, in Native American terms, between spiritualism and Western logic. Inevitably, the Native American detective fad has attracted a lot of stories where the Native American elements are superficial, serving New Age, antirational, and even anti-intellectual agendas. However, it has also produced excellent writers like Margaret Coel, Richard Parrish, Thomas Perry, Aimée and David Thurlo, Naomi Stokes, and Mark Sullivan, who are investigating the limits of the genre, finding new ways to raise issues of social justice, manipulation of the law, minority status, and the like, all problems of crucial interest to the Native American community. We can expect more of this testing of the genre in the future, especially of the potential for two visions of reality, the spiritual and the rational, to be in collision.

The recent acceptance of Indian visions of horror can be regarded as an openness to non-European ways of seeing the world, a recognition that a spiritual world existed on the continent long before the arrival of Christianity, and a search for parallels in European culture, even some as far afield as Irish second sight and leprechauns in stories like those of James Doss. The problem, of course, is that readers don't want their horror explained (then it isn't horrible!); they want to feel it deep in the bone. Consequently, although Native American stories and traditions can open up a new world of horror possibilities from shape-shifters to malevolent dwarfs or cannibalistic giants, unless they are in some way related to part of the existing tradition of ghosts and witches and werewolves, they lack the gut force needed to succeed. As a result, we can expect interesting blends like Muriel Gray's *Trickster*, with Christian and Indian overlaid, or Martin Cruz Smith's *Nightwing*, with scientific technology played off against the Hopi spirit world. This, too, is an area that we can hope more Native American writers like Louis Owens, Louise Erdrich, and Joseph Bruchac will exploit. Here, there is much to teach the mainstream readership about the hazards of blind faith in the visible and material to the exclusion of all else, in recognizing that words like "power" and "medicine" speak to more than literal effects and things. America's stunning success with the mechanical and the utilitarian has often blinded its citizens to anything beyond the physical. In particular, legitimate Indian ways could offer curbs and restraints on the contrasting extreme, the absurd excesses of New Age spiritualism, with its effortless, no-cost approaches to what should be hard-won insights.

Science fiction, of course, is the classic American means of speculating about what might be; it is our way of testing out future moral and social cruxes. As with the horror genre, there are fascinating opportunities for informing the classic conventions with new perspectives, for illustrating dramatically and forcefully what political rhetoric does so indifferently: the hazards of following a given technological or scientific direction simply because the capacity exists to do so. Native American culture has not always been well served by a preoccupation with the past, but neither has mainstream America by its infatuation with the future, with all costs of change written off as the price of progress. The possibilities of science fiction, though amazingly varied, are unpredictable. We can certainly expect more of the prehistory utopias with their strong female heroines rewriting the (nonexistent) prehistory of the past, and every new archaeological discovery about ancient peoples, from cave drawings to Neanderthal remains, is bound to generate fictive re-creations of their lives and times. Furthermore, the Indian as a model for encounters with the Other offers inexhaustible possibilities for fantasies on other worlds, in other times, with other humanoids, as in the work of Ursula LeGuin. Time travel, too, offers a chance to mix the Western genre with the sci-fi as creatures/aliens or humanoids from the future come back to the past to observe, to interfere in history, or otherwise to change the course of events. Perhaps the most likely direction sci-fi will take is toward more alternative futures, what-if speculation about changing history: What if William Byrd had convinced the colonists that intermarriage with Native Americans was a good solution to cultural difference? How would America's relationships with the Native peoples have been different? Would mainstream America today be a true amalgam of the European and the Native American, an American synthesis as a product of the "wilderness marriage," or some unpredictable hybrid, more like Brazil in its mix of cultures and people?

Yet, for all these changes, the Native American is still seen in terms and under conditions set by the white, mainstream community. Acceptance, despite all good intentions, is not the same thing as authenticity or even fairness. As Robert Berkhofer (in *The White Man's Indian*) and many other later commentators have shown, images of Native Americans have been manipulated, molded, and fictionalized to serve mainstream functions in innumerable ways. From the earliest days, these fictive images sprang directly from mainstream needs: to warn against the moral and spiritual dangers of "going native," to provide a means for escaped or exchanged white Indians/captives to win sympathy and acceptance upon returning or being returned to white society, to justify the westward expansion and the decimation of natives seen as obstacles, and later to idealize the loss of a frontier way of life and of the freedoms of living outside the boundaries of official government control. Today, new fictive images serve other functions: to provide a distanced forum for modern issues like feminism,

New Age spiritualism, urban versus rural values, environmental awareness, endangered species, multiculturalism, ethnicity, and so forth. In fact, the Indian story has become a catchall for pushing all sorts of messages—ecological, feminist, ethnic, religious, political, ad infinitum.

Some of this imaging of the Other is the inevitable result of numbers and market forces. Just as Chinua Achebe writes his novels in English rather than in his native Igbo in order to reach as many readers as possible in Nigeria, in Africa, and around the world, so even the most committed and dedicated writer, Native or white, may find herself or himself struggling to reconcile a legitimate vision with the need to reach many readers, to sell the book, to communicate broadly. The ready-made image of the Indian provides a quick way of communicating with a vast and far-flung readership, even as it sacrifices tribal particulars and specific regional ways. We should also recognize how difficult it is to reconcile a traditional way of life with the modern in a convincing fashion. Philbert, the hero of the film *Powwow Highway* (based on David Seals's book of the same name), uses a Hershey bar as a religious tribute on a holy mountain and discusses Cheyenne sacred figures on his CB radio, a wonderful use of the new to pay homage to the old. However, Mercedes Lackey's description in *Sacred Ground* of her heroine's odd mix of Osage traditions from the past with white accoutrements from the present suggests the absurdities that may result:

She sat down cross-legged on the wooden floor, boards that had been sanded as smooth as satin underneath her bare thighs. It didn't matter to her—or more importantly, to Grandfather—that this sweatlodge was really a commercially made portable sauna; that the rocks were heated by electricity and not in a fire; that the sweetgrass and cedar smoke were from incense bought at an esoteric bookstore in Tulsa. Or even that the sweatlodge as a place for meditation was more common among the Lakotah Sioux than the Osage; Grandfather had borrowed judiciously from other nations to remake the ways of the Little Old Men into something that worked again. *The destination is what matters*, he had told her a thousand times, *and the path you take to get there. Not whether your ritual clothing is of tradecloth or buckskin, the water you drink from a stream or a spring—or even the kitchen tap. Sometimes ancient ways are not particularly wise, just old.*

So they had this contrivance of the *I'n-Shta-Heh*, the "Heavy Eyebrows," installed in what had been the useless half-bath at the back of the house she and Grandfather shared. Most of the time it served as nothing more esoteric than anyone else's sauna, useful for aching muscles and staving off colds.

Sometimes it served purposes the *I'n-Shta-Heh* who built it would never have dreamed of. (1–2)

The passage raises a thorny question: When a culture ceases to have any material connection with its origins, is it the same culture? Plato's boat analogy asked the same question: If all the boards and other boat parts are replaced with new ones, does the same boat remain? Are, as Grandfather asserts in the passage, paths and destinations all that count?

Different views of the world formulate different answers to the question. The answers matter, for they are not simply philosophical teasers, but rather elements of identity, as we have suggested since the beginning of this discussion. Who we are is the ultimate human question, or at least the ultimate one for modern folk, especially for Americans. Our national identity has always been in a state of negotiation, violently in the Revolutionary War and the Civil War, with less force but in constant flux thereafter. The generic Indian long ago became a part of the American identity, if only as a role to play, and the Indian is still integral, though differentiating more as awareness of Native American realities increases; Native Americans themselves have changed, and must accommodate the modern world which has encircled them, at least in being able to communicate with it.

Can native ways of seeing the world be rescued from the near oblivion that afflicts many tribes? Can assimilation be reversed and ethnic authenticity be recaptured? Certainly not by outsiders writing pulp fiction and mass market popular novels, but perhaps native writers can create change. Other groups have faced similar problems of cultural obliteration. Cajun French came within a generation or two of disappearing entirely from south Louisiana, and while strenuous efforts to arrest its decline have produced mixed results, the jury is still out as to the future of this centuries-old dialect and way of life. In Great Britain, speakers of Old Irish, Welsh, and Gaelic have fought back the hegemony of English, and with the languages come the literatures and entire visions of reality. We can note that Scottish culture suffered a similar fate, first a near destruction by military forces, then a sentimental-romantic rebirth begun by Sir Walter Scott when the real thing was gone or safely under control. Now, attempts are being made to recapture the original language and culture.

In a way, the generic Indian of popular fiction has, in mainstream American culture, become what King Arthur has become for the English: a multifaceted fictive creation serving a multitude of functions. What Neil Fairbairn says of King Arthur in his opening to *A Traveller's Guide to the Kingdoms of Arthur* sums up our dilemma as writers of this book:

Say the words "King Arthur" . . . and you conjure up a vision of knights and maidens, quests and adventures, good and evil. . . .

It is tempting to begin a search for a "real" King Arthur by peeling away this romantic veneer, but the truth does not lie immediately beneath the surface. Indeed, the task of stripping away the myths and legends about Arthur is like unwrapping the huge "present" that consists merely of one gaily wrapped box inside another. In our search for the gift we believe to be within, we . . . risk . . . ending up with a tiny empty box. Arthur has as many faces as this practical joke has cartons. Somewhere there is a real man, but there is also a giant, a tyrant, a huntsman, an emperor—even a god. The purist who wishes to remove all those colorful layers is left peering at a figure so tiny that all detail is lost. Arthur may have been a sixth-century chieftain, but his importance to European culture lies not in what the truth was but in what he became. The wrapping is worth far more than the gift. (9)

Native Americans are not "tiny"—here the analogy breaks down, for their community is as large as many small countries recognized by the United Nations—but the central point remains: the Indian figure has as many meanings are there are writers willing to use it, and it has only a tangential connection to the authentic Native American people. Say the word *Indian* and you conjure up mixed visions, positive and negative—strong, wild peoples, free as the wind, untamed by civilization, seemingly welded to the steeds they sit astride, long, straight black hair tossed by the wind, their skins bronze, their war cry fierce—figures of demonic savagery or ancient spiritual and environmental wisdom.

Nevertheless, it is as impossible to find the "real" Indian in these images as it is to find the "real" King Arthur. In terms of Fairbairn's metaphor, within our literary genres it is the wrapping that attracts and dominates, but, unlike King Arthur, Native Americans still exist, inevitably different from the ancestors our fiction derides, defends, eulogizes, and reconstructs. Thus, unlike the British, Americans have both the myth and the reality, and modern popular fiction provides possible ways of finding the one through the other, of narrowing the gulf of separation that has so long run through American culture. The first residents of the continent have always provided a sense of authenticity missing in the tumultuous mix of immigrant peoples, a loss felt but often deflected into the more malleable figure of the Indian, one less demanding of identity shifts if reshaped into forms that served mainstream agendas. Many commentators have pointed out the American phenomenon of feeling unfinished, of striving to reinvent both the national and the personal character (Deloria, 191). We are historically the land of the second chance, and popular fiction offers new opportunities to reconcile the opposition of Indian and European, to rediscover meanings in our closest Other.

Glossary

animal guardian spirits. During the "time of the beginnings," animal spirit beings emerged who were the prototypes for the animal kingdom. They are the intermediaries between the earth realm and the spirit realm.

animalism. In hunting cultures, the mysterious relation between humans and animals, manifested in the idea of spirits in animal form.

Beauty Way. A Navajo ritual healing complex.

berdache. A person who was viewed as a third gender by a wide variety of Native American tribes. The *berdache* combined the best qualities of both male and female in one body.

bilaganna. A Navajo term for whites.

Blessing Way. A Navajo song and prayer ceremony; also a pattern of life that is in harmony with Navajo beliefs.

bone picker. A specialized role among the Choctaw; leader of the burial rites.

Buffalo Woman. Spirit messenger to the Sioux. She bestows the Sacred Pipe, the ritual object used in the seven sacred ceremonies of the Sioux.

cedar. Cedar necklaces are worn and cedar bark is used in ceremonies because the plant is thought to have powerful properties.

chindi. A Navajo term for the evil part of a person that remains on Earth when someone dies.

clowns and clowning societies. Associated with curing but also known for their acts of defiling or mocking (gluttony, simulated sexual activities, pranks, burlesques of rituals and ceremonies, satires). Examples are the Hopi and Zuñi mud-head clowns and the Koshare, the black-and-white-striped clowns.

cornmeal/corn pollen. Used extensively among Navajo in rituals to bless health and life.

to count coup. A sign of high achievement by a warrior. He touches the body of his enemy and then retreats, leaving the enemy forever shamed in the eyes of his people.

country wife. Frontier term for an Indian wife.

Coyote Trickster. A spirit being in the mythology of all Native American tribes. He is necessary to the finalizing of the Creation process. He is a powerful and often feared teacher whose tricks can have life-and-death consequences. Coyote is only one of his manifestations.

Crow. An animal guardian spirit who often functions as a messenger from the realm of the dead.

datura. A plant with narcotic and hallucinogenic properties used in special ceremonies. *See* jimsonweed.

Diné/dineh. A Navajo term for themselves; the "people."

dream catcher/spirit catcher. Small circular frame with a web stretched across it that is attached to an infant's cradle board. It is used as protection against frightening dreams or influences.

earth diver. One of the five traditional types of Creation stories in world mythology. It emphasizes the joining of the sky realm with the watery depths in a combined effort to bring forth the Earth's surface.

emergence myth. Myth about the emergence of mankind from the underworld.

fetish. Object giving off supernatural power.

flute. The Lakota Sioux considered the flute a love charm; throughout the Southwest the humpbacked Kokopelli plays his flute.

ghost board. Tool used by Quinault shamans.

Ghost Dance. A round dance that was supposed to bring back the dead and the good times of the past; the present world would be rolled up (including whites). This dance originated with the Paiute of Nevada and California (1870–1890) and spread to the Plains Indians. It led to clashes between the Sioux and the U.S. military.

grandfather tobacco. Used in the Sacred Pipe. As it is transformed from leaf to smoke, it actualizes the connection between the material and the spiritual planes.

grass dance. A strenuous and competitive men's social dance.

Great Mystery. A term used by some Native American tribes to designate the ultimate spiritual reality. It is meant to be an inclusive term for the being from which all living beings emerge and to which they return.

guardian spirit. The helping spirit (often animal) that aids a young person on a vision quest or in times of special need.

hataalii. Navajo for a "singer" who conducts healing ceremonies.

Hee man eh. Cheyenne dances performed by members of the half-men/half-women society.

hogan. The round, clay-and-stick home of the Navajos; the door faces east.

jimsonweed. A poisonous plant from which datura is derived.

kachina. An ancestor or rain spirit portrayed by a masked Pueblo dancer; also the figure representing this spirit.

kiva. Pueblo ceremonial chamber that is built below ground level, indicating the connection with the Creation story that describes the emergence of the Pueblo people from the Earth's depths.

mahuts. Four sacred arrows given by Maiyun to the Cheyenne prophet Sweet Medicine. Two of the arrows held power over the buffalo, and two held power over human beings.

Maiyun. The Cheyenne name of the Supreme Being.

medicine. Supernatural power received from a personal protective spirit.

medicine bag/bundle/pouch. A bag made from animal skin and used to hold the sacred "medicines" (pieces of animal bones, claws, hooves, pollen, meal, feathers, or other objects that are centers of sacred power). The "medicines" may be those of an individual, a clan, or a society; they may be put together following the instructions of guardian spirits appearing in dreams or visions, or they may be inherited from previous generations. Medicine bags may be described as fetishes.

medicine society. A society made up of those blessed by the same supernatural curative power.

Milky Way. Spirit road, road taken by the dead.

Misshepechu. The Chippewa water god featured in Louise Erdrich's "Fleur."

moccasin game. A variation on the modern-day shell game.

Nightland. Cherokee region where magic and witchcraft hold sway.

night walkers. Cherokee witches from the west.

NumumBi Pygmies. Spirits of evil disposition who bring injury and destruction to those foolish enough to stumble upon them or their underground dwellings at night (*nynmbi* in Shoshone).

Otter People. A Northwest Coast concept of beings who disguise themselves as humans coming to rescue the survivors of capsized boats. Once they feed their unsuspecting victims fish and seaweed, the rescued become Otter People and inhabit lakes and waterways.

parfleche. A bag made of buffalo hide and used to store food and clothing (like a movable chest of drawers); sometimes highly decorated with patterns particular to a clan or family group.

pemmican. Thin strips of buffalo meat or venison dried in the sun and pounded with nuts.

Peyotism. A religion based on the use of peyote, a psychedelic drug from the buttons of the mescal cactus.

Pitukupf. A benign Ute dwarf spirit.

potlatch. Ceremony of honor given at special times, such as marriage, naming, or coming of age. Vast quantities of goods were given away to those in attendance, who acted as the official witnesses to the life transition.

powwow. A social and religious gathering, usually involving several tribes.

puberty quest. A vision quest at the onset of puberty.

Quetzalcoatl. The name for both a Toltec and an Aztec god who manifested himself as a plumed serpent.

Raven. A powerful animal guardian spirit; a trickster figure for the tribes in the Pacific Northwest.

sachem. Honorable title or position; chief (especially of a confederation); a member of the governing body of the League of Iroquois.

Shalako. The great Zuñi ritual at the end of the year. The *shalako* spirits are powerful *kachinas.*

shaman. One who has passed through an initiation that allows direct access to the spirit realm. With the aid of guardian spirits, the shaman often travels either to the sky world or to the watery depths in search of remedies for both personal and tribal difficulties. Associated with supernatural powers and healing, shamans who use ritual techniques to treat the sick or injured or psychologically disturbed may also be called medicine man/medicine woman or healer, though a healer may be simply an herbalist.

shamanism. Rituals, tales, and beliefs concentrated around the shaman.

shape-shifters. Individuals who can transform themselves from human to animal form and back again.

shape-shifting. Changing shape or appearance (human to wolf or owl or cougar); an ability associated with a hero's power but also with witchcraft or malevolence.

Shipap. In the Pueblo Creation story, the place of emergence from the Earth's depths.

sipapu. In Pueblo religion, a sacred hollow in a cult chamber, representing the *Shipap.*

sits-beside-him-woman/-wife. The favorite wife, usually the first wife, with the power to direct the other wives and the right to sit next to her husband at important gatherings.

skinwalkers. Navajo witches.

soul catcher. See dream catcher.

Spider Woman. A creator figure associated with duality, a helper who is dangerous; she taught humans to weave.

spirit canoe. A ritual instrument which might carry a shaman on a spirit journey.

spirit journey. An entranced shaman's journey to bring back a lost or stolen life force from the Nightland or from an enchanter.

spirit warrior. A spirit being who is manifested as a human being in the warrior's role.

Standing People. Fictive name given to the Anasazi gods.

stomp dance. A night dance performed by purified men; the national dance of the Seminoles and Creeks.

Stone People. Fictive name given to the Anasazi people, perhaps in connection with their mode of dwelling.

Straight pipe/sacred pipe. A ritual object used as a means of purification and initial address to the spirits before any ceremony.

Sun Dance. The annual Plains Indian summer ceremony of world renewal. It often required a flesh offering by those seeking a special blessing. Sometimes a buffalo head was placed on an elevated structure to evoke visions; sometimes a cottonwood tree was used as the center pole in the Sun Dance lodge.

sweat lodge. A small enclosure in which stones are heated and splashed with water to create steam; a place of purification, teaching, praying, and communing.

sweet grass. Sweet sedge, an herb used during ceremonies.

Sweet Medicine. Cheyenne prophet who journeyed to the sacred mountain in Montana.

tepee/tipi. The buffalo skin tent of Plains Indians.

totem poles. Northwest Coast Indian heraldic poles that celebrate an important person's new title or new name, commemorate a feast or ceremonial occasion, or memorialize a dead person's remains. The poles portray guardian spirits and ancestors.

totem spirit. A powerful animal guardian spirit that manifests itself to an individual as a special protector.

Trail of Tears. The forced removal of the Cherokee people from Georgia and Tennessee to Oklahoma in 1838–1839.

vision quest. Males at puberty or in early youth seek a guardian spirit through a ritual quest that involves fasting, purification in a sweat lodge, and a journey.

Wakan Tanka. Cheyenne/Sioux term for the Great Spirit or Great Mystery. A collective term for supernatural beings that sometimes verges on the concept of a Supreme Being.

washichan. Sioux term for whites.

White Buffalo. A powerful animal guardian spirit. When the Sioux Buffalo Woman departs for the spirit realm, she is transformed into a black, then a red, then a yellow, and finally a white buffalo. The reappearance of the White Buffalo signals an event equal in significance to Buffalo Woman's first appearance to the Sioux.

windigo (witiko/wittago). Anthropomorphic cannibal giants with hearts of ice and the power to turn people into cannibals; demons of ice, mud, or stone.

winkte. Sioux for a man-woman or transvestite.

Wolf. The chief of the Shoshone myth world.

Wolf Clan. A subdivision of a tribal society that has the wolf as its animal guardian spirit.

World Tree. The cosmic tree that reaches through the worlds of sky, earth, and underworld, and that symbolizes the cosmic center or *Wakan Tanka*. The World Tree serves as a channel for communications between humans and the sky powers.

Bibliography

PRIMARY SOURCES

Detective Fiction (series detectives in parentheses)

Babula, William. *According to St. John*. New York: Carol Publishing, 1989. (Chief Moses)

———. *St. John and the Seven Veils*. New York: Carol Publishing, 1991. (Chief Moses)

———. *St. John's Baptism*. New York: Citadel Press, 1988. (Chief Moses)

———. *St. John's Bestiary*. Aurora: Colo.: Write Way, 1994. (Chief Moses)

Barker, Rodney. *The Broken Circle: A True Story of Murder and Magic in Indian Country*. New York: Ballantine Books, 1992.

Bowen, Peter. *Coyote Wind*. New York: St. Martin's Press, 1994. (Du Pré)

———. *Long Son*. New York: St. Martin's Press, 1999. (Du Pré)

———. *Notches*. New York: St. Martin's Press, 1997. (Du Pré)

———. *Specimen Song*. New York: St. Martin's Press, 1995. (Du Pré)

———. *Thunder Horse*. New York: St. Martin's Press, 1998. (Du Pré)

———. *Wolf, No Wolf*. New York: St. Martin's Press, 1996. (Du Pré)

Brown, Sinclair. *The Last Song Dogs*. New York: Bantam, 1999. (Ellis)

———. *The Sporting Club*. New York: Bantam, 2000. (Ellis)

Coel, Margaret. *The Dream Stalker*. New York: Berkley, 1997. (Holden)

———. *The Eagle Catcher*. New York: Berkley, 1995. (Holden)

———. *The Ghost Walker*. New York: Berkley, 1996. (Holden)

———. *The Lost Bird*. New York: Berkley, 1999. (Holden)

———. *The Spirit Woman*. New York: Berkley, 2000. (Holden)

———. *The Storyteller*. New York: Berkley, 1998. (Holden)

Davis, Val. *Track of the Scorpion*. New York: St. Martin's Press, 1996.

Dawkins, Cecil. *Clay Dancers*. New York: Random House, 1994. (Martinez)

———. *The Santa Fe Rembrandt*. New York: Random House, 1993. (Prettyfield)

Delving, Michael. *The Devil Finds Work*. New York: Scribner's, 1960.

———. *A Shadow of Himself*. New York: Scribner's, 1972.

———. *Smiling the Boy Fell Dead*. New York: Scribner's, 1968.

Doss, James D. *The Shaman Laughs*. New York: St. Martin's Press, 1995. (Moon; Perika)

———. *The Shaman Sings*. New York: St. Martin's Press, 1994. (Perika)

———. *The Shaman's Bones*. New York: St. Martin's Press, 1997. (Perika)

———. *The Shaman's Game*. New York: St. Martin's Press, 1998. (Perika)

Estleman, Loren. *The Stranglers*. New York: Doubleday, 1984.

Garfield, Brian. *Relentless*. New York: World, 1972.

———. *The Threeperson Hunt*. New York: Evans, 1974.

Gorman, Ed. *Hawk Moon*. London: Headline, 1995. (Rhodes)

Grove, Fred. *Warrior Road*. New York: Doubleday, 1974.

Guthrie, A. B., Jr. *The Genuine Article*. Boston: Houghton Mifflin, 1977.

Hackler, Micah S. *Coyote Returns*. New York: Bantam Doubleday, 1996.

———. *The Dark Canyon*. New York: Bantam Doubleday, 1998.

———. *Legend of the Dead*. New York: Bantam Doubleday, 1995. (Anasazi/Zuñi)

———. *The Shadow Catcher*. New York: Bantam Doubleday, 1997.

Hager, Jean. *The Fire Carrier*. New York: Warner Books, 1996. (Bushyhead)

———. *Ghostland*. New York: Warner Books, 1992. (Bushyhead)

———. *The Grandfather Medicine*. New York: Warner Books, 1989. (Bushyhead)

———. *Night Walker*. New York: Warner Books, 1990. (Bushyhead)

———. *Ravenmocker*. New York: Warner Books, 1994. (Bearpaw)

———. *The Redbird's Cry*. New York: Warner Books, 1994. (Bearpaw)

———. *Seven Black Stones*. New York: Warner Books, 1995. (Bearpaw)

———. *The Spirit Caller*. New York: Warner Books, 1997. (Bearpaw)

Hillerman, Tony. *The Blessing Way*. New York: Harper & Row, 1970. (Leaphorn)

———. *Coyote Waits*. New York: Harper & Row, 1990. (Chee)

———. *Dance Hall of the Dead*. New York: Harper & Row, 1973. (Leaphorn)

———. *The Dark Wind*. New York: Harper & Row, 1981. (Chee)

———. *The Fallen Man*. New York: Harper & Row, 1997. (Chee & Leaphorn)

———. *The First Eagle*. New York: Harper & Row, 1998. (Chee & Leaphorn)

———. *Fly on the Wall*. New York: Harper & Row, 1983. (Leaphorn)

———. *The Ghostway*. New York: Harper & Row, 1984. (Chee)

———. *Listening Woman*. New York: Harper & Row, 1978. (Leaphorn)

———. *People of Darkness*. New York: Harper & Row, 1980. (Chee)

———. *Sacred Clowns*. New York: Harper & Row, 1993. (Chee & Leaphorn)

———. *Skinwalkers*. New York: Harper & Row, 1986. (Chee & Leaphorn)

———. *Talking God*. New York: Harper & Row, 1989. (Chee & Leaphorn)

———. *A Thief of Time*. New York: Harper & Row, 1988. (Chee & Leaphorn)

Hirsh, M. E. *Dreaming Back*. New York: St. Martin's Press, 1993.

Hoeg, Peter. *Smilla's Sense of Snow*. New York: Farrar Straus Giroux, 1993.

Hoyt, Richard. *Fish Story*, New York: Viking Press, 1985.

Kelman, Judith. *Where Shadows Fall*. New York: Berkley, 1987.

Lane, Christopher. *Elements of a Kill*. New York: Avon, 1998. (Attla)

———. *Season of Death*. New York: Avon, 1999. (Attla)

MacDonald, William Colt. *The Comanche Scalp*. New York: Thorndike, 1998.

MacGregor, Ron. *Hawk Moon*. New York: Simon and Schuster, 1996.

————. *Prophecy Rock.* New York: Simon and Schuster, 1995.

Matheson, Richard. *Shadow on the Sun.* New York: Evans, 1994.

Matteson, Stefanie. *Murder on High.* New York: Berkley Publishing, 1994.

McClendon, Lise. *The Bluejay Shaman.* New York: Walker, 1996.

Medawar, Mardi. See under Native American Literature.

Miles, John. *Tenoclock Scholar.* New York: Walker, 1993. (Johnnie Baker)

Moody, Skye Kathleen. *Rain Dance.* New York: St. Martin's Press, 1998.

Owens, Louis. See under Native American Literature.

Padgett, Abigail. *Child of Silence.* New York: Time Warner, 1993. (Bradley)

————. *The Dollmaker's Daughters.* New York: Time Warner, 1997. (Bradley)

————. *Moonbird Boy.* New York: Time Warner, 1997. (Bradley)

————. *Strawgirl.* New York: Time Warner, 1994. (Bradley)

————. *Turtle Baby.* New York: Time Warner, 1995. (Bradley)

Page, Jake. *The Deadly Canyon.* New York: Random House, 1994.

————. *The Knotted Strings.* New York: Random House, 1995.

————. *The Lethal Partner.* New York: Random House, 1996.

————. *Shoot the Moon.* New York: Hobbs, 1997.

————. *The Stolen Gods.* New York: Random House, 1993.

Parrish, Richard. *Abandoned Heart.* New York: Dutton, 1997. (Rabb)

————. *The Dividing Line.* New York: Dutton, 1993. (Rabb)

————. *Nothing but the Truth.* New York: Dutton, 1995. (Rabb)

————. *Our Choice of Gods.* New York: Dutton, 1997. (Rabb)

————. *Versions of the Truth.* New York: Dutton, 1994. (Rabb)

————. *Wind and Lies.* New York: Dutton, 1996. (Rabb)

Patten, Lewis B. *Death Stalks Yellowhorse.* New York: G. K. Hall, 1997.

Perry, Thomas. *Blood Money.* New York: Random House, 2000. (Whitefield)

————. *Dance for the Dead.* New York: Random House, 1996. (Whitefield)

————. *The Face-Changers.* New York: Random House, 1998. (Whitefield)

————. *Shadow Woman.* New York: Random House, 1997. (Whitefield)

————. *Vanishing Act.* New York: Random House, 1995. (Whitefield)

Peterson, Geoff. *Medicine Dog.* New York: St. Martin's Press, 1989.

Prowell, Sandra West. *By Evil Means.* New York: Walker, 1993. (Siegel)

————. *The Killing of Monday Brown.* New York: Walker, 1994. (Siegel & Wolf)

————. *When Wallflowers Die.* New York: Walker, 1996. (Siegel & Wolf)

Reynolds, Brad, S.J. *A Ritual Death.* New York: Avon, 1997. (Townsend)

————. *The Story Knife.* New York: Avon, 1996. (Townsend)

Sanders, William. *Blood Autumn.* New York: St. Martin's Press, 1995. (Taggart Roper)

Sands, Marella. *Serpent and Storm.* New York: Forge, 1999.

————. *Sky Knife.* New York: Forge, 1997.

Satterthwait, Walter. *At Ease with the Dead.* New York: St. Martin's Press, 1990.

————. *Wall of Glass.* New York: St. Martin's Press, 1987.

Seals, David. *Powwow Highway.* New York: Plume Press, 1990.

Sibley, Celestine. *Dire Happenings at Scratch Ankle.* New York: HarperCollins, 1993.

Smith, Martin Cruz. See under Horror/Supernatural.

Stabenow, Dana. *Blood Will Tell.* New York: Putnam's, 1996. (Shugak)

————. *Breakup.* New York: Putnam's, 1997. (Shugak)

————. *A Cold-blooded Business.* New York: Berkley, 1994. (Shugak)

————. *A Cold Day for Murder.* New York: Berkley, 1992. (Shugak)

———. *Dead in the Water*. New York: Berkley, 1993. (Shugak)

———. *A Fatal Thaw*. New York: Berkley, 1993. (Shugak)

———. *Killing Ground*. New York: Berkley, 1998. (Shugak)

———. *Play with Fire*. New York: Berkley, 1995. (Shugak)

Stern, Richard Martin. *Death in the Snow*. New York: Simon and Schuster, 1973. (Ortiz)

———. *Missing Man*. New York: Simon and Schuster, 1990. (Ortiz)

———. *Murder in the Walls*. New York: Simon and Schuster, 1971. (Ortiz)

———. *Tangled Murders*. New York: Simon and Schuster, 1988. (Ortiz)

Stout, Rex. *Red Threads*. New York: Farrar, 1939.

Straley, John. *The Curious Eat Themselves*. New York: Bantam, 1993. (Younger)

———. *Death and the Language of Happiness*. New York: Bantam, 1997. (Younger)

———. *The Music of What Happens*. New York: Bantam, 1996. (Younger)

———. *The Woman Who Married a Bear*. New York: Bantam, 1994. (Younger)

Sullivan, Mark T. *Ghost Dance*. New York: Avon, 1999.

———. *The Purification Ceremony*. New York: Avon, 1997.

Thurlo, Aimée. *Breach of Faith*. New York: Harlequin, 1992.

———. *Redhawk's Heart*. New York: Harlequin, 1999.

———. *Shadow of the Wolf*. New York: Harlequin, 1993.

———. *Timewalker*. New York: Harlequin, 1994.

See ROMANCE for more Thurlo entries.

Thurlo, Aimée, and David Thurlo. *Bad Medicine*. New York: Tom Doherty Associates, 1997. (Clah)

———. *Blackening Song*. New York: Tom Doherty Associates, 1995. (Clah)

———. *Death Walker*. New York: Tom Doherty Associates, 1996. (Clah)

———. *Enemy Way*. New York: Tom Doherty Associates, 1998. (Clah)

———. *Second Shadow*. New York: Tom Doherty Associates, 1993. (Clah)

Trainor, J. F. *Corona Blue*. New York: Kensington, 1994.

———. *Dynamite Pass*. New York: Kensington, 1993.

———. *High Country Murder*. New York: Kensington, 1995.

———. *Target for Murder*. New York: Kensington, 1991.

———. *Whiskey Jack*. New York: Kensington, 1994.

Truman, Margaret. *Murder at the FBI*. New York: Arbor House, 1985.

Westbrook, Robert. *Ghost Dancer*. New York: Signet, 1998. (Howard Moon Deer)

———. *Warrior Circle*. New York: Signet, 1999. (Howard Moon Deer)

Yarbro, C(helsea). Q. *Blood Games*. New York: Berkley, 1992. (Spotted Moon)

———. *Cat's Claw*. New York: Berkley, 1992. (Spotted Moon)

———. *Music When Sweet Voices Die*. New York: Putnam's, 1979. (Spotted Moon); reprinted as *False Notes*. New York: Putnam's, 1979. (Spotted Moon)

———. *Ogilore, Tallant and Moon*. New York: Putnam's, 1976. (Spotted Moon); reprinted as *Bad Medicine*. New York: Berkley, 1991. (Spotted Moon)

———. *Poison Fruit*. New York: Putnam's, 1991. (Spotted Moon)

Young, Scott. *Murder in a Cold Climate*. New York: Penguin, 1988. (Inuk Matthew "Mateesie" Kitologitak of the Royal Canadian Mounted Police)

———. *The Shaman's Knife*. New York: Viking Press, 1993. (Kitologitak)

First People Stories

Allan, Margaret. *Keeper of the Stone*. New York: Dutton NAL, 1993.

———. *The Last Mammoth*. New York: Dutton NAL, 1994.

———. *The Mammoth Stone*. New York: Dutton NAL, 1992.

———. *Spirits Walking Woman*. New York: Dutton NAL, 1997.

Auel, Jean. *The Clan of the Cave Bear*. New York: Crown Publishers, 1994.

———. *The Mammoth Hunters*. New York: Crown Publishers, 1996.

Gear, Kathleen, and Michael Gear. *People of the Earth*. New York: Tom Doherty Associates, 1992.

———. *People of the Fire*. New York: Tom Doherty Associates, 1991.

———. *People of the Lakes*. New York: Tom Doherty Associates, 1994.

———. *People of the Lightning*. New York: Tom Doherty Associates, 1995.

———. *People of the Masks*. New York: Tom Doherty Associates, 1997.

———. *People of the Mist*. New York: Tom Doherty Associates, 1997.

———. *People of the River*. New York: Tom Doherty Associates, 1993.

———. *People of the Sea*. New York: Tom Doherty Associates, 1994.

———. *People of the Silence*. New York: Tom Doherty Associates, 1996.

———. *People of the Wolf*. New York: Tom Doherty Associates, 1990.

Gordon, Noah. *Shaman*. New York: Dutton NAL, 1992.

Harrison, Sue. *Brother Wind*. New York: Morrow, 1994.

———. *Cry of the Wind*. New York: Avon, 1998.

———. *Mother Earth, Father Sky*. New York: Avon, 1991.

———. *My Sister the Moon*. New York: Avon, 1993.

———. *Song of the River*. New York: Avon, 1997.

McKee, Lynn Armistead. *Spirit of the Turtle Woman*. New York: Dutton NAL, 1999.

Prentiss, Charlotte. *Children of the Ice*. New York: Onyx, 1993.

———. *The Island Tribe*. New York: Onyx, 1996.

———. *The Ocean Tribe*. New York: Onyx, 1999.

———. *People of the Mesa*. New York: Onyx, 1994.

Robbins, Judith Redman. *Coyote Woman*. New York: Onyx, 1996.

———. *Sun Priestess*. New York: Onyx, 1998.

Sarabande, William. The First Americans series

> *Beyond the Sea of Ice*. No. 1. New York: Bantam, 1986.
>
> *Corridor of Storms*. No. 2. New York: Bantam, 1987.
>
> *Forbidden Land*. No. 3. New York: Bantam, 1988.
>
> *Walkers in the Wind*. No. 4. New York: Bantam, 1989.
>
> *The Sacred Stones*. No. 5. New York: Bantam, 1990.
>
> *Thunder in the Sky*. No. 6. New York: Bantam, 1991.
>
> *The Edge of the World*. No. 7. New York: Bantam, 1992.
>
> *Shadow of the Watching Star*. No. 8. New York: Bantam, 1994.
>
> *Face of the Rising Sun*. No. 9. New York: Bantam, 1995.
>
> *Time Beyond Beginning*. No. 10. New York: Bantam, 1997.
>
> *Wolves of the Dawn*. No. 11. New York: Bantam, 1997.

Scott, Theresa. Hunters of the Ice Age series

  Dark Renegade. New York: Dorchester, 1994.

  Broken Promise. New York: Dorchester, 1995.

  Yesterday's Dawn. New York: Dorchester, 1998.

Shuler, Linda Lay. *Let the Drum Speak.* New York: Morrow, 1996.
———. *She Who Remembers.* New York: Morrow, 1988.
———. *Voice of the Eagle.* New York: Morrow, 1992.
Thom, James Alexander. *The Children of First Man.* New York: Ballantine, 1994.
Wolf, Joan. *Daughter of the Red Deer.* New York: Dutton NAL, 1997.
———. *The Horsemasters.* New York: Dutton NAL, 1996.
———. *The Reindeer Hunters.* New York: Dutton NAL, 1995.
Young Bear, Ray. *See under Native American Literature.*

Historical Captivity Stories

Axtell, James. "The White Indians of Colonial America." *William and Mary Quarterly,*
    3rd ser., 32 (1975): 55–88.
Bab, Dot. *In the Bosom of the Comanches.* Dallas, Tex.: Press of John F. Worley, 1923.
Baker, Alice C. *True Stories of New England Captives Carried to Canada during the
    Old French and Indian Wars.* Cambridge, Mass.: Press of E. A. Hall, 1897.
Bartlett, John R. *Personal Narrative.* 2 vols. New York, 1854.
Bleecker, Ann Eliza. *The History of Maria Kittle.* Hartford, Conn.: Elisha Babcock, 1797.
    Reprinted in *The Garland Library of Narratives of North American Indian Cap-
    tivities.* Vol. 2. New York: Garland Press, 1978.
Boller, Henry A. *Among the Indians: Four Years on the Upper Missouri, 1858–1862.*
    Ed. Milo Milton Quaife. Lincoln: University of Nebraska Press, 1972.
Brush, Edward Hale. *Iroquois Past and Present.* Buffalo, N.Y.: Baker, Jones, 1901.
    Reprinted New York: AMS Press, 1977.
Coleman, Emma Lewis. *New England Captives Carried to Canada, Between 1677 and
    1760.* 2 vols. Portland, Me.: 1925. Reprinted North Stratford, N.H.: Ayer, 1977.
Demos, John. *The Unredeemed Captive: A Family Story from Early America.* New York:
    Alfred A. Knopf, 1994.
Dennis, T. S., and Mrs. T. S. Dennis, eds. *F. M. Buckelew, Life of . . . as Related by
    Himself.* Bandera, Tex.: T. S. Dennis, 1924.
Derounian-Stodola, Kathryn Zabelle, and James Arthur Levernier. *The Indian Captivity
    Narrative, 1550–1900.* New York: Twayne, 1993.
Drake, Samuel G. *Indian Captivities; Or Life in the Wigwam.* Auburn: Derby and Miller,
    1899. Reprinted New York: AMS Press, 1975.
———. *Tragedies of the Wilderness, or True and Authentic Narratives of Captives.*
    Boston: Antiquarian Bookstore and Institute, 1841.
Drimmer, Frederick, ed. *Captured by the Indians: 15 Firsthand Accounts, 1750–1870.*
    Toronto: General Publishing Co., 1961.
Eastman, Edwin. *Seven and Nine Years Among the Comanches and Apaches; An Auto-
    biography.* Jersey City, N.J.: C. Johnson, 1873.
Frost, John. *Indian Battles, Captivities, and Adventures.* New York: Ayer, 1859.
———. *Pioneer Mothers of the West; or Daring & Heroic Deeds of American Women.
    Comprising Thrilling Examples of Courage, Fortitude, Devotedness & Self-*

Sacrifice. Boston: Lee and Shepard, 1869. Reprinted New York: Arno Press, 1974.

Gangi, Rayna M. *Mary Jemison: White Woman of the Seneca*. Peter Jemison, Epilogue. Santa Fe, N.M.: Clear Light, 1995.

Gardner, Jeanne LeMonnier. *Mary Jemison, Seneca Captive*. New York: Harcourt, Brace, and World, 1966.

The Garland Library of Narratives of North American Indian Captivities. Selected and arranged by Wilcomb E. Washburn. 111 vols. New York: Garland, 1976–1978.

Harrison, Emily Haines. "Reminiscences of Early Days in Ottawa County." *Kansas Historical Collections*, 10 (1907–1908): 627–628.

Hunter, John Dunn. *Memoirs of a Captivity Among the Indians of North America*. 1824. Ed. Richard Drinnon. New York: Schocken Books, 1973.

Kelly, Fanny. *My Captivity Among the Sioux Indians*. Hartford, Conn.: Mutual Publishing, 1872. Reprinted Secaucus, N.J.: Citadel Press, 1973.

Lehmann, Herman. *Nine Years Among the Indians*. Ed. J. Marvin Hunter. Austin, Tex.: Van Boeckmann-Jones, 1927. Reprinted Albuquerque: University of New Mexico Press, 1993.

Lenski, Lois. *Indian Captive: The Story of Mary Jemison*. New York: Frederick A. Stokes, 1941. Reprinted Friday Harbor, Wash.: Turtleback, 1994.

Merrill, Arch. *The White Woman and Her Valley*. Interlaken, N.Y.: Empire State Books, 1987.

Methvin, Rev. J. J. *Andele, or the Mexican-Kiowa Captive*. Louisville, Ken.: Pentacostal Herald Press, 1899. Reprinted as *Andele, the Mexican-Kiowa Captive: A Story of Real Life Among the Indians*. Albuquerque: University of New Mexico Press, 1996.

Moore, Robin. *My Life with the Indians: The True Story of Mary Jemison*. 1988. Reprinted Parsippany, N.J.: Silver Burdett Press, 1998.

Nystel, Ole T. *Lost and Found; or Three Months with the Wild Indians*. Dallas, Texas: Willmans Brothers, 1888. Republished as *From Bondage to Freedom; or Three Months with Wild Indians*. Keen, Tex., 1930.

Parker, James W. *Narrative of the Perilous Adventures, Miraculous Escapes and Sufferings of Rev. James W. Parker, During a Frontier Residence in Texas, of Fifteen Years . . . to Which Is Added a Narrative of the Capture, and Subsequent Sufferings of Mrs. Rachel Plummer. . . .* Louisville, Ky.: 1844.

Pierce, Roy Harvey. "The Significances of the Captivity Narrative." *American Literature*, 19 (1947): 1–20.

Roop, Connie, and Peter Roop, eds. *In My Own Words: The Diary of Mary Jemison*. New York: Benchmark Books, 2000.

Rowlandson, Mary. *A True History of the Captivity & Restoration of Mrs. Mary Rowlandson*. London: Joseph Poole, 1682.

Ruster, Carl Coke. *Comanche Bondage: Beale's Settlement of La Villa De Dolores on Las Moras Creek in Southern Texas of the 1830's and Sarah Ann Horn's Narrative*. Lincoln: University of Nebraska Press, 1989.

Schultz, James Willard. *My Life as an Indian: The Story of a Red Woman and White Man in the Lodges of the Blackfeet*. New York: Doubleday, 1907. Reprinted New York: Corner House Historical Publications, 1996.

Seaver, James Everett. *Captured by Indians: The Life of Mary Jemison*. Ed. Karen Zeinert. North Haven, Conn.: Linnet Books, 1995.

———. *Deh-He-Wa-Mis: or, A Narrative of the Life of Mary Jemison*. Batavia, N.Y.: W. Seaver and Son, 1842. Reprinted Buffalo, N.Y.: Matthews and Warren, 1877; New York: Putnam's, 1898.

———. *The Life of Mary Jemison*. New York: C. M. Saxton, Barker and Co., 1860.

———. *A Narrative of the Life of Mrs. Mary Jemison*. Canandaigua, N.Y.: J. D. Bemis, 1824. Reprinted Howden, U.K.: R. Perkin, 1826; Buffalo, N.Y.: Matthews and Warren, 1877. Ed. Allen Trelease. New York: Corinth Books, 1961; reprinted Syracuse, N.Y.: Syracuse University Press, 1990.

Shields, James T. *Cynthia Ann Parker: The Story of Her Capture at the Massacre of the Inmates of Parker's Fort*. St. Louis: James T. Shields, 1886.

Smith, Derek G. *The Adventures and Sufferings of John R. Jewitt, While held as Captive Among the Nootka, Indians of Vancouver Island, 1803–1805*. Middletown, Conn.: Loomis and Richards, 1815. Reprinted Edinburgh: A. Constable, 1824; Ramona, Calif.: Ballena Press, 1975.

Smith, James. *Scoouwa: James Smith's Indian Captivity Narrative*. Columbus: Ohio Historical Society, 1978.

Slotkin, Richard. *Regeneration Through Violence: The Mythology of the American Frontier, 1600–1860*. New York: HarperCollins, 1996.

VanDerBeets, Richard, ed. *Held Captive by Indians: Selected Narratives, 1642–1836*. Knoxville: University of Tennessee Press, 1973; reprinted 1994.

Vaughan, Alden, and Daniel K. Richter. "Crossing the Cultural Divide: Indians and New Englanders, 1605–1763." *American Antiquarian Society Proceedings*, 90 (1980): 23–99.

Vaughan, Alden, and Edward W. Clark, eds. *Puritans Among the Indians: Accounts of Captivity and Redemption, 1676–1724*. Cambridge, Mass.: Harvard University Press, 1982.

Whalen, Will W. *The Red Lily of Buchanan Valley*. Orrtanna, Pa.: White Squaw Publishing, 1923.

Williams, Eleazer. *The Life of Te-ho-ra-gwa-ne-gen, alias Thomas Williams*. Albany, N.Y.: J. Munsell, 1859.

Horror/Supernatural

Barron, T. A. *The Ancient One*. New York: Tom Doherty Associates, 1992.

Bendell, Don. *Eagle*. New York: Signet, 1996.

Bird, Robert Montgomery. *Nick of the Woods*. Philadelphia, Pa.: Carey, Lee, and Blanchard, 1837.

Brown, Charles Brockden. *Edgar Huntly: Or the Memoirs of a Sleepwalker*. 1799. Reprinted New Haven, Conn.: College and University Press, 1973.

Dawson, Saranne. *Heart of the Wolf*. New York: Leisure Books, 1993.

Drake, Samuel. See under Historical Captivity Stories.

Flynn, Connie. *Shadow of the Wolf*. New York: Topaz, 1998.

———. *Shadow on the Moon*. New York: Topaz, 1997.

Gray, Muriel. *Trickster*. New York: St. Martin's Press, 1995.

Hackler, Micah. See under Detective Fiction.

Herbert, Frank. *Soul Catcher*. New York: Putnam's, 1973.

King, Stephen. *Pet Sematary*. New York: Doubleday, 1983.

————. *The Shining*. New York: Doubleday, 1977.

Lackey, Mercedes. See under Science Fiction.

L'Amour, Louis. *The Haunted Mesa*. New York: Bantam, 1987.

————. *The Lonesome Gods*. New York: Bantam, 1983.

Monteleone, Thomas F. *Night Things*. New York: Fawcett, 1980.

————. "Spare the Child." In *The Year's Best Horror Stories 11*. Ed. Karl Edward Wagner. New York: DAW, 1983.

————. "Wendigo's Child." In *Monster Tales*. Ed. Roger Elwood. Chicago: Rand McNally, 1973.

Murray, Earl. *Ghosts of the Old West*. New York: St. Martin's Press, 1997.

Owens, Louis. See under Native American Literature.

Roberts, James Hall. *The Burning Sky*. New York: Morrow, 1966.

Simms, William Gilmore. *The Cassique of Kiawah: A Colonial Romance*. New York: Redfield, 1859.

————. "The Two Camps." In *The Wigman and the Cabin*. New York: Wiley & Putnam, 1845.

————. *The Yemassee: A Romance of Carolina*. 1835. 2 vols. Reprinted New York: Harper & Brothers, 1853.

Smith, Martin Cruz. *Nightwing*. New York: Random House, 1977. (Duran)

Somtow, S. P. *Moon Dance*. New York: Tom Doherty Associates, 1989.

Stein, Garth. *Raven Stole the Moon*. New York: Simon and Schuster, 1988.

Stokes, Naomi. *The Listening Ones*. New York: Tom Doherty Associates, 1997. (Tidewater)

————. *The Tree People*. New York: Tom Doherty Associates, 1995. (Tidewater)

Strieber, Whitley. *The Wolfen*. New York: Morrow, 1978.

Thurlo, Aimée. See under Romance.

Weiner, Eric. *Heart of the Hunter*. New York: Simon and Schuster, 1997.

Native American Literature

Alexie, Sherman. *Indian Killer*. New York: Warner Books, 1998. (Spokane/Coeur d'Alene)

————. *The Lone Ranger and Tonto Fistfight in Heaven*. New York: Atlantic Monthly Press, 1993.

————. *Reservation Blues*. New York: Warner Books, 1995.

Allen, Paula Gunn. *A Cannon Between My Knees*. New York: Strawberry Press, 1981. (Laguna Pueblo/Sioux)

————. *Grandmothers of the Light: A Medicine Woman's Sourcebook*. Boston: Beacon Press, 1991. (nonfiction)

Armstrong, Jeanette. *Slash*. Penticton, B.C.: Theytus Books, 1985. (Okanogan)

Black Elk, Wallace, and William S. Lyon. *Black Elk: The Sacred Ways of the Lakota*. San Francisco: HarperSanFrancisco, 1990. (Black Elk-Oglala Lakota Sioux)

Bloom, Harold, ed. *Native American Women Writers*. Broomall, Pa.: Chelsea House, 1998.

Broker, Ignatia. *Night Flying Woman: An Ojibway Narrative*. St. Paul: Minnesota Historical Press, 1983. (Ojibway)

Bruchac, Joseph. *A Boy Called Slow: The True Story of Sitting Bull.* New York: Philomel Books, 1994. (Abenaki) (biography)

———. *Between Earth and Sky: Legends of Native American Sacred Places.* New York: Harcourt Brace, 1996.

———. *Dawn Land: A Novel.* Golden, Colo.: Fulcrum, 1992.

———. *Dog People: Native Dog Stories.* Golden, Colo.: Fulcrum, 1995.

———. *Long River: A Novel.* Golden, Colo.: Fulcrum, 1995. (sequel to *Dawn Land*)

———, ed. *Aniyunwiya/Real Human Beings: An Anthology of Contemporary Cherokee Prose.* Greenfield Center, N.Y.: Greenfield Review Press, 1995.

———, ed. *New Voices from the Longhouse: Anthology of Contemporary Iroquois Writing.* Greenfield Center, N.Y.: Greenfield Review Press, 1989.

———, ed. *Smoke Rising: The Native North American Literary Companion.* Detroit: Visible Ink Press, 1995.

———, ed. *When the Chenoo Howls; Native American Tales of Terror.* New York: Walker, 1999.

Bullchild, Percy. *American Indian Genesis.* Ulysses Press, 1985; 1998. (Blackfoot)

———. *The Sun Came Down.* San Francisco: Harper & Row, 1985.

Campbell, Maria. *Halfbreed.* Lincoln: University of Nebraska Press, 1982. (biography)

———. *Stories of the Road Allowance People.* Penticton, B.C.: Theytus Books, 1995. (Métis/Cree)

Carter, Forrest. *The Education of Little Tree.* New York: Delacorte Press, 1979. (Cherokee)

———. *Gone to Texas.* New York: Delacorte Press, 1975.

———. *Josey Wales: Two Westerns by Forrest Carter.* Albuquerque: University of New Mexico Press, 1986.

———. *The Outlaw Josey Wales.* New York: Delacorte Press, 1973.

———. *The Vengeance Trail of Josey Wales.* New York: Delacorte Press, 1976.

———. *Watch for Me on the Mountain.* New York: Delacorte Press, 1978. Reissued as *Cry Geronimo.* New York: Dell, 1980.

Conley, Robert J. *The Actor.* New York: Leisure Books, 1999. (Cherokee)

———. *Border Line.* New York: Pocket Books, 1993.

———. *Captain Dutch.* New York: Pocket Books, 1995.

———. *Colfax.* New York: Evans, 1989.

———. *Crazy Snake.* New York: Pocket Books, 1994.

———. *The Dark Island.* New York: Doubleday, 1995.

———. *Geronimo: An American Legend.* New York: Pocket Books, 1993. (biography)

———. *Go-ahead Rider.* New York: Evans, 1990.

———. *Incident at Buffalo Crossing.* New York: Dorchester, 1998.

———. *Killing Time.* New York: Evans, 1988.

———. *The Long Trail North.* New York: Pocket Books, 1993.

———. *Mountain Windsong: A Novel of the Trail of Tears.* Norman: University of Oklahoma Press, 1992.

———. *Ned Christie's War.* New York: Evans, 1991.

———. *Nickajack.* New York: Doubleday, 1992.

———. *Outside the Law.* New York: Pocket Books, 1995.

———. *Quitting Time.* New York: Evans, 1989.

———. The Real People series

#1 *The Way of the Priests.* New York: Doubleday, 1992.

#2 *Dark Way.* New York: Doubleday, 1993.

#3 *The White Path.* New York: Doubleday, 1993.

#4 *The Way South.* New York: Doubleday, 1993.

#5 *The Long Way Home.* New York: Doubleday, 1994.

#6 *Dark Island.* New York: Doubleday, 1995.

#7 *The War Trail North.* New York: Doubleday, 1995.

#8 *War Woman.* New York: St. Martin's Press, 1998.

#9 *The Peace Chief.* New York: St. Martin's Press, 1998.

————. *The Saga of Henry Starr.* New York: Doubleday, 1989.

————. *Strange Company.* New York: Pocket Books, 1991.

————. *To Make a Killing.* New York: Pocket Books, 1994.

————. *The Way of the Priests, The Dark Way, The White Path. Three Novels of the Real People.* New York: Quality Paperback Book Club, 1995.

————. *Wilder and Wilder.* New York: Pageant Books, 1988.

————. *The Witch of Goingsnake and Other Stories.* Norman: University of Oklahoma Press, 1988.

————. *Zeke Proctor: Cherokee Outlaw.* New York: Pocket Books, 1994.

Cook-Lynn, Elizabeth. *From the River's Edge.* New York: Arcade, 1991. (Lakota/Crow)

————. *The Power of Horses and Other Stories.* New York: Arcade, 1990.

Culleton, Beatrice. *In Search of April Raintree.* Winnipeg, Man.: Pemmican Publications, 1987. Reprinted Grand Forks, N.D.: Peguis Publications, 1992. (Métis)

————. *Spirit of the White Bison.* Winnipeg, Man.: Pemmican Publications, 1985; Summertown, Tenn.: Book Publishing, 1989.

Curtin, Jeremiah. *Creation Myths of Primitive America.* Boston: Little, Brown, 1898. Reprinted New York: B. Blom, 1969.

DeLoria, Ella Cara. *Buffalo People.* Albuquerque: University of New Mexico Press, 1994. (Yankton Sioux)

————. *Waterlily.* Lincoln: University of Nebraska Press, 1988.

Dorris, Michael. *Morning Girl.* New York: Hyperion Books for Children, 1992. (Modoc)

————. *A Yellow Raft in Blue Water.* New York: Holt, 1987.

Dorris, Michael, and Louise Erdrich. *Crown of Columbus.* New York: HarperCollins, 1991.

Downing, [George] Todd. *The Case of the Unconquered Sisters.* Garden City, N.Y.: Doubleday, 1936. (Choctaw)

————. *The Cat Screams.* Garden City, N.Y.: Doubleday, 1934.

————. *Death Under the Moonflower.* Garden City, N.Y.: Doubleday, 1938.

————. *The Last Trumpet: Murder in a Mexican Bull Ring.* Garden City, N.Y.: Doubleday, 1937.

————. *The Lazy Lawrence Murders.* New York: Doubleday, 1941.

————. *The Mexican Earth.* New York: Doubleday, 1940.

————. *Murder on the Tropic.* Garden City, N.Y.: Doubleday, 1935.

————. *Murder on Tour.* New York: Putnam's, 1933.

————. *Night over Mexico.* Garden City, N.Y.: Doubleday, 1937.

————. *Vultures in the Sky.* Garden City, N.Y.: Doubleday, 1935.

Erdoes, Richard, and Afonso Ortiz, eds. *American Indian Myths and Legends*. New York: Pantheon Books, 1984.

Erdrich, Louise. *Antelope Woman*. New York: HarperCollins, 1998. (Ojibway)

————. *Beet Queen*. New York: Henry Holt, 1986.

————. *Bingo Palace*. New York: HarperCollins, 1994.

————. "Fleur." In *New Worlds of Literature: Writings from America's Many Cultures*. Ed. Jerome Beaty and Paul Hunter. New York: W. W. Norton, 1994.

————. *Love Medicine*. New York: Henry Holt, 1984.

————. *Tracks*. New York: Henry Holt, 1988.

Gish, Robert Franklin. *Bad Boys and Black Sheep: Fateful Tales from the West*. Reno: University of Nevada Press, 1996. (Cherokee)

————. *Dreams of Quivira*. Santa Fe, N.M.: Clear Light, 1996.

————. *First Horses: Stories of the New West*. Reno: University of Nevada Press, 1993.

————. *When Coyote Howls: A Lavaland Tale*. Albuquerque: University of New Mexico Press, 1994.

Glancy, Diane. *Claiming Breath*. Lincoln: University of Nebraska Press, 1992. (Cherokee)

————. *Drystalks of the Moon*. Tulsa, Okla.: Hadassah Press, 1981.

————. *Firesticks: A Collection of Stories*. Norman: University of Oklahoma Press, 1993.

————. *Pushing the Bear: A Novel of the Trail of Tears*. San Diego: Harcourt Brace, 1996.

————. *Trigger Dance*. Boulder, Colo.: Fiction Collective Two, 1990.

————. *The West Pole*. Minneapolis: University of Minnesota Press, 1997.

Goodwill, Jean Cuthand. *John Tootoosis: Biography of a Cree Leader*. Ottawa: Golden Dog Press, 1982. (from Little Pine Reserve, Saskat)

Hale, Janet Campbell. *The Jailing of Cecelia Capture*. Albuquerque: University of New Mexico Press, 1987. (Coeur d'Alene)

————. *The Owl's Song*. Garden City, N.Y.: Doubleday, 1974.

Hogan, Linda. *Mean Spirit*. New York: Atheneum, 1990. (Chickasaw)

————. *Solar Storms*. New York: Scribner's, 1995.

Horn, Gabriel (White Deer of Autumn). *Native Heart: An American Indian Odyssey* (autobiography). San Rafael, Calif.: New World Library, 1993. (Wampanoag)

Johnston, Basil. *The Bear-Walker and Other Stories*. Toronto: Royal Ontario Museum, 1995. (Ojibway)

————. *The Manitous: The Spiritual World of the Ojibway*. New York: HarperCollins, 1995. (Folklore)

————. *Ojibway Ceremonies*. Toronto: McClelland and Stewart, 1987. (in Ojibway) Printed in English, Lincoln: University of Nebraska Press, 1990.

————. *Ojibway Tales*. Omaha: University of Nebraska Press, 1993. First published as *Moose Meat and Wild Rice*, 1978.

————. *The Star Man and Other Tales*. Toronto: University of Toronto Press, 1996.

King, Thomas. *Coyote Columbus*. Toronto: University of Toronto Press, 1992. (Blackfoot)

————. *Green Grass, Running Water*. Boston: Houghton Mifflin, 1993.

————. *Medicine River*. Markham, Ont.: Viking, 1990.

————, ed. *All My Relations: An Anthology of Contemporary Canadian Native Fiction*. Norman: University of Oklahoma Press, 1992.

Kingsolver, Barbara. *Animal Dreams*. New York: HarperCollins, 1990. (Cherokee)

———. *Pigs in Heaven*. New York: HarperCollins, 1993.

LaDuke, Winona. *Last Standing Woman*. Stillwater, Minn.: Voyageur Press, 1997. (Ojibway)

Maracle, Lee. *Ravensong*. Vancouver, B.C.: Press Gang, 1995.

———. *Sojourner's Truth*. Vancouver, B.C.: Press Gang, 1990.

———. *Sundogs: A Novel*. Penticton, B.C.: Theytus Books, 1992.

Markoosie. *Harpoon of the Hunter*. Montreal: McGill-Queen's University Press, 1970. (Inuit)

Marshall, Joseph III. *Winter of the Holy Iron*. Santa Fe, N.M.: Red Crane Books, 1994. (Lakota)

McLuhan, T. C., compiler. *Touch the Earth*. New York: Outerbridge and Dienstfrey, 1971.

McNickle, D'Arcy. *The Hawk Is Hungry and Other Stories*. Ed. Birgit Hans. Tucson: University of Arizona Press, 1992. (Cree/Salish/Kootenai)

———. *Runner in the Sun: A Story of Indian Maize*. New York: Holt, Rinehart & Winston, 1954.

———. *The Surrounded*. New York: Dodd, Mead, 1936.

———. *Wind from an Enemy Sky*. New York: Harper & Row 1978.

———, and Harold E. Fey. *Indians and Other Americans: Two Ways of Life Meet*. New York: Harper & Row, 1970.

Medawar, Mardi Oakley. *Death at Rainy Mountain*. New York: St. Martin's Press, 1996. (Eastern Band Cherokee) (mystery)

———. *The Misty Hills of Home*. New York: Dutton Signet, 1998. (romance)

———. *Murder at Medicine Lodge*. New York: St. Martin's Press, 1999. (mystery)

———. *People of the Whistling Waters*. Encampment, Wyo.: Affiliated Writers of America, 1993. Reprinted New York: Doubleday, 1997. (western)

———. *Remembering the Osage Kid*. New York: St. Martin's Press, 1997.

———. *The Witch of Palo Duro*. New York: St. Martin's Press, 1997. (mystery)

Momaday, N. Scott. *The Ancient Child*. New York: Doubleday, 1989. (Kiowa)

———. *Circle of Wonder: A Native American Christmas Story*. Santa Fe, N.M.: Clear Light, 1994.

———. *House Made of Dawn*. New York: Harper & Row, 1968.

———. *The Way to Rainy Mountain*. Tucson: University of Arizona Press, 1996.

Neihardt, John G., ed. *Black Elk Speaks*. New York: Morrow, 1932. Reprinted as *Black Elk Speaks. Being the Life Story of a Holy Man of the Oglala Sioux*. Lincoln, NE: University of Nebraska Press, 1979. (Black Elk—Oglala Lakota Sioux)

Northrup, Jim (Chibenashi). *The Rez Road Follies: Canoes, Casinos, Computers and Birch Bark Baskets*. Tokyo: Kodansha International, 1997. Reprinted Minneapolis: University of Minnesota Press, 1999. (Chippewa/Anishinaabe)

———. *Walking the Rez Road*. Stillwater, Minn.: Voyageur Press, 1993.

Ortiz, Simon J. *Fightin': New and Collected Stories*. Chicago: Thunder's Mouth Press, 1983. (Acoma Pueblo)

———. *Howbah Indians*. Tucson, Ariz.: Blue Moon Press, 1978.

———. *Men on the Moon; Collected Short Stories*. Tucson: University of Arizona Press, 1999.

———, ed. *Earth Power Coming: Short Fiction in Native American Literature*. Tsaile, Ariz.: Navajo Community College Press, 1983.

Owens, Louis. *Bone Game: A Novel*. Norman: University of Oklahoma Press, 1994. (Choctaw/Cherokeee)

————. *Dark River: A Novel*. Norman: University of Oklahoma Press, 1999.

————. *Mixed Blood Messages: Literature, Film, Family, Place*. Norman: University of Oklahoma Press, 1998.

————. *Nightland*. New York: Dutton NAL, 1996.

————. *Other Destinies: Understanding the American Indian Novel*. Norman: University of Oklahoma Press, 1994.

————. *The Sharpest Sight: A Novel*. Norman: University of Oklahoma Press, 1992.

————. *Wolfsong*. Norman: University of Oklahoma Press, 1995.

————, ed. *American Indian Novelists: An Annotated Critical Bibliography*. New York: Garland, 1985.

Power, Susan. *The Grass Dancer*. New York: Putnam's, 1994. (Standing Rock Sioux)

Querry, Ron. *The Death of Bernadette Lefthand*. Red Crane Books, 1993. (Sixtown Clan Choctaw)

Quintasket, Christine (Mourning Dove/Humishuma). *Coguwea: The Half-Blood, a Depiction of the Great Montana Cattle Range*. Caldwell, Idaho: Caxton Printers, 1927. Reprinted Lincoln: University of Nebraska Press, 1981. (Colville/Okanogan/Salish) (The first novel by an American Indian woman)

————. *Coyote Stories*. Caldwell, Idaho: Caxton Printers, 1933. Reprinted Lincoln: University of Nebraska Press, 1990.

Reid, Bill, and Robert Bringhurst. *The Raven Steals the Light*. Boston: Shambhala, 1996. (Haida)

Sarris, Greg. *Keeping Slug Woman Alive: A Holistic Approach to American Indian Texts*. Berkeley, Calif.: University of California Press, 1993. (Pomo/Miwak)

————. *Watermelon Nights*. New York: Hyperion, 1998.

————, ed. *The Sound of Rattles and Clappers: A Collection of New California Indian Writing*. Tucson: University of Arizona Press, 1994.

Seals, David. *Powwow Highway*. Sturgis, S.D.: Sky and Sage Books, 1979. Reprinted New York: Plume Press, 1990. (Huron)

————. *Sweet Medicine*. New York: Orion Books, 1992. (sequel)

————. *Thunder Nation*. Sturgis, S.D.: Sky and Sage Books, 1996.

Silko, Leslie Marmon. *Almanac of the Dead*. New York: Penguin Books, 1992. (Laguna Pueblo)

————. *Ceremony*. New York: Viking Press, 1977.

————. *Gardens in the Dunes*. New York: Simon and Schuster, 1997.

————. *Storyteller*. New York: Seaver/Arcade, 1981.

————. *Yellow Woman and Beauty of the Spirit: Essays on Native American Life Today*. New Brunswick, N.J.: Rutgers University Press, 1993.

Simon, Lorne. *Stones and Switches*. Penticton, B.C.: Theytus Books, 1994. (Mi'kmaqi)

Slipperjack, Ruby. *Honour the Sun*. Singing Shield Productions, 1986. Reprinted Winnipeg, Mann.: Pemmican, 1987. (Ojibway)

————. *Silent Words*. Saskatoon, Sask.: Fifth House, 1992.

Sneve, Virginia Driving Hawk. *The Chichi Hoohoo Bogeyman*. Lincoln: University of Nebraska Press, 1993. (Lakota Sioux)

————. *Jimmy Yellow Hawk*. New York: Holiday House, 1977.

Strete, Craig (Kee). *The Bleeding Man and Other Science Fiction Stories*. New York: Greenwillow, 1977. (Cherokee)

———. *Burn Down the Night.* New York: Warner Books, 1982.

———. *Dreams That Burn in the Night.* New York: Doubleday, 1982.

———. *If All Else Fails.* New York: Doubleday, 1980.

Swann, Brian, ed. *Coming to Light: Contemporary Translations of the Native Literatures of North America.* New York: Random House, 1996.

Ticasuk, Emily Ivanoff Brown. *The Longest Story Ever Told: Qayaq, the Magical Man.* Anchorage: Alaska Pacific University Press, 1981.

Trafzer, Clifford E. (as Richard Red Hawk). *Grandfather's Story of Navajo Monsters.* Sacramento, Calif.: Sierra Oaks, 1988. (Wyandot)

———, ed. *Blue Dawn, Red Earth: New Native American Storytellers.* New York: Anchor Books, 1996. (Craig S. Womack, "The Witches of Eufaula, Oklahoma"; Annie Hansen, "Spirit Curse")

———. *Earth Song, Sky Spirit: Short Stories of the Contemporary Native American Experience.* New York: Doubleday, 1992. (Gerald Vizenor, "The Moccasin Game"; LeAnne Howe, "Danse d'Amour, Danse de Mort"; Joseph Bruchac, "Bone Girl"; Craig Womack, "Lucy, Oklahoma, 1911")

Trout, Lawana, ed. *Native American Literature: An Anthology.* Lincolnwood, Ill.: NTC Publishing Group, 1999. (John Bierhorst, "The Vampire Skeleton Onondaga Story"; Louis Owens, "Soul-catcher")

Vizenor, Gerald Robert. *Bearheart: The Heirship Chronicles.* Minneapolis: University of Minnesota Press, 1990. (Choctaw)

———. *Darkness in Saint Louis: Bearheart.* St. Paul, Minn.: Track Press, 1973.

———. *Dead Voices: Natural Agonies in the New World.* Norman: University of Oklahoma Press, 1992.

———. *Earthdivers: Tribal Narratives on Mixed Descent.* Minneapolis: University of Minnesota Press, 1981.

———. *Griever: An American Monkey King in China.* New York: Fiction Collective, 1987.

———. *The Heirs of Columbus.* Hanover, N.H.: Wesleyan University Press/University Press of New England, 1991.

———. *Hotline Healers: An Almost Browne Novel.* Hanover, N.H.: University Press of New England, 1997.

———. *Shadow Distance: A Gerald Vizenor Reader.* Hanover, N.H.: University Press of New England, 1994.

———. *The Trickster of Liberty: Tribal Heirs to a Wild Baronage.* Minneapolis: University of Minnesota Press, 1988.

———. *Wordarrows: Indians and Whites in the Fur Trade.* Minneapolis: University of Minnesota Press, 1978.

———, and Ishmael Reed, eds. *Native American Literature: A Brief Introduction and Anthology.* New York: HarperCollins, 1995.

Walters, Anna Lee. *Ghost Singer.* Albuquerque: University of New Mexico Press, 1988. (Pawnee/Oto)

———. *The Sun Is Not Merciful.* Ithaca, N.Y.: Firebrand Books, 1985.

———, ed. *Neon Pow-wow: New Native American Voices of the Southwest.* Flagstaff, Ariz.: Northland, 1993.

Weeks, Rupert. *Pachee Goyo: History and Legends from the Shoshone.* Laramie, Wyo.: Jelm Mountain Press, 1981. (Shoshone)

Welch, James. *Confluence*. Ed. Ron McFarland. Lewiston Idaho Confluence Press, 1986.
(Blackfeet/Gros Ventre)

———. *The Death of Jim Loney*. New York: Harper & Row, 1979.

———. *Fool's Crow*. New York: Harper & Row, 1986.

———. *The Indian Lawyer*. New York: W. W. Norton, 1990.

———. *Killing Custer: The Battle of the Little Bighorn and the Fate of the Plains
Indians*. New York: W. W. Norton, 1994.

———. *Winter in the Blood*. New York: Harper & Row, 1974.

Wheeler, Jordan. *Brothers in Arms*. Winnipeg, Man.: Pemmican, 1989. (Cree/Ojibway)

Winnie, Lucille Jerry. *Sah-Gan-De-Oh: The Chief's Daughter*. New York: Vantage Press,
1969. (Seneca/Cayuga)

Young Bear, Ray. *Remnants of the First Earth*. New York: Grove/Atlantic, 1997. (Mes-
quakie Fox)

Youyouseyah, and Tawa Mana. *When Hopi Children Were Bad: A Monster Story*. Sacramento, Calif.: Sierra Oaks, 1989. (Hopi/Tewa)

Zithala-Sa (Gertrude Bonnin). *American Indian Stories*. Omaha: University of Nebraska
Press, 1985. (Dakota Sioux)

New Age

Andrews, Lynn V. *Flight of the Seventh Moon*. New York: HarperCollins, 1984.

———. *Jaguar Woman*. New York: HarperCollins, 1985.

———. *Medicine Woman*. New York: Harper & Row, 1981.

———. *Star Woman*. New York: Warner Books, 1986.

Castañeda, Carlos. *The Fire from Within*. New York: Simon and Schuster, 1991.

———. *Journey to Ixtlan: The Lessons of Don Juan*. New York: Simon and Schuster,
1991.

———. *A Separate Reality: Further Conversations with Don Juan*. New York: Simon
and Schuster, 1991.

———. *Tales of Power*. New York: Simon and Schuster, 1991.

———. *The Teachings of Don Juan: A Yaqui Way of Knowledge*. Los Angeles: University of California Press, 1968.

———, and Florinda Donner-Grau. *The Witches' Dream: A Healer's Way of Knowledge*.
New York: Simon and Schuster, 1997.

Hughes-Calero, Heather. *Circle of Power*. Cottonwood, Ariz.: Higher Consciousness
Books, 1993.

———. *Demystifying Shamanism*. Cottonwood, Ariz.: Higher Consciousness Books,
1996.

———. *Dialogues with a Shaman Teacher: Into the Silence*. Cottonwood, Ariz.: Higher
Consciousness Books, 1996.

———. *The Flight of Winged Wolf*. Cottonwood, Ariz.: Higher Consciousness Books,
1991.

———. *The Sedona Trilogy*: Book 1, *Through the Crystal*; Book 2, *Doorways between
the Worlds*; Book 3, *Land of Nome*. Cottonwood, Ariz.: Higher Consciousness
Books, 1990.

———. *Woman Between the Wind; The Power of Resistance; An Eagle's Viewpoint of a Shaman's Entry Through the First Door*. Cottonwood, Ariz.: Higher Consciousness Books, 1990.

Lackey, Mercedes. See under Science Fiction.

Rain, Mary Summer. *Spirit Song*. Norfolk, Va.: Hampton Roads, 1985.

Steiger, Brad. *American Indian Medicine Dream Book*. New York: Schiffer, 1997.

Twofeathers, Manny. *The Road to Sundance: My Journey into Native Spirituality*. New York: Hyperion, 1997.

Romance

Archer, Jane. *Out of the West*. New York: Simon and Schuster, 1996.

Archibald, Catherine. *Hawk's Lady*. New York: Dorchester, 1997.

Baker, Jeanette. *The Reckoning*. New York: Kensington, 1997.

Baker, Madeline. *Apache Flame*. New York: Dorchester, 1999.

———. *Apache Runaway*. New York: Dorchester, 1995.

———. *Chase the Wind*. New York: Dorchester, 1996.

———. *Cheyenne Surrender*. New York: Dorchester, 1996.

———. *Comanche Flame*. New York: Dorchester, 1996.

———. *Feather in the Wind*. New York: Dorchester, 1997.

———. *First Love, Wild Love*. New York: Dorchester, 1994.

———. *Forbidden Fires*. New York: Dorchester, 1996.

———. *Hawk's Woman*. New York: Topaz Dutton, 1998.

———. *Lacey's Way*. New York: Dorchester, 1990.

———. *Lakota Renegade*. New York: Dorchester, 1995.

———. *Love Forevermore*. New York: Dorchester, 1997.

———. *Love in the Wind*. New York: Dorchester, 1997.

———. *Midnight Fire*. New York: Dorchester, 1992.

———. *Prairie Heat*. New York: Dorchester, 1991.

———. *Reckless Desire*. New York: Dorchester, 1995.

———. *Reckless Heart*. New York: Dorchester, 1995.

———. *Reckless Love*. New York: Dorchester, 1995.

———. *Renegade Heart*. New York: Dorchester, 1996.

———. *The Spirit Path*. New York: Dorchester, 1996.

———. *Spirit's Song*. New York: Dorchester, 1999.

———. *Under a Prairie Moon*. New York: Dorchester, 1998.

———. *Warrior's Lady*. New York: Dorchester, 1997.

———. *A Whisper in the Wind*. New York: Dorchester, 1991.

Barbieri, Elaine. *Captive Ecstasy*. New York: Dorchester, 1981, 1997.

———. *Dangerous Virtues: Purity*. New York: Dorchester, 1997.

———. *Eagle*. New York: Leisure Books, 1999.

———. *Untamed Captive*. New York: Dorchester, 1987.

Barton, Beverly. *Lone Wolf's Lady*. New York: Silhouette, 1998.

Bennett, Constance. *Moonsong*. New York: Harlequin, 1992.

Bird, Beverly. *A Man Without a Wife*. New York: Jove, 1995.

———. *The Pony Wife*. New York: Jove, 1995.

———. *Touch the Sun*. New York: Jove, 1994.

———. *Walk into the Night*. New York: Kensington, 1996.

Bishop, Sandra. *Beloved Savage*. New York: Kensington, 1990.

Bittner, Rosanne. *Comanche Sunset*. New York: Kensington, 1994.

———. *Indian Summer*. New York: Forge, 1995.

———. *Mystic Dreamers*. New York: Forge, 1999.

———. Savage Destiny series

  #1 *Sweet Prairie Passion*. New York: Kensington, 1988; reprinted 1996.

  #2 *Ride the Free Wind*. New York: Kensington, 1989.

  #3 *River of Love*. New York: Kensington, 1990; reprinted 1996.

  #4 *Embrace the Wild Land*. New York: Kensington, 1991; reprinted 1996.

  #5 *Climb the Highest Mountain*. New York: Kensington, 1992.

  #6 *Meet the New Dawn*. New York: Kensington, 1986.

  #7 *The Eagle's Song*. New York: Kensington, 1997.

———. *Savage Horizons*. New York: Kensington, 1987.

———. *Sioux Splendor*. New York: Kensington, 1995.

———. *Song of the Wolf*. New York: Doubleday, 1991.

———. *Tame the Wild Wind*. New York: Doubleday, 1996.

———. *Thunder on the Plains*. New York: Doubleday, 1992.

Blacke, Veronica. *Sioux Sunrise*. New York: Dutton NAL, 1994.

Brooks, Betty. *Comanche Sunset*. New York: Kensington, 1998.

———. *Warrior's Destiny*. New York: Kensington, 1995. (Vikings meet Native Americans)

Brown, Dee. *Creek Mary's Blood*. New York: Holt, Rinehart and Winston, 1980.

Brown, Sandra. *Honor Bound*. New York: Silhouette, 1986.

Camp, Deborah. *Cheyenne's Shadow*. New York: Avon, 1994.

———. *Lone Wolf's Woman*. New York: Avon, 1995.

Carr, Bernadette. *A Woman's Touch*. New York: Dorchester, 1998.

Dailey, Janet. *Legacies*. New York: Warner Books, 1995.

———. *Night Way*. New York: Pocket Books, 1981.

———. *The Proud and the Free*. New York: Warner Books, 1994.

———. *Ride the Thunder*. New York: Pocket Books, 1980.

Darnell, Berde. *Passion's Whisper*. New York: Kensington, 1987.

Dellin, Genell. *After the Thunder*. New York: Avon, 1998. (Choctaw trilogy)

———. *Cherokee Dawn*. New York: Avon, 1990. (Cherokee trilogy)

———. *Cherokee Nights*. New York: Avon, 1991. (Cherokee trilogy)

———. *Cherokee Sundown*. New York: Avon, 1992. (Cherokee trilogy)

———. *Comanche Flame*. New York: Avon, 1994. (Comanche trilogy)

———. *Comanche Rain*. New York: Avon, 1995. (Comanche trilogy)

———. *Comanche Wind*. New York: Avon, 1993. (Comanche trilogy)

———. *Passion's Storm*. New York: Avon, 1995.

———. *Red Sky Warrior*. New York: Avon, 1996. (Choctaw trilogy)

———. *The Renegades*. New York: Avon, 1999.

———. *Silver Moon Song*. New York: Avon, 1996. (Choctaw trilogy)

———. *Tame the Wild Wind*. New York: Avon, 1995.

Dillon, Catherine. *Beloved Prisoner*. New York: New American Library, 1980.

Donnell, Susan. *Pocahontas*. New York: Berkley, 1991.

Drymon, Kathleen. *Blaze of Desire*. New York: Kensington, 1999.
———. *Gentle Savage*. New York: Kensington, 1990.
———. *Legend of Desire*. New York: Kensington, 1998.
———. *Savage Heaven*. New York: Kensington, 1990.
———. *Velvet Savage*. New York: Kensington, 1989.
———. *Warrior of the Sun*. New York: Kensington, 1992.
Duquette, Anne Marie. *In the Arms of the Law*. New York: Harlequin, 1997.
Eagle, Kathleen. *Carved in Stone*. New York: Silhouette, 1987.
———. *Dream Catchers*. New York: Harlequin, 1996.
———. *Fire and Rain*. New York: Avon, 1994.
———. *The Last True Cowboy*. New York: Avon, 1998.
———. *Medicine Woman*. New York: Harlequin, 1989.
———. *The Night Remembers*. New York: Avon, 1997.
———. *Reason to Believe*. New York: Avon, 1995.
———. *Sunrise Song*. New York: Avon, 1996.
———. *This Time Forever*. New York: Avon, 1992.
———. *What the Heart Knows*. New York: Avon, 1999.
Edwards, Cassie. *Bold Wolf*. New York: Topaz/Dutton Signet, 1998.
———. *Enchanted Enemy*. New York: Zebra, 1988.
———. *Flaming Arrow*. New York: Topaz/Dutton Signet, 1997.
———. *Lone Wolf*. New York: Topaz/Dutton Signet, 1998.
———. *Rolling Thunder*. New York: Topaz/Dutton Signet, 1996.
———. The Savage series

Savage Bliss. New York: Jove, 1991; reprinted 1997.

Savage Dance. New York: Jove, 1991; reprinted 1997.

Savage Dream. New York: Jove, 1991; reprinted 1997.

Savage Eden. New York: Dorchester, 1996.

Savage Embers. New York: Dorchester, 1994.

Savage Heat. New York: Dorchester, 1998.

Savage Heart. New York: Zebra, 1985.

Savage Illusion. New York: Dorchester, 1993.

Savage Innocence. New York: Dorchester, 1997.

Savage Longings. New York: Dorchester, 1997.

Savage Mists. New York: Dorchester, 1992.

Savage Obsession. New York: Zebra, 1985; reprinted 1997.

Savage Paradise. New York: Zebra, 1987.

Savage Passions. New York: Dorchester, 1996.

Savage Persuasion. New York: Dorchester, 1993.

Savage Pride. New York: Dorchester, 1995.

Savage Promise. New York: Dorchester, 1992; reprinted 1995.

Savage Secrets. New York: Dorchester, 1995.

Savage Shadows. New York: Dorchester, 1996.

Savage Spirit. New York: Dorchester, 1994.

Savage Splendor. New York: Dorchester, 1996.

Savage Sunrise. New York: Dorchester, 1993.

Savage Surrender. New York: Dorchester, 1996.

Savage Tears. New York: Dorchester, 1997.

Savage Torment. New York: Dorchester, 1997.

Savage Whispers. New York: Jove, 1989.

Savage Wonder. New York: Dorchester, 1999.

———. *Silver Wing.* New York: Topaz/Dutton Signet, 1999.
———. *Touch the Wild Wind.* New York: Dorchester, 1993.
———. *White Fire.* New York: Topaz/Dutton Signet, 1997.
———. The Wild series

Wild Abandon. New York: Topaz/Dutton Signet, 1994.

Wild Bliss. New York: Topaz/Dutton Signet, 1995.

Wild Desire. New York: Topaz/Dutton Signet, 1994.

Wild Ecstasy. New York: Topaz/Dutton Signet, 1992.

Wild Embrace. New York: Topaz/Dutton Signet, 1993.

Wild Rapture. New York: Topaz/Dutton Signet, 1992.

Wild Splendor. New York: Topaz/Dutton Signet, 1993.

Wild Thunder. New York: Topaz/Dutton Signet, 1995.

Wild Whispers. New York: Topaz/Dutton Signet, 1996.

Edwards, Susan. *White Flame.* New York: Dorchester, 1998.
———. *White Wolf.* New York: Dorchester, 1999.
Faraday, Tess. *Blue Rain.* New York: Berkley, 1999.
Faulkner, Colleen. *Captive.* New York: Kensington, 1994.
———. *Fire Dancer.* New York: Kensington, 1997.
———. *Flames of Love.* New York: Kensington, 1993.
———. *Savage Surrender.* New York: Kensington, 1992.
Finch, Carol. *Apache Knight.* New York: Zebra, 1994.
———. *Apache Wind.* New York: Zebra, 1993.
———. *Captive Bride.* New York: Zebra, 1987.
———. *Cheyenne Moon.* New York: Zebra, 1999.
———. *Comanche Promise.* New York: Kensington, 1998.
Ford, Jessie. *A Different Breed.* New York: Random House, 1988.
Fox, Kathryn. *Bright Morning Star.* New York: Zebra, 1998.
French, Judith E. *Fire Hawk's Bride.* New York: Avon, 1997.
———. *Moon Dancer.* New York: Avon, 1991.
———. *Moonfeather.* New York: Avon, 1990.
———. *Shawnee Moon.* New York: Avon, 1995.
———. *Sundancer's Woman.* New York: Avon, 1996.
———. *Windsong.* New York: Avon, 1988.
Gayle, Roberta. *Sunshine and Shadows.* New York: Pinnacle/Arabesque, 1995. (Black/Ute)

Gentry, Georgina. *Apache Caress*. New York: Zebra, 1991.

———. *Apache Tears*. New York: Zebra, 1999.

———. *Cheyenne Captive*. New York: Zebra, 1987; reprinted 1994.

———. *Cheyenne Caress*. New York: Zebra, 1986.

———. *Cheyenne Princess*. New York: Zebra, 1987.

———. *Cheyenne Song*. New York: Zebra, 1998.

———. *Cheyenne Splendor*. New York: Zebra, 1994.

———. *Comanche Cowboy*. New York: Zebra, 1988.

———. *Half-breed's Bride*. New York: Zebra, 1993.

———. *Nevada Dawn*. New York: Zebra, 1993.

———. *Quicksilver Passion*. New York: Zebra, 1990.

———. *Sioux Slave*. New York: Zebra, 1992.

———. *Song of the Warrior*. New York: Zebra, 1995.

———. *Timeless Warrior*. New York: Zebra, 1996.

———. *Warrior's Prize*. New York: Zebra, 1997.

Gluyas, Constance. *The Passionate Savage*. New York: New American Library, 1980.

Hallam, Elizabeth. *Spirit Catcher*. New York: Jove, 1998.

Harrington, Kathleen. The Dream Seekers trilogy

Warrior Dreams. New York: Avon, 1992.

Dream Catcher. New York: Avon, 1996.

Fly with the Eagle. New York: Avon, 1997.

Hart, Catherine. *Charmed*. New York: Kensington, 1996.

———. *Night Flame*. New York: Dorchester, 1995.

———. *Silken Savage*. New York: Dorchester, 1985.

———. *Summer Storm*. New York: Dorchester, 1987.

Hawkins, Paul A. *Crow Feather*. New York: Signet, 1995.

Hill, Sandra. *Sweeter Savage Love*. New York: Dorchester, 1997.

Hudson, Janis Reams. The Apache series

Apache Flame. New York: Zebra, 1996.

Apache Heartsong. New York: Zebra, 1996.

Apache Legacy. New York: Zebra, 1994.

Apache Magic. New York: Zebra, 1991; reissued 1999.

Apache Promise. New York: Zebra, 1992; reissued 1999.

Apache Temptation. New York: Zebra, 1993; reissued 1995, 1996.

———. *Hawk's Woman*. New York: Zebra, 1998.

———. *Warrior's Song*. New York: Zebra, 1996.

———. *Winter's Touch*. New York: Zebra, 1999.

Jackson, Helen Hunt. *Ramona*. 1884. Reprinted New York: Avon, 1984.

Johnston, Joan. *Comanche Woman*. New York: Simon & Schuster, 1989.

Kay, Karen. *Gray Hawk's Lady*. New York: Avon, 1997.

———. *Lakota Princess*. New York: Avon, 1995.

———. *Lakota Surrender*. New York: Avon, 1994.

———. *Night Thunder's Bride*. New York: Avon, 1999.

————. *Proud Wolf's Woman*. New York: Avon, 1996.

————. *White Eagle's Touch*. New York: Avon, 1998.

Kitzmiller, Chelley. *Embrace the Wind*. New York: Topaz/Dutton, 1997.

————. *Fires of Heaven*. New York: Topaz/Dutton, 1994.

Lane, Elizabeth. *Apache Fire*. New York: Harlequin, 1998.

Langen, Ruth. *Malachite*. New York: Harlequin, 1998.

Lanzoni, Fabio, with Eugenia Riley. *Comanche*. New York: Avon, 1995.

Layton, Edith. *The Indian Maiden*. New York: Signet, 1995.

London, Cait. *The Cowboy and the Cradle*. New York: Silhouette, 1996.

————. *The Groom Candidate*. New York: Silhouette, 1998.

————. *The Seduction of Fiona Tallchief*. New York: Silhouette, 1998.

————. *The Seduction of Jake Tallchief*. New York: Silhouette, 1995.

————. *Tallchief's Bride*. New York: Silhouette, 1994.

————. *Tallchief for Keeps*. New York: Silhouette, 1997.

Lowell, Elizabeth. *Warrior*. New York: Harlequin, 1991; reprinted 1999.

Mason, Connie. *A Promise of Thunder*. New York: Dorchester, 1996.

————. *Shadow Walker*. New York: Dorchester, 1997.

————. *Wind Rider*. New York: Dorchester, 1995.

Macdonald, Elisabeth. *Bring Down the Sun*. New York: Avon, 1996.

McCall, Dinah. *Dreamcatcher*. New York: HarperCollins, 1996.

————. *Legend*. New York: HarperCollins, 1998.

————. *Tall-Chief*. New York: HarperCollins, 1997.

McCarthy, Candace. *Heaven's Fire*. New York: Zebra, 1995.

————. *Warrior's Caress*. New York: Kensington, 1996.

————. *White Bear's Woman*. New York: Zebra, 1997.

Merritt, Emma F. *Autumn's Fury*. New York: Kensington, 1989.

Mills, Anita. *Comanche Moon*. New York: Topaz, 1995.

O'Banyon, Constance. *Dakota Dreams*. New York: Kensington, 1988.

————. *Savage Autumn*. New York: Kensington, 1988.

————. *Savage Desire*. New York: Kensington, 1983.

————. *Savage Splendor*. New York: Kensington, 1983.

————. *Savage Spring*. New York: Kensington, 1986.

————. *Savage Summer*. New York: Kensington, 1986.

————. *Savage Winter*. New York: Kensington, 1988.

Orwig, Sara. *Comanche Temptation*. New York: Kensington, 1996.

————. *Warrior Moon*. New York: Kensington, 1995.

Palmer, Diana. *The Savage Heart*. New York: Fawcett, 1997.

Pelton, Sonya. *Heavensent*. New York: Kensington, 1995.

Riefe, Barbara. *For Love of Two Eagles*. New York: Tom Doherty Associates, 1996.

————. *Mohawk Woman*. New York: Tom Doherty Associates, 1995.

————. *The Woman Who Fell from the Sky*. New York: Tom Doherty Associates, 1995.

Ronander, Jane. *Warrior's Heart*. New York: Simon and Schuster, 1997.

Ross, Dana Fuller. *Wyoming!* New York: Thorndike Press, 1979.

Ross, David William. *Beyond the Stars*. New York: Avon, 1990.

Sanders, Leonard. *Light on the Mountain*. New York: Bantam, 1986.

Sandifer, Linda. *Embrace the Wind*. New York: Kensington, 1993.

Scott, Fela Dawson. *Black Wolf*. New York: Dorchester, 1994.

————. *Ghost Dancer*. New York: Dorchester, 1992.

———. *Spirit of the Mountain*. New York: Dorchester, 1995.

Scott, Theresa. *Apache Conquest*. New York: Dorchester, 1996.

———. *Captive Legacy*. New York: Dorchester, 1996.

———. *Savage Betrayal*. New York: Dorchester, 1996.

———. *Savage Revenge*. New York: Dorchester, 1997.

Smith, Bobbi. *Half-Breed's Lady*. New York: Dorchester, 1998.

———. *Renegade's Lady*. New York: Dorchester, 1997.

Sommerfield, Sylvie. *Captive Embrace*. New York: Kensington, 1986.

———. *Night Walker*. New York: Kensington, 1998.

———. *Savage Rapture*. New York: Kensington, 1982.

Taylor, Janelle. *Chase the Wind*. New York: Kensington, 1994.

———. Ecstasy Saga (based on the lives and loves of Lakota warrior Gray Eagle, his white wife Alisha Williams, and their heirs, 1776–1873)

    Bittersweet Ecstasy. New York: Kensington, 1987; reissued 1992.

    Brazen Ecstasy. New York: Kensington, 1983; reissued 1991.

    Defiant Ecstasy. New York: Kensington, 1982; reissued 1991.

    Endless Ecstasy. New York: Kensington, 1988.

    Forbidden Ecstasy. New York: Kensington, 1982; reissued 1991.

    Forever Ecstasy. New York: Kensington, 1991.

    Savage Ecstasy. New York: Kensington, 1981; reissued 1991.

    Stolen Ecstasy. New York: Kensington, 1985; reissued 1992.

    Tender Ecstasy. New York: Kensington, 1983; reissued 1991.

———. *First Love, Wild Love*. New York: Kensington, 1984; reissued 1992.

———. *Follow the Wind*. New York: Kensington, 1991.

———. *Lakota Winds*. New York: Kensington, 1998.

———. *Savage Conquest*. New York: Kensington, 1985; reissued 1992.

———. *Sweet Savage Heart*. New York: Kensington, 1986; reissued 1998.

Thompson, Victoria. *Winds of Destiny*. New York: Kensington, 1993.

Thurlo, Aimée. *Black Mesa*. New York: Harlequin, 1990.

———. *Breach of Faith*. New York: Harlequin, 1992.

———. *Cisco's Woman*. New York: Harlequin, 1996.

———. *Expiration Date*. New York: Harlequin, 1989.

———. *Fatal Charm*. New York: Harlequin, 1995.

———. Four Winds trilogy

    Her Destiny. New York: Harlequin, 1997.

    Her Hero. New York: Harlequin, 1996.

    Her Shadow. New York: Harlequin, 1998.

———. *Shadow of the Wolf*. New York: Harlequin, 1993.

———. *Spirit Warrior*. New York: Harlequin, 1993.

———. *Strangers Who Linger*. New York: Harlequin, 1991.

———. *Suitable for Framing*. New York: Harlequin, 1990.

Van Every, Dale. *Bridal Journey*. New York: Simon and Schuster, 1950.

Vaughan, Vivian. *Chance of a Lifetime*. New York: Kensington, 1999.

Warfield, Teresa. *Cherokee Bride*. New York: Jove, 1994.

Wilde, Lauren. *Beloved Captive*. New York: Kensington, 1997.

Wimberly, Clara. *Cherokee Wind*. New York: Kensington, 1997.

Wyan, Michele. *Night Singer*. New York: Kensington, 1995.

Science Fiction

Arnason, Eleanor. *A Woman of the Iron People*. New York: William Morrow, 1991.

Becko, Peggy. *The Winged Warrior*. New York: Doubleday, 1977.

Benét, Stephen Vincent. *By the Waters of Babylon*. 1898. Reprinted Mankato: The Creative Co., 1990.

Broxon, Mildred. "Walk the Ice." In *The Best Science Fiction of the Year 11*. Ed. Terry Carr. New York: Pocket Books, 1982.

Canter, Mark. *Ember from the Sun*. New York: Bantam Doubleday, 1996.

Crowley, John. *Engine Summer*. New York: Doubleday, 1979.

Darney, Arsen. *The Karma Affair*. New York: St. Martin's Press, 1978.

Edmonson, G. C. *The Aluminum Man*. New York: Berkley, 1975.

———. *Chapayeca*. New York: Doubleday, 1971.

Fast, Howard. "The Mohawk." In *Time and the Riddle: Thirty-One Zen Stories*. Pasadena, Calif.: Ward Ritchie Press, 1975.

Green, Sharon. *The Warrior Within*. New York: Daw Books, 1982.

Haldeman, Jack Carroll, and Jack Dann. *High Steel*. New York: Tom Doherty Associates, 1993.

Haldeman, Jack, with Jack Dann. "High Steel," in *Fantasy and Science Fiction* (February 1982).

Huxley, Aldous. *Brave New World*. London: Chatto and Windus; New York: Doubleday, 1932.

Ing, Dean. *Anasazi*. New York: Ace, 1980.

Jones, Douglas C. *The Court-Martial of George Armstrong Custer*. New York: Scribner's, 1976.

Lackey, Mercedes. *Burning Water*. New York: Tom Doherty Associates, 1989.

———. *Sacred Ground*. New York: Tom Doherty Associates, 1994.

LeGuin, Ursula K. *Always Coming Home*. New York: Harper & Row, 1985.

McIntyre, Vonda Neel. *Superluminal*. Boston: Houghton Mifflin, 1983. (expanded version of her short story "Aztec")

McQuinn, Donald E. *Warrior*. New York: Ballantine, 1990.

Nasnaga. *Indian's Summer*. New York: Harper & Row, 1975.

Norman, John. *Ghost Dance*. New York: Ballantine, 1970.

Norton, Andre. *The Beast Master*. New York: Harcourt Brace, 1959.

———. *Defiant Agents*. Cleveland, Ohio: World, 1962.

———. *Galactic Derelict*. Cleveland, Ohio: World, 1959.

———. *Key Out of Time*. Cleveland, Ohio: World, 1963.

———. *Lord of Thunder*. New York: Harcourt Brace, 1962.

———. *The Sioux Spaceman*. New York: Ace, 1960.

———. *Star Gate*. New York: Harcourt Brace, 1958.

———. *The Time Traders*. Cleveland, Ohio: World, 1958.

Page, Jake. *Apacheria: An Epic of Alternate History*. New York: Random House, 1998.

Rotsler, William. *The Far Frontier*. New York: Playboy Press, 1980.

Silverberg, Robert. "Sundance." In his *Sundance and Other Science Fiction Stories*. Nashville, Tenn.: Thomas Nelson, 1974.

Smith, Martin Cruz. *The Indians Won*. New York: Nordon, 1962.

Starhawk. *The Fifth Sacred Thing*. New York: Bantam, 1993.

Stewart, George Rippey. *Earth Abides*. New York: Random House, 1949.

Sucharitkul, Somtow. *The Aquiliad*. New York: Pocket Books, 1983.

Utley, Steven, with Howard Waldrop. "Custer's Last Jump." In *Universe 6*. Ed. Terry Carr. New York: Doubleday, 1976.

Verrill, Alpheus Hyatt. *The Trail of the White Indians*. New York: Dutton, 1920. (for children)

Watson, Ian. *The Martian Inca*. New York: Ace, 1978.

Williams, Paul. *An Ambush of Shadows*. New York: Ballantine, 1983.

———. *The Breaking of Northwall*. New York: Ballantine, 1981.

———. *The Dome in the Forest*. New York: Ballantine, 1981.

———. *The Ends of the Circle*. New York: Ballantine, 1981.

———. *The Fall of the Shell*. New York: Ballantine, 1982.

———. *The Song of the Axe*. New York: Ballantine, 1984.

Western

Adams, Gerald Drayson. *Son of the Sioux*. New York: Tower, 1981.

Allen, Henry. *The Apache Kid*. New York: Bantam, 1961. (originally *El Niño*, as Clay Fisher)

———. *Chiricahau*. New York: Lippincott, 1972. (as Will Henry)

———. *Warbonnet*. New York: Bantam, 1952. (as Clay Fisher)

Andrews, Patrick. E. *Blood of Apache Mesa*. New York: Kensington, 1988.

Arnold, Elliott. *Blood Brother*. New York: Hawthorn, 1953; University of Nebraska Press, 1979.

———. *Broken Arrow*. New York: Hawthorn, 1954.

———. *The Camp Grant Massacre*. New York: Simon and Schuster, 1976.

Ballas, Jack. *Apache Blanco*. New York: Berkley, 1994.

———. *Tomahawk Canyon*. New York: Berkley, 1992.

Barry, Jane. *A Time in the Sun*. 1929. New York: Doubleday, 1962.

Bean, Frederic. *Rivers West: Pecos River*. New York: Doubleday, 1995.

Bellah, James. *The Apache*. New York: Fawcett, 1951.

———. *Massacre*. New York: Lion, 1950.

———. *A Thunder of Drums*. New York: Bantam, 1961.

Bendell, Don. *Blazing Colts*. New York: Signet, 1999.

———. *Chief of Scouts*. New York: Signet, 1993.

———. *Colt*. New York: Signet, 1994. (*Chief of Scouts*, vol. 3)

———. *Coyote Run*. New York: Signet, 1994.

———. *Horse Soldiers*. New York: Signet, 1993. (*Chief of Scouts*, vol. 2).

———. *Justis Colt*. New York: Signet, 1995.

———. *Matched Colts*. New York: Signet, 1997.

———. *War Bonnet*. New York: Signet, 2000.

———. *Warrior*. New York: Signet, 1995.

Berger, Thomas. *Little Big Man*. New York: Dial Press, 1960.

Blackburn, Glen. *Apache Half-breed*. New York: Modern Promotions, 1971.

Blackburn, Tom W. *A Good Day to Die*. New York: Dorchester, 1995.

Blake, Michael. *Dances with Wolves*. New York: Fawcett, 1988.

Blakely, Mike. *Comanche Dawn*. New York: Forge, 1998.

Bodine, Jack. *The Pecos Kid—Apache Moon*. New York: HarperCollins, 1993.

Bower, Terrell. *Cheyenne Brothers*. New York: Bouregy, 1986.

———. *Iron Claw's Revenge*. New York: Bouregy, 1988.

Brand, Max. *The Legend of Thunder Moon*. New York: Dorchester, 1999.

———. *The Revenge of Broken Arrow*. New York: Street & Smith, 1929.

Braun, Matt. *Black Fox*. New York: Fawcett, 1972.

———. *Bloody Hand*. New York: Popular Library, 1975. Reprinted Pinnacle, 1985, 1996.

———. *Indian Territory*. New York: Pinnacle, 1985.

———. *The Last Stand*. New York: St. Martin's Press, 1998.

Brown, Dee. *Killdeer Mountain*. New York: Washington Square Press, 1984.

Burchardt, Bill. *The Lighthorsemen*. New York: Doubleday, 1981.

———. *Medicine Man*. New York: Doubleday, 1980.

Burleson, Frank. The Apache Wars trilogy

> *Desert Hawks*. New York: Signet, 1994.
>
> *Devil Dance*. New York: Signet, 1997.
>
> *Night of the Cougar*. New York: Signet, 1997.

———. *Savage Frontier*. New York: Signet, 1995.

———. *War Eagles*. New York: Signet, 1995.

———. *White Apache*. New York: Signet, 1996.

Burroughs, Edgar Rice. *Apache Devil*. New York: Tarzana, Calif.: Burroughs, 1933.

———. *The War Chief*. Chicago: A.C. McClurg and Co., 1927; Mattituck, New York: Amereon Ltd, 1945. Reprinted Cutchogue, New York: Buccaneer Books, 1976.

Cameron, Kate. *Orenda: A Novel of the Iroquois Nation*. New York: Random House, 1991.

Camp, Will. *Cold Justice*. New York: HarperCollins, 1998.

Capps, Benjamin. *A Woman of the People*. New York: Duell, Sloan, and Pearce, 1966.

Carter, Forrest. See under Native American Literature.

Clayton, Paul. *Calling Crow Nation*. New York: Berkley, 1995.

Coburn, Walt. *La Jornada*. South Yesmouth, Mass.: Curley 1961; reprinted 1990.

Coldsmith, Don. *Bearer of the Pipe*. New York: Doubleday, 1995.

———. *Bride of the Morning Star*. New York: Doubleday, 1991.

———. *Buffalo Medicine*. New York: Doubleday, 1981.

———. *The Changing Wind*. New York: Doubleday, 1990.

———. *Child of the Dead*. New York: Doubleday, 1994.

———. *Daughter of the Eagle*. New York: Doubleday, 1984.

———. *The Elk-Dog Heritage*. New York: Doubleday, 1982.

———. *The Flower in the Mountains*. New York: Doubleday, 1988.

———. *Follow the Wind*. New York: Doubleday, 1983.

———. *Fort De Chastaigne*. New York: Doubleday, 1990.

———. *Man of the Shadows*. New York: Doubleday, 1983.

———. *Medicine Hat*. Norman: University of Oklahoma Press, 1997.

———. *The Medicine Knife*. New York: Doubleday, 1988.

————. *Moon of Thunder.* New York: Doubleday, 1985.

————. *Pale Star.* New York: Doubleday, 1986.

————. *Quest for the White Bull.* New York: Doubleday, 1990.

————. *Return of the Spanish.* New York: Doubleday, 1993.

————. *Return to the River.* New York: Doubleday, 1987.

————. *River of Swans.* New York: Doubleday, 1986.

————. *Rivers West: The Smokey Hill.* New York: Bantam, 1996.

————. *Runestone.* New York: Doubleday, 1995.

————. *The Sacred Hills.* New York: Doubleday, 1985.

————. *Song of the Rock.* New York: Doubleday, 1989.

————. *Southwind.* New York: Doubleday, 1999.

————. *Tall Grass: A Novel of the Great Plains.* New York: Bantam, 1997.

————. *Thunderstick.* New York: Doubleday, 1993.

————. *Track of the Bear.* New York: Doubleday, 1994.

————. *Trail from Taos.* New York: Doubleday, 1988.

————. *Trail of the Spanish Bit.* New York: Doubleday, 1980.

————. *Walks in the Sun.* New York: Doubleday, 1992.

————. *World of Silence.* New York: Doubleday, 1992.

Cole, Judd. *Cheyenne Giant: Blood on the Arrows.* New York: Dorchester, 1995.

————. The Cheyenne series

Cheyenne #1: Arrow Keeper. New York: Dorchester, 1992.

Cheyenne #2: Death Chant. New York: Dorchester, 1992.

Cheyenne #3: Renegade Justice. New York: Dorchester, 1993.

Cheyenne #4: Vision Quest. New York: Dorchester, 1993.

Cheyenne #5: Blood on the Plains. New York: Dorchester, 1993.

Cheyenne #6: Comanche Raid. New York: Dorchester, 1993.

Cheyenne #7: Comancheros. New York: Dorchester, 1993.

Cheyenne #8: War Party. New York: Dorchester, 1993.

Cheyenne #9: Pathfinder. New York: Dorchester, 1994.

Cheyenne #10: Buffalo Hiders. New York: Dorchester, 1994.

Cheyenne #11: Spirit Path. New York: Dorchester, 1994.

Cheyenne #12: Mankiller. New York: Dorchester, 1994.

Cheyenne #13: Wendigo Mountain. New York: Dorchester, 1995.

Cheyenne #14: Death Camp. New York: Dorchester, 1995.

Cheyenne #15: Renegade Nation. New York: Dorchester, 1995.

Cheyenne #16: Orphan Train. New York: Dorchester, 1996.

Cheyenne #17: Vengeance Quest. New York: Dorchester, 1996.

Cheyenne #18: Warrior Fury. New York: Dorchester, 1996.

Cheyenne #19: Bloody Bones Canyon. New York: Dorchester, 1996.

Cheyenne #20: Renegade Siege. New York: Dorchester, 1996.

Cheyenne #21: River of Death. New York: Dorchester, 1997.

Cheyenne #22: Desert Manhunt. New York: Dorchester, 1997.

Combs, Harry. *Brules.* New York: Delacorte Press, 1995.

———. *Legend of the Painted Horse.* New York: Delacorte Press, 1996.

———. *The Scout.* New York: Delacorte Press, 1995.

Comfort, Will Levington. *Apache.* New York, E. P. Dutton and Co., 1931.

Cox, William. *Comanche Moon.* New York: New American Library, 1959.

Coyle, Harold. *Savage Wilderness.* New York: Simon and Schuster, 1997.

Cunningham, Chet. *Apache Ambush.* New York: Carousel, 1979.

———. *Cheyenne Blood Storm.* New York: Dorchester, 1988.

———. *Comanche Massacre.* New York: Dorchester, 1987.

———. *Comanche Moon.* New York: Dorchester, 1988.

———. *Sioux Showdown.* New York: Dorchester, 1988.

———. *Sioux Slaughter.* New York: Dorchester, 1988.

———. *Slaughter at Buffalo Creek.* New York: Dorchester, 1987.

Curry, Tom. *Guns of the Sioux.* New York: Arcadia House, 1945.

Dalton, Kit. *Apache Rifles.* New York: Dorchester, 1990.

———. *Buckskin Double: Gold Town Gal/Morgan's Squaw.* New York: Dorchester, 1997.

Dawson, Peter. *The Half-Breed.* New York: Bantam, 1962.

Duncan, Terence. *Apache Raiders.* New York: Kensington, 1987.

———. *Mustang Warriors.* New York: Kensington, 1987. (Quanah Parker)

Edmonds, Walter Dumaux. *Drums Along the Mohawk.* New York: Bantam, 1936, reprinted 1947.

Edwards, Hank. *Apache Sundown.* New York: HarperCollins, 1996.

Ell, Flynn J. *Dakota Scouts.* New York: Walker, 1992.

Englade, Ken. Tony Hillerman's Frontier series

　　#1 *People of the Plains.* New York: HarperCollins, 1995.

　　#2 *Tribes.* New York: HarperCollins, 1996.

　　#3 *The Soldiers.* New York: HarperCollins, 1997.

　　#4 *Battle Cry.* New York: HarperCollins, 1997.

　　#5 *Brothers in Blood.* New York: HarperCollins, 1998.

Englade, Ken, and Will Camp. #6 *Comanche Trail.* New York: HarperCollins, 1999.

Fast, Howard. *The Last Frontier.* New York: Duell, Sloan, and Pearce, 1941.

Fisher, Clay. See under Allen, Henry.

Gall, Grant. *Apache: The Long Ride Home.* New York: Sunstone Press, 1988.

Garland, George. *Apache Warpath.* New York: New American Library, 1959.

Gear, Kathleen O'Neal. *Sand in the Wind.* New York: Tor Books, 1990.

———. *This Widowed Land.* New York: Tom Doherty Associates, 1993.

Gear, Michael. *Coyote Summer.* New York: Forge, 1997.

———. *Long Ride Home.* New York: Tor Books, 1991.

———. *Morning River.* New York: Forge, 1996.

Gilman, Julia M. *William Wells and MacOnaquah: White Rose of the Miamis.* New York: Jewel, 1985.

Goodman, Charles R. *Black Cheyenne.* New York: Halloway House, 1993.

Gordon, Noah. *Shaman.* New York: Signet, 1993.

Gray, Judson. *Hunter's Run.* New York: Penguin, 1998.

Grove, Frederick. *Comanche Captives*. New York: Ballantine, 1961.
———. *Flame of the Osage*. New York: Pyramid, 1958.
———. *Phantom Warrior*. New York: Doubleday, 1981.
———. *Sun Dance*. New York: Ballantine, 1958.
Gulick, Bill. *Northwest Destiny*. New York: Doubleday, 1988.
Guthrie, A(lfred) B(ertman), Jr. *The Big Sky*. New York: Sloane, 1947. Reprinted Sentry Edition, Boston: Houghton Mifflin, 1965.
———. *The Way West*. Boston: Houghton Mifflin, 1949; reprinted 1993.
Haas, Benjamin. *Apache Raiders*. New York: Belmont Tower, 1970.
Halleran, Eurene. *Indian Fighter*. New York: Ballantine, 1964.
———. *Shadow of the Big Horn*. New York: Ballantine, 1960.
———. *Summer of the Sioux*. London: Hammond, 1965.
Haseloff, Cynthia. *Man Without Medicine*. New York: Dorchester, 1999.
Hawkins, Doug. *Comanche Reckoning*. New York: Dorchester, 1998.
———. *Keelboat Carnage*. New York: Dorchester, 1998.
Hawkins, Paul A. Ben Tree saga

   The Legend of Ben Tree. New York: Signet, 1993.

   The Vision of Benjamin One Feather. New York: Signet, 1993.

   White Moon Tree. New York: Signet, 1994.

Henry, Will. *The Bear Paw Horses*. New York: Leisure Books, 1991.
Hewson, Ed. *Apache Sundown*. New York: Fanjoy and Bell, 1996.
Hill, Ruth Beebe, and Chunksa Yaha. *Hanta Yo: An American Saga*. New York: Doubleday, 1979.
Hogan, Ray. *Soldier in Buckskin*. New York: Dorchester, 1998.
Holmes, Llewellyn Perry. *Apache Desert*. New York: Doubleday, 1952.
———. *Black Sage*. New York: Doubleday, 1950.
———. *Modoc, the Last Sundown*. New York: Dodd, Mead, 1959.
Hotchkiss, Bill. *Crow Warrior*. New York: Bantam, 1982.
———. *Dance of the Coyote*. New York: Bantam, 1987.
———. *Fire Woman*. New York: Bantam, 1987.
———. *The Medicine Calf*. New York: Bantam, 1981.
———. *People of the Sacred Oak*. New York: Bantam, 1986.
———. *Shoshone Thunder*. New York: Bantam, 1983.
———. *Soldier Wolf*. New York: Bantam, 1982.
———. *Spirit Mountain*. New York: Bantam, 1984.
———, with Judith Shears. *Pawnee Medicine*. New York: Banbury Books, 1983.
Hunter, E. J. White Squaw series

   #1 *Sioux Wildfire*. New York: Kensington, 1982.

   #2 *Boomtown Bust*. New York: Kensington, 1983.

   #3 *Virgin Territory*. New York: Kensington, 1984.

   #4 *Hot Texas Tail*. New York: Kensington, 1985.

   #5 *Buckskin Bombshell*. New York: Kensington, 1985.

   #6 *Dakota Squeeze*. New York: Kensington, 1985.

   #7 *Abilene Tightspot*. New York: Kensington, 1985.

#8 *Horn of Plenty.* New York: Kensington, 1985.

#9 *Twin Peaks—or Bust.* New York: Kensington, 1986.

#10 *Solid as a Rock.* New York: Kensington, 1986.

#11 *Hot-Handed Heathen.* New York: Kensington, 1986.

#12 *Ball and Chain.* New York: Kensington, 1986.

#13 *Track Tramp.* New York: Kensington, 1987.

#14 *Red Top Tramp.* New York: Kensington, 1987.

#15 *Here Comes the Bride.* New York: Kensington, 1987.

#16 *Redskin Rosebud.* New York: Kensington, 1988.

#17 *Bullwhipped Beauty.* New York: Kensington, 1988.

#18 *Hot Pursuit.* New York: Kensington, 1989.

#19 *Badman's Climax.* New York: Kensington, 1989.

#20 *Bareback Beauty.* New York: Kensington, 1990.

#21 *Arizona Laydown.* New York: Kensington, 1990.

#22 *Desert Climax.* New York: Kensington, 1991.

#23 *Comanche Come Down.* New York: Kensington, 1992.

#24 *Rough and Ready.* New York: Kensington, 1992.

Jessup, Richard. *Comanche Vengeance.* New York: Fawcett, 1957.

John, James Steward. *Dream Catchers: Journey into Native American Spirituality.* Nashville, Tenn.: Premium Press American, 1999.

Johnson, Dorothy. *All the Buffalo Returning.* New York: Dodd, Mead, 1979. Reprinted Lincoln: University of Nebraska Press, 1996.

———. *The Bloody Bozeman: The Perilous Trail to Montana's Gold.* New York: McGraw-Hill, 1971. Reprinted Missoula, Mont.: Mountain Press, 1983.

———. *Buffalo Woman.* New York: Dodd, Mead, 1977. Reprinted Lincoln: University of Nebraska Press, 1994; Thorndike, Me.: G. K. Hall, 1997.

———. *A Man Called Horse.* New York: Ballantine, 1949. (Formerly *Indian Country*)

Johnston, Terry C. *Black Rain.* New York: Bantam, 1993.

———. *Buffalo Palace.* New York: Bantam, 1996.

———. *Carry the Wind.* New York: Green Hill, 1982.

———. *Crack in the Sky.* New York: Bantam, 1997.

———. *Cries from the Earth.* New York: Bantam, 1999.

———. *Cry of the Hawk.* New York: Bantam, 1993.

———. *Dance on the Wind.* New York: Bantam, 1996.

———. *Dream Catcher.* New York: Bantam, 1994.

———. *One-Eyed Dream.* New York: Bantam, 1989.

———. The Plainsman series

Book I. *Sioux Dawn.* New York: St. Martin's Press, 1988.

Book II. *Red Cloud's Revenge: Showdown on the Northern Plains, 1867.* New York: St. Martin's Press, 1989.

Book III. *The Stalkers: The Battle of Beecher Island, 1868.* New York: St. Martin's Press, 1990.

Book IV. Black Sun: The Battle of Summit Springs, 1869. New York: St. Martin's Press, 1991.

Book V. Devil's Backbone. New York: St. Martin's Press, 1991.

Book VI. Shadow Riders: The Southern Plains Uprising. New York: St. Martin's Press, 1991.

Book VII. Dying Thunder: The Fight at Adobe Walls and the Battle of Palo Duro Canyon, 1874–1875. New York: St. Martin's Press, 1992.

Book VIII. Blood Song: The Battle of Powder River and the Beginning of the Great Sioux War of 1876. New York: St. Martin's Press, 1993.

Book IX. Reap the Whirlwind: The Battle of the Rosebud, June 1876. New York: St. Martin's Press, 1994.

Book X. A Cold Day in Hell: The Spring Creek Encounters, the Cedar Creek Fight with Sitting Bull's Sioux, and the Dull Knife Battle, November 25, 1876. New York: St. Martin's Press, 1996.

Book XI. Trumpet on the Land: The Sibley Scout, the Skirmish at Warbonnet Creek, the Battle of Slim Buttes and Crook's "Horse-Meat March"—The Aftermath. New York: St. Martin's Press, 1995.

Book XII. Wolf Mountain Moon. New York: St. Martin's Press, 1997.

Book XIII. Ashes of Heaven: The Lame Deer Flight, May 7, 1877, and the End of the Great Sioux War. New York: St. Martin's Press, 1998.

———. *Whisper of the Wolf.* New York: Bantam, 1991.
———. *Winter Rain.* New York: Bantam, 1993.
Johnstone, William W. *Absoroka Ambush.* New York: Pinnacle, 1993.
———. *Blood Bond.* New York: Zebra, 1989.
———. *Blood of the Mountain Man.* New York: Zebra, 1992.
———. *Cry of Eagles.* New York: Kensington, 1999.
———. *The First Mountain Man: Blood on the Divide.* New York: Pinnacle, 1992.
Jones, Douglas C. *Arrest Sitting Bull.* New York: Scribner's, 1977.
———. *A Creek Called Wounded Knee.* New York: Scribner's, 1978.
———. *Gone the Dreams and Dancing.* New York: HarperCollins, 1984.
———. *The Search for Temperance Moon.* New York: Henry Holt, 1991.
———. *Season of Yellow Leaf.* New York: Holt Rinehart, 1983.
———. *This Savage Race.* New York: HarperCollins, 1994.
———. *Winding Stair.* New York: Holt Rinehart, 1979.
Jones, Robert F. *Tie My Bones to Her Back.* New York: Farrar, Straus, 1996. Reprinted as *The Buffalo Runners.* New York: St. Martin's Press, 1998.
Judd, Cameron. *Cherokee Joe.* New York: Doubleday, 1992.
Kelton, Elmer. *The Wolf and the Buffalo.* New York: Doubleday, 1980.
Killdeer, John. *The Savage Land.* New York: Bantam, 1995.
Knott, William Cecil (as Jon Sharpe). *The Golden Hawk.* New York: New American Library, 1986.
———. The Trailman series

#18 *Cry the Cheyenne.* New York: New American Library, 1983.

#51 *Sioux Captive.* New York: New American Library, 1986.

#59 *Thunderhawk*. New York: New American Library, 1986.

#70 *Hostage Arrows*. New York: New American Library, 1987.

#104 *Comanche Crossing*. New York: New American Library, 1990.

#108 *Pawnee Bargain*. New York: New American Library, 1990.

———. *White Savage*. New York: New American Library, 1984.

L'Amour, Louis. *Hondo*. New York: Bantam, 1953.

———. *Kiowa Trail*. New York: Bantam, 1964.

———. *Last Stand at Papago Wells*. New York: CBS Publications, 1957.

———. *To Tame a Land*. Greenwich, Conn.: Fawcett, 1955; reprinted 1984, 1987.

Lampman, Evelyn Sibley. *Squaw Man's Son*. New York: Atheneum, 1978.

———. *White Captives*. New York: Atheneum, 1975.

Lassiter, Karl. *First Cherokee Rifles*. New York: Kensington, 1999.

Lederer, Paul. Indian Heritage series

#1 *Manitou's Daughter*. New York: New American Library, 1982.

#2 *Shawnee Dawn*. New York: New American Library, 1982.

#3 *Seminole Skies*. New York: New American Library, 1983.

#4 *Cheyenne Dreams*. New York: New American Library, 1985.

#5 *Way of the Wind*. New York: New American Library, 1985.

#6 *North Star*. New York: New American Library, 1987.

#7 *Far Dreamer*. New York: New American Library, 1987.

———. *Tecumseh*. New York: New American Library, 1982.

Levin, Beatrice. *John Hawk: White Man, Black Man, Indian Chief*. Austin, Tex.: Eakin
    Press, 1988.

London, David. *Sun Dancer*. New York: Simon and Schuster, 1996.

Loomis, Noel Miller. *Cheyenne War Cry*. New York: Avon, 1959.

Macdonald, Elisabeth. *Voices on the Wind*. New York: Avon, 1994.

Manfred, Frederick. *Conquering Horse*. New York: McDowell Obolensky, 1959.

———. *King of Spades*. New York: Simon and Schuster, 1976.

———. *Lord Grizzly*. New York: McGraw-Hill, 1954.

———. *Scarlet Plume*. New York: Simon and Schuster, 1964.

Marriott, Alice. *Indian Annie: Kiowa Captive*. New York: McKay, 1965.

May, Karl. *Winnetou*. New York: Seabury, 1977.

McCarthy, Gary. *Blood Brother*. New York: Leisure Books, 1999.

———. *Grand Canyon*. New York: Pinnacle, 1996.

McCurtin, Peter. *Gold Strike*. New York: Dorchester, 1980.

———. *The Savage*. New York: Dorchester, 1979.

McGowan, Wynema. *Beyond the River*. New York: Pinnacle, 1997.

McMasters, Jake. Cheyenne series

#14 *Blood on the Arrows*. New York: Dorchester, 1995.

#15 *Renegade Nation*. New York: Dorchester, 1995.

———. White Apache double editions

Hangman's Knot/Warpath. New York: Dorchester, 1997.

Warrior Born/Quick Killer. New York: Dorchester, 1997.

———. White Apache series

#1 *Hangman's Knot*. New York: Dorchester, 1993.

#2 *Warpath*. New York: Dorchester, 1994.

#3 *Warrior Born*. New York: Dorchester, 1994.

#4 *Quick Killer*. New York: Dorchester, 1994.

#5 *Bloodbath*. New York: Dorchester, 1994.

#6 *Blood Treachery*. New York: Dorchester, 1995.

#7 *Blood Bounty*. New York: Dorchester, 1995.

#8 *The Trackers*. New York: Dorchester, 1995.

#9 *Desert Fury*. New York: Dorchester, 1995.

#10 *Hanged*. New York: Dorchester, 1996.

McMurtry, Larry. *Comanche Moon*. New York: Simon and Schuster, 1997.

Mills, Robert E. *The Cheyenne's Woman*. New York: Dorchester, 1983.

Moore, Brian. *Black Robe*. New York: Fawcett, 1986.

Moss, Robert. *The Firekeeper: A Narrative of the Eastern Frontier*. New York: Tom Doherty Associates, 1995.

Munn, Vella. *Daughter of the Mountain*. New York: Tom Doherty Associates, 1993.

———. *River's Daughter*. New York: Forge, 1996.

———. *Seminole Song*. New York: Forge, 1997.

———. *Spirit of the Eagle*. New York: Forge, 1996.

Murray, Earl. *Flaming Sky: A Novel of the Little Big Horn*. New York: Tom Doherty Associates, 1995.

———. *Free Flows the River*. New York: Tom Doherty Associates, 1994.

———. *High Freedom*. New York: Tom Doherty Associates, 1992.

———. *The River at Sundown*. New York: Tom Doherty Associates, 1997.

———. *Savage Whisper*. New York: Tom Doherty Associates, 1998. (romance)

———. *Song of Wovoka*. New York: Tom Doherty Associates, 1992.

———. *Spirit of the Moon*. New York: Tom Doherty Associates, 1992. (romance)

———. *Thunder in the Dawn*. New York: Tom Doherty Associates, 1994.

———. *Whisper on the Water*. New York: Forge, 1988. (romance)

Newcomb, Kerry. *Scalpdancers*. New York: Bantam, 1990.

Norman, John. *Ghost Dance*. New York: Ballantine, 1970.

Olsen, Theodore V. *Arrow in the Sun*. New York: Leisure Books, 1996.

———. *Blood of the Breed*. New York: Leisure Books, 1997.

———. *The Stalking Moon*. New York: Doubleday and Co., 1965.

O'Meara, Walter. *Last Portage*. Boston: Houghton Mifflin, 1961.

O'Reilly, Jackson. *Cheyenne Raiders*. Wayne, Pa.: Banbury Books, 1982.

Overholser, Wayne. *Summer of the Sioux*. New York: Dell, 1967.

Paine, Lauran. *The Renegade*. New York: Thorndike Press, 1995.

———. *Spirit Meadow*. New York: Walker, 1987.

———. *The Squaw Men*. New York: Walker, 1992.

Parkinson, Dan. *Blood Arrow*. New York: Zebra, 1985.

Patten, Lewis B. *The Killings at Coyote Springs—The Trail of the Apache Kid*. New York: Dorchester, 1994.

Payne, Oliver. *Warpath*. New York: Berkley, 1982.

Porter, Donald Clayton. *Kiowa Fires*. New York: Banbury Books, 1983.

————. White Indian series

> #1 *White Indian*. New York: Thorndike Press, 1983.
>
> #2 *The Renegade*. New York: Thorndike Press, 1983.
>
> #3 *War Chief*. New York: Thorndike Press, 1983.
>
> #4 *The Sachem*. New York: Thorndike Press, 1983.
>
> #5 *Renno*. New York: Thorndike Press, 1983.
>
> #6 *Tomahawk*. New York: Thorndike Press, 1983.
>
> #7 *War Cry*. New York: Thorndike Press, 1984.
>
> #8 *Ambush*. New York: Thorndike Press, 1985; reprinted 1993.
>
> #9 *Seneca*. New York: Thorndike Press, 1985; reprinted 1994.
>
> #10 *Cherokee*. New York: Thorndike Press, 1985; reprinted 1991.
>
> #11 *Choctaw*. New York: Thorndike Press, 1985.
>
> #12 *Seminole*. New York: Thorndike Press, 1986.
>
> #13 *War Drums*. New York: Thorndike Press, 1986.
>
> #14 *Apache*. New York: Thorndike Press, 1987.
>
> #15 *Spirit Knife*. New York: Thorndike Press, 1988.
>
> #16 *Manitou*. New York: Thorndike Press, 1988; reprinted 1990.
>
> #17 *Seneca Warrior*. New York: Thorndike Press, 1989.
>
> #18 *Father of Waters*. New York: Thorndike Press, 1989.
>
> #19 *Fallen Timbers*. New York: Thorndike Press, 1990.
>
> #20 *Sachem's Son*. New York: Thorndike Press, 1990.
>
> #21 *Sachem's Daughter*. New York: Thorndike Press, 1991.
>
> #22 *Seneca Patriots*. New York: Thorndike Press, 1992.
>
> #23 *Hawk's Journey*. New York: Thorndike Press, 1992.
>
> #24 *Father and Son*. New York: Thorndike Press, 1993.
>
> #25 *War Clouds*. New York: Thorndike Press, 1994.
>
> #26 *Red Stick*. New York: Thorndike Press, 1994.
>
> #27 *Creek Thunder*. New York: Thorndike Press, 1995.
>
> #28 *Medicine Shield*. New York: Thorndike Press, 1996.

Powell, James. *Apache Moon*. Garden City, N.Y.: Doubleday, 1983.

Preeble, John E. C. *The Buffalo Soldiers*. London: Secker & Warburg, 1959.

Proctor, George W. *Blood of My Blood: A Novel of Quanah Parker*. New York: Doubleday, 1996.

————. *Walks Without a Soul*. New York: Doubleday, 1995.

Quarles, Johnny. *Fool's Gold*. New York: Avon, 1993.
———. *Spirit Trail*. New York: Avon, 1995.
Randisi, Robert Joseph (as J. R. Roberts). *Apache Gold*. New York: Charter, 1988.
———. *Geronimo's Trail*. New York: Charter, 1987.
———. *Navaho Dust*. New York: Charter, 1985.
Reasoner, James L. *Cossack Three Ponies*. New York: Berkley, 1997. (Blackfeet allied with Cossacks)
Richman, Roe. *Mojave Guns*. New York: Arcadia House, 1952.
Richter, Conrad. *A Country of Strangers*. New York: Knopf, 1966.
———. *Light in the Forest*. New York: Knopf, 1953.
Riddle, Paxton. *Lost River*. New York: Berkley, 1999. (part Modoc)
Roberts, J. R. *Apache Raid*. New York: Jove, 1998.
Robson, Lucia St. Clair. *Light a Distant Fire*. New York: Ballantine, 1988.
———. *Ride the Wind: The Story of Cynthia Ann Parker, and the Last Days of the Comanche*. New York: Ballantine, 1982.
———. *Walk in My Soul*. New York: Ballantine, 1985.
Ross, David William. *Beyond the Stars*. New York: Avon, 1990.
———. *Eye of the Hawk*. New York: Avon, 1994.
———. *Savage Plains*. New York: Avon, 1996.
———. *War Cries*. New York: Avon, 1995.
Sandoz, Mari. *Cheyenne Autumn*. New York Avon, 1953. Reprinted Lincoln: University of Nebraska Press, 1992.
Sealsfield, Charles. *The Indian Chief, or Tokeah and the White Rose*. Philadelphia: Carey, Lea, and Carey, 1829. Reprinted Hildesheim: Olms Press, 1972.
Sharpe, Jon. *Apache Arrows*. New York: Signet, 1996.
———. *Kiowa Command*. New York: Signet, 1995.
———. Trailsman Western series

    #187 *Sioux War Cry*. New York: Signet, 1997.

    #196 *Kansas Carnage*. New York: Signet, 1998.

    #197 *Utah Uprising*. New York: Signet, 1998.

    #208 *Arizona Renegades*. New York: Signet, 1999.

    #211 *Badlands Bloodbath*. New York: Signet, 1999.

    #212 *Sioux Stampede*. New York: Signet, 1999.

    #213 *Apache Wells*. New York: Signet, 1999.

    #214 *Texas Hellion*. New York: Signet, 1999.

Sherman, Jory. *The Columbia River*. New York: Bantam, 1996.
———. *The Medicine Horn*. New York: Bantam, 1992.
———. *Song of the Cheyenne*. Garden City, N.Y.: Doubleday, 1987.
———. *The South Platte*. New York: Bantam, 1998.
———. *Trapper's Moon*. New York: Forge, 1994.
Shirreffs, Gordon D. *The Apache Hunter*. New York: Dorchester, 1995.
———. *Bold Legend*. New York: Fawcett, 1982.
———. *The Ghost Dancers*. New York: Dorchester, 1995.
———. *The Untamed Breed*. New York: Dorchester, 1994.
Skimin, Robert. *Apache Autumn*. New York: St. Martin's Press, 1993.

Stuart, Colin. *Walks Far Woman*. New York: Dial, 1976.

Thom, James Alexander. *Follow the River*. New York: Random House, 1981.

———. *Panther in the Sky*. New York: Ballantine, 1989.

———. *The Red Heart*. New York: Ballantine, 1997.

Thompson, David. Davy Crockett series

    #1 *King of the Mountain*. New York: Dorchester, 1990.

    #2 *Lure of the Wild*. New York: Dorchester, 1990.

    #5 *Tomahawk Revenge*. New York: Dorchester, 1991; reprinted 1993.

    #6 *Comanche Country*. New York: Dorchester, 1998.

    #10 *Sioux Slaughter*. New York: Dorchester, 1997.

    #12 *Apache Blood*. New York: Dorchester, 1992.

    #16 *Blood Truce*. New York: Dorchester, 1993.

    #28 *The Quest*. New York: Dorchester, 1999.

Thorpe, Raymond W., and R. Bunker. *Crow Killer: Jeremiah Johnson*. New York: Dutton NAL, 1980.

Tobin, Greg. *Prairie: An Epic of the West*. New York: Book Creations (Random House), 1997.

Tolbert, Frank Xavier. *The Staked Plain*. New York: Harper & Row, 1958.

Tubb, Edwin Charles (as E. F. Jackson). *Comanche Capture*. London: Spencer, 1955.

Tuttle, Wilbur Coleman. *The Medicine Man*. London: Collins, 1925.

Tyler, Dodge. Dan'l Boone, the Lost Wilderness series

    #2 *Algonquin Massacre*. New York: Leisure Books, 1996.

    #4 *Apache Revenge*. New York: Leisure Books, 1997.

    #6 *Comanche Country*. New York: Leisure Books, 1998.

    #8 *Taos Death Cry*. New York: Leisure Books, 1998.

Ude, Wayne Richard. *Becoming Coyote*. Amherst, Mass.: Lynx House Press, 1981.

———. *Buffalo and Other Stories*. Amherst, Mass.: Lynx House Press, 1975; revised edition, 1991.

———. *Three Coyote Tales*. Petersham, Mass.: Lone Oak Press, 1989.

Ulyatt, Kenneth. *North Against the Sioux*. New York: Popular Library, 1965.

Vance, William E. *Apache War Cry*. New York: Popular Library, 1955.

———. *Death Stalks the Cheyenne Trail*. Garden City, N.Y.: Doubleday, 1980.

———. *The Raid at Crazy Horse*. New York: Ace, 1967.

Vaughan, Carter. *The Seneca Hostage*. New York: Popular Library, 1969.

Waldo, Anna Lee. *Sacajawea*. New York: Avon, 1979.

Walsh, W. W. B. *The Four-Colored Hoop*. New York: Putnam's, 1976.

Weber, Sherman S. *Black Robe: A Novel*. Anaheim, Calif.: Lincoln, 1981.

Wellman, Broncho. *Apache*. New York: Macmillan, 1952.

———. *The Comancheros*. New York: Doubleday, 1952.

Wells, Angus (as William S. Brady). *Comanche!* London: Fontana, 1981.

——— (as Charles R. Price). *Vengeance Hunt*. London: Mayflower, 1976.

West, Charles G. *Bitter Root*. New York: Signet, 1999.

———. *Black Eagle*. New York: Signet, 1998.

————. *Cheyenne Justice*. New York: Signet, 1999.

————. *Stone Hand*. New York: Signet, 1997.

————. *Wind River*. New York: Signet, 1999.

Wheeler, Richard S. *Badlands*. New York: Tom Doherty Associates, 1992.

————. *Dodging Red Cloud*. New York: Evans, 1987.

————. Skye's West series

#1 *Sun River*. New York: Tom Doherty Associates, 1989.

#2 *Bannack*. New York: Tom Doherty Associates, 1989.

#3 *The Far Tribes*. New York: Tom Doherty Associates, 1990.

#4 *Yellowstone*. New York: Tom Doherty Associates, 1990.

#5 *Bitterroot*. New York: Tom Doherty Associates, 1991.

#6 *Sundance*. New York: Tom Doherty Associates, 1992.

#7 *Wind River*. New York: Tom Doherty Associates, 1993.

#8 *Santa Fe*. New York: Tom Doherty Associates, 1994.

#9 *Rendezvous*. New York: Forge, 1997.

————. *The Two Medicine River*. New York: Doubleday, 1993.

————. *Where the River Runs*. New York: Evans, 1990.

Wisler, G. Clifton. *Among the Eagles*. New York: Random House, 1989.

————. *Comanche Crossing*. New York: Paperjacks, 1987.

————. *Comanche Summer*. New York: Zebra, 1987.

————. *Lakota*. New York: Evans, 1989.

————. *Massacre at Powder River*. New York: Berkely, 1997.

————. Medicine Trail Series

#1 *The Buffalo Shield*. New York: Kensington, 1991; reprinted 1992.

#2 *Stone Wolf's Vision*. New York: Kensington, 1991.

#3 *Dreaming Wolf*. New York: Kensington, 1992.

————. *Spirit Warrior*. New York: Zebra, 1986.

Wright, Harold Bell. *The Mine with the Iron Door*. New York: D. Appleton, 1923.

Zietlow, Edward. *The Indian Maiden's Captivity* and *The Heart of the Country*. Hermosa, S.D.: Lame Johnny Press, 1978.

War

L'Amour, Louis. *The Last of His Breed*. New York: Bantam, 1986.

Stone, Scott C. S. *Song of the Wolf*. New York: Arbor House, 1985.

Other

Barth, John. *The Sot-Weed Factor*. New York: Doubleday, 1960.

Borland, Hal. *When the Legends Die*. New York: Bantam, 1972.

Byrd, William. "History of the Dividing Line." (1728). In *The Prose Works of William*

Byrd of Westover. Ed. Louis B. Wright. Cambridge, Mass.: Harvard University Press, 1966.

Catlin, George. *Letters and Notes on the Manners, Customs, and Conditions of the North American Indians.* 1832. Vols. 1 and 2. New York: Dover Publications, 1973.

Cooper, James Fenimore. *The Last of the Mohicans: A Narrative of 1757.* New York: Scribner's, 1986.

———. *The Prairie.* New York: New American Library, 1964.

Crèvecoeur, J. Hector St. Jean de. *Letters from an American Farmer.* 1782. Reprinted New York: Dutton, 1990.

Dodge, Richard Irving. *Our Wild Indians: Thirty-three Years Personal Experience Among the Red Men of the Great West.* 1883. Reprinted Freeport, N.Y.: Gallery Books, 1983.

Eastlake, William. *Dancers in the Scalp House.* New York: Viking Press, 1975.

Fergus, Charles. *Shadow Catcher.* New York: Soho Press, 1991.

Franklin, Benjamin. Letter to Peter Collinson, May 9, 1753. In *Papers of Benjamin Franklin.* Ed. Leonard W. Labanee. Vol. 4. New Haven, Conn.: Yale University Press, 1961.

Hawthorne, Nathaniel. *The Works of Hawthorne.* Ed. Norman Holmes Pearson. New York: Modern Library, 1937.

Huffaker, Clair. *Nobody Loves a Drunken Indian.* New York: McKay, 1967.

Kesey, Ken. *One Flew over the Cuckoo's Nest.* New York: Viking Press, 1962.

LaFarge, Oliver. *The Enemy Gods.* Boston: Houghton Mifflin, 1937.

———. *Laughing Boy.* Boston: Houghton Mifflin, 1929.

Lott, Milton. *Dance Back the Buffalo.* Boston: Houghton Mifflin, 1959.

Moody, Ralph. *Geronimo: Wolf of the Warpath.* New York: Random House, 1958.

Morison, Samuel Eliot, ed. *The Parkman Reader: From the Works of Francis Parkman.* Boston: Little, Brown, 1955.

Munger, David, ed. *80 Readings.* New York: HarperCollins, 1992.

Parkman, Francis, and George Bancroft. *The Oregon Trail.* 1849. Reprinted London: Oxford University Press, 1996.

SECONDARY SOURCES

Anderson, Eric Gary. *American Indian Literature and the Southwest: Contexts and Dispositions.* Austin: University of Texas Press, 1999.

Barnett, Louise K. *The Ignoble Savage: American Literary Racism, 1790–1890.* Westport, Conn.: Greenwood Press, 1975.

Beam, John, Barbara Brenstad, and Jack Marden. *The Native American in Long Fiction: An Annotated Bibliography.* New York: Scarecrow Press, 1996.

Beidler, Peter G. "The Contemporary Indian Romance: A Review Essay." *American Indian Culture and Research Journal* 15 (4) (1991): 97–125.

———. "Indians in Martin Cruz Smith's *Nightwing*: A Review Article." *Albuquerque Quarterly* 4 (1979): 155–159.

Berkhofer, Robert. *Salvation and the Savage: An Analysis of Protestant Missions and American Indian Response, 1787–1862.* Lexington: University Press of Kentucky, 1965.

————. *The White Man's Indian: Images of the American Indian from Columbus to the Present.* New York: Knopf, 1978.

Bird, Elizabeth, ed. *Dressing in Feathers: The Construction of the Indian in American Popular Culture.* Boulder, Colo.: Westview Press, 1996.

Buscombe, Edward, ed. *The BFI Companion to the Western.* New York: Atheneum, 1988.

Cawelti, John G. *Adventure, Mystery, and Romance: Formula Stories as Art and Popular Culture.* Chicago: University of Chicago Press, 1976.

————. *The Six-Gun Mystique.* Bowling Green, Ohio: Bowling Green State University Popular Press, 1984.

Chahta-Ima (Father Adrien Rouquette). *La nouvelle Atala.* New Orleans, 1897.

Chavkin, Allan Richard, and Lavonne Brown Ruoff, eds. *The Chippewa Landscape of Louise Erdrich.* Birmingham: University of Alabama Press, 1999.

Churchill, Ward. *Fantasies of the Master Race: Literature, Cinema, the Colonization of American Indians.* Ed. M. Annette Jaimes. Monroe, Me.: Common Courage Press, 1992; San Francisco: City Lights Books, 1998. (Creek/Cherokee/Métis)

Davis, Mary, ed. *Native America in the Twentieth Century: An Encyclopedia.* Hamden, Conn.: Garland, 1994, reprinted 1996.

Deloria, Philip J. *Playing Indian.* New Haven, Conn.: Yale University Press, 1998.

Donovan, Kathleen M. *Feminist Readings of Native American Literature: Coming to Voice.* Tucson: University of Arizona Press, 1998.

Ebersole, Gary L. *Captured by Texts: Puritan to Postmodern Images of Indian Captivity.* Charlottesville: University Press of Virginia, 1995.

Fairbairn, Neil. *A Traveller's Guide to the Kingdoms of Arthur.* London: Evans Brothers, 1983.

Fairchild, Hoxie Neale. *The Noble Savage: A Study in Romantic Naturalism.* New York: Columbia University Press, 1928.

Freeman, James. *Ishi's Journey: From the Center to the Edge of the World.* Happy Camp, Calif.: Naturegraph, 1992.

French, Philip. *Westerns: Aspects of a Movie Genre.* London: Secker & Warburg, 1973.

Gill, Sam, and Irene F. Sullivan. *Dictionary of Native American Mythology.* New York: Oxford University Press, 1992.

Goetzmann, William H., and William N. Goetzmann. *The West of the Imagination.* New York: W. W. Norton, 1986.

Hagan, William T. *Quanah Parker, Comanche Chief.* Norman: University of Oklahoma Press, 1993.

Hall, Edward T. *The Silent Language.* New York: Doubleday/Anchor, 1973.

Heard, J. Norman. *White into Red: A Study of the Assimilation of White Persons Captured by Indians.* Metuchen, N.J.: Scarecrow Press, 1973.

Hilger, Michael. *The American Indian in Film.* New York: Scarecrow Press, 1986.

————. *From Savage to Nobleman: Images of Native Americans in Film.* New York: Scarecrow Press, 1995.

Holt, Patricia. "Tony Hillerman." *Publishers Weekly* (October 24, 1980): 6–7.

Hultkrantz, Ake. *Native Religions of North America: The Power of Visions and Fertility.* San Francisco: Harper & Row, 1987.

Jensen, Margaret Ann. *Love's Sweet Return: The Harlequin Story.* Bowling Green, Ohio: Bowling Green State University Popular Press, 1984.

Jordan, Winthrop D. *White over Black: American Attitudes Toward the Negro, 1550–1812*. Chapel Hill: University of North Carolina Press, 1968.

Jung, C. S. "Psychology of the Unconscious." In *Two Essays on Analytical Psychology*. Trans. R. F. C. Hull. In *The Collected Works of C. S. Jung*. Vol 7. 1943. Reprinted in Bollingen series. Princeton, N.J.: Princeton University Press, 1972.

Kaplan, Robert B. "Cultural Thought Patterns in Intercultural Education." *Language Learning* 16 (1966): 1–20.

Kaplan, Robert D. "Kissinger, Metternich, and Realism." *Atlantic Monthly* (June 1999): 73–82.

Keiser, Albert. *The Indian in American Literature*. New York: Oxford University Press, 1933.

Kilpatrick, Alan. *Night Has a Naked Soul: Witchcraft and Sorcery Among the Western Cherokee*. Syracuse, N.Y.: Syracuse University Press, 1997.

Klein, Kathleen, ed. *Diversity and Detective Fiction: Race, Gender, Ethnicity*. Bowling Green, Ohio: Bowling Green State University Popular Press, 1999.

Klein, Laura E., and Lillian A. Ackerman. *Women and Power in Native North America*. Norman: University of Oklahoma Press, 1995.

Kovel, Joel. *White Racism: A Psychohistory*. New York: Random House, 1970.

Krentz, Jayne Ann, ed. *Dangerous Men and Adventurous Women: Romance Writers on the Appeal of the Romance*. Philadelphia: University of Pennsylvania Press, 1992.

Kroeber, Theodora. *Ishi in Two Worlds: A Biography of the Last Wild Indian in America*. Los Angeles: University of California Press, 1962.

————, and Robert F. Heizer, eds. *Ishi the Last Yahi: A Documentary History*. Los Angeles: University of California Press, 1979.

Lamar, Robert, ed. *The New Encyclopedia of the American West*. New Haven, Conn.: Yale University Press, 1998.

Levernier, James, and Hennig Cohen. *The Indians and Their Captives*. Westport, Conn.: Greenwood Press, 1977.

Macdonald, Ross. "The Writer as Detective Hero." In *On Crime Writing*. Santa Barbara, Calif.: Capra Press, 1973.

Mack, John E. *Abduction: Human Encounters with Aliens*. New York: Scribner's, 1994.

Matteson, Patricia. "A Stain on the Blood: Indian-Loving and Nineteenth-Century Women's Literary Strategies." Ph.D. diss., University of Colorado, Boulder, 1996.

McCleary, Timothy P. *The Stars We Know: Crow Indian Astronomy and Lifeways*. Prospect Heights, Ill.: Waveland Press, 1997.

McFarland, Ron, ed. *James Welch*. Lewiston, Idaho: Confluence, 1986.

McNickle, D'Arcy, and Harold E. Fey. *Indians and Other Americans: Two Ways of Life Meet*. New York: Harper & Row, 1970.

Mihesuah, Devon A. *American Indians: Stereotypes and Realities*. Atlanta: Clarity Press, 1996.

Miller, Dorcas S. *Stars of the First People*. Boulder, Colo.: Pruett, 1997.

Miller, James, Carlota Cardenas de Dwyer, et al. *United States in Literature*. Glenview, Ill.: Scott, Foresman, 1982.

Miller, Perry. *The American Puritans—Their Prose and Their Poetry*. Garden City, N.Y.: Doubleday/Anchor, 1956.

Mitchel, Lee Clark. *Westerns: Making the Man in Fiction and Film*. Chicago: University of Chicago Press, 1996.

Modleski, Tania. *Loving with a Vengeance: Mass Produced Fantasies for Women*. Hamden, Conn.: Archon Books, 1982.

Moon, Sheila. *A Magic Dwells: A Poetic and Psychological Study of the Navaho Emergence Myth*. Middletown, Conn.: Wesleyan University Press, 1970.

Mussell, Kay. *Fantasy and Reconciliation: Contemporary Formulae of Women's Romantic Fiction*. Westport, Conn.: Greenwood Press, 1984.

Namias, June. *White Captives: Gender and Ethnicity on the American Frontier*. Chapel Hill: University of North Carolina Press, 1993.

Nemanic, Gerald. "The Indians of the Midwest: A Partially Annotated Bibliography." *Great Lakes Review*, 2 (1976): 2, 54–74.

Newcomb, William W., Jr. *North American Indians: An Anthropological Perspective*. Santa Monica, Calif.: Goodyear, 1974.

Nussbaum, Martin. "Sociological Symbolism of the 'Adult Western.' " *Social Forces*, 39 (October 1960): 25–28.

Osterreich, Shelley Anne. *The American Indian Ghost Dance, 1870–1890: An Annotated Bibliography*. Westport, Conn.: Greenwood Publishing, 1991.

Pearce, Roy Harvey. *The Savages of America: A Study of the Indian and the Idea of Civilization*. Baltimore: John Hopkins University Press, 1953.

Pfitzer, Gregory M. "The Only Good Alien Is a Dead Alien: Science Fiction and the Metaphysics of Indian-Hating on the High Frontier." *Journal of American Culture*, 18 (Spring 1995): 51–67.

Ponicsan, Darryl. *Tom Mix Died for Your Sins: A Novel Based on His Life*. New York: Delacorte Press, 1975.

Pronzini, Bill, and Martin H. Greenberg, eds. *The Ethnic Detectives: Masterpieces of Mystery Fiction*. New York: Dodd, Mead, 1985.

Purchas, Samuel. *Hakluytas Posthumus; or Purchas his Pilgrimes*. London: H. Fetherston, 1625.

Purdy, John Lloyd. *The Legacy of D'Arcy McNickle: Writer, Historian, Activist*. Norman: University of Oklahoma Press, 1994.

Radin, Paul. *The Trickster*. Westport, Conn.: Greenwood Press, 1969.

Radway, Janice. *Reading the Romance: Women, Patriarchy, and Popular Literature*. Chapel Hill: University of North Carolina Press, 1984.

Riley, Glenda. *Women and Indians on the Frontier, 1825–1915*. Albuquerque: University of New Mexico Press, 1984.

Roberts, Elizabeth, and Elias Amidon, eds. *Earth Prayers from Around the World*. San Francisco: HarperSanFrancisco, 1991.

Rollins, Peter, and John O'Connor. *Hollywood's Indian: The Portrayal of the Native American in Film*. Lexington: University Press of Kentucky, 1998.

Roscoe, Will. *The Zuñi Man-Woman*. Albuquerque: University of New Mexico Press, 1991.

Rose, Alan Henry. *Demonic Vision*. Hamden, Conn.: Archon Press, 1976.

Ruoff, A. LaVonne Brown. *American Indian Literature: An Introduction, Review, and Selected Bibliography*. New York: Modern Language Association, 1990.

Sadler, Geoff, ed. *Twentieth-Century Western Writers*. Chicago: St. James Press, 1991.

Sapir, E. *Language*. New York: Harcourt Brace, 1921.

Scheick, William J. *The Half-Blood: A Cultural Symbol in 19th Century American Fiction*. Lexington: University Press of Kentucky, 1979.

Simmons, Marc. *Witchcraft in the Southwest: Spanish and Indian Supernaturalism on the Rio Grande*. Omaha: University of Nebraska Press, 1980.

The Spirit World. One vol. in *The American Indians*. Series ed. Henry Woodhead. Alexandria, Va.: Time-Life Books, 1992.

Stensland, Anna Lee. *Literature by and About the American Indian: An Annotated Bibliography*. Urbana, Ill.: NCTE, 1979.

Stratton, Joanna. *Pioneer Women: Voices from the Kansas Frontier*. New York: Simon and Schuster, 1981.

Tedlock, Dennis, and Barbara Tedlock, eds. *Teachings from the American Earth: Indian Religion and Philosophy*. New York: Liveright, 1975.

Thompson, Jon. *Fiction, Crime, and Empire*. Chicago: University of Illinois Press, 1993.

Thurston, Carol. *The Romance Revolution: Erotic Novels for Women and the Quest for a New Sexual Identity*. Urbana: University of Illinois Press, 1987.

Tilton, Robert S. *Pocahontas: The Evolution of an American Narrative*. Cambridge: Cambridge University Press, 1994.

VanDerBeets, Richard. *The Indian Captivity Narrative: An American Genre*. Lanham, Md.: University Press of America, 1984.

———. "A Surfeit of Style: The Indian Captivity Narrative as Penny Dreadful." *Research Studies*, 32 (December 1971): 197–306.

Van Lent, Peter. "Her Beautiful Savage: The Current Sexual Image of the Native American Male." In Elizabeth Bird, ed., *Dressing in Feathers*. Boulder, Colo.: Westview Press, 1996.

Velie, Alan R. "American Indian Literature in the Nineties: The Emergence of the Middle-Class Protagonist." *World Literature Today*, 66 (Spring 1992): 264–268.

Wall, Leon, and William Morgan. *Navajo-English Dictionary*. New York: Hippocrene Books, 1994.

Waters, Frank. *Book of the Hopi*. New York: Penguin Books, 1977.

The Way of the Warrior. One vol. in *The American Indians*. Series ed. Henry Woodhead. Alexandria, Va.: Time-Life Books, 1993.

Weatherford, Jack. *Native Roots: How the Indians Enriched America*. New York: Fawcett Columbine, 1991.

Wild, Peter. *James Welch*. Boise, Idaho: Boise State University Press, 1983.

Williams, Walter L. *The Spirit and the Flesh: Sexual Diversity in American Indian Culture*. Boston: Beacon Press, 1986.

Winks, Robin. "Tony Hillerman." *Washington Post Book World* (May 27, 1990): 12.

Wissler, Clark, and D. C. Duvall. *Mythology of the Blackfoot Indians*. 1908. Reprinted Lincoln: University of Nebraska Press, 1995.

Witalec, Janet, ed. *Native North American Literature*. Detroit, Michigan: Gale Research Inc., 1994.

The Woman's Way. One Vol. in *The American Indians*. Series ed. Henry Woodhead. Alexandria, Va.: Time-Life Books, 1995.

www.pbs.org/lewisandclark/archive/index.htm.

Index

Boldface page numbers indicate sections that specifically involve the topic listed.

About the Authors

ANDREW MACDONALD teaches English at Loyola University. He is the author of *Howard Fast: A Critical Companion* (Greenwood, 1996).

GINA MACDONALD teaches English at Loyola University. She is the author of *James Clavell: A Critical Companion* (Greenwood, 1996) and *Robert Ludlum: A Critical Companion* (Greenwood, 1997).

MARYANN SHERIDAN has taught in the Religious Studies Department at Loyola University.

Recent Titles in
Contributions to the Study of Popular Culture